# WILLIAM HICKLING PRESCOTT

## A BIOGRAPHY

Wm. H. Prescott

# WILLIAM HICKLING PRESCOTT

## A BIOGRAPHY

By C. Harvey Gardiner

*Introduction by Allan Nevins*

UNIVERSITY OF TEXAS PRESS

AUSTIN AND LONDON

Standard Book Number 292–70005–9
Library of Congress Catalog Card No. 72–96223
Copyright © 1969 by C. Harvey Gardiner
All Rights Reserved

Printed by The University of Texas Printing Division, Austin
Bound by Universal Bookbindery, Inc., San Antonio

# CONTENTS

01056

# PREFACE

This is the first biography of William Hickling Prescott in more than sixty years. In the first decade of the second century since his death, Prescott deserves attention because:

1) he wedded history and literature, widening the historian's public and challenging succeeding generations of historians,

2) he turned American interest to wider worlds in a period too given to narrow nationalism and isolation,

3) he won the first significant international reputation ever accorded an American historian—while contributing to the internationalization of the nascent literature of his country,

4) he is the most widely translated and frequently published of American historians,

5) he introduced historical practices,—for example, careful and full documentation, multiarchival research, and biobibliographical essays, which basically have enriched American historiography,

6) he represents the self-educated and magnificent amateur historian at his best,

7) he represents inspiring triumph over a vast array of obstacles,

8) he is still considered the finest historian of the Hispanic world produced by the Anglo-Saxon world,

9) he produced the "classic" accounts of the conquests of Mexico and Peru, and

10) his works are alive today—published, bought, read, and authoritative.

The present biography, based on more than a decade of study of materials in America and Europe, attempts to present a full and balanced view of William Hickling Prescott in every significant aspect of his life. Here is appreciation of the Salem in which he was born, and the Boston in which he lived more than a half century. Here is the nature of his parents and their households. Here, too, is the boy at play and in school, the young traveler in Europe, the searcher for a career. In years of maturity he is seen as dependent son, young husband, doting parent, clubman, conversationalist, literary lounger. Economic interests, political outlook, intellectual activities—all are brought in. The writer is viewed in his apprenticeship and his achievement, his works assessed as history and as literature.

The full view of William Hickling Prescott indicates that he was a moody, changing, and complex person, much more so than previous biographers have revealed. George Ticknor, who published his *Life of William Hickling Prescott* in 1864, was an intimate, lifelong friend of the historian. Accordingly his work exhibits advantages and disadvantages. Marring his superior knowledge of the man, his family, his intellectual milieu, are these limitations: writing as a contemporary for contemporaries, he fails to meet the modern reader's need of background, because he took for granted and omitted much that a removed generation must have; writing within the framework of genteel nineteenth-century biography, which so pivots on the public life of the subject as to exclude real awareness of the personal side of the man, Ticknor was so busy hoisting Prescott higher on his pedestal that he failed to inject the breath of life into him; writing in a period when the "life and letters" approach to biography was common, Ticknor produced a book which, in many places, is interlarded and padded rather than written. For a modern, Ticknor's *Prescott* is a rich storehouse of information, not biography. Yet Ticknor's name and relationship to Prescott frightened away other biographers. Forty years passed before Rollo Ogden published *William Hickling Prescott,* in 1904. Leaning very heavily upon Ticknor, and intending to supplement rather than supplant his biography, Ogden principally desired to offer a fuller view of Prescott's personality. His book is peppered with additional references to the major collection of the historian's papers. In 1905 Harry Thurston Peck published *William Hickling Prescott,* the last full account of the historian. Shorter than either Ticknor's or Ogden's work, Peck's biography is the least acceptable of the three. He made no use of primary sources, much less digging out new ones. His only contribution is his consideration of Prescott's style.

All three biographers ignored vast masses of papers. None related Prescott to his times in any full and continuing sense. None understood or set forth the agonizing development of Prescott the historian —to Ticknor, student of Spanish literature, Ogden, newspaperman, and Peck, professor of literature, the education and practice of the historian were mysteries to be left veiled.

In manner of presentation, as well as in fullness of treatment, the present biography attempts to reconstruct the life of William Hickling Prescott. Because he was a great narrative historian, much of the biography is narrative. Because Prescott exercised critical faculties, critical evaluation is employed. Prescott was a marvelous conversationalist, and because some correspondence approximates recorded conversation, the conversationalist is reawakened through direct quotations. Because he was simultaneously active on many fronts—as husband-parent-socialite-investor-writer—a kaleidoscopic awareness of his nature must be at work. Because he was brilliant and dull, hilarious and serious, sick and well, and much else of polar nature, there are highs and lows, unique and repetitious things. In essence it is hoped that in broad design the biography reflects much of the man's nature, even as, in specific detail, it mirrors the pattern of his life.

For the promotion of reader comprehension and the achievement of more attractive format, two types of liberties have been taken with certain quotations in this book. Where Prescott and others, writing in haste, employed "mg," "wld," "F," "ys," "fr," and so on, I have spelled out the words "morning," "would," "Ferdinand," "years," "from." Secondly, for better integration of direct quotations within the text, I have dispensed with most initial and terminal ellipses. In no instance, needless to say, have I altered the meaning of quoted passages.

C. H. G.

*"The Oaks"*
*Murphysboro, Illinois*

# ACKNOWLEDGMENTS

This biographical study of William Hickling Prescott is based upon the generous cooperation of many individuals and institutions.

The late Roger Wolcott, of Milton, Massachusetts, a great-grandson of William Hickling Prescott and the owner of the largest and most significant collection of Prescott papers, once more has accorded the present writer the widest access and the most unrestricted use of the papers of his famous kinsman. Mr. Wolcott's cooperation, indispensable to the fulfillment of this project, is deeply appreciated.

Similar sentiments of indebtedness and gratitude are directed to the Massachusetts Historical Society, the depository of this richest collection of materials about Prescott. In the Society's library the William H. Prescott papers are admirably supplemented by almost a dozen other collections which impinge upon Prescott's career. For access to and for assistance while working with these materials, thanks are directed to the Massachusetts Historical Society, director Stephen T. Riley, Winifred Collins, John D. Cushing, Malcolm Freiberg, and Warren G. Wheeler.

At Harvard University, where numerous other collections touch Prescott's career, words of appreciation are extended to the late William A. Jackson, librarian of Houghton; to Carolyn E. Jakeman, in charge of the reading room of The Houghton Library; to Kimball C. Elkins, senior assistant in the Harvard University Archives; and to the photographic services of Harvard College Library.

Boston Public Library, another holder of multiple collections related to the life of Prescott, is deserving of sincere expressions of thanks. Foremost there among those who aided the present project are Zoltán Haraszti, late keeper of rare books, John Alden, keeper of rare books,

Edith A. Wright, editorial assistant, Sarah W. Flannery and Marjorie G. Bonquet, deputy supervisors of reference and research services, and B. J. O'Neil, coordinator of general reference services.

In addition to the three leading depositories of Prescott materials, the assistance of the following institutions and individuals is gratefully acknowledged: The Academy of Natural Sciences of Philadelphia and Venia T. Phillips, manuscript librarian; the Alderman Library, University of Virginia and Robert E. Stocking, acting curator of manuscripts; the American Academy of Arts and Sciences and Frances Burhoe, assistant to the executive officer; the American Antiquarian Society and Clifford K. Shipton, director; the American Philosophical Society, Whitfield J. Bell, Jr., associate librarian, Gertrude D. Hess, assistant librarian, and Murphy D. Smith, manuscripts librarian; Sir Ian Douglas Campbell, 11th Duke of Argyll, Inveraray Castle; the library of the Boston Athenaeum and Anne Palmer; the Boston Museum of Fine Arts and Thomas N. Maytham, assistant in the Department of Paintings; the Bowdoin College Library, Richard Harwell, librarian, and Dale C. Gresseth, assistant librarian; the British Museum and T. A. J. Burnett, assistant keeper, Department of Manuscripts; the Brown University Library, John R. Turner Ettlinger, in charge of special collections, and Mary W. Ranby, manuscript assistant; the University of California General Library, Donald Coney, university librarian, and Eliza Hart Pietsch, Rare Books Department; Lady Esme, the Dowager Countess of Carlisle, Naworth Castle; the Chicago Historical Society and Archie Motley, manuscript librarian; The Church Historical Society and Archivist Virginia Nelle Bellamy; the William L. Clements Library, The University of Michigan and Howard H. Peckham, director; the Colby College Library, Edwin Arlington Robinson Treasure Room, F. Elizabeth Libbey, associate librarian, and Richard Cary, curator of rare books and manuscripts; the Columbiana Library, Low Memorial Library, Columbia University and Alice H. Bonnell; The Connecticut Historical Society and Thompson R. Harlow, director; the Dartmouth College Library, Edward Connery Lathem, associate librarian, Kenneth C. Cramer, college archivist, and Ethel J. Martin, associate archivist; Charles E. Feinberg, Detroit; Professor J. D. M. Ford, Cambridge; the Frick Art Reference Library and assistant librarian Mildred Steinback; the Georgia Historical Society and Lilla M. Hawes, director; the Hakluyt Society and R. A. Skelton, honorary secretary; Harper & Brothers, Eugene Exman, Vice-President and Dorothy B. Fiske; the Haverford College Library, A. T. Haakinson, supervisor of The Treasure Room, and Thomas E. Drake, curator; The Hispanic Society of America and Clara L. Penney; The Historical Society of Pennsylvania and R. N. Williams, II, director; Houghton Mifflin Company; the Humanities Research Center, The University of Texas and Ann Bowden, librarian; the Henry E. Huntington Library and Art Gallery, Robert O. Dougan, librarian, and Helen S. Mangold, assistant, Department of Manuscripts; the University of Illinois Library and Robert F. Delzell, library administrative assistant; Professor Joseph Jones, Department of English, The University of Texas; the University of Kansas Library, Special Collections Department; the Margaret I. King Library, University of Kentucky and Jacqueline Bull, archivist; the Lehigh University Library, James D. Mack, librarian, and Robert S. Taylor, associate librarian; The Library Company of Philadelphia and Lillian Tonkin; The Library of Congress and David C. Mearns, chief, Manuscript Division; The Lilly Library, Indiana University, Doris M. Reed, curator of manuscripts, and E. L. Craig, reference librarian; J. B. Lippincott Company and President Howard K. Bauernfeind; the Maryland Historical Society, Archives, and John D. Kilbourne, librarian; the Massachusetts Institute of Technology, Microreproduction Laboratory; The Metropolitan Museum of Art and Emma N. Papert; The Pierpont Morgan Library, Frederick B. Adams, Jr., director, and Herbert Cahoon, curator of autograph manuscripts; Professor Samuel Eliot Morison, Boston; the Morristown National Historical Park, Morristown, N.J., and Francis S. Ronalds, superintendent; the National Library of Scotland, the trustees of the National Library of Scotland, and J. S. Ritchie, assistant keeper, Department of Manuscripts; A. Newman, Department of History, University of Leicester; The New York Historical Society and James J. Heslin, director; The New York Public Library, Robert W. Hill, keeper of manuscripts, and Paul R. Rugen, first assistant, Manuscript Division; The New York Society Library and Sylvia C. Hilton, librarian; The New York *Times;* Sir Hugh Algernon Percy, 10th Duke of Northumberland, Alnwick Castle; the Peabody Institute of the City of Baltimore and Frank N. Jones, director of library; the Perkins School for the Blind, Edward J. Waterhouse, director, and Nelson Coon, librarian; The Phillips Exeter Academy, Davis Library, and Rodney Armstrong, librarian; the Probate Court, Suffolk County, Massachusetts, Louis F. Musco and John F. Collins, registers, and John A. Griffin and Arthur A. Kelly, assistant registers; the Redwood Library and Athenaeum, Newport, R. I., and Donald T. Gibbs, librarian; The Rhode Island Historical Society and Clarkson A. Collins, III, librarian; the University of Rochester Library, John R. Russell, director of libraries, and Ruth Hollis; the Rosenberg Library, Galveston, Texas, Charles O'Halloran, director, and Mildred Stevenson, reference librarian; the Rev. Herbert Boyce Satcher, D. D., Philadelphia; The William Henry Smith Memorial Library of The Indiana Historical Society and librarian Caroline Dunn; The South Caroliniana Library, University of South Carolina and director E. L. Inabinett; the Southern Illinois University Library, Ralph E. McCoy, director of libraries, Hensley C. Woodbridge, bibliographer, Ralph Bushee, rare book librarian, and Alan M. Cohn, humanities librarian; Sutherland Estates Office and J. M. L. Scott; The State Historical Society of Wisconsin, Josephine L. Harper, manuscripts librarian, and Margaret Gleason, reference librarian; the Wellesley College Library and Hannah D. French, research librarian; College of William and Mary Library and archivist H. L. Ganter; and the Yale University Library, David R. Watkins, chief reference librarian, and Dorothy W. Bridgwater, assistant head, Reference Department.

# INTRODUCTION

A genuinely comprehensive and searching biography of William Hickling Prescott is long overdue. Fortunately, the task of filling the gap has fallen to an author with special scholarly preparation, critical insight, and the ability to appraise the great New England historian against the cultural background of the early republic. He is equally well qualified to assess his achievements in the bold line of romantic historians running down from Prescott, Motley, Bancroft, and Parkman to the appearance of Henry Adams and a more sober, thoughtful, and analytical school of writers upon the New World. Prescott has received fuller study, to be sure, than his fellow historian John Lothrop Motley, but this is only because Motley's long foreign residence, together with the marriage of his daughter—who held his papers—to an Englishman of distinguished and active family, sequestered many of his letters and other essential papers and impeded the use of household memories and Bostonian traditions. Then too, the study of Prescott's career suffered from the relatively early appearance of a half-dozen inferior biographies, the products of prentice hands, which obscured the need for a really thorough and incisive examination of his lustrous activities and attainments, so representative of some of the best elements in early American thought and intellectual activity.

One volume alone proved worthy of the varied, robust, and distinguished theme offered by Prescott's writings. He will be well remembered as one of the more illustrious American historians and as author of an enduring classic of the English language, *The Conquest of Mexico*, which has never been out of print or unobtainable in any leading Western country since its publication in 1843, and which grows in interest and cosmopolitan appeal as the development of both

Latin and English-speaking America proceeds, and as the two peoples become more closely interlinked; but he was also one of the pioneers in opening to study the worldwide field of Colonial history, still inadequately explored, in comprehending the importance of Hispanic life, conquest, and thought to our whole Western continent, and in substituting a broadly humane cosmopolitanism of outlook for a narrow nationalism. The one biography hitherto worthy of Prescott's varied and abundant career (though the short life by Rollo Ogden also deserves mention because of Ogden's Latin American training and sense of kinship) has been that of his close friend, supporter, and admirer George Ticknor. Ticknor had the insight and sympathy to realize that Prescott was most memorable, not for his high literary gifts, but for his still more impressive and exemplary traits of character, making him, as Ticknor wrote, "a man whose life for more than forty years was one of almost constant struggle—of an almost constant sacrifice of impulse to duty, of the present to the future." But Ticknor's life appeared in 1863, and the 106 years since then have not only given us better perspective, but have added a vast heap of bright new treasures to the memoranda, notes, and criticisms preserved in Prescott's papers in the Massachusetts Historical Society, which, since his death, have been amplified in many another collection. Moreover, Ticknor confined himself too largely, in his thirty chapters of some five hundred duodecimo pages, to a pleasing but inadequate portraiture of the historian, illustrated by copious anecdotal memories, biographic if sometimes rather stilted letters, and contemporaneous commentaries.

Mr. Gardiner has avoided Ticknor's restrictive and old-fashioned selection of materials, adopting a wider and livelier examination of the facts. He has also brought to his work a much more sympathetic temperament than Ticknor possessed, for Ticknor held a set of the best Brahmin prepossessions and preferences, and inclined more closely toward Whig respectability and Websterian conservatism than Prescott, always at heart healthfully radical, had ever done. Mr. Gardiner has, moreover, brought to his subject a deeper learning than any previous writer, for he not only knows such oldtime historians as Robertson and the Abbé Clavigero, along with the most colorful Spanish and Hispanic American chroniclers, more fully than any of his predecessors, but he also possesses a unique knowledge of modern Hispanic American politics, intellectual activity, and ideology, gained through long residence and travel in Latin America, that is of the utmost value to his readers. He can write of Aztec life, beliefs, and tendencies far more expertly than Prescott could in his unwieldy if often glamorous opening sections in *The Conquest of Mexico*, just as he can treat with a fuller grasp of Spanish and European politics the gripping story of the progress toward a unified Spain told in *Ferdinand and Isabella,* Prescott's first spectacular success. No scholar has worked more assiduously in collecting Prescott's materials, studying his modes of approach to Latin American history, and analyzing his notes and reflections than Mr. Gardiner, as he has shown in the two valuable volumes of *The Literary Memoranda of William Hickling Prescott*, published in 1961. He is thus able to comprehend completely the ardor and gusto that Prescott brought to the writing of *Ferdinand and Isabella, The Conquest of Mexico*, and the harsher, less compelling, but at times admirable story told in *The Conquest of Peru*. Mr. Gardiner is able to estimate, but does not exaggerate, the occasional element of stiffness and priggishness in Prescott's nature, which accompanied his natural gaiety and gusto, and to understand why his presentation of history, while often highly romantic, could also be at times unhappily didactic. He can describe better than any other biographer the tremendous obstacles, some physical in nature, especially his blindness, and some intellectual, like his paucity of interest in archeological ideas, though he was a friend of John Lloyd Stephens, and his neglect of economic factors, which he had to overcome in writing his first brilliantly successful volumes, and then in pressing on, amid grave doubts and modest humility, in what he intended to be his greatest work, his *Philip II*. In a sentence, his newest biography enables us to understand, as never before, Prescott's aims, his methods, and his heroic mastery of impediments that would have daunted a Von Ranke or Gibbon. He presents, too, a constant conflict in Prescott's mind between his nationalism, so characteristic of Jacksonian America and of newly flowered New England, and his stronger internationalism, based on long study and observation.

Mr. Gardiner's depiction of Prescott is also consistently pleasing and interesting in its portraits of his many joyous, always completely vital associates. His friends included such diverse personalities as the Spanish exile Pascual de Gayangos; the severe scientist Sir Charles Lyell, so much admired by Henry Adams; the Earl of Carlisle, who entertained Prescott in London; such hard-grained Yankees as Nathaniel Bowditch and N. L. Frothingham; such eminent Britons as Tennyson's friend Henry Hallam; such magisterial Europeans as Leopold von Ranke in Berlin, a man whose work on the *Spanish Empire* he wished to get reprinted; the mercurial Richard Henry Dana of *Two Years Before the Mast*; the lively Charles Dickens, who helped popularize Mme. Calderón de la Barca's *Life in Mexico* at Prescott's request; and the great religious leader William Ellery Channing. Mr. Gardiner's biography is a gallery full of picturesque, salient, and memorable personages. Prescott himself, despite his ailments, was full of spontaneity and imagination. Gardiner shows him staying up until two o'clock in the morning to watch dancing before Queen Victoria, and shows him swept by gusts of hope and fear as he awaited the verdict of the British and American critics on his *Ferdinand and Isabella*, his *Conquest of Mexico*, and other books. One good friend was the lively British travel writer Richard Ford. Among other friends were the learned Georg Heinrich Pertz of the Royal Library in Berlin; the explorer and archeologist John Lloyd Stephens, pioneer in Central American excavations and studies; and the great reformer Edward Everett, "who also spoke" at Gettysburg.

Prescott, when he gave himself leisure, excelled as a letter writer, and Mr. Gardiner's biography profits on every page from the fact. The book, weighty with learning, is at the same time full of vitality and is occasionally even exciting. We may surmise whether Prescott would not have fared damagingly at the hands of the newer historians of our time who emphasize the psychological study of such leaders as Isabella and Pizarro, who see the economic forces at work in discovery, daring conquest, and dynastic change, and who would levy upon ethnology, archeology, and primitive sociology to draw a portrait of Montezuma quite different from Prescott's. But as a narrative historian working in the restrictions of his era, Prescott was in some respects unequalled.

Prescott declared that the greatest happiness in life consists in per-

manent immersion in some subject of great intellectual interest. That
happiness Prescott had in eminent degree. He was unsurpassed as a
narrative historian until Francis Parkman appeared, and still remains
in some ways unmatched. His work will not only live, but catch new
glints from the passage of time. His life will not cease to seem both
psychologically and factually exciting. This laboriously compiled and
carefully wrought book should long rank among the major American
biographies, and no reader of Van Wyck Brooks's *The World of Washington Irving*—which was also the world of Cooper, Prescott, Bryant,
the younger Hawthorne, and Whitman—will wish to neglect it.

ALLAN NEVINS

# WILLIAM HICKLING PRESCOTT

## A BIOGRAPHY

I

## Mr. and Mrs. Prescott request the honour . . .

WITH CHARACTERISTIC ACTIVITY, Boston seethed that summer, the summer that ushered in the third year of the second war between Englishmen and Americans.[1] Gliding to and from the wharves on the east and northeast side of town were sailing vessels of the world. India Wharf identified one dimension of her commerce; and Long Wharf hinted at the draining and filling which would enlarge the town at the expense of the Atlantic. In adjacent shipyards hammers and saws noisily increased the merchant tonnage of the eighteen-state American Union. Beacon Hill, already shorn of its light, was losing altitude to an antlike procession of two-wheeled tipcarts. In 1814 expanding Boston was home to thirty-odd thousand citizens.

The community keenly sensed the issues behind this second struggle with England. To many Federalists the war was the catastrophic climax to the misguided policies of territorial acquisition and commercial restriction which favored boisterous newer sections of the country.

---

[1] The composite glimpse of Boston which follows derives from the newspapers *Boston Daily Advertiser, Boston Gazette, Boston Patriot, Columbian Centinel, Evening Gazette and General Advertiser, Independent Chronicle, New-England Palladium, The Repertory, The Weekly Messenger, The Yankee*; Justin Winsor, ed., *The Memorial History of Boston*, 4 vols. (Boston, 1881), vol. 4; and Walter Muir Whitehill, *Boston: A Topographical History* (Cambridge, 1959).

Recently, on Independence Day, such men had enthusiastically toasted, "President Madison's Administration—Loans, internal taxes, double duties, non-intercourse, embargoes and war—ruinous to ourselves, harmless to our enemies."[2] Social, economic, and intellectual chasms accentuated the political gulf between the Republicans and these Federalists. Augmenting the summer heat were partisan blasts in the half-score newspapers. Boasting classical learning and solutions to contemporary problems, vigorous writers masqueraded behind such names as Menillus, Sicinius Velutus, Brutus, and Gustavus. Rumors, then the terms, of the peace in Europe which released more English manpower for the struggle in America accompanied news of the battles of Chippawa and Lundy's Lane. The humiliation of American arms in the Washington-Baltimore area stifled any exultation over successes along the Canadian frontier.

Most Bostonians, however great their political lament and military uncertainty, continued to immerse themselves in their workaday worlds. Despite shifting workers and capital, money was sufficiently plentiful that numerous duly authorized lotteries—financing cultural institutions, systems of transportation, and new industries—were intent upon siphoning off a portion of it. Extravagant advertising baited the gambling instinct.

The faithful of Boston often heard such memorable sermons that printed copies of them soon appeared in the bookstores. Munroe & Francis, booksellers at Four Cornhill, were plumbing the potential market for a second printing of "Pleas for Friendship & Patriotism." Occasionally, too, a pewholder wearied of what he heard, or found himself about to depart the community. For one such reason a fine pew in the broad aisle of the Federal Street Church, the church of the Reverend Mr. William Ellery Channing, was for sale.

From infancy to the grave, the health of the citizenry received attention. Healthy young married women with good breasts of milk wished to nurse children. Surgeon-dentist Levi S. Parmly offered his professional services between the hours of 6 A.M. and 10 P.M. Painlessly, at the price of one dollar, he whitened teeth; and in the course of "regulating" children's teeth, he extracted all broken and decayed

---

[2] *Boston Gazette*, July 18, 1814, p. [1].

ones, without charge. By means of initialed testimonials, druggist Cyrus Holbrook, at the sign of St. Luke's Head in Hanover Street, was extolling Dr. Hunter's Pills for the cure and prevention of venereal disease—price, one dollar. Another common treatment prompted an advertisement for several thousand leeches. In short supply, the blood-suckers commanded an extra price.

War, politics, business, religion, health—none extinguished the desire for amusement. Throughout the summer season, on fair evenings, brilliant illuminations and the music of the Italian Band awaited those who paid the admission charge of twenty-five cents. Among the varied fare greeting the curious at the Muscum Boylston Hall were six new cases containing thirty birds of North and South America.

Anticipating the end of term, unruly collegians beyond the Charles River were greeting the summer with pranks. Shortly after midnight on August 3, a goodly number of disguised students had set fire to a brewhouse and a carpenter's shop. The college authorities, taking their customarily dim view of such antics, meted out a tongue-lashing in chapel. One newspaper, viewing the destruction of property about which the civil authorities had done nothing, carped, "Had it been a Republican College instead of a Federal College, you would have heard another story."[3] Andrews Norton performed another ritual when he notified all gentlemen having volumes which belonged to Harvard University to return them. When John Thornton Kirkland, Harvard's affable bachelor president, announced that all candidates for degrees at the next commencement should appear at the college, Boston was looking toward Cambridge, and Cambridge to the climax of its academic year.

2

As usual, commencement season at Harvard opened with "Exhibition." Although performed by juniors, it nonetheless commanded the attention of the graduating class and its friends and families.[4] Between

[3] *Boston Patriot,* August 6, 1814, p. [2].

[4] The commencement season is treated in "Order of Performances for Exhibition" (August 23, 1814) and "Order of Exercises" (August 31, 1814), Archives, Harvard College; Invitation, July 26, 1814, Prescott papers; [Har-

the opening philosophical oration and a dialogue, both in Latin, was a four-man conference on "novels, poetry, history, and criticism." In terms of his teenage tastes, this probably constituted the highlight for one senior, eighteen-year-old William Hickling Prescott. With appropriate fervor, a student closed Exhibition with an oration "On National Pride." The following day, hundreds of miles to the south, the theme might better have been "On National Ignominy." That Wednesday, August 24, raw American militia, incompetently led, broke and ran at Bladensburg, exposing the national capital to the invading British. A week later it was Commencement Day in Cambridge.

The procession formed in Boston under clear skies. Led by Lieutenant Governor William Phillips, it included Spanish diplomat Luis de Onís, several consuls, and some distinguished strangers. The Boston Light Dragoons dutifully escorted this cavalcade. At Philosophy Hall the candidates for degrees and a band swelled the marching throng. A few minutes after ten, at the Meeting-house, President Kirkland opened the ceremonies with prayer.

The official Order of Exercises listed thirty-five of the sixty-two candidates for the bachelor's degree, and two who were winning master's degrees. Except for the salutatory and valedictory orations, both of which were in Latin, limited honor attached to participation in this nervous parade. Unrelieved by any music, the program consisted of compositions, conferences, dissertations, colloquies, philosophical disputations, orations, poems, forensic disputations, and deliberative discussions—enough to satisfy anybody and weary everybody.

vard University], *Quinquennial Catalogue of the Officers and Graduates of Harvard University 1636–1900* (Cambridge, 1900), pp. 15, 137–138; George Ticknor, *Life of William Hickling Prescott* (Boston, 1864), pp. 26–27; Anna Eliot Ticknor, ed., *Life of Joseph Green Cogswell as sketched in his letters* (Cambridge, 1874), pp. 7, 33; Francis F. Beirne, *The War of 1812* (New York, 1949), pp. 280–286; Rev. Dr. John Pierce, ed. Charles C. Smith, "Some Notes on the Harvard Commencements, 1803–1848," Massachusetts Historical Society *Proceedings*, 2nd ser., 4 (1889–1890): 178–179; *Boston Daily Advertiser,* September 1, 1814, p. [2]; and *Columbian Centinel,* September 3, 1814, p. [1].

Arthur Middleton, Prescott's classmate since the hot August day three years earlier when they had taken their entrance examinations together, orated in French regarding the French Revolution. The paths of this genial South Carolinian and his Boston friend parted that day, but twenty years later diplomat Middleton was in the right place at the right time for Prescott's purposes. Edward Everett, then an M.A. candidate and destined later to aid Prescott's labors repeatedly, spoke "On the Restoration of Greece." Subsequently Everett distinguished himself in many fields, but oratory always was his forte. Appraising Walter Scott's poetry, a subject which generously overlapped Prescott's interests, was his lifelong friend Francis W. P. Greenwood. Soon to enter the ministry, Greenwood continued his love of literature. Just short of the twenty-fifth anniversary of this commencement, he would publish a laudatory review of Prescott's first book.

Late in the program all eyes focused on Prescott. A shock of brown hair topped his clean-cut face. Of medium build and slightly above average height, he carried himself well. However, the gravity of the occasion, stifling his effervescent nature, had given rise to nervous mannerisms. Still, though, the word for him, at a glance, was "handsome," the word that friend and stranger, male and female alike, applied to him all his life. The official program styled him William Hickling Prescott, which he soon would shorten to William H. Prescott.

Moving to the center of the platform, William delivered his original poem "Ad Spem." Possibly his proudest hearer, with due allowance for his relatives, was Dr. John S. J. Gardiner, the friendly instiller of William's love of Latin. Beaming, too, was George Ticknor. How and at what length William expressed himself on hope, we do not know. Many years later the speaker sought unsuccessfully his copy of this schoolboy verse. However, one attentive listener, Dr. John Pierce, recording impressions of his thirtieth commencement, mentioned only Prescott's offering by title. Four exercises later the formal program ended, and Harvard graduated her sons of 1814.

Time proclaimed those graduates of 1814 above the Harvard average. In years, they ranged from Charles Keating, whose death in 1817 precluded his welcoming the Era of Good Feelings, to Ebenezer Gay, who witnessed the close of the Era of Reconstruction. As adolescents they had contributed to bedlam in Cambridge; as men they achieved considerable distinction. One of the most boyish, William H. Prescott became the most manly. In the Quinquennial Catalogue of Alma Mater, his name inspired more lines and listed more honors and degrees than did that of any of his classmates. On August 31, 1814, however, no such promise was evident. As the mixed throng streamed from the old Meeting-house, some went to dine in new University Hall, others attended private parties.

In honor of their elder son, the William Prescotts offered the most elaborate affair of the day. A leading Federalist and one of Harvard's overseers, lawyer Prescott, growing in reputation, community esteem, and earning power, had seized the opportunity to arrange a memorable banquet. Catherine Greene Hickling Prescott seconded her husband's social instinct. Both sensed aright that their teenage son, already somewhat of a social butterfly, would be pleased. Hundreds received printed invitations.[5]

In order to shield their guests from the heat of that late summer day, the Prescotts had arranged for a canvas canopy. Fixed securely by poles, pegs, and lines, it looked like a circus setting except that the side flaps were omitted, the better to insure the circulation of air. The tables were set upon the grass, and the throng of more than five hundred that toasted young Prescott sat down to dinner.

For ebullient young William, this was a capital moment. Surrounding him were friends, among them those special intimates William Howard Gardiner and George Ticknor. Relieved from the formality of Exercises and the nervous tension attending "Ad Spem," he was the buoyant, gay social extrovert he had grown to be among these people. The moment probably passed without serious reflection, but had the honored youngster thought for an instant, he would have agreed: the joy of the day he owed to his father, the opportunities that Harvard had afforded he owed to his father, the classical discipline of his preparatory schooling he owed his father. On the verge of choosing a lifetime career, William was—and always would be—peculiarly the son of William Prescott.

[5] Invitation, July 26, 1814, Prescott papers.

3

William Prescott also had attended Harvard, but, unlike his children, he had encountered hardship in his formative years.[6] Born in 1762 in the farmhouse at Pepperell which he loved all his life, he was the only son of Colonel William Prescott. The Colonel had fastened his name to history at Bunker Hill on June 17, 1775. After studying under Master Moody at Byfield Academy during the early years of the American Revolution, the Colonel's son had entered Harvard in 1779.

His hurried departure to take charge of a school at Pomfret, Connecticut, absented William Prescott from the commencement activities for the class of 1783. This hasty launching of his career derived from both an ambitious nature and parental improvidence. The Colonel's

[6] For the Prescott family, prior to 1808, see the following: Catherine Greene Hickling, Journal, 1786–1789 and Catherine G. Prescott, Notebook, 1791–1814, Prescott papers; C. Harvey Gardiner, ed., *The Literary Memoranda of William Hickling Prescott,* 2 vols. (Norman, Okla., 1961), 2: 137–139, 211–212; [Anon.], "Brief Memoirs and Notices of Prince's Subscribers," *The New England Historical and Genealogical Register,* 6 (July, 1852): 274; [Harvard], *Quinquennial Catalogue,* pp. 118–119; Ticknor, *Prescott,* pp. 1–7; Roger Wolcott, *Family Jottings* (Boston, 1939), pp. 79–84; Samuel Eliot Morison, *The Life and Letters of Harrison Gray Otis, Federalist,* 1765–1848, 2 vols. (Boston and New York, 1913), 1: 24; Samuel Eliot Morison, *The Maritime History of Massachusetts 1783–1860* (Boston, 1921), pp. 79–81; James Duncan Phillips, *Salem and the Indies* (Boston, 1947), pp. 194, 219, 270, 289, 369; William Bentley, *The Diary of William Bentley, D.D.,* 4 vols. (Salem, 1905–1914), 2: 399, and 3: 293, 361–363; B. F. Browne, "An Account of Salem Common and the Levelling of the Same in 1802, with short notices of the Subscribers," Essex Institute *Historical Collections,* 4, no. 1 (February, 1862): 7; Joseph B. Felt, *Annals of Salem,* 2nd ed., 2 vols. (Salem, 1845, 1849), 1: 458, and 2: 377, 565; Capt. George Henry Preble, USN, "The First Cruise of the United States Frigate Essex," Essex Institute *Historical Collections,* 2nd ser., 10, pt. III (1870): 4–5; Robert S. Rantoul, "Some Notes on Old Modes of Travel," Essex Institute *Historical Collections,* 11, pt. I (April, 1871): 34–35; Oliver Thayer, "Early Recollections of the Upper Portion of Essex Street," Essex Institute *Historical Collections,* 21 (1884): 212; Henry Wheatland, "Historical Sketch of the Philosophical Library at Salem, with Notes," Essex Institute *Historical Collections,* 4, no. 4 (August, 1862): 177–180, and 4, no. 6 (December, 1862): 279–280; [Anon.], "Memorials of the Washington Rangers," Essex Institute *Historical Collections,* 6, nos. 5–6 (October–December, 1864): 203; John B. Derby, *A Few Reminiscences of Salem, Massachusetts* (Boston, 1847), pp. 6, 10.

generous hospitality had so exceeded his income and burdened the
Pepperell property with mortgages that William simply was facing
harsh realities as he hastened to fend for himself. A year later he left
Pomfret for Beverly, Massachusetts, where he coupled the operation
of a private school with the study of law under Nathan Dane. In
Beverly, in addition to laying the foundation for his professional
career, William Prescott formed lasting friendships with the Cabots,
Thorndikes, and other powerful families. Admitted to the bar in
1787, he practiced law in Beverly for two years before moving to
busier Salem.

Keen rival of Boston, Salem, sixth city of the young nation, lived
by the sea in every sense. A hundred years after the black magic of
witchcraft, Salem reveled in the golden magic of world commerce.
In Salem's heyday William Prescott, brilliantly methodical in the
planning and presentation of his cases, prospered. He retired the indebtedness on the Pepperell property, in which his father and mother
continued to live until their respective deaths in 1795 and 1821.

Outside his profession, wherein his integrity and ability quickly
commanded respect, the lawyer identified himself with many community developments. He was cofounder and loyal supporter of the
Philosophical Library Company and clerk of the Essex Bridge Company. He subscribed one thousand dollars to the fund that built the
frigate *Essex* in 1798; and he served as major and third ranking officer
in the regiment Salem organized in 1801. William Prescott also was a
director of a marine insurance company and a founder of Jacob Knapp's
private school. In addition he was elected, on occasion, spokesman for
his town and county. Grave in his church pew, modest at his work,
he was, and always would be, a gentleman whose old-school manners
concealed a warm and friendly nature, a man whom a political oppo-
nent commended for his "probity, sound sense and discretion."[7]

In Salem the young lawyer met and wooed Catherine Greene Hickling. Five years younger than William, Catherine had a background
unlike his. Born into a merchant's family in Boston, where she had
lived during the Revolution, she was quite young when her mother

[7] William W. Story, ed., *Life and Letters of Joseph Story*, 2 vols. (Boston,
1851), 1: 97–98.

died. Even then her father, Thomas Hickling, was spending most of his time in the Azores. Reared in the Massachusetts home of grandfather Rufus Greene, Catherine had sailed to the Azores at eighteen and passed two years there, as well as eighteen months in and about London.

Those years abroad matured Catherine into the kind of woman she would be the rest of her life. Gay and adaptable, she met people easily, making and appreciating friends. She exuded energy—riding, walking, and dancing. In the Azores, curiosity led her to study Portuguese. There, too, although a devout Protestant, she observed and was tolerant toward Roman Catholicism. She liked music but lacked any accomplishment in it. In London her love of Shakespeare carried her regularly to the Covent Garden and Drury Lane theaters, to see Sarah Siddons and John Kemble. Her spelling was as erratic as her humanitarian inclinations were consistent. Both in the Azores and England the underprivileged and afflicted drew full measures of her concern and pity. Of one citizen of the Portuguese possession she exclaimed, "How delightful to be so useful a member of society."[8] Decades later countless persons said the same about her. Considerably sooner, however, she represented a molding force in the lives of her children. At all times Catherine was both like and unlike her husband, matching his love of books and, as a traveler, surpassing his provincial experience. Late in 1793, newly married, William and Catherine established their home in Salem.

In a neighborhood distinguished by its clergymen and public officials, the comfortably large Prescott residence stood on Upper Essex Street, shuttered windows adorning the first and second floors of the three-storied frame dwelling. An ample lawn, fenced at the sidewalk and dotted with large trees, stretched between the house and passing traffic. During their Salem years Catherine bore seven children, only three of whom lived beyond the age of one.

Eldest of the surviving trio, William Hickling, bearing names in honor of both sides of his family, was born on May 4, 1796. Sister Catherine Elizabeth, known at home and abroad as Lizzie, was born on November 12, 1799. Brother Edward Goldsborough, born Janu-

---

[8] C. G. Hickling, Journal, 1786–1789, p. 55, Prescott papers.

ary 2, 1804 and often called Ned, was William's junior by almost
eight years.

Before Ned's birth, when play no longer consumed all his days,
William attended Miss Mehitable Higginson's school. A little later
he studied under Jacob Newman Knapp, the ablest master obtainable
by lawyer Prescott. William's love of books grew rapidly in this period,
as did a passion for fun and mischief. Zest for reading notwithstanding, William never demonstrated for Master Knapp, or any succeeding
teacher, any real love of study. In early youth his outspoken forthrightness, inspired by his father, often offended schoolmates.

Neither the best of students nor the most popular of boys, William
went his way, tempering reading with horseplay. Practical jokes and
puns early crept into his concept of fun. A gay, warm personality usually won him speedy forgiveness. There were instances, however—for
example, he once sprang forth suddenly and almost frightened a serving girl out of her wits—when father disciplined son. Mother Prescott occasionally converted to agonizing punishment the family pleasure
of reading aloud. One evening William had to read one of Mr. Channing's sermons. "Mother, if I am ever a bad boy again, won't you set
me to reading that sermon?" the tearful child chokingly asked through
quivering lips.[9] In early years at Salem the likes and dislikes, the social
nature, the animal energy—all these and more forecast the mold of the
man.

Although all Salem reeked of salt air, not everyone delved in commerce as much as the Grays, Peabodys, Derbys, and Pickmans. Some
men of Salem were en route to intellectual distinction—Joseph Story
as jurist, Nathaniel Bowditch as mathematician, John Pickering as classicist. Like Boston, Salem at turn of century harbored commercial and
intellectual activities in happy combination. Social intercourse also
thrived, and the gregarious Prescotts, satisfying their own adult instincts, entertained often enough to insure the inheritance of their
social natures by their children. None received that inheritance more
willingly or completely than young William.

As you have been in Boston sometime [twelve-year-old William wrote

9 Ticknor, *Prescott*, p. 5.

his sister on May 10, 1808] and as I am desirous of receiving a letter from you, I now take up my pen to write a few lines to you, in hopes, that you will return me a speedy answer. I understand by your letter . . . that Dr. Randall has extracted a few of your *grinders*, which I am very glad to hear; I also congratulate you, that you conducted yourself so much like a *heroine*, whilst under the painful but useful operation of the Doctor's instruments. I very well remember, how I behaved when Dr. Treadwell, two or three years ago, took a couple of tusks out of my jaw; I now think, that I shall be perfectly willing, when necessity requires it, to have a handful of my teeth nipped out by *Dr. Randall*, but by *no one* else. Yesterday, my Father, Mr. Knapp, Capt. Peabody, Augustus, and myself went up to the Circus, where I was both delighted and astonished, by the dangerous and extraordinary feats of horsemanship which the members of the Circus performed.[10]

This, the earliest of William H. Prescott's extant letters, reveals traits of a lifetime: affection for Lizzie, companionship with father, humor, romantic air, love of correspondence.

Shortly thereafter, after nineteen years in Salem—years which included service in the state legislature as representative from Salem and as senator from Essex County, as well as a refusal to accept appointment to the bench of the Supreme Court of Massachusetts—prospering William Prescott moved his family. In search of larger opportunities, he took them to Boston.

Catherine, recording tidbits concerning family activities, wrote, "September 13, 1808—We began to remove our furniture from Salem to Boston. Saturday 17 we removed our family, and took possession of the front house in Bumstead place, at 750 dollars a year." At once Mrs. Prescott sought servants.

For all the family, life in the house facing Boston Common at Tremont Street and Bumstead Place quickly resembled that which they had enjoyed in Salem. They read aloud regularly within the family circle; and they often entertained. As in Salem, so in Boston, the Prescotts immediately sought the best educational opportunities for their children. Four days after the change of residence, William enrolled in Parson Gardiner's school; on September 26 he entered Mr. McThean's

[10] C. Harvey Gardiner, ed., *The Papers of William Hickling Prescott* (Urbana, Ill., 1964), p. 3.

school; and on October 3, he began his studies at Mr. Tancon's French school. In January 1809, suggestive that the fees were quarterly ones, his father paid $25.00 to Gardiner, $10.60 to McThean, and $33.83 to Tancon, the last sum including books as well as instruction.[11] Carefully schooled in Latin and Greek, Prescott felt it time for William to come under the instruction of a master of classical learning. More than he could have hoped for he found in John S. J. Gardiner.

4

When the Prescotts thus came to know him, the Reverend Mr. John S. J. Gardiner was rector of Trinity Church.[12] Earlier, while assistant to the rector of that Episcopal congregation, he also had opened a private school. To love of children and teaching, he brought the love of classical learning imparted to him in England by the famous Dr. Samuel Parr.

Gardiner's school was justly acclaimed. To his excellent command of Greek he added possibly the most complete mastery of Latin enjoyed

[11] C. G. Prescott, Notebook, 1791–1814, unnumbered pages, Prescott papers.
[12] For the period 1808–1814, see the following: C. G. Prescott, Notebook, 1791–1814, Prescott papers, WHP to William B. Sprague, December 21, 1848, in William B. Sprague, *Annals of the American Pulpit*, 9 vols. (New York, 1857–1869), 5: 365–367; [WHP], "Obituary Notice of the Rev. Dr. Gardiner," *Columbian Centinel*, September 11, 1830, p. [1]; [Scott H. Paradise], "John Sylvester John Gardiner," in Allen Johnson and Dumas Malone, eds., *Dictionary of American Biography*, 20 vols. (New York, 1928–1936), 7: 137–138; Harvard University, *Laws of Harvard College* (Cambridge, 1814); [Harvard], *Quinquennial Catalogue*, pp. 15, 80, 117, 120, 136–141; George S. Hillard, ed., *Life, Letters, and Journals of George Ticknor*, 5th ed., 2 vols. (Boston, 1876), 1: 8; James Jackson, *Another Letter to a Young Physician* (Boston, 1861), pp. 131–132; Morison, *Otis*, I, 318; Samuel Eliot Morison, *Three Centuries of Harvard 1636–1936* (Cambridge, 1946), pp. 94–95, 181–182, 195–197; Porcellian Club, *Catalogue of the Honorary and Immediate Members of the Porcellian Club* (Cambridge, 1819), pp. 14–17; Josiah Quincy, *The History of the Boston Athenaeum* (Cambridge, 1851), pp, 1, 3, 5–6, 23, 42, 45, 53, 54; Josiah Quincy, *The History of Harvard University*, 2 vols. (Boston, 1860), 2: 327–328; Ticknor, *Prescott*, pp. 7–8, 12–14, 15n., 19, 20–23, 25–26; Charles A. Wagner, *Harvard—Four Centuries and Freedoms* (New York, 1950), pp. 73–75; Wolcott, *Jottings*, p. 85; Andrew P. Peabody, *Harvard Reminiscences* (Boston, 1888), pp. 9–10, 13.

by anyone of his day in New England. When he read a passage his modulated tones, careful pronunciation, and sonorous voice elevated the commonplace and embellished the excellent. Sharing in friendly fashion his love of the beauty and perfection of the classics, he made learning contagious. One of the fortunate, William H. Prescott daily settled down to studies in the Gardiner library in Franklin Place. Accentuating the relaxed atmosphere, his ruddy-complexioned teacher generally sat by the fireside in slippers and dressing gown. Kind and hospitable, yet blunt and exacting, he taught the rules of Latin and English composition. Simultaneously he extolled the beauties of classical literature. Much later some of Prescott's concern about combining truth and beauty in his own writing, as well as many of his classical allusions, derived from three years of study with Gardiner.

William Howard Gardiner, near Prescott's age and the clergyman's only son, strengthened the ties between the two families. For fifty years William H. Gardiner was one of the closest friends of William H. Prescott—the one to whom he wrote when first abroad, for whom he named his first son, and in whose hands he left the administration of his estate.

Another lasting and significant friendship came Prescott's way through the Gardiner circle. When, at noon, the younger boys left the rector's library, George Ticknor entered for an hour of private instruction. George, five years older than young Prescott, later remarked, in characteristic and shielding understatement, concerning the rambunctious side of his young friend, "Probably he was too much indulged."[13]

Gardiner's teaching challenged Prescott, and he came closer to indulging in hard work than in any other period of his schooling. For many reasons the rector was his finest and most cherished teacher, and his impact on Prescott was genuine. Of the four friends about whom he wrote biographical sketches, Dr. John S. J. Gardiner alone was twice his subject.

A third friendship initiated in Boston was with William Amory,

[13] Ticknor, *Prescott,* p. 8.

son of the merchant Thomas C. Amory. Unlike the balanced Will
Gardiner and the bookish George Ticknor, young Amory—eight
years Prescott's junior—especially answered his friend's physical and
social needs. Through him Prescott met all the Amorys, including
Susan, who, in 1820, became Mrs. Prescott.

For years the two Wills, Prescott and Gardiner, were almost inseparable. Inspired by a circus, they instituted their own performances—
until a cat scorching rang down the curtain. Their pistol shooting disrupted a quiet neighborhood and almost laid low one of the Prescott
horses. Much given to playing games, they doted on battles, inspired
by deft storytelling as well as by study of ancient history and hearsay
knowledge of the American Revolution. On occasion the combatants
added dramatic intensity to their struggles by donning pieces of old
armor. Apparently they borrowed it, without permission, from the
Boston Athenaeum, to which Will Gardiner, like Prescott, had access
through his father.

Neither the assignments of Gardiner nor the books in the family
library satisfied William H. Prescott's insatiable appetite for reading.
At an early moment the Boston Athenaeum, the community's newest
effort to stimulate and satisfy intellectual curiosity, attracted him.
When the Athenaeum purchased a house in Tremont Street, it located
within the proverbial stone's throw of the Prescott residence. Sub-
scriber William Prescott held two tickets of admission, one of which
was transferable. In all probability his son, in curious moments, availed
himself of it and browsed in Boston's finest library. Yet Boston, for all
it offered and had come to mean to the Prescotts, did not absorb their
every moment.

Lawyer Prescott's childhood, rooted in country life at Pepperell,
insured his taking his family there repeatedly, forty miles northward,
near the New Hampshire line. The hero of Bunker Hill had died, but
grandmother Abigail Prescott lived on, too attached to Pepperell to
consider living in the hurly-burly of Boston.

Going to Pepperell was going to father's birthplace, to grandfather's
grave, grandmother's house—and fun in the country. Later, William
H. Prescott's three small children counted their weeks at Pepperell

among the joys of annual routine, and in time so did his grandchildren. It was the same when he, as one of three small children, had responded to the lure of hills and woods and ponds, of winding lanes and countless other charms of nature.

During those years when neutrality became increasingly burdensome to the United States and Jefferson's Embargo and Madison's Non-Intercourse Act and other legislation failed to insulate America from the clashing world of the Napoleonic era, the Prescotts lived in a small world of their own—a home in Boston, visits to Pepperell, and a triangle of friendships bounded by Pepperell, Beverly, and Boston. However often his reading carried him beyond the horizon, this was the real world of young Prescott.

By late summer of 1811 three years of instruction under Rector Gardiner, buttressed by last-minute tutoring by Levi Frisbie of the Harvard faculty, had readied William for college. To win advanced standing, he faced an examination. Also scheduled for that ordeal on Thursday, August 22, was Arthur Middleton, a sixteen-year-old South Carolinian who boasted a grandfather who had signed the Declaration of Independence. At eight in the morning the quaking pair reported to the home of President Kirkland. Professors Frisbie and Ware, with prying inquiries and sober countenances, were so many inquisitors. President Kirkland, however, thoughtfully sent in a dish of pears, the munching of which helped to ease the situation. The amiable Levi Frisbie subjected their Latin to lengthy examination.

Because the morning did not suffice, the boys returned in the afternoon. Then the interrogation came from the Reverend Henry Ware, Hollis Professor of Divinity. Somewhere in the flow of questions and answers on Grotius's *De Veritate Religionis Christianae,* a required Monday morning exercise for freshmen, young William queried the professor. The good-natured man who had been a sophomore the year that Prescott's father had graduated convulsed with laughter. About mid-afternoon the examination ended; Prescott and Middleton were declared sophomores. Eager to report to his father in detail, as he did by letter the following day, William sought out Professor Frisbie.

"Did I appear well in my examination, sir?" Prescott asked.

"Yes," the professor replied.

William pressed him, "Did you think that I appeared very well, sir?"

"Why are you so particular, young man?" Frisbie countered, "Yes, you did yourself a great deal of credit."[14] Feeling as though he had shed a twenty-pound burden, William hurried with his good news to a dinner engagement at the Gardiners.

Harvard of 1811 differed but little from that which Prescott's father had known. When he entered college, he had paid his fees to young Steward Caleb Gannett; young Prescott handed his fees to a veteran Gannett. Sturdy, red-brick Hollis Hall, now one of few eighteenth-century structures in the Yard, had been the "new" dormitory in William Prescott's day. Thirty years later his son also roomed in monastic Hollis. Then, and for years to come, the furnishings of a room in Hollis included "a pine bedstead, washstand, table, and desk, a cheap rocking-chair, and from two to four other chairs of the plainest fashion . . ."[15] Few carpets were in evidence. Each room had its own fireplace, and maintaining the fire was often as tedious as the lighting of one's lamp by means of flint, steel, and tinderbox.

The sophomore curriculum, admitting of no substitutions, consisted of Greek and Latin, geometry, rhetoric, logic, and mathematics. In the first term, which extended to the Christmas season, William had eleven out of sixteen weekly class periods in Greek and Latin. Professor Ashur Ware taught the Greek and Levi Frisbie the Latin. An inclination toward classical studies endeared these subjects to Prescott, but his excellent preparation in them helped him to the leisure that confirmed his playboy nature. Neither affection nor achievement marked his identification with mathematics and geometry, taught by Professor John Farrar. Capable of exciting other students, Farrar kindled no fires of enthusiasm in Prescott. Logic was taught by Levi

---

[14] Gardiner, ed., *Papers*, p. 4. The text of this letter, as printed in Ticknor, *Prescott*, pp. 14–15, illustrates Ticknor's handling of Prescott's papers. Therein he corrected spelling, added and deleted words, introduced paragraphing and punctuation, reduced names to initials, and injected emphasis through underscoring.

[15] Peabody, *Harvard Reminiscences*, pp. 196–201.

Hedge, and the jovial Reverend Mr. Joseph McKean, founder of the Porcellian Club, in which Prescott soon gained membership, taught sophomore rhetoric. On Saturday at nine, sophomores had a weekly exercise in history, all that Harvard offered them in that field, and at ten came declamations.

Harvard placed other demands upon young Prescott. He attended chapel morning and evening, and church on Sunday. His attendance at the public declamations by the juniors and seniors was compulsory. In the commons, at tables seating eight to ten students, he ate ample but unappetizing meals. Permitted to withdraw two books from the library at a time, he did so at a stated moment on a designated day. At noon on Saturday the educational operation ceased, and the library closed until Monday. Saturday at sundown Prescott was expected to put aside all diversions, retire to his room, and ready himself spiritually for the Sabbath.

Harvard's entering students were commonly in their middle teens, prematurely adult only in reference to classical studies. Many young bloods, outwardly searching for the hallmark of the gentleman, bubbled inwardly with the energy which stamped them a breed of juvenile jackasses, eager to kick up their heels. For some, including Prescott, college especially invited riotous behaviour during initial release from parental supervision. The punishment promised those guilty of instigating bonfires, illuminations, and displays of fireworks hinted that such activities were commonplace. Because the waiters in commons were expected to report rowdyism and destruction of property, prankish natures rose to the challenge. Ordered to spend Saturday evening in quiet meditation in your room, that night was the obvious one for a Porcellian Club feast on roast pig at some forbidden tavern. A clear recollection of his own dissipation at college probably prompted many of the admonitions Prescott later gave his elder son.

In 1812 William won membership in the Porcellian Club, already Harvard's most aristocratic social organization. Dedicated to physical pleasures, the Porcellian, or Pig Club as it commonly was known from its members' predilection for roast pig, undertook little that smacked of intellectual activity. Two years within P.C. meant that William spent much of his campus life in company with approximately forty young aristocrats. For P.C. good times were the first order of business, but from its ranks also came many members of Phi Beta Kappa and more than a few valedictorians. A few years later, when serious literary interests drew a band of youthful Bostonians together, William H. Prescott counted among them more than a half-dozen P.C. members of his own college days.

Like the Gardiner circle earlier, Harvard rewarded the socially precocious Prescott with enduring acquaintances and friends. During his sophomore year he entered the world of seniors Franklin Dexter and Jonathan M. Wainwright. Before the end of the decade young Dexter, a lawyer in the wake of a distinguished father, married Lizzie Prescott. Wainwright, one of the university's gifts to the clergy, was a warm friend and frequent host to Prescott in later years. That same season several juniors entered Prescott's world. Decades later the scholarly precision of Charles Folsom served Prescott well in the critical reading of his manuscripts and galley proofs. Charles's editorial pencil improved all of William's books. The humorous Henry Warren, the future Dr. John Ware, and the short-lived William Jones Spooner, a trio of Prescott's literary friends a few years later, also belonged to the class of 1813. In his own sophomore class, in addition to Arthur Middleton and F. W. P. Greenwood, his classmates included the gentle Thomas Bulfinch, another longtime friend.

Mathematics, a subject in which William was deficient in training, interest, and ability, provided one of the classic stories of the academic side of his Harvard years. His sophomore experience with Professor Farrar inspired it. For a time he laboriously memorized propositions and processes in geometry and reproduced them in class exactly as they appeared in the textbook. Wearying, however, of the drudgery which stamped him acceptable to his teacher but grossly ignorant of the subject, Prescott confided his secret to Farrar. Convincing the professor of the impossibility of his mastering the subject, he was told that regular attendance, without recitation, would suffice. A lifetime underscored the truth that simple arithmetic often defied him: his notebooks contain repeated miscalculations in writing schedules, his correspondence indicates errors on his part in accounts with his publishers, and the prospect of treating the mathematical achievements of the native

Mexicans in one of his books almost threw him into panic. Along with additional Greek and Latin, Prescott, as a junior, studied metaphysics, theology, natural philosophy, and, for three one-hour sessions weekly during the third term, mathematics. If one did not study Hebrew, he could study any one of three substitute languages. Later, Prescott never indicated any knowledge of Hebrew, leading one to believe that he elected either French or additional Greek and Latin. One thing is certain—he avoided additional mathematics. As in the previous year, he was, as a junior, a social rather than an academic success. The summer of 1813 the student body at Harvard mounted its annual crescendo of horseplay. Then it was that William, nearing the close of his junior year, suffered the accident that eventually shaped his life.

In University Hall, which housed the commons, some of the rowdyism inspired elsewhere infected student protests about food. Flying gobs of gravied mashed potatoes and chunks of crisp bread often enlivened mealtime. One evening during such a melee, William H. Prescott, standing, received a surprise blow which did not permit him to close the lid before a crust of bread crashed against his left eye. Ticknor, who did not witness the accident, said that it occurred in commons—and well it might have. Gus Peabody, as yet unborn but destined to become a walking encyclopedia of Harvard lore, always insisted it happened in the Porcellian Club—and well it might have.

The blow felled William from pain rather than force. He vomited and exhibited the immediate symptoms of a concussion of the brain. Instantly sobered, some boys hurried him to his home in Boston. There Dr. James Jackson, the family physician for decades to come, attended him. The left eye, though insensible to light, carried no external evidence of severe injury. Admitting of no active treatment, the case led Dr. Jackson to prescribe complete rest. After a few days William's system recovered from the shock and within a few weeks he returned to college. The damaged retina showed no outward sign of injury. Nothing noticeable, in color or movement, differentiated the injured left eye from the good right one. In later years many people did not know of the condition of the left eye, and Prescott commonly presented it to the public in his portraits, perhaps accidentally.

The weeks of convalescence at home greatly changed William's approach to college during the year 1813–1814. Reinforced by sobering words from his parents, the quiet moments encouraged the lotus-eater's resolve that deeper purpose attend his remaining college days. As social incentive to intellectual labor, his parents promised him a party at commencement. Returning to campus as a senior, William, a blend of social and intellectual appetites, did his best work. That year he studied natural philosophy, mathematics, moral and political philosophy, and theology. Election to Phi Beta Kappa was one recognition of his achievement; participation in the Exercise on Commencement Day was another.

As Prescott moved toward graduation, successive classes beneath him added to his intimates. In the class immediately below him were William Havard Eliot, John Gorham Palfrey, Theophilus Parsons, and Jared Sparks, a quartet whose literary and intellectual interests brightened his life. Also in that class was a scion of a sophisticated planter family of Virginia, Benjamin Ogle Tayloe, whom Prescott later visited repeatedly on the Potomac. George Parkman, whose widely publicized murder touched the Prescotts in 1849, likewise was in the class of 1815. Two years behind William, in addition to Will Gardiner, came his Salem friend Joseph Augustus Peabody, with whom he had attended circus in 1808. Far in the future another generation would renew the Peabody-Prescott ties. At the moment, however, Will and Augustus joined him in Porcellian fellowship. Among the freshmen when Prescott was senior were Samuel Atkins Eliot and George Bancroft, the latter with intellectual interests to inspire the friendship of any potential historian.

Then came the climax of August 31—his Latin poem, the A.B. degree, best wishes of friends at the banquet—and Harvard was behind the boy turning man.

## II

*Your description of men and places is very entertaining...*

IN THE AUTUMN OF 1814 young Prescott embarked upon preparatory study for his career.[1] By way of background he first read widely
in historical literature. A year of that and he would enter his father's
office for training. Across the years William Prescott's idea that his
elder son would follow in his footsteps was taken for granted by all
the Prescotts.

The same autumn weeks brought fifty-two-year-old William Prescott
to one of the climactic moments of his career, his attendance at the
Hartford Convention. Its agenda included public grievances and concerns, defense against the enemy, and preliminary steps looking toward
revision of the Constitution of the United States. The twenty-six
spokesmen for New England met twice daily, six days a week, from

[1] For this interval in late 1814 and early 1815 the sources are: WHP to
C. E. Prescott, March 12, 1816, Prescott papers; W. Prescott to Lowell, August
14, 1834, Harvard College; Gardiner, ed., *Papers,* pp. 5–12; Theodore Dwight,
*History of the Hartford Convention* (New York and Boston, 1833); Henry
Adams, *History of the United States of America, 1801–1817,* 4 vols. (New
York, 1940), bk. VIII, 292; M. A. DeWolfe Howe, ed., *The Articulate Sisters*
(Cambridge, 1946), pp. 12–14 *passim*; Jackson, *Another Letter,* pp. 133–141;
James Jackson, "On Rheumatism in the Heart, Eyes, &c.," *The New-England
Journal of Medicine and Surgery,* 5 (April, 1816): 143–146.

December 15, 1814, to January 5, 1815, in secret session in the council chamber of the old State House in Hartford. Like the others, Prescott expressed his opinions and helped to formulate reports. He subscribed to the resolution which permitted the summoning of another meeting of the convention, but no second meeting took place. Twenty years later, however, he continued to endorse the labors of the Hartford body as he contributed money and otherwise promoted publication of its history.

Changing prospects came early in 1815 for both father and son. The terms of the Treaty of Ghent, which exalted the Madison administration, cast over the Hartford Convention an unpatriotic pall bordering on treason. The resultant Republican surge forecast doom for the Federalists. Ill health, meanwhile, had upset the activities of the embryonic lawyer in the Prescott household. Eighteen months had elapsed since the accident to William's left eye, when mild inflammation of the right eye led him, on January 15, to consult the family physician. Dr. Jackson treated him with leeches and a saturnine lotion on the temple, simple remedies for what he considered a passing complaint. The next morning, however, the inflammation mounted.

I called in consultation my friend Dr. John C. Warren [Dr. Jackson wrote]. For five days the inflammation continued with great fury; and during this time he lost by general and local bleeding more than seven pounds of blood, was purged abundantly, was blistered freely, was kept in the dark, on the lowest diet; also the vessels of the conjunctiva were divided twice, with a view to arrest the disease in the cornea.[2]

At the end of a week the inflammation subsided and William was much improved, except for sight.

Seemingly on the road to recovery, William suddenly complained of pain, attended by redness and swelling, in his right knee. This pleased the previously baffled doctor. Apparently the inflammation, basically rheumatic, was a form of acute rheumatism. For three months the larger joints of the lower legs suffered this attack. Occasional pains also attacked William's neck and loins. In the same period his vision ex-

---

[2] Jackson, *Another Letter*, p. 134. The medical history of Prescott's case, by virtue of Jackson's extensive writings, is unusually full.

perienced two more attacks, each less serious than the preceding one. In every instance, however, blindness was complete for a time. Along with additional bleeding and blistering, Dr. Jackson experimented with antimonials, opium, and cinchona. Surprisingly, William never developed dyspepsia. Until early May the extreme pain in his ankles and knees confined him to his bed.

In late April, when light streamed generously into William's room for the first time, he realized that restoration of perfect vision had not accompanied the departure of pain. As there was no sign of injury to the cornea, it was concluded that the successive inflammations had affected the retina. In mid-spring electrical shocks on the head three times daily were added to the treatment, as well as moderate use of calomel. Dr. Jackson's study of the rheumatic propensity in the Hickling family—it plagued at least three, including Catherine Prescott —led to the conclusion that William had inherited rheumatic tendencies. His complaint was destined to recur frequently in subsequent years.

Meanwhile intimates who visited him found the same gay, loquacious companion they always had known. Denied any other social activity, he improved his French. In neighboring Brookline and at Pepperell the Prescotts sought conditions which would restore his health. Pepperell was kind, even partially restorative. However, the haunting fear of the Boston winter, as well as the paucity of medical specialists for the eyes, encouraged the family to consider a long trip abroad for the afflicted teenager. The healthful climate of the Azores, coupled with the attention of a doting grandparent, suggested a leisurely visit to the Hicklings. For the young man whose world, till then, scarcely had exceeded the bounds of his native state, high adventure loomed.

2

The American brig *Legal Tender,* Captain Lindsay, cleared Boston harbor under a fair wind on September 26, 1815, her passengers including nineteen-year-old Prescott.[3] "Completely initiated into the

---

[3] For the voyage to the Azores the sources are: WHP to his parents, October 7, 17, November 13, 1815, and WHP to C. E. Prescott, November 13, 1815, Prescott papers.

science of seasickness," his second and third days out, he quickly recovered and enjoyed good health the remainder of the voyage, despite certain discomfitures.

Life in his cabin proved an endless battle. Because of poor fittings, and because it opened directly on the deck, the cabin caught generous quantities of wind and water. The latter threatened to exacerbate the voyager's rheumatic condition. And when the rays of the patent binnacle were not in his eyes or water under his feet, bedbugs demanded attention. To break the monotony of the voyage, William checked his wardrobe and quickly noted that he had left behind something much desired, his knee buckles!

On deck, "battling with democrats" became a favorite pastime. For Prescott, accustomed to servants, the Negro cook supplemented the meager shipboard services by doubling as his *valet de chambre* and as his supporter in political arguments.

"I cannot be thankful enough to heaven, that it has not cased in these rheumatic shackles the navigating soul of a Cook or a Columbus," he wrote, summarizing his initial shipboard experience, "for I am very sure that if a fifth quarter of the globe depended upon me for its exposure, it would remain *terra incognita* forever."[4] Later, across all his creative years, Prescott penned lines suggestive of real affection for the open sea in letters as well as in accounts of Columbus, Cortés, Pizarro, and the Battle of Lepanto. But the truth was: Prescott detested the sea. That, however, was but one of numerous contradictions between the man and the writer.

3

Hurrying ashore at Ponta Delgada, the weary passenger stepped into a strange world.[5] On the quay to welcome him stood a pair of previously unmet uncles who quickly whisked him through the quaint community and three miles beyond to grandfather Hickling's place at

[4] WHP to his parents, November 13, 1815, Prescott papers.
[5] The account of WHP in the Azores derives from the following: WHP, Journal, 1815–1821, pp. 1–5, and WHP to his parents, sister, and brother, October 17, 18, 30, November 13, 14, 20, 1815, March 12, April 1, 4, 1816, Prescott papers; Gardiner, ed., *Papers*, pp. 5–12; and Ticknor, *Prescott*, pp. 33–41.

Rosto de Cão. Yankee Hall, the recently remodeled country home of the expatriate New Englander, was a joy. Enhancing its valley setting was the approach by way of a long avenue of box trees and a flight of fifty stone steps. There, within a patriarchal household of enormous proportions, the gregarious visitor soon felt at ease.

Much of the joy and comfort experienced by William during the ensuing six months derived from the personality of grandfather Hickling. To gentlemanly deportment and an affectionate nature, that septuagenarian added frankness and liberality. Several of William's aunts, like his grandfather in his second marriage, had wed natives of the islands. Aunt Fanny's husband, "wonderfully clever for a Portuguese,"[6] was a graduate of the University of Coimbra who divided his time between medical practice and orange groves. Conversing in French, William grew fond of him. Of Aunt Charlotte's husband, however, he entertained a contrary opinion. Son of a *morgado*, the heir to an entailed estate, he was intensely jealous and educated to nothing.

Always susceptible to feminine charms, William quickly found some of his most pleasant associations with two young aunts, Amelia and bright-eyed Harriet. Amelia accompanied him on a ride the day following his arrival. The scenery, enriched by classical allusions, transported young Prescott via "boxwood cypress and myrtle . . . to the ages of Horace and Anacreon"[7] and almost inspired poetic sentiments which, though felt, remained unexpressed.

On one occasion the fragrance of an orange grove grew doubly delightful because of his companion, Maria, "a little belle with pretty hands, and roguish eyes, all of which I explained to her . . . in very bad Portuguese."

William's enjoyment of people and places—rides and walks by day and evenings with song and guitar—abruptly changed. A slight inflammation brought on, he thought, by seafaring discomfits, had plagued him when he landed. Complicating matters, as he accommodated himself to brighter sunlight and native diet, William had left his supply of medicines aboard ship. To lessen the strain on his

[6] WHP to C. E. Prescott, March 12, 1816, Prescott papers.
[7] WHP to his parents, November 13, 1815, Prescott papers.

eyes, Aunt Amelia penned his first letter to his parents. The affliction he had experienced in Boston recurred and for the three months following November 1, 1815, his journal carried the single word "d-a-r-k-n-e-s-s."

Life in a darkened room began anew at Yankee Hall, but Thomas Hickling concluded that his house in Ponta Delgada would better serve the invalid's needs. In the port town, in a room facing the north, the windows of which had varying thicknesses of baize over them, the ailing visitor was much more at ease. Aunt Amelia penned additional letters, some to William's parents, others to his sister, brother, and friends. Sister Lizzie learned that the state of her brother's vision precluded his keeping his promise to correspond with her in French. Of her he asked the favor, "Beg your sweet friend C. [Caroline Preble] at least to oblige me with a postscript."[8] To his brother Edward, not quite twelve years old, then studying Latin and Greek under one of William's former teachers, he wrote in waggish and admonitory vein.

In January a severe cold and rheumatic pains in knee and ankle added their own restrictions to those of the already confining inflammation. That same month James Collis arrived from London as Grandfather's new clerk. Because business was dull that season, he allowed William to use him as his private and confidential secretary. Collis' assistance enabled Prescott to touch on matters which he had withheld while his kinsman served as secretary. He also reported more fully. Indeed he wrote at that great length which so characterized his lifetime use of secretaries as to cause him once to exclaim, "I can't write a short one."[9] Relieved of secretarial duty, Amelia read him Greek and Roman history. Harriet, whom William quickly regarded as a second sister, read aloud Scott, Shakespeare, the *Iliad* and *Odyssey,* and travel books about England and Scotland. William also worked his way three times through much of a Portuguese grammar.

As remedies for what ailed him, beefsteaks and grandfather's universal nostrum, old Madeira, failed. William speedily reverted to a diet of bread, milk, and gruel, accompanied by applications of blisters for the relief of the inflammation of the eyes. His spirits and bodily

8 WHP to C. E. Prescott, November 13, 1815, Prescott papers.

9 Gardiner, ed., *Literary Memoranda,* 2: 96.

vigor sustained, William, as earlier in Boston, paced literally hundreds of miles in his darkened room. Occasionally he walked on the piazza, wearing a pair of borrowed goggles around which he tied a handkerchief to reduce the light.

Most unpleasant of all the thoughts running through his mind was "the probable necessity of abandoning a profession, congenial with my taste, and recommended by such favorable opportunities."[10] This was the first articulated hint that his search for health might not succeed sufficiently to permit the resumption of the study of law.

As before, the illness ran its course and disappeared more rapidly than it had come. For the remainder of his island stay, William, despite continuing weak vision, enjoyed good health. Even before the scales informed him that he weighed 154 pounds, he was suffering embarrassment—his coat refused to button.

Once more he spent considerable time in the saddle. "Since my recovery," he told his sister, "I may be compared to bottled beer which . . . imprisoned a long time, burst forth with tremendous explosion." The details of one memorable excursion, to Furnas, he colorfully reported in terms reminiscent of Radcliffe and Scott. They also forecast the histories which transported Prescott's readers to the time and place of colorful action.

Coupled with his love of nature was an insatiable, yet tempered, curiosity about people. Often, in the name of friendship, someone who remembered his mother heartily embraced William in the native manner, which, he confessed, "I am not quite Portuguese enough to relish."[11] In his jaundiced view of Roman Catholicism, the ruddy cheeks of the monks, he was certain, derived more from feasting than fasting. Yet his pity for nuns blended with frank admiration of the gilded and carved churches under candlelight.

The islanders both attracted and repelled William. Jealousy, pride, and ignorance, he thought, constituted the essential ingredients of the Portuguese character. The condition of the poor—who shared their rooms with their animals, subsisted on corn bread and vegetables, and wore a minimum of rough clothing—greatly distressed him. Their

[10] Gardiner, ed., *Papers,* pp. 6–7.
[11] WHP to C. E. Prescott, March 12, 1816, Prescott papers.

degradation provoked his condemnation of monopolies, the wealth of the Church, and the stagnation of industry on countless saints' days.

To his study of the history and government of the islands, Prescott added close observation of the customs of the islanders. He concluded, a month before his departure,

Whatever opinion I had formed of the Portuguese, I could have no idea of the debasement which our capacities may suffer when crampt by an arbitrary government and Papal superstition. Indeed, I believe there is an original inferiority in the nature of the Portuguese, and if it were possible to dissect the Soul, I suspect in three fourths of the nation, the anatomy would be composed solely of knavery and stupidity, with an equal chance, which of these two ingredients should predominate.[12]

The Azores introduced William to variety in historical and cultural influence, even as they momentarily prodded him into postures of cultural arrogance and religious intolerance. For the historian that he became, the experience in the Azores is important in that it demonstrates how much the callow youth had to put aside to attain the objectivity of adulthood. In this initial foreign experience Prescott also had learned what the careful observer must look for and what a writer must include to give his writing a breath-of-life appeal. Perhaps Prescott's insistence upon utilizing travelers' accounts in his historical research stemmed, in part, from the inescapable significance of his own visit to the Azores, the only moment that he studied an Iberian culture face to face.

4

Tearful best wishes attended William's departure from the Hickling clan on April 8.[13] The passage to Dover proved tedious, calms and

[12] Gardiner, ed., *Papers*, pp. 8–10.

[13] For WHP's voyage to and initial stay in England, the sources are: WHP, Journal, 1815–1821, pp. 5–22, WHP to his parents and sister, April 4, May 26, June 7, 9, 10, 20, July 28, 1816, W. and C. G. Prescott to WHP, March 2, June 7, 10, 11, 15, July 14, August 6, 8, 10, 19, 20, September 4, 1816, Prescott papers; Gardiner, ed., *Papers*, pp. 14–17; John Quincy Adams, ed. Charles Francis Adams, *Memoirs of John Quincy Adams, comprising portions of his diary from 1795 to 1848*, 12 vols. (Philadelphia, 1874–1877), 3: 385; Dorothie Bobbe, *Mr. & Mrs. John Quincy Adams: An Adventure in Patriotism* (New York, 1930), pp. 97, 184, 186; Grose Evans, *Benjamin West*

headwinds alternately reaffirming his aversion to seafaring. Four days out, his eyes once again became inflamed and "the sun . . . which invited others to remain upon deck induced me to remain *solus* in the cabin," he wrote his parents. Regaining his stamina, he greeted the white cliffs of Dover with unfeigned joy. The ugly port town detained him just long enough to be cheated by a guide. Then, by stagecoach, he hurried toward London. Encouraged by fine weather, William ignored the seat he had purchased inside the coach and shared the coachman's box as they swung along toward Canterbury. From his airy perch he tapped the coachman's knowledge of the country while enjoying the best possible view of it. The deep green of Kent pleased him; and the elegant antiquity of Canterbury stirred him.

Of his visit to the site of the former shrine to Thomas à Becket in the cathedral, Prescott recalled, "I immediately threw myself on my knees on the very spot, . . . much to the astonishment of my poor guide, though, if the truth were known, not so much from religious veneration, as from my respect to antiquity."

"I had here also," he continued, "the honor of sitting in the same chair in which the Kings of Kent formerly reposed their royal *breeches,* at their Coronation."[14]

A less colorful stagecoach ride brought him to London, via Gravesend and Greenwich, late on his twentieth birthday. Employing one of his many letters of introduction, he gained assistance in locating comfortable lodgings in the West End in Pall Mall. His eyesight, the chief reason for his visit to London, at once led him to use other letters.

On Dr. Jackson's recommendation, Prescott took his problem to Astley Cooper and Dr. John Richard Farre. The latter prescribed such a succession of medicines that William lost all patience. "I soon found," he wrote, "I was to be the through-fare of half the Apothecary's Shop, . . . I had neither time or inclination for such a process, and still more, . . . I had no faith in its efficacy."[15] Ready to drop this

*and the Taste of His Times* (Carbondale, 1959), pp. 42–47, 67–74; Roger Wolcott, ed., *The Correspondence of William Hickling Prescott 1833–1847* (Boston and New York, 1925), p. 206.

[14] WHP to his parents, June 7, 1816, Prescott papers.

[15] *Id.* to *id.*, May 26, 1816, Prescott papers.

treatment after three weeks, he asked Cooper to recommend an oculist. Cooper suggested Sir William Adams.

Sir William's examination indicated that the injured left eye, paralyzed, never could be completely restored. However, the oculist believed that under treatment it could improve. Believing that his patient's abstemious diet had increased his susceptibility to inflammation, the doctor prescribed generous portions of meat and fish for him, along with a wine tonic. The extreme regularity with which William catalogued his wine consumption for years thereafter suggests his enthusiastic endorsement of that part of the new regimen. Dr. Adams also applied lotions and unguents to the lid as well as to the eye because he found it in need of medication.

Sir William's diagnosis and treatment won his patient's complete confidence and led him to settle in London. At his doctor's suggestion, he changed his lodgings, going still farther west to rooms overlooking Regent's Park. The quiet and the free circulation of air there counted as aids to recovery. Frowning upon tight goggles, the doctor replaced them with glasses and a side screen of silk, which William soon discarded.

"My eye is entirely free from inflammation and it has already acquired considerable strength under Sir William Adams's treatment," he reported to his parents in mid-June via the pen of McCandlish, to whom he was paying twelve dollars monthly for secretarial services.[16]

Letters in hand, William had called promptly upon Minister and Mrs. John Quincy Adams at Boston House, their spacious place in suburban Ealing. He subsequently shared many social occasions, including breakfasts and dinners, with the Adamses. In company with them he visited Windsor Castle and gained admission to private royal apartments which the public normally did not see. Later in life, in pursuit of highly inaccessible manuscripts, he remembered that diplomats work miracles.

"I dine with some friend or other, almost every day," he wrote, "as they know my weak part, and allow me to shade the candles."[17] His contacts often concealed future significance. One day he met Colonel

[16] *Id.* to *id.*, June 10, 1816, Prescott papers.
[17] *Id.* to *id.*, June 20, 1816, Prescott papers.

and Mrs. Thomas Aspinwall. The late commander of the Ninth Infantry of Massachusetts in the War of 1812 was then embarking upon a long career in the American consular service. Two decades later Aspinwall became Prescott's literary agent in London.

William also sought out the "lions"—Richmond Hill, Hampton Court, Eton, The Tower, the Houses of Parliament, St. Paul's, Westminster Abbey, Greenwich Observatory, and many others. Curiosity also took him to Miss Linwood's needlework exhibition, DuBourg's cork models, Polito's menagerie, Bullock's Museum, the Stevens-Robinson boxing match, races at Epsom, Weeks's mechanical exhibition, a performance of Indian jugglers, a shoe factory, pony races, the docks, and the funeral of an alcoholic Cabot. In Hyde Park, Kensington Gardens, Regent's, and St. James's, he passed pleasant hours. The love of walking inculcated at his father's side in Boston and at Pepperell helped him to enjoy London outdoors.

Some attractions drew him time and again. None did so more often than the British Museum. For William the Elgin marbles constituted the Museum's greatest attraction. Once, as he was leaving the apartment containing the marbles, he "discovered a small fragment of marble which had been broken off of a Corinthian column. I immediately took possession of it."[18] Westminster Abbey also called for repeat visits. His classical studies had prepared him for the Elgin marbles, and wide reading of English literature accounted for much of his interest in the Abbey. The pure Latinity of Addison's epitaph he copied on the spot, sending it to his schoolboy brother. The twenty-year-old sightseer whose historical writings at somewhat more than twice that age carried numerous poetic excerpts and even more poetic sentiments went often to the Poets' Corner, to commune, as it were, with his own love of beauty.

Possibly earlier, and then again perhaps on this trip, Prescott developed the interest in painting which London first permitted him to indulge. After attending a special exhibition of Benjamin West's works, including his *Christ Rejected by the Jews* and *Christ Healing*

[18] *Id.* to *id.,* June 7, 1816, Prescott papers; John Quincy Adams, Diary, Reel 32 (August 1, 1813–May 31, 1816), p. 452, Reel 33 (June 1, 1816–December 31, 1818), pp. 29–30, Adams papers.

*the Sick in the Temple,* he keenly desired to meet the renowned American. The handsome seventy-eight-year-old president of the Royal Academy welcomed his curious young countryman to his studio for a lengthy morning visit. West was then working on another mammoth religious work for public exhibition, *The Opening of the Seals.* What Prescott told his dignified host is not known, but in a letter to his parents he confided, "Such allegorical subjects never please me."[19]

Beyond Prescott's desire to meet another famous person—and some special delight that this one was an American—the possibility of underlying kinship of spirit between the old man and the youngster heightens interest in their meeting. Throughout the various periods in West's long career, from ancient to modern themes and back to Biblical ones, he often had interpreted notable historical episodes. Later, historian Prescott, similarly attracted to grand personalities and notable events, adapted his themes to episodic treatment. This parallel between men working in oil and words might have been sheer coincidence, but Prescott himself strengthens the suspicion that his love of painting influenced his approach to history. Later he would proclaim, "The historian, the greatest of painters."[20]

A commission by his father, as well as his own interest, took William to countless bookshops, especially on Paternoster Row. Of their high prices he complained, but then added, "I take great delight in looking into their scarce and valuable editions, collections such as I have never before witnessed."[21] Years later, when he needed the assistance of a bookseller in Europe, Prescott's recollection of the wealth of London possibly helped him fix his choice there.

Complying with another of his father's charges, William repeatedly attended court to study the English processes of justice. "I have heard some excellent arguments in the cockpit, the Court of Appeal from the Colonies, and Admiralty decisions," he reported.[22] Henry Brougham he remembered for his aquiline nose, twitching muscles, and acute ar-

---

[19] WHP to his parents, July 28, 1816; [Mantle Fielding], "Benjamin West," *Dictionary of American Biography,* 20: 6–9.

[20] Gardiner, ed., *Literary Memoranda,* 2: 67.

[21] WHP to his parents, June 10, 1816, Prescott papers.

[22] *Id.* to *id.,* June 7, 1816, Prescott papers.

gument; Sir William Scott, for his Roman head and feeble voice. At the King's Bench, Baron Edward Law Ellenborough presiding, he found the points of law obscure and the proceedings dull.

The House of Commons disappointed him, but George Canning's powers as a speaker deeply impressed him. At the other extreme he recorded, "I have heard Mr. [William] Wilberforce or Saint Wilberforce as they call him, prose for a couple of hours, amid more groans than commonly attend an execution." Sitting in the gallery of the House of Lords, through Lord Shaftsbury's generosity, he again experienced disappointment.[23]

Meanwhile, exasperation attended his transatlantic correspondence. In the Azores shipping opportunities had been few and often so indirect as to be shunned. William's illness additionally encouraged him to delay letters in the hope that soon he could send good news. In London he again procrastinated, hoping to report progress under Sir William's treatment. Yet another reason for delay was his willingness to transmit letters by individuals, some of whom postponed their sailings and others of whom experienced unduly long voyages.

The Prescotts in Boston, first disappointed, then anxious, finally became indignant. Once William Prescott wrote that they had received no word from him for five months. While his father worried through sleepless nights, his mother, humiliated that she had no answer when solicitous friends inquired, wrote a blistering letter.

Had it not been for the attention of our friends [she said] we should not even have heard of your arrival in London; does the amusements of that gay city, and the pleasures that surround you, banish from your remembrance the Parents, who promoted your going there, the father who dailly labours to support you there, and the friends who feel so much anxiety for you, no that can not be, yet I am weary of conjecture, and tired of apologizing.[24]

The force of Catherine Prescott's ideas, like her character, soared beyond limitations of expression.

The explanations of frugal parents that their letters were short be-

[23] *Id.* to *id.,* July 28, 1816, Prescott papers.
[24] C. G. Prescott to WHP, July 14, 1816, Prescott papers.

cause of postage rates and, better yet, entrusted to traveling acquaintances to escape postage entirely were likewise unacceptable to the
lonesome traveler.

When the flow of mail became mutually satisfactory, Mrs. Prescott crowded pages with social gossip and Mr. Prescott posted his son
on state and national politics. Prescott also admonished William to
write full accounts of men and places and things. "Furnish us," he
wrote, "with a narrative that will enable us to trace your journey, and
in imagination accompany you in it, and to partake of the various and
strong sensations which the novelty of the objects continually presented to your view must produce." Twenty years later William H.
Prescott applied this dictum to historical writing. Anticipating readers
and critics decades later, his mother wrote, "Your description of men
and places is very entertaining."[25]

Young Prescott quickly drew some conclusions about the English
people. English ladies, he thought, were prone to be proud, timid, and
reserved. "The men are universally known as repulsive in their manners," he wrote. Time, amending early estimates, led him to say "It is
only by being domesticated with them that you can appreciate the
value of an English heart."[26]

By late July he completed plans for his departure from England.
First he would go to Paris, in company with N. Amory. From there
Bostonian John Chipman Gray would accompany him on a tour of
Italy. All plans, of course, evolved from Sir William's treatment and
recommendations. Believing that blisters did not benefit his patient,
the doctor substituted a cold water remedy. At the slightest hint of
inflammation, the application of cold water was in order. The physician's desire that young Prescott escape the rigors and risks of a cold
winter coincided with the traveler's plans. Italy, it was hoped, might
eliminate the lingering rheumatism.

Supplied with written instructions on diet and medication, William
could follow Sir William's orders abroad as easily as in London. If his
orders were obeyed, the oculist believed that his patient's vision would

[25] W. Prescott to WHP, August 19, 1816, and C. G. Prescott to WHP, August 10, 1816, Prescott papers.
[26] WHP to his parents, June 7, July 28, Prescott papers.

continue to improve gradually. Yet, even as he hoped for the best, Prescott prepared for the worst.

On July 27 he heard for the first time "of a new invented machine by which blind people were enabled to write." A week later, having hurried to purchase one from patentee Ralph Wedgwood, Jr., in the Strand, he added a noctograph to his baggage. Years later, describing his *modus operandi* as historian to his friend George E. Ellis, William deftly pictured the noctograph.

It consists of a frame of the size of a sheet of paper, traversed by brass wires, as many as lines are wanted on the page, and with a sheet of carbonated paper, such as is used for getting duplicates, pasted on the reverse side. With an ivory or agate stylus the writer traces his characters between the wires on the carbonated sheet, making indelible marks, which he cannot see, on the white page below.[27]

5

Hurrying down the road between Calais and Paris, Amory and young Prescott glimpsed Boulogne, Montreuil, Abbeville, Grandvilliers, and Beauvais.[28] Yellow brick houses, stone staircases, and singing beggars caught William's eye, as did French females. In provincial Grandvilliers their mobcaps and neat aprons intrigued him; and on the boulevards of Paris he positively capitulated, declaring, "I am delighted with the ladies."[29]

Never one to go it alone, William speedily found a circle of Americans among whom he circulated constantly during his two months in Paris. The smallness of his circle in Paris stemmed, in part, from a

[27] *Ibid.*; WHP to George E. Ellis, June 1, 1857, Ellis papers, and in Massachusetts Historical Society *Proceedings,* 13 (1875): 246–249 and Gardiner, ed., *Papers,* pp. 379–382. Now a permanent exhibit of the Massachusetts Historical Society, the noctograph permitted seventeen lines of writing. The paper for it approximated 7¾ x 10 inches. The leather case which enclosed the noctograph fitted, in turn, into a box which allowed one to carry a supply of paper, as well as lock up the entire apparatus.

[28] The account of WHP in France in 1816 derives from the following: WHP, Journal, 1815–1821, pp. 23–45, WHP to his parents, August 24, October 4, November 15, 1816, Prescott Papers; and Gardiner, ed., *Papers,* pp. 22–30.

[29] WHP to his parents, August 24, 1816, Prescott papers.

background which contributed to his being ill at ease among the French. In addition, his desire to protect his vision encouraged his using only those letters of introduction which acquainted him with people among whom he could safeguard his eyes.

The health precautions were necessary. For three days, almost immediately upon arrival in Paris, inflammation plagued him. Once more his extreme sensitivity to change had evidenced itself. However, he recovered quickly and experienced no further trouble with his eyes in Paris.

In France he used the noctograph for the first time when he wrote, on August 24, to his parents. The initial operation of it he found tedious, but he readily admitted, "The invention, however, is certainly a very fortunate one for me." In view of the fact that Prescott composed sizable portions of every one of his books on the noctograph, generations of his readers echo that sentiment.

William called upon Albert Gallatin, but he did not develop with the American minister such friendly ties as he had in London with the Adamses. Far in the future, in the mid-1840's, it would be different. Then Prescott and Gallatin, sharing an interest in the Mexicans, engaged in a friendly correspondence. In Paris he also met John Chipman Gray. Descendant of an old Salem shipping family, Gray had graduated from Harvard the August that Prescott took his entrance examination. As soon as they agreed on the route for their Italian tour, William planned the remainder of his stay in Europe, scheduling his return to Boston for the autumn of 1817.

For two months the City of Light drew William to her museums, churches, parks, palaces, schools, and libraries. The Bibliothèque du Roi and the library of the French Institute overwhelmed him with their holdings and organization. The bookstalls of Paris, however, did not receive as much attention as had the shops of Paternoster Row.

"The other day," he wrote, "I was introduced to the Institute, where I had the pleasure of meeting the most celebrated literary characters in France. . . . there are actually among them at the present period, more men, remarkable for their researches in science, mathematicks [sic], botany and chemistry particularly than in all the world." High regard for the French Institute remained with Prescott. Thirty years later, when he could claim a score, he settled for a few select honors on the title pages of his works, that of the French Institute always heading the list.

A letter to Daniel Parker introduced the young American to life in a French château. On two occasions he spent a few days with Parker, at Draveil, about five leagues from Paris. There the park was "noble," the riding "romantic," and other activities equally memorable.[30]

Product of a society dedicated to law and order, and son of a man whose very livelihood smacked of judicial processes, William H. Prescott had gone to France basically anti-French. He gradually altered his thinking so much that he felt constrained to explain. "Do not suspect, however, dear parents," he wrote, "that my admiration of the French is in the least inconsistent with the honest sentiments in which I have been educated."[31]

On October 7 Prescott set out eastward in company with Gray and their Swiss manservant Fribourg. Ahead was the prospect of meeting Lafayette, to whom both Americans carried letters. This journey introduced Prescott and Gray to both the comfort and the expense of travel by chariot. Lined throughout with green, the front blind always raised, this vehicle afforded the needed protection and its side windows, views of the countryside. Purchased in Paris, their chariot cost two thousand francs.

The road to La Grange was execrable, the visit there, a joy. Hospitably received at the six-century-old, ivy-clad castle, the young Americans must have evoked memories for their fifty-nine-year-old host. At William's age, Lafayette had pledged his sword to the cause of American independence. After passing the night at La Grange, Prescott and Gray inspected the superb lawn, the farmland, and the Merino flock of the Marquis before bidding him adieu. In 1825, when Lafayette included Boston on his triumphal tour of America, no Bostonian more eagerly rolled out the welcome mat than did William H. Prescott.

For ten days the young travelers rolled toward the Italian border, via Avallon, Autun, Mâcon, Lyon, Bourgoin, Chambéry, and St. Jean

[30] *Id.* to *id.,* October 4, 1816, Prescott papers.
[31] *Id.* to *id.,* August 24, 1816, Prescott papers.

de Maurienne. "I found none of those charms in the petits Savoyards that Goldsmith had taught me to expect,"[32] he remarked, adverting to his literary recollections. At a miserable little inn on Mt. Cenis he remembered and fulfilled a promise to drink to Caroline Preble's health atop the Alps.

6

The prodigal son of Biblical days rushed homeward with no greater anticipation than moved Prescott from Alpine heights into Piedmont.[33] In a very real sense, Italy was for him an intellectual home. In the course of his study of Latin, first with clergyman Gardiner and then at Harvard, he had developed sincere affection for Caesar, Ovid, Virgil, Horace, Livy, Cicero, and other classical writers. "I never expect to feel again similar emotions to those I felt when I set foot on this sacred land," he confessed.[34] Gray being similarly inclined, the two dug favorite authors out of their baggage in preparation for their classical pilgrimage.

"It is a noble river, and well deserves the immortality to which Ovid has consigned it," he wrote of the Po after stooping to bathe his hands in it at Turin. The highway to Genoa, notorious for robbers, buttressed his negative opinion of modern Italians. Quickly, however, the dusky loveliness of white-veiled Genoese women counteracted the disparagement. Marengo recalled Napoleon's great victory; but in the nearby towns of Asti and Novi, Prescott himself fought losing battles to the extraordinary local breed of fleas. Crossing the battlefield on which Francis I had surrendered to Charles V, the travelers moved on toward Milan, which served as base for trips to lakes Maggiore and Como. To test the Milanese echo, which was reputed to reverberate fifty times, the Bostonians "fired off a brace of pistols, and it sounded

---

[32] *Id.* to *id.,* November 15, 1816, Prescott papers. The reference to Goldsmith apparently is to the poem "The Traveller or A Prospect of Society."

[33] WHP's tour of Italy derives from: WHP, Journal, 1815–1821, pp. 46–98, 166, WHP to his parents, November 15, December 11, 20, 1816, January 18, February 14, 20, 25, March 19, April 29, 1817, Prescott papers; Gardiner, ed., *Papers,* pp. 18–20, 22–30; and Ticknor, *Prescott,* pp. 45–48.

[34] WHP to his parents, November 15, 1816, Prescott papers. The quotations which follow immediately are also from this letter.

like a general discharge of our militia on election day." The amphitheater at Verona, occupied at the moment by a circus, carried William back to ancient times, as did visits to Livy's townhouse and the birthplaces of Catullus and Pliny. Near Mantua, Virgil and his farm came to mind. South of the Po, the Americans saw Modena and Bologna before arriving at Florence.

Ten days in the Tuscan center offered Prescott and Gray new opportunities, for letters of introduction gained them admittance to cosmopolitan society. After less than a week, during which he had met the Swedish and Russian ministers, the Marquis of Silva and the Countess of Alfieri, Prescott declared, "Italian society is in its perfection at Florence." That city also evoked the praise, "It is the modern Athens; and the arts seem to have selected it, as their last retreat."

In Florence he visited Rafaello Morghen. Joining those already appreciative of Morghen's genius, Prescott bought ten of his engravings for 180 francs and wished that he could afford more. His purchases focused on classical themes—Diana and Aurora—and works by Raphael, Murillo, and Correggio and such men of Italian letters as Tasso, Ariosto, Petrarch, and Dante. Prescott's urge to acquire more engravings by Morghen triumphed, because the inventory that he made upon his return to Boston listed fifteen works by that master.

Health was never an issue during the seven weeks between Paris and Rome, owing in part to Gray's kind attentions. John read the classical references which interested both; and in Florence he accepted the invitations to balls and to the theater while Prescott attended only breakfasts and dinners. Aside from mild touches of rheumatism, William felt fine as he entered Rome. When the dome of St. Peter's came into view, he remarked, "Roma pulcherrima rerum."[35]

The Hôtel d'Europe in the Piazza di Spagna was headquarters during the next seven weeks. Except for one slight cold, which affected neither his eyes nor his rheumatic legs, William enjoyed good health. The excellent state of his eyes he attributed to his medicines, his exercise, and the somber colors of Italian buildings.

[35] WHP, Journal, 1815–1821, p. 62, Prescott papers; [Michael Bryan], *Bryan's Dictionary of Painters and Engravers,* 5 vols. (London and New York, 1903–1905), 3: 366–368.

"Rome has three principal subjects of curiosity," he informed his parents, "its antiquities, arts, and splendid mummeries."[36] He gave attention to everything—amphitheaters, bridges, baths, churches, circuses, fountains, grottoes, Masses, paintings, palaces, temples, tombs, villas, and more. The Tiber drew the laconic observation, "very muddy."[37] More words and feeling he accorded the "charming legs—feet —fine busts of the Roman women."

In Rome, as in every other place in which he spent much time, Prescott developed a circle of acquaintances. He sampled Italian social life with the Duchess of Bracciano, the Countess of Marascotti, and Signor Trebbi. Among fellow Americans he dined, attended balls, and passed pleasant evenings, some of which testified to his improved physical well-being. Most of his prowling, however, he undertook alone. In reverie and in communion with his love of antiquities, he preferred it that way. On occasion he wrote, "Spent the day in the Forum."

At this stage of his long trip, Prescott's expenditures were running in excess of his allowance, medical expenses alone having amounted to £100. Parisian gowns and Florentine engravings were his only extravagances. When Rome tempted him with another, he decided against it. After arranging to be presented to His Holiness Pius VII, he and several American friends decided that the expense of appropriate dress—cut in a manner that made it useless for any other purpose— rendered the honor so dubious that they decided to forego it. In Naples, soaring prices, which he attributed to the deluge of English travelers, led William to move several times in the course of a four-week stay.

Rich in historical and literary associations, Naples proved fascinating. From there William excursioned to Portici, Vesuvius, Pozzuoli, Pompeii, Cumoe, Salerno, Eboli, and Baia. "Shoes burnt, feet blistered, exceedingly fatigued—but much gratified," he wrote of his ascent to the crater of Vesuvius.

The accommodations at Eboli he termed the *"ne plus ultra"* of his Italian experience.

[36] WHP to his parents, December 11, 1816, Prescott papers.
[37] WHP, Journal, 1815–1821, p. 63, Prescott papers. The quotations which follow immediately are from *ibid.,* pp. 74, 70, 81, 85.

We were lodged at Eboli at the most wretched inn, of the most wretched village in Italy [he wrote] . . . squeezed into a small chamber which had been appropriated for the last century to potatoes and corn-stocks. . . . dinner was served upon a washing bench; seats were out of the question, but as I felt somewhat fatigued, and had forgotten the Italian for a chair, I squatted down in different parts of the room, and endeavoured to make the good landlady comprehend by pantomime what I could not by words. She nodded very sagaciously and returned in about five minutes with a large basket of eggs. . .[38]

On Naples and its citizens, William's appraising eye fell with mixed reactions. Lower class Neapolitans he found indolent and dishonest; the aristocracy he considered libertine and profligate. Entertained by nobility, William also had his pockets picked, by lazzarone.[39] The unrivaled beauty of the bay, meanwhile, was, in part, Prescott's undoing. Early in February 1817 inflammation confined William for four days. The brilliant sky and the reflections on the water he considered the principal causes.

As winter waned, Prescott trekked northward; in Rome he consumed several days in farewell glimpses of his favorite Italian city. By way of Siena, he returned to Florence. After a parting social flourish there, William and John journeyed down the Arno Valley toward Pisa and Leghorn.

On March 12 the Americans sailed from Leghorn, concluding their five-month Italian tour. As they coasted past Genoa, Nice, and Toulon under a light breeze, Prescott had time for shipboard musings. If he bothered to hark back, possibly he related recent Italian experiences to schoolboy studies. If he looked ahead, it was merely to Paris and London, because at that point it was impossible for him to anticipate the continuing significance of Italy in his life. However, his love for it soon would lead him to modern Italian literature, to focus on the

[38] WHP to his parents, April 29, 1817, Prescott papers.

[39] In *History as Romantic Art—Bancroft, Prescott, Motley, and Parkman* (Stanford, 1959), pp. 113, 249 n.45, David Levin is too occupied categorizing Prescott to realize that he based his statement about Neapolitan dishonesty on experience: WHP had been overcharged in hotels, his pocket had been picked, and he had been gouged on posting charges.

epic. The epic, in turn, would influence for all time his approach to history.

7

As he resumed touring in Marseilles, Prescott found that his eyes, for the first time, had benefited from a sea voyage.[40] Ashore, however, new hazards awaited, among them indigestion and runaway horses. Northward the American pair headed their chariot for Avignon, to visit Laura's tomb and Petrarch's house. In haste to re-establish themselves in Paris, they gave Fontainebleau scant attention. As they entered the French capital, Prescott felt ill.

For a week an inflammation kept him indoors at the Hotel de Montmorency. He barely had recovered when George Ticknor, fresh from studies at Göttingen, checked into the same hotel. That evening they strolled the boulevards, deep in conversation, one teeming with two years of German experience, the other with vivid Italian memories. George also spoke of his appointment as professor of Spanish at Harvard. After dining together, they returned to the Montmorency. There, suddenly ill with fever, William remained for three weeks, under a doctor's care. In this bleak period George Ticknor passed many hours with him. From April 1817 dated the special intimacy which the two men enjoyed for more than forty years.

Full of thoughts which he wanted to share with his parents, Prescott again employed a secretary. One letter penned by Busson filled forty-nine pages. As he recounted his travels, William also totaled his expenses. The account which, from Paris, anticipated his short second visit to England as best it might, indicated that his two years of travel represented an expenditure of £1,100, plus passage. He had traveled like a special kind of gentleman, an invalided one.

Recovering his health, Prescott visited Madame de Staël and other Parisian hostesses, revisited certain stellar attractions, and shopped feverishly to fulfill commissions. Aside from medical expenses and this shopping, he economized, in quixotic fashion. He abandoned the

---

[40] For WHP's second visits to France and England, see: WHP, Journal, 1815–1821, pp. 90–125, WHP to his parents, March 19, April 11, 29, May 15, 24, June 23, July 5, 29, 1817, WHP to E. G. Prescott, May 28, 1817, Prescott papers; and Ticknor, *Prescott*, pp. 46–48.

luxury of a fire in his room, but kept servant Fribourg to slide the warming pan into his bed. Most enjoyable, one suspects, were the days at Draveil with Parker. They were physically and mentally ideal for William before he set out for the Channel coast.

Selling their trusty chariot to another junketing American for 1,250 francs, William and John left Paris for Dieppe in an open cabriolet. At that coastal fishing village, William bade France farewell.

London, once more, was many things to the youthful visitor—consultations with Sir William Adams, social activities with friends, shopping for himself and his father, second looks at certain attractions against critical insights born of Continental experience, plans for an excursion to Scotland, and arrangements for the homeward voyage.

Although William saw Dr. Adams, he did not desire treatment. His eyes and general health were at their best. Rather it was a matter of reporting and winning approval of his own handling of his ailments. For months young Prescott had adhered to the nutritious diet, shielded his eyes, applied astringent lotions, and sipped wine tonic. The last item in the regimen had encouraged his tasting every kind of wine he encountered. Rationed to two glasses per day, he had relished the wine so much that he invariably ordered his served in the largest glasses available. To his doctor's formula Prescott had added one thing, regular exercise. By the time of this visit to Sir William, after an absence of nine months, the daily exercise program included a stint of walking which ranged between four and eight miles. Dr. Adams did not alter the program. All of his years Prescott remained an enthusiastic pedestrian.

As before, the Scottish tour was dropped to lengthen his stay in London. There, after ten months with Gray, Prescott was on his own. He minimized his social contacts. Once more he lived in the West End and had secretary McCandlish handle his correspondence. As the daily routine took form, McCandlish also assumed other duties.

I rise at half past six A.M. [William wrote] . . . at least a good hour before my Secretary summons up sufficient courage to open his eyes; from eight till two we are closeted, from two till six I am running about the town as a man of business, from six to eight in the important occupation of dinner.

... as the Sun goes down I return to my lodgings and am occupied with my Secretaire until eleven.[41]

In addition to penning letters, McCandlish regularly read to him, it being the young traveler's desire to supplement his own impressions.

Shortly after his return to London, William booked passage on friend Hinckley's vessel *Triton*. Until the *Triton*'s scheduled departure, in late July or early August, excursioning was in order. By public stagecoach he visited Oxford, Blenheim, Gloucester, the Wye, Bristol, and Salisbury in a counterclockwise circuit which consumed one week.

In mid-July, armed with letters of introduction to various fellows and professors, Prescott visited Cambridge. There the last instance of acquisitiveness in the romantic traveler who already had fragments of the Elgin marbles and Juliet's tomb evidenced itself. "In the gardens of Christ Church is a mulberry tree planted by Milton," he wrote. "I plucked a sprig to add to Lizzy's literary collection."[42] Returned to London with stronger vision and without rheumatism, he said his farewells and left, on July 30, for Liverpool and the *Triton*.

[41] WHP to his parents, June 23, 1817, Prescott papers.
[42] *Id.* to *id.*, July 29, 1817, Prescott papers.

**III**

*By the time I am 30, (God willing) I propose . . .*

T HE CHANGES OF TWO YEARS were upon William H. Prescott, his family, friends, and Boston.[1] The basic objective of his long trip —a return to good health—had not materialized. However, the assurance that every effort had been made did console all the Prescotts. Having concluded that self-discipline, in diet, exercise, social affairs, use of eyes, and all else, would be more helpful than medicines, William found that his efforts at disciplined living would show varying results.

A second side of his trip, the grand tour, was a success. His curiosity, the family's queries and expectations, and his own classical education

[1] The sources for the Prescotts, their friends, and Boston in the period 1815–1817 are these: W. and C. G. Prescott to WHP, August 10, 19, September 4, 1816, June 1, 1817, W. Prescott to WHP, March 2, June 10, 15, August 6, October 13, November 24, 1816, January 4, April 12, 1817, C. G. Prescott to WHP, June 7, July 14, August 8, September 15, 22, October 10, 12, 16, 27, November 6, 29, 1816, January 1, 9, March 3, 10, 19, May 18, 1817, C. E. Prescott to WHP, September 15, December 29, 1816, Prescott papers; George S. Hillard, "Prescott," in *Little Journeys to the Homes of American Authors* (New York, 1896), p. 84; Caroline Gardiner Curtis, *Memories of Fifty Years in the Last Century* (Boston, 1947), p. 12; Annie Haven Thwing, *The Crooked & Narrow Streets of the Town of Boston, 1630–1822* (Boston, 1920), p. 180; William B. Sprague, *Annals of the American Unitarian Pulpit* (New York, 1865), pp. 439–440.

had converted months in England, France, and Italy into a rich experience. Stimulated by intelligent travel, William had replaced hasty generalizations about nations with refined and more precise conclusions. Intolerance had lessened, odious and unthinking comparisons diminished. He had appraised English, French and Italian life in relation to history, geography, and other variables that fashion nationality.

But what of the future? Unable to pursue law, William put himself on record as not desiring to become a merchant. Contempt did not dictate the decision. His father had married the daughter of a merchant; and he would do likewise. Will Prescott simply found the world of the merchant, as a possible career, unappealing. When the older Prescott realized that Will could not pursue his profession, he had written, "You must be turning your attention to something else."[2] William was doing nothing of the kind.

Meanwhile William Prescott, frail, smooth-shaven, and quite bald, was at the height of his powers, a recognized leader of his profession. Conservative in outlook, manners, and dress—he requested black cloth when his son brought British woolens to him—William Prescott, though a generous parent and host, consistently impressed everyone with the virtue of economy. His wife also had public and private sides to her nature. In all Catherine was friendly, direct, honest, and economical. Her purse and her labor helped to support activities of the Female Asylum.

Elizabeth changed considerably in her brother's absence. Not quite sixteen when William went abroad, and possessed of the intellectual instincts of her parents as well as their love of society, Lizzie did more than merely dabble at painting and French. She read avidly, and, after Will's return, her love of reading put her eyes increasingly at his service. As she moved from sweet young girl to poised young lady, the special affection which had led to her writing Will, on September 15, 1816, "You have been absent 1,115,118 minutes,"[3] deepened.

Less than twelve years of age when his older brother departed, Ned Prescott grew rapidly during the ensuing two years. At times scholastically indifferent, even lazy, Ned occasionally surprised and pleased

[2] W. Prescott to WHP, August 19, 1816, Prescott papers.
[3] C. E. Prescott to WHP, September 15, 1816, Prescott papers.

his parents. The gap of almost eight years between Will and Ned made difficult any comradeship between them in this period.

The first summer of William's absence the Prescotts rented a house, which Mrs. Prescott named "The Wigwam," in the Jamaica Plains district. Her husband's health had prompted the move. When mid-autumn returned the family to their Summer Street residence, the head of the family was in much better health. However, the Prescotts did not live much longer on Summer Street. About Christmas time they made arrangements to buy an old-fashioned house on the north side of Pond Street. In a central location, the big square yellow brick house was more remarkable for its isolation than for its architecture. Only a narrow strip of earth separated it from the unpaved street, but much more ground lay at the sides and rear of the house. Horse chestnuts and elms of considerable size shaded it. At the rear of the lot stood an ample brick stable. In view of the lawyer's love of nature, the earthen street, the sprawling yard, the stately elms, and the distance to his immediate neighbors were unmistakable assets.

To win Catherine Prescott's approbation, the house met various re-quirements—space for her husband's library, a parlor suitable for their social requirements, spare bedrooms for guests. One of the front upper chambers was William's, the other Elizabeth's. When informed of the remodeling of his unseen room, William had written from Paris, "I hope it has blinds, shutters, and curtains, that the Sun never has the audacity to enter it, that it has a fire place or a stove, which is a much more sensible contrivance, that the bed is furnished with curtains and the floor with a carpet. You will think me whimsical, but these re-quests may lie all resolved into bad eyes and the rheumatism."[4]

On the Sabbath most of the Prescotts dutifully attended two Uni-tarian services in nearby New South Church. Its high tapering steeple rose a short distance east of their neighborhood, as convenient to them from Pond Street as it had been from Summer. Sunday also fitted into the social life of the Prescotts. On that day they regularly entertained the small groups which they variously termed their "Sunday evening circle" and "roast beef set." For months William would be a special focus of attention and conversation at these intimate gatherings.

[4] WHP to his parents, May 1, 1817, Prescott papers.

Of the changing worlds of some friends, William learned in direct correspondence; of others his family kept him informed. Will Gardiner, after graduation from Harvard in 1816, was reading history at home, preparatory to studying for the bar with lawyer Prescott. Franklin Dexter—Frank to his friends—was enjoying life to the full, professionally as the law partner of C. G. Loring.

Meanwhile, in the heart of Boston, frame buildings were giving way to brick and stone. Politically, life was less hectic than it had been during the late war. Governor John Brooks, a Federalist, had won another term, to the satisfaction of the Prescotts, among others. Boston's special contribution to the American intellectual scene, the *North American Review,* had as its new editor a friend of young Prescott.

2

The bright welcome and Will's light front room quickly changed. Besieged by old torments, he suffered even more because of the light colors of the wallpaper and painted surfaces. More somber colors replaced them. Failing to respond at home, he moved to a house in the country close at hand. There the dampness multiplied his rheumatic complaint. Quicker than he had departed it, he returned to town. William spent the winter of 1817–1818 in close confinement, painfully restricted to his darkened room. Day after day Will Gardiner, then reading law with the senior Prescott, read classics to the invalid. When Will departed, Lizzie took over. She usually read novels and other light literature. Reading and discussion deepened their common love of literature.

By the spring of 1818, eyes, joints, and spirit encouraged young Prescott to tabulate his wine consumption. When the severest weather had passed, he ventured outside, but pain often drove him back indoors. In May inflammation struck again—"God knows how," he said. In desperation he experimented with a vegetable diet and decided to forego wine until July, except at parties. Before that month, however, he resumed his daily wine allotment, increased his walks, and gradually withdrew the protective blinds from his windows. In this period his journal carried the note: "*Colds*—principal evil to be dreaded." Physical recovery proving tedious, he routinized his day. Seven days a week, with Sunday varying slightly from the others, he set aside certain intervals for intellectual matters.

Prescott's first literary effort dates from this period. Inspiration for it stemmed not only from a growing love of letters but also from Lizzie's encouragement and from the stimulus of a literary-minded group of young men with whom he had organized the nucleus of a club. William was the leading architect of the organization. Simply called "Club" and eventually counting twenty-four—half of whom were Porcellians—the group first met on June 13, 1818, with a membership of nine. The renewal of strength and spirit which permitted movement beyond his family circle enabled William to attend the hearty sessions of Club which combined eating, smoking, drinking, and talking. The last derived, in part, from the original papers which they read and criticized within the group.[5] Yet another stimulus which urged Prescott to write for publication was the nearness of the *North American Review.*

In secrecy which he shared only with Lizzie, he wrote and sent to its editors an anonymous article. Joyfully anticipating the publication of his material, they suffered crushing disappointment when the piece was rejected. "There! it is good for nothing," he exclaimed. "They refuse it. I was a fool to send it."[6] This initial rebuff notwithstanding,

[5] WHP, Journal, 1815–1821, pp. 181, 185, Prescott papers. With the date signifying graduation from Harvard, and the letter "P" denoting membership in the Porcellian Club, the full membership of Club eventually included: Alexander Bliss, John Brazer (1813), George Augustus Frederick Dawson (1818), Franklin Dexter (1812), Samuel Atkins Eliot (1817, P), William Havard Eliot (1815, P), Charles Folsom (1813), William Howard Gardiner (1816, P), John Chipman Gray (1811, P), Francis William Pitt Greenwood (1814), Enoch Hale (1813), Charles Greely Loring (1812), William Powell Mason (1811), John Gorham Palfrey (1815, P), Theophilus Parsons (1815, P), Octavius Pickering (1810), William Hickling Prescott (1814, P), Jared Sparks (1815), William Jones Spooner (1813, P), Jonathan Mayhew Wainwright (1812, P), John Ware (1813), Henry Warren (1813), Martin Whiting (1814), Francis William Winthrop (1817, P).

For a number of these young men it is apt to say "The interest of Boston Federalists in literature was, principally, a cryptic expression of their alienation from the commercial strain in American life." See Jane Maloney Johnson, "Through Change and Through Storm: A Study of Federalist-Unitarian Thought, 1800–1860" (Ph.D. diss., Radcliffe College, 1958), p. 33.

[6] Ticknor, *Prescott,* p. 51.

he continued with literary criticism and his apprenticeship at writing. By January 1, 1819, this dictum was shaping Will's intellectual life: "Once in 3 months for the club 3 sheets—not opinion—never more or less—Elizabeth's writing.

"Never print or write to publish or show my writing out of the club—or talk of my writing out of the club."[7] Diligence and modesty walked hand in hand.

### 3

Although uncertainty shrouded William's present and future, it was otherwise with his father. In addition to conspicuous public service in this period—as overseer of Harvard, judge of the Court of Common Pleas, and delegate to a state constitutional convention—William Prescott was quietly establishing a substantial fortune. He believed and invested in the rising prospects of New England industry, transportation, and insurance. His long identification with port towns and his friendships with many shippers and merchants likewise prompted speculation in imported goods, especially in the India trade. In partnership with his friend David Sears, he had invested in Maine land.[8]

### 4

During the second half of 1818, improved health permitted young Prescott to mingle more in society. He avoided hot, stuffy rooms and did his best daily to get out of bed at 6 A.M. and into it by 10:30 P.M. He was among those who, on the evening of Friday, August 14, drove out to the beautiful Brookline establishment of James Perkins, where Eliza Susan Quincy found him an agreeable dancing partner.[9] Will's nature required such contacts, and their renewal quickened his physical improvement. Because he still had colds and read only with the greatest caution, he continued to use Lizzie's eyes. As the setbacks lessened in number and severity, and the winter social season advanced, he

[7] WHP, Journal, 1815–1821, p. 184, Prescott papers.
[8] William T. Davis, *Bench and Bar of . . . Massachusetts,* 2 vols. (Boston, 1895), 1: 279; Statements of William Prescott's adventures in the ships *Glide* and *George,* December 31, 1818, Prescott papers; and Morison, *The Maritime History,* pp. 218–220.
[9] Howe, *Articulate Sisters,* p. 31.

cautiously attended some balls. In mid-December he noted worriedly, "too late at a ball—Sears." Less than two weeks later he wrote, in evident exultation, "lights and lamps at home."

In early 1819 Prescott's intellectual diet scheduled 4½ hours of work 6 days a week, and 3 hours on Sunday; and his social schedule responded directly to his physical state. One social highlight for him was the ball given by his parents at their home on snowy February 16. Socially he was himself once again—gay to the point of hilarity, full of the social grace of manhood without surrendering his addiction to puns and practical jokes. Club continued to command William's attention. So, too, did reading and writing—at which he often abused his eyes and regretted it. In May he boasted of walking three miles without the silken screens on his glasses. That same month he also complained, "weak from reading and writing."[10] Meanwhile he was adhering to his wine diet with ritualistic precision.

Most of the summer he spent at Cohasset. On occasion the names Cohasset and Miss Susannah Amory—not seventeen until October 8— were linked. "Susan" to her friends, she gradually became more than Will's favorite dancing partner. The annoucement of the Amory-Prescott engagement cast William in twin roles, punster and classicist, as he declared "Omnia vincit amor, et nos cedamos Amori." While his heart increasingly belonged to Susan, he was seeking new areas of the physical discipline so important to his happiness. That same summer he issued to himself the dictum, "Never smoke a cigar that is not positively weak—and leave off when affected by it."[11]

Even as love came to William, Franklin Dexter was preparing to lead Lizzie to the altar. For her wedding Lizzie selected a day in September six weeks in advance of her twentieth birthday.

In October, William, battling a series of colds, concluded, "Better take tea for a real cold." The following month he enunciated a new rule, born of experience, "Never read a *syllable* by candlelight after the eye feels it."[12]

[10] WHP, Journal, 1815–1821, pp. 154, 176, 177, Prescott papers.
[11] Ticknor, *Prescott,* p. 50 n.2; and WHP, Journal, 1815–1821, p. 151, Prescott papers.
[12] *Ibid.,* pp. 148, 149.

Sometime in 1819, at various moments one suspects, Will cata-logued the holdings of the growing Prescott library, under four head-ings: English classics, French classics, Greek and Roman classics, and Italian classics. Untrue to these designations, however, he grouped the works by the languages in which they were printed rather than by the nationalities of their authors. Accordingly Tacitus was listed as both English and Roman literature, and Voltaire as both French and English. At the time the Prescott library contained about 666 vol-umes. Most heavily represented among the British authors were Dr. Samuel Johnson, John Dryden, Henry St. John Bolingbroke, Edmund Burke, Oliver Goldsmith, Walter Scott, Francis Bacon, Robert Southey, Jonathan Swift, John Milton, Joseph Addison, David Hume, Edward Gibbon, and William Robertson. The principal French writers were Voltaire, Molière, Jean Baptiste Racine, Jean François Marmontel, and Bernard le Bovier de Fontenelle. The leading ancient authors in the library were Homer, Cicero, Livy, Ovid, Virgil, and Tacitus. Un-known is the degree of William's personal acquaintance with these works at that time, but later labors reflected his wide use of the library.

## 5

Club, having met three times in December 1819 to refine an ex-citing idea, bent every effort in the new year to establish a publication to feature original contributions by its members. Appropriately named *The Club-Room*, its first and only editor was young Prescott, almost twenty-four and so lacking a career that some of his friends had dubbed him "the gentleman." Will conscientiously set about lining up con-tributors. On January 12, Theophilus Parsons, William H. Gardiner, and Dr. John Ware all agreed "to furnish 6 pages printed at a week's notice, once in three weeks for the year 1820."[13] Frank Dexter made a similar pledge, but on a fortnight's notice. In reserve and without specific promises as to size or frequency of contribution were Henry Warren, John Chipman Gray, John Gorham Palfrey, Francis W. P. Greenwood, and William Jones Spooner.

Counting Prescott, the corps which not only promised but delivered

---

[13] WHP, Commonplace Book, 1820–1822, p. 3, Prescott papers.

the copy for more than 90 per cent of all the issues of *The Club-Room* counted ten in number. All were William's contemporaries at Harvard. Professionally they were lawyers, clergymen, doctors, and curious young men in search of their lifework. More than half eventually led such achieving lives that Alma Mater conferred honorary degrees upon them.

Marked by the same high humor and keen wit which prevailed at the Tuesday evening meetings of Club, Henry Warren, in an unsigned article—as indeed all were in every issue—set forth in the initial issue the *raison d'être* of the new publication. A note on the back cover indicated that *The Club-Room* would appear at irregular intervals, carrying indefinite quantities of original matter—light or grave, prose or poetry, excluding only serious criticism. The price would vary with the size of the number, the first one selling for 37½ cents. Copyrighted late in January and published on February 5, 1820, it appeared in octavo, to facilitate binding. The titles of the articles in that forty-page issue, of which five hundred copies were printed, hinted at their light and predominantly fictional nature: "Happiness" by Parsons, "Recollections" by Dexter, and "Castle Building" by Ware. In a moment of editorial confidence, Prescott told Jared Sparks, "As the literary merits of most of our members have already been decided by their public performances, we have little reason to doubt our ability to support such a work."[14]

The second number of *The Club-Room*, five articles aggregating forty-four pages, appeared on March 10. The editor opened it with a rambling and half-humorous seven-page discussion of the choice of name for the paper. Will Gardiner contributed "Lake George" and Theophilus Parsons discussed "Ennui." Of Francis W. P. Greenwood's fictional piece "The Village Grave-Yard," Prescott entertained the highest regard, terming it "exquisitely beautiful and tender. It is in my opinion above anything Irving had reached A.D. 1820."[15] The direct and simple account of a traveler's musings in the world of the

---

[14] *The Club-Room,* No. 1 (February, 1820); and Gardiner, ed., *Papers,* p. 31.

[15] *The Club-Room,* No. 2 (March, 1820); and WHP, Commonplace Book, 1820–1822, p. 8, Prescott papers.

spirits pleased Prescott. The concluding piece in the second number, "Calais," was Prescott's. For this tale of a traveler's nighttime terror, the author seemed to hark back to his own European experience. This undistinguished writing again aligned his personal taste with fiction smacking of the mysterious and supernatural.

Looking beyond the first two numbers of *The Club-Room*, its editor undertook to broaden the range of its content and to lengthen its list of contributors. To Fitz-Greene Halleck, he wrote, "I find no difficulty as the editor in obtaining compositions in prose; but it is otherwise in poetry, which, as it is not necessary to publish, we feel unwilling to publish unless it is particularly good; and I know of no source from whence I could be so likely to obtain this as from the author of 'Fanny.' "[16] Halleck apparently ignored Prescott's appeal.

The fat third issue, containing fifty-four pages and six pieces, emerged on April 26. Because of its size, the price rose to forty-five cents. The fifth selection, "The Vale of Alleriot," was Prescott's third and last contribution to *The Club-Room*. Like "Calais," its setting was a European region known to Prescott, this time a Burgundian valley north of Lyons. Like "Calais," it did not represent real life experience; and like "Calais," it associated a traveler with a mysterious episode. In "The Vale of Alleriot" Prescott combined his affection for the mysterious and the melancholy.

The regularity with which an avowedly irregular paper had appeared, plus the expanded size of the third issue, suggested, at first glance, that *The Club-Room* was on the road to success and long life. A closer view, however, suggested the contrary. Whereas seven different members had contributed the nine items in the first two numbers, only one additional author contributed to the third issue. In fact, the labor of writing and publishing the paper was falling upon such a small number that they could not sustain it. Consequently contributions by nonmembers Edward Everett and J. C. Fisher won space in the third number. Quantitatively the literary output of the Tuesday evening

[16] Gardiner, ed., *Papers*, pp. 32–33. Altered, the letter appears in James Grant Wilson, *The Life and Letters of Fitz-Greene Halleck* (New York, 1869), pp. 238–239.

group had fallen below the expectations on which they had launched the paper.

Three months elapsed before the fourth and final issue of *The Club-Room* appeared, on July 19. Pieces by Gardiner and Dexter filled its thirty-nine pages. "And here," the editor mused, "ended this precious publication."[17] Never again did William H. Prescott edit anything. Although Club never made any effort to revive its publication program, it did continue its social and literary camaraderie. Yet even as Prescott and friends never outgrew their desire for companionship of that order, the early death of *The Club-Room* attested the essential dilettantism of most members.

Finances had nothing to do with the collapse of the paper, witness Prescott's statement, "Each number has considerably more than paid its expenses—but out of town it has not been well managed." From youth, Prescott, who twenty-nine years later as an eminent historian insisted that "advertising is the breeze that carries an edition off," knew the role of promotion in the success of any published work.[18] The failure of *The Club-Room* to win a wider public contributed, meanwhile, to its editor's willingness to abandon it. Of the fifteen published items written by Club, Prescott, his brother-in-law, and his closest friend had contributed eight. Perhaps the editor's special demands upon Dexter and Gardiner had enabled him to stave off an earlier demise.

Despite the labors imposed by *The Club-Room* in early 1820, the social whirl continued to lure William. Before the end of January his social life inspired the note, "Theatre, late Balls, smoking, supper parties always pernicious—ergo, not go—or not stay long."[19] Nevertheless, balls, suppers, and Club crowded the succeeding months, as

[17] WHP, Commonplace Book, 1820–1822, p. 9, Prescott papers. WHP's three articles in the publication may be identified fully as follows: "Club-Room," *The Club-Room,* no. 2 (March, 1820), pp. 43–50; "Calais," *The Club-Room,* no. 2 (March, 1820), pp. 78–84; and "The Vale of Alleriot," *The Club-Room,* no. 3 (April, 1820), pp. 130–137.

[18] Gardiner, ed., *Papers,* p. 34; and C. Harvey Gardiner, *Prescott and His Publishers* (Carbondale, 1959), p. 174.

[19] WHP, Journal, 1815–1821, pp. 144, 146, Prescott papers.

did colds and ailing eyes. To strengthen his will and improve his health, Prescott reduced certain rules to writing. When dyspeptic, he would eat moderately—one dish per meal, neither a pastry nor a heavy food, taking nothing between meals and omitting supper. Wine he would limit to one glass; and he would eliminate smoking except at Club. He would shut his eyes outdoors in the presence of snow and when riding. Sleigh rides were taboo. Balls were to be left by 11 P.M. or after 2½ hours attendance; and Club could hold him only till midnight. He would write everything by noctograph; and his reading, with judicious pauses, must be laid aside at the first sign of fatigue. How helpful it would have been if a stronger will than William's had enforced these resolves!

6

"It is so long since the bet became due that I ought to pay interest," William wrote the amiable Theophilus Parsons, "but such a thing I believe is contrary to the code of honor, and is still more contrary to the laws of love, which have a right to preside over our bet. However if I have lost my money I have got my wife, and I am very willing to pay it as a discount upon the high prize."[20] Prescott's marriage to Susan Amory would coincide with his twenty-fourth birthday.

Thomas Coffin Amory, Susan's father, had succeeded capitally as merchant. Long before his death in 1812, he had amassed the wealth which spelled comfort for his widow and children. Susan's mother was the former Hannah Linzee, whose father, as commander of the British frigate *Falcon*, had shelled the position occupied by William's grandfather and his men on Bunker Hill that memorable day in 1775. William Amory, not quite sixteen, was the Amory with the social zest to match that of William H. Prescott.

Neither then nor later was Susan Amory's personality the kind that attracted attention. She lacked the extrovert qualities of her father and exhibited little of the fighting spirit of grandfather Linzee. Her re-

[20] Gardiner, ed., *Papers*, p. 34. For this section, also see: W. Prescott, Last Will and Testament, July 29, 1844, Probate Court, Suffolk County, Massachusetts; John Gould Curtis, *History of the Town of Brookline Massachusetts* (Boston, 1933), p. 188; W. G. Prescott to S. A. Prescott, September 29, 1849, Prescott papers; and Ticknor, *Prescott*, p. 53.

tiring nature abhorred the idea of moving about in society. On more than one count the attraction between her and William was that of opposites. Seventeen-year-old Susan could dutifully conform to the way of life of her twenty-four-year-old husband in all but religion. Of stanch Episcopalian stock, Susan was accustomed to hearing Dr. John S. J. Gardiner at Trinity Church in nearby Summer Street. The Prescotts, meanwhile, like many leading families of Boston, had shifted to Unitarianism. Like Susan, William could not turn his back on his church, so they compromised. A compact between them provided for their alternating between the Unitarian and Episcopal churches. Though impossible to assess precisely, some of the religious tolerance in Prescott's histories possibly stemmed from this compact.

The evening of May 4, 1820, drew three generations of kinsmen and friends of the Amorys and Prescotts to the marriage festivities at Twenty-one Franklin Place. As when Lizzie married Frank, a supper followed the marriage service. When William departed with his teenage bride, he took her but a short distance—two blocks south to the home of his parents.

Meek and impressionable, Susan never had a real chance to develop a strong personality. For the next twenty-four years she and her husband occupied an apartment in the residence owned, occupied, and managed by William and Catherine Prescott. While bearing and rearing her children, Susan helped William maintain the rules of health which heretofore had been broken too frequently, joined the corps of readers whose eyes were invaluable to him, and augmented the family circle which pampered him. Prescott's accommodations to marriage were few, Susan's many. Ever addicted to schedules, he soon wrote into the record, "from after dinner to one hour after sundown, with Susan."[21]

May swept the newlyweds to a series of suppers, dances, dinners, and visits. Nothing, however, usurped William's loyalty to Club, which he attended at Palfrey's place on May 16. During the summer months, junkets to Brookline, Watertown, and Nahant interrupted life in Boston. Cigars troubled William in June; and the following

---

[21] WHP, Journal, 1815–1821, p. [187], Prescott papers. The quotations that follow immediately are from *ibid.*, pp. 128, 136, 138, 139.

month, despite a renewed effort at methodical care, he irritated his eyes
at least twice—once from too much wine, and once, he said, "I think
from playing chess." In August he diagnosed one indisposition "too
much wine or snuff." In mid-summer William also dictated a new set
of admonitions for himself. "Late hours bad . . . One Ball a week
enough . . . One dinner party in five days enough . . . Exercise of walking when there is no sun or wind the best kind of exercise." His diet
included light breakfasts, temperate dinners of simple food and little
variety, light teas, and no suppers. Wine he restricted to "excellent,
and old" and reading to large print when his right eye was in trim. In
a few months Susan had fathomed the changeable, dependent, and
sympathy-loving nature of her husband.

When autumn confined William and Susan more completely to
Boston, he observed, "Country alone not bracing enough—requires
sea air." In time this observation, repeated, influenced his pattern of
summertime residence, accounting for the roles that Nahant and Lynn
later played. As Boston, six months after William's marriage, moved
into another social season, benedict Prescott was unchanged. Drinker
of wine, taker of snuff, attender of Club, patron of suppers, dinners,
and the theater, player of cards and chess, he remained a gay young
blade.

7

Appearances to the contrary, the social was but one side of Prescott's
nature. Even more rigid than the calendaring of balls and dinners was
his work schedule. At this time he promised 5½ hours to his work in
what he termed the A.M.—either 8:30–2:00 or 9:00–2:30 P.M.—and
two more hours in the P.M., either 4–6 or 5–7. Thus his daily objective
was 7½ hours. Turning from one writer to another in an analysis of
style, Prescott crowded his notes with succinct judgments. In close
array stood essayists and sermon writers—vigorous and polished, nervous and inverted, plain and artificial, involved and easy-flowing, terse
and prolix, labored and free, chaste and ornate. Perhaps Prescott called
them as he saw them, but his recourse to historical surveys of literature
possibly led to some parroting.

His reading and study included Thomas Hooker's *Ecclesiastical*

*Polity* and volumes of sermons by Isaac Barrow, John Tillotson, Jeremy Taylor, and Samuel Clarke. They influenced him spiritually as well as stylistically, because he soon summarized yet another personal religious inquiry. "I believe after due examination," he wrote. "1. In the truth of the Christian religion, 2. That there is much authority for believing in the inspiration of the Apostles, and I believe in it, 3. There is much authority for relying on the authenticity of the whole Pentateuch, and I am willing to rely on its authenticity." All was not certainty, however. On the subject of Trinitarian versus Unitarian doctrine, he concluded, "the general spirit of the volume [ the Holy Bible] seems to accord with the Unitarian faith, and . . . although I am not satisfied with the fallacy of the Trinity, I am not convinced of its truth."[22]

In one of several reactions to European educational practice, William looked askance at the annual lectures of the Collège de France for men who had concluded their formal education. However, George Ticknor, carrying enthusiasms born of his Göttingen experience to his teaching of Spanish and French at Harvard, happily seized upon that idea. After parting from William in Paris in 1817, George had spent two additional years in Europe, in Spain among other places. He had entered upon his appointment at Harvard full of ideas for his courses, his department, and indeed, the university. At twenty-eight he mirrored the man he always would be: benign of countenance, frank and friendly of disposition, cultivated in his tastes, elegant of manner, inquiring of mind, a voracious reader, a man with a large head and a big heart. In time he wooed Anna Eliot, youngest daughter of another successful merchant. In September 1821 both George and Anna brought comfortable fortunes to their marriage. Meanwhile, George was establishing precedents at Harvard. When Ticknor gave a series of four lectures on the language and literature of France, at which interested graduates of Harvard were welcome, Prescott delighted in his majestic surveys of the four periods, 1150–1550, 1550–1624, 1624–1778, and 1778 to the present. Unknowingly William was subjected

---

[22] WHP, Commonplace Book, 1820–1822, p. 84, Prescott papers. For this section, also see: WHP, Journal, 1815–1821, pp. 37, 106, [187], and WHP to his parents, July 5, 1817, Prescott papers.

to the first of several influences by which Ticknor gave both direction and stimulus to his intellectual pursuits.

Prescott's course of study in October 1821 consisted of principles of grammar and correct writing, the history of North America, English prose writers from Roger Ascham to the present, and Latin classics. He gave the Latin classics the least attention, the English authors, the most. By the following spring, his growing desire to study Western European literature took shape.

I am now 26 years of age (nearly) [he wrote]. By the time I am 30, (God willing) I propose with what stock I have already on hand to be a *very well read English scholar*, to be acquainted with the *classical* and useful authors (prose and poetry) in *Latin, French*, and *Italian*, especially *History*. I do not mean a critical or profound acquaintance. The two following years, 31–32, I may hope to learn and to have read the classical *German* writers— and the translations, (if my eye continues weak) of the *Greek*.

Listing fifteen Latin authors and emphasizing a *multum, non multa* approach to them, William hoped to relish "the *peculiar* beauties of some of the most eminent Poets, and Prose writers." In reference to twenty-one French writers, he said, "My object is to *form* not to *revive* as in the Latin, an *intimacy* with the best writers." Speaking of seventeen Italian writers he had selected, Prescott indicated, "My object is the same as with the French." One conclusion, written and canceled, read, "Historians, and philosophers, I have for the most part excluded, in these three languages, they must be studied hereafter." Concluding on a unifying note, he insisted, "All these languages I would know as a *gentleman;* not as a *critic*."[23]

Prescott tackled this gigantic program as he had conceived it, with enthusiasm and energy. Even without specific details, it is quite evident that Judge Prescott, sometime before William's marriage, had agreed to underwrite his son's scholarly pursuits. Individual readings led the beginning scholar to pull together masses of miscellaneous quotations and anecdotes; but his collective reading prompted numerous not so

[23] [Jeremiah D. M. Ford], "George Ticknor," *Dictionary of American Biography*, XVIII, 525–528; Robert Means Lawrence, *Old Park Street and Its Vicinity* (Boston, 1922), pp. 90–91; WHP, Commonplace Book, 1820–1822, pp. 48–51, Prescott papers. The canceled lines are in WHP's record.

miscellaneous reflections. Most of the resultant twenty-six reflections, meticulously set down, strongly motivated his subsequent life, many serving as cardinal intellectual influences. They depicted both the man that he was and the man that he wanted to become.[24]

8

To a person who read widely, thought deeply, and studied style, an interest in writing came naturally. No longer the editor of an assured outlet for his literary efforts, Prescott now turned to the respected *North American Review* and its editor, Edward Everett, who brought to that post a rich background, sound scholarship, renown as a speaker, and a magnetic personality.

The first of Prescott's many contributions to the "Old North," as he affectionately termed the quarterly, introduced him to the art of book reviewing.[25] As he assessed the second edition of Lord Byron's book-length letter concerning Bowles's indictment of Alexander Pope, he immediately exhibited many of the current reviewing techniques: writing at inordinate length, using the title under consideration as a springboard to a demonstration of his own wide reading and erudition, and garnishing—padding is another word for it—the review with numerous excessively long direct quotations. Quite possibly the anticipated pleasure of seeing himself in print also invited his wordiness. Furthermore, for a person who, at twenty-five, was earning his first dollar, the prospect of payment-by-the-page was another invitation to prolixity. Studded with a feeling for poetry, love of Pope, admiration for Byron, awareness of the literature regarding a dispute of long duration, and demonstrations of his own intellectual independence, Prescott's unsigned review constituted his American bow to a national audience.

His next contribution quickly followed. Indeed, between 1821 and

[24] *Ibid.,* pp. 76–61 (*sic*).

[25] [Henry G. Pearson], "Edward Everett," *Dictionary of American Biography,* 6: 223–226; [WHP], "Byron's Letter on Pope," *North American Review,* 13 (October, 1821): 450–473. For this section also see Josiah Quincy, *A Municipal History of the Town and City of Boston, during Two Centuries* (Boston, 1852), pp. 30, 31, 33, 40, 434, 436–440, 442.

1832 every year found at least one review by Prescott in the *North American Review*. In his second review article William assessed his own defunct paper, *The Club-Room*.[26] At the same time he passed judgment on another short-lived periodical, *The Idle Man,* published in New York by Richard Henry Dana. Exhibiting more objectivity than normally might be expected of an editor criticizing his own publication—and of a Bostonian looking at anything from New York— William tossed six pages of brickbats and bouquets at *The Club-Room*. Among its weaknesses he counted the disadvantageous comparison with *The Sketch Book* which it deservedly had incurred, a want of finish in its immature contributors, and a lack of that unity which sustains reader interest. He praised three pieces "of considerable pretension both to beauty of composition, and to originality of invention."[27] These were "The Village Grave-Yard" by Greenwood, "Recollections" by Dexter, and "A Voyage of Discovery" by Gardiner. Perhaps William sincerely believed those pieces to be well written. On the other hand, reviewer Prescott, destined ever to say agreeable things about the writings of his intimates, quite possibly had adopted already the practice of rewarding the published works of close friends with the coin of hearty public commendation.

The months of 1821–1822 which thus had introduced William to the readers of the *North American Review* provided some of Judge Prescott's finest service to Boston. He was one of the thirteen men whose report precipitated the balloting by which Boston changed its legal status from town to city. (A lesser change affected the Prescott address; in February 1821 Pond Street became Bedford.) Within the first city administration, that of Mayor John Phillips, Judge Prescott served as one of four councilmen from the Ninth Ward. In addition, he served as president of the Common Council, a body of forty-seven men. The judge's son-in-law, Franklin Dexter, served as councilman for the same ward in 1825, and his younger son, Edward Goldsborough Prescott, did likewise in 1830. For Edward's brother, however, politics held no attractions, despite his civic consciousness.

[26] [WHP], "Essay Writing," *North American Review,* 14 (April, 1822): 319–350.
　[27] *Ibid.,* p. 335.

William's identification with community affairs increased with his service on the Committee of Managers of the Boston Asylum for Indigent Boys. Counterpart of the Female Asylum, which his mother served, this charity, founded in 1814, provided for male orphans. When William learned that the annual maintenance of each boy cost fifty dollars and the average earnings of each boy—from knitting stockings, pasting covers for bookbinders, and making steel chains—was no more than two dollars, he concluded that the institution could operate more successfully if it moved from the city and engaged in a farming operation. Greatly exceeding his association with the Asylum, young Prescott's awareness of his community reflected itself in rambling letters to absent friends.[28]

Like his reading program, William's writing for the *North American Review* required rules. Given his disposition, they speedily appeared.

Mem. I will write a Review [he told himself] no oftener than once in three Numbers of the *North American Review*—*no oftener,* and print only what I think will *add* to my reputation. . . . I will follow a course of reading, and make the subjects of my Reviews, as far as I can, fall in with this course, or with what I have before read. Provide for the next subject so as to allow 3 months preparation. Pursue this course untill I am thirty. . . . Mem. I will never engage to write for a Number.[29]

Most of these rules he broke sooner or later. On occasion Prescott wrote for consecutive issues, and apparently everything that he penned added to his reputation because he never failed to send to the "Old North" any item which he originally had planned for it. On the other

[28] George F. Weston, Jr., *Boston Ways—High, By, and Folk* (Boston, [1957]), p. 238; Gardiner, ed., *Papers*, pp. 38–40; Caleb Snow, *A History of Boston* (Boston, 1825), p. 360; WHP to W. H. Gardiner, January 24, 1822, Gardiner papers; [Anon.], *A Record of the Streets, Alleys, Places, Etc. in the City of Boston* (Boston, 1910), pp. 44, 371; and [Boston], *Minutes of the Selectmen's Meetings from September 1, 1818, to April 24, 1822* (Boston, 1909), p. 182.

[29] WHP, Commonplace Book, 1820–1822, p. 17, Prescott papers. The quotations that follow in this section are in *ibid.,* pp. 39, 45–47, 81–82, 83. The collection of librarian C. D. Ebeling (1741–1817) of Hamburg was at Harvard.

hand, most reviews did relate to his reading program. To the end he persisted in his refusal to have schedules thrust upon him.

Method in his relations with editors could mean little without method in the composition of his writings. Accordingly Prescott promptly engineered a second set of maxims. "Turn over the subject *generally* in my own mind," he told himself, "in order to get *original* views of it and also, to *direct* my course of *reading,* that it may not be wasted." Facts and useful quotations would occupy him first, then reflection could set in, still considering the theme in its general aspects. When the facts and leading ideas began to fall in line, he would peruse again the whole of his material preparatory to writing a certain segment of it. As reading and organization led to writing, Prescott said, "then *sit down,* and *keep your chair* all the rest of the day." The acceptability of words, epithets, figures, and allusions depended upon whether they lent clarity and strength to his writing. Harmony in the whole became another early and persistent objective.

William insisted that writing should flow freely, without any concern about eventual correction. To think deeply enough to keep his writing flowing, he resolved to work alone under conditions which minimized the likelihood of interruption. "You can write, after proper reflection, from 1 to 2 pages of the *North American Review* in a day," he concluded. For reviews he established a minimum of fifteen and a maximum of twenty-five pages. Among those from whom he might expect helpful suggestions he counted Gardiner, Dexter, Ticknor, and Parsons.

Prescott predicated every schedule of reading and writing upon the good health which continued to be a serious concern. His major exercise came from walking, and in good weather he was a pedestrian par excellence. Although he used stylus and noctograph to write the successive drafts of his reviews, he depended upon his own sight to correct his manuscripts. He minimized such reading and studiously avoided it when his vision flagged. Some writing, such as correspondence, notebook entries, and the like, defied use of the noctograph. He performed it in keeping with his rule, "Write a large and straight and unequivocal, and broad hand—black ink."

The interest in history which he had suppressed repeatedly in the organization of his reading programs insistently recurred. Before long he established a general reading program in history. Except for the Holy Land, that historical interest proceeded forward from the Middle Ages and apparently embraced all of Europe except the Balkans. Vaguely he promised some attention to North and South America.

In his customary manner of developing a general view first, Prescott gained much of his introduction to Western Europe from Henry Hallam. Once he acquired an initial awareness of the pattern of major historical events, he planned to turn to John Bigland and Voltaire concerning the study and philosophy of history. Prescott intended that his study of history mushroom into a big and consuming intellectual activity.

History has always been a favorite study with me [he admitted] "and I have long looked forward to it, as a subject on which I may one [day] exercise my pen. It is not rash, in the dearth of well written American history, to entertain the hope of throwing a light upon this matter—especially with the rich materials which are now buried in pedantic lumber, and foreign languages in the Ebeling Collection. This is my hope. But it requires time and a long time, before the mind can be sufficiently prepared for this department of writing. 1. An easy style, and familiarity with composition must be first obtained by practice: skirmishing occasionally in the Reviews, is the best discipline for this purpose. A Review is the proper gymnasium of a writer, in which he may try his strength before he comes into the world, upon his own credit. 2. The understanding must be ripened by reflection and experience. Poets may be born, but historians are made. 3. The memory must be enriched and the taste improved by a wide cultivation of polite letters; (I do not mean a critical or profound acquaintance with them.) 4. When all this is attained, and not till then, the man is prepared to investigate the *particular* subject of his intended history. After this, some years of careful, deep, and accurate research into whatever has a relation to this subject can alone authorise him to come before the public as an Historian. These are at least, my notions upon the matter. I think 35 years of age full soon enough to put pen to paper. The preceding years may be devoted to the objects above enumerated. Gibbon, and Hume were both more than 40 years old, when they commenced their Great Histories—and Robertson was

I believe nearly of the same age. I have said nothing of travelling, though I think, from obvious reasons, every Historian should be personally acquainted with the country concerning which he is to write.

Only a distant future could determine whether Prescott, adhering to this program and timetable, would become a historian.

IV

*Down the stream of Italian narrative poetry
we have wandered . . .*

THE EARLY 1820's were kind to the Prescotts. Terminating more than a decade of service to Harvard as overseer, Judge Prescott, as he commonly was called, had assumed the responsibilities of fellow. As lawyer, he was enjoying the professional success which enabled him to retire before the end of the decade. Upon his elder son he generously had settled income-producing property which gave a semblance of dignity to the young scholar's continuing dependence. Catherine Prescott superintended the household which now bore the address Twenty-two Bedford Street. She also continued to dedicate astonishing fervor and energy to the support and direction of the Boston Female Asylum and to what became the Lying-in-Hospital. In 1821 grandmother Abigail Prescott went to her grave, but even as death carried off one generation, birth introduced a new one. William Prescott Dexter, son of Lizzie and Frank, brought joy to his parents, pride to Judge and Mrs. Prescott, and possibly a tinge of envy to William and Susan who, as yet, were childless.

In mid-1822 the Athenaeum moved once more, to bigger quarters. Both William and William H. Prescott continued to support and frequent it. In 1823 they each subscribed fifty dollars to its building program; and a few years later each donated one hundred dollars. In 1823 Ticknor became a trustee, a role which William H. Prescott later assumed.

On the other hand, Prescott said and did nothing in support of Ticknor's valiant but unsuccessful efforts to effect general reform at Harvard.[1] In fact, except for attendance at Ticknor's public lectures, William divorced himself from Cambridge, apparently believing that college was something that a grown man should put behind him.

2

In another matter, however, William did show much concern. So good was his general health and the state of his vision that neither 1823 nor 1824 provided a record of complaint. Guarded diet, sensible social habits, luck, and the protection and aid extended by wife, parents, reader-secretaries, and servants combined to promote this happy state. It was August 1825, before brief reference to "eye unwell" and "touch of dyspepsia" interrupted, and then not for long, his methodical study of European literature.[2]

System came, by June 1823, to yet another aspect of Prescott's intellectual endeavor. At that time he started what eventually became a thirty-five-year record of such activity. When he recorded the first of these literary memoranda, he was studying the poetry of the Middle Ages and earlier times. A few months later he was concentrating overwhelmingly on a single national literature, the Italian.

One of Prescott's approaches to mastery of a literature was the simultaneous study of general, critical historical surveys and individual titles. For the former he early turned to Jean C. L. Sismondi's *Literature du Midi de l'Europe*, which he admired, and to John Colin Dun-

---

[1] For this section see: Quincy, *Boston Athenaeum*, pp. 88 n., 104 n., 105 n.; Samuel Eliot Morison, "The Great Rebellion in Harvard College, and the Resignation of President Kirkland," Colonial Society of Massachusetts *Transactions*, 27 (November, 1927–November, 1928): 54–112; Hillard, ed., *Life, Letters, and Journals*, 1: 355–356, 360–361. Another indication of Judge Prescott's interest in education is in James G. Carter, *Letters to the Hon. William Prescott, LLD. on the Free Schools of New England, with Remarks upon the Principles of Instruction* (Boston, 1824).

[2] Gardiner, ed., *Literary Memoranda*, 1: 63. For background to this chapter, see *ibid.*, pp. 3–69, 232–241.

lop's *History of Prose Fiction,* which, though useful, was labored and dry. The more he read the comprehensive surveys of Italian literature, the more he entertained the thought: "The English are behind every cultivated language in Europe, in similar works of general literary criticism. A fine field this, therefore, for a scholar."[3] This was but one of many instances in which his active mind consciously sought the themes which might convert reading program into research project.

Of greater value to Prescott, however, were the conclusions that he reached through direct sampling of Italian literature. Because many of the works which he read were available to him in translation as well as in Italian, and because, too, his command of Italian—exceedingly limited earlier, in Italy—is not known precisely, the language in which he read some titles cannot be determined. Needless to say, as his Italian studies progressed, he increasingly used the language which he warmly admired for its many beauties. The autobiography of Benvenuto Cellini he relished. Although he next turned to the *Decameron* of Boccaccio for more prose, Italian poetry quickly challenged his attention.

Before the end of September 1823, Prescott was enjoying the Italian literary form which made the most lasting impression on him, the epic. He early read Torquato Tasso's *Gerusalemme Liberata* and met Dante, Francesco Berni, Matteo Boiardo, and Luigi Pulci through their writings as well as by means of criticism in major English reviews and in Pierre Louis Ginguené's *Histoire littéraire d'Italie.* This reading program, coupled with the poverty of the Prescott library and the wealth of George Ticknor's holdings in the Italian field, insured a deeper intellectual tie between William and George. Sharing with Ticknor thoughts inspired by his study of Italian literature, he wrote, "As to Cary, I think Dante would have given him a place in his ninth heaven, if he could have foreseen his Translation."[4] Detailed study

---

[3] *Ibid.,* p. 9.

[4] Ticknor, *Prescott,* p. 67. Also see *ibid.,* pp. 62–68; Hillard, ed., *Life, Letters, and Journals,* 1: 341–344; and WHP to G. Ticknor, December 17, 1823, Rare Book Department, Boston Public Library. Ticknor, failing to publish that portion of Prescott's correspondence which indicates the slender basis of knowledge from which William was writing, did much to cast an aura of sophisticated criticism about the exchange.

of the *Gerusalemme Liberata* encouraged William to explore earlier and later periods both in and out of Italy. Soon he was busily summarizing, simply for his own edification, his conclusions on "certain characteristics of different literatures."[5] The distinctions between the ancient and modern epic especially interested him. For weeks, even as he read Ludovico Ariosto's *Orlando Furioso* and *La Divina Commedia* and other poetry by Dante, Prescott expressed himself about the epic. At some length, he undertook a comparative analysis of Ariosto and Tasso. Early in 1824 his critical attention focused on Dante's masterwork. Next, adhering to patterns of study derived from the literary surveys, he gave Vittorio Alfieri, Jacopo Sannazaro, Giovanni Battista Guarini, Angelo Poliziano, Gabriello Chiabrera, Carlo Innocenzo Frugoni, and a host of other Italian writers his hurried attention.

He turned to works which demanded more detailed consideration. Luigi Pulci's *Il Morgante Maggiore,* an epic crowded with details of everyday living—such as Prescott would later put into his histories—drew lengthy comment from him. The epics *Orlando Innamorato* by Boiardo and Berni evoked the comparison which their similar titles invited. Through the spring of 1824 William continued his study of the Italian language and literature. At times he picked up additional titles, as Niccolò Forteguerri's *Ricciardetto*. On occasion, too, he returned to and dug deeper into familiar pages. The Orlando theme of Ariosto, Boiardo, and Berni was one such favorite. "If I were to find a fault in the general plan of this epic [Ariosto's *Orlando*]," Prescott commented, "I should point out the want of some great object, and some leading personage who might form a sort of central rallying point to the subordinate objects and characters."[6]

At first glance, as he terminated his concentrated study of Italian literature in 1824, it might seem that Prescott merely had consumed another segment of his European literary program. Any such assessment, however, would deny the relationship of this preparatory period to the climax of his career as historian. Medieval and Renaissance

---

[5] Gardiner, ed., *Literary Memoranda,* 1: 20.
[6] *Ibid.*, pp. 29, 44–45.

Italian literature had served to move Prescott toward and into the magnificent sixteenth century on which he later expended his own energies. Italian epic poetry developed for him many of the classic and heroic proportions which he incorporated into his own writings. In terms of the mold which he unconsciously fastened upon himself by means of these Italian influences, it is readily understood why the heroic Great Captain and his Italian operations received the measure of attention and kind of treatment accorded them—why the *Conquest of Mexico,* its leading character, and great object fitted the epic mold perfectly; why in both character and time the apparently similar *Conquest of Peru* troubled Prescott endlessly; why an unhappy central figure and thematic disunity frustrated him in his study of Philip II. In 1824 Prescott put his systematic study of Italian literature behind him, but the influences derived therefrom affected his entire creative life. Italian poetry, especially the epic, had struck a powerful aesthetic note in Prescott's nature.

3

In this period William's published writings were exclusively in the field of reviewing. He based his first piece on two recent five-act tragedies, one French, the other English.[7] The former was Étienne Jouy's *Sylla,* the latter the Rev. George Croly's *Cataline.* Two-thirds of the review article discussed the nature, history, and present state of tragedy in English and French drama. When Croly's plot abused history, Prescott chided him. Jouy's plot he deemed "feeble and uninteresting."[8] Apparently the two mediocre plays triggered a summarization of some of the thoughts which he had derived from his reading program.

Eighteen months later, the "Old North" carried one of the briefest reviews that William ever published. In the section entitled "Miscellaneous Notices," he considered the rimed lines of Charles Sprague,

----

[7] [WHP], "The French and English Tragedy," *North American Review,* 16 (January, 1823): 124–156. For this section see also: William H. Prescott, *Biographical and Critical Miscellanies* (New York, 1845), pp. 410–485; Deed, December 7–10, 1823, American Antiquarian Society; WHP to J. Sparks, May 10, 1824, Sparks papers.

[8] [WHP], "The French and English Tragedy," *North American Review,* 16 (January, 1823): 155.

a banker-poet of Boston.[9] All Boston knew that Sprague, writing in honor of Shakespeare, had won the competition sponsored by the managers of the Boston Theatre. Dutifully noticing the verses of the local author, Prescott, with genuine love of poetry, endorsed the picturesque and the romantic. Balancing his commendation was his criticism of the "unwieldy epithets and useless allegory."[10] On the latter subject William still entertained the condemnatory sentiments which he had turned upon Benjamin West's painting in London.

Better than his consideration of either French and English tragedy or American poetry was his next review, an evaluation of W. S. Rose's translations of Berni's *Orlando Innamorato* and Ariosto's *Orlando Furioso*.[11] Once more the review prompted a related essay, but this time William's writing showed marked improvement. The fifty-page article, by far his longest to date, essentially summarized his study of Italian narrative poetry in all ages and forms, with particular reference to the epic.

Down the stream of Italian narrative poetry, we have wandered into so many details . . . that we have little room, and our readers, doubtless, less patience left for a discussion of the poems, which form the text of our article. . . . The translations have been noticed in several of the English journals, and we perfectly accord with the favorable opinion of them, which has been so often expressed, that it needs not here be repeated.[12]

In form, this review article differed from William's earlier writings in two respects: greater synthesis on his part reduced the number and extent of direct quotations; and the footnote appeared for the first time in his writing. Although, in terms of an earlier dictum, all of these reviews presumably contributed to William's reputation, the essay on Italian narrative poetry was the first piece for which he himself felt continuing affection. This selection, wherein he publicly affirmed his love of the epic, was chronologically the earliest item to go into the

[9] [WHP], "Mr. Sprague's Prize Poems," *North American Review*, 19 (July, 1824): 253–256.

[10] *Ibid.*, p. 254.

[11] [WHP], "Italian Narrative Poetry," *North American Review*, 19 (October, 1824): 337–389.

[12] *Ibid.*, p. 389.

volume which reprinted in the mid-1840's many of his contributions to periodicals.

A changing, maturing individual in his intellectual life, Prescott, in this period, also metamorphosed economically and socially. Living under the roof of conservative yet speculative Judge Prescott, William naturally followed his father in economic matters. As an intelligent investor, Judge Prescott was an incorporator, in this decade, and subsequently a director (1823–1827) and long-term president (1828–1842) of the Massachusetts Hospital Life Insurance Company. Destined to become "one of the largest financial institutions in Boston in the nineteenth century, the Massachusetts Hospital Life was an important supplier of funds for industrial growth in New England."[13] Some of the property settled upon William at the time of his marriage had enabled the budding scholar to develop the keen awareness of financial matters which otherwise might seem completely alien to his life of letters.

Meanwhile the 3 P.M. dinner party of May 11, 1824, is illustrative of the activity which blended his social and intellectual proclivities. The small group invited that day to Bedford Street included George and Anna Ticknor and Jared Sparks. George and Anna, whose marriage followed that of Susan and William by more than a year, lived in elegant ease. George avidly immersed himself in intellectual matters while Anna dedicated energies to learning, travel, family, society, and charities. Whereas stay-at-home Susan participated in her husband's intellectual interests only to the extent of helping to maintain ideal working conditions for him, Anna was a more direct participant in her husband's varied activities. And as William's love for Susan was constant, so was his admiration of Anna. In 1824 the Ticknor household knew the joy of an infant daughter born the previous year. Little Anna, or Anika, as "Uncle" William affectionately called her, increased the bonds between the Ticknors and the Prescotts.

With Jared Sparks, William's relationship was similar, yet different.

[13] Gerald T. White, *A History of the Massachusetts Hospital Life Insurance Company* (Cambridge, Mass., 1955), pp. xiii, 1, 10–11, 169; and W. Prescott, Last Will and Testament, July 29, 1844, Probate Court, Suffolk County, Massachusetts.

Two years older than George and William's senior by seven years, Jared, robust and brown-eyed, had dedicated himself to both religion and history after graduating from Harvard in 1815. As Ticknor had become Harvard's first professor of modern languages, so Jared, late in the 1830's, became its first professor of history. Meanwhile, he shared, without the financial means of either, the intellectual curiosity of both Ticknor and Prescott. Four years had convinced the handsome Sparks that his literary interests exceeded his dedication to church. Accordingly he initiated, on borrowed money, a half-dozen years as owner-editor of the *North American Review,* to earn income as well as to satisfy himself intellectually. In addition to shifting the quarterly from its dilettantish origins, Jared blazed new trails of reader interest as he read and wrote about contemporary Latin-American affairs. Few Americans did as much as Sparks to direct American attention to newly independent Latin America at the time of the proclamation of the Monroe Doctrine. For the curly-haired bachelor editor, whose Roman nose enhanced his air of distinction, Prescott had written, just two days before, his review of Sprague's poetry. Ticknor soon would publish a lengthy piece about Lafayette in the "Old North."[14] The tenor of conversation in the Prescott home that May day a week after William's twenty-eighth birthday is not difficult to imagine. Select, small dinner parties, sometimes attended by both sexes but often entirely masculine, sometimes at Twenty-two Bedford Street yet often in public establishments, increasingly became an ingredient of William's social life.

On September 24 Susan gave birth to her first child, a daughter. The happy father announced the joyous news in these words to Theophilus Parsons: "Miss ——— Prescott, aged 22 hours (9 lb. weight,) sends her love to the learned editor of the *U. S. Literary Gazette.* All are doing well. *Valete et plaudite.*" Honoring William's mother, the child was named Catherine.

Parsons was another member of Club whose literary interests inevitably included an editorship. After graduating in Sparks's class at Harvard, Theop, as he was to friends, had studied law with Judge

---

[14] [George Ticknor], "Lafayette," *North American Review,* 20 (January, 1825): 147–180; and [Samuel Eliot Morison], "Jared Sparks," *Dictionary of American Biography,* 17: 430–434.

Prescott. At this time the young lawyer was even newer as editor, having but recently succeeded to that post for *The United States Literary Gazette.* When William was editing *The Club-Room,* Theop, as one of the quartet of dependable contributors, had supplied articles for two of the four issues. Now it was time for William to help Theop fill his pages. "I can let you have on Monday morning if you desire it for your next Literary Gazette," wrote Prescott, " a rambling Essay on the *Cui Bono?* to the amount of about seven of your columns. If that is too long it can be better shortened than divided. I wish you would let me know and I will make a fair copy for your devils."[15] The unseen article interested Theop. As he sent the clean copy, William attached a string to it. "I promised Gray to furnish his half hours Club reading on Tuesday, week from to-day," he informed the editor, "and I should like to make use of this 'cui bono' affair for that purpose if you have no objection."[16]

Resembling every other periodical article by Prescott, "Cui Bono" was unsigned; but, in several respects, it was unlike any other article he ever wrote. This essay, the earliest of a considerable number of previously unidentified published writings by Prescott, differed from both the reviews written for the *North American Review* and the mystery fiction published in *The Club-Room.* This essay on utility—its subtitle translated the Latin as "What's the use of 't?"—reveals some of the struggle then raging within the careerless twenty-eight-year-old. Citing scientists, philosophers, businessmen, and antiquarians to illustrate his point, William declared, "In short, every profession reciprocates a most cordial contempt for its opposite." It distressed him that Americans increasingly tended "to estimate every thing upon the scales of the *cui bono.*" Focusing attention on authors, he wondered if writers

[15] WHP to T. Parsons, September 25, 1824, Mellen Chamberlain Autograph Collection; and [Charles Fairman], "Theophilus Parsons," *Dictionary of American Biography,* 14: 273–274. The original MS of this note, like many others to intimates in his own hand, illustrates WHP's addiction to abbreviations.

[16] WHP to T. Parsons, September 28, 1824, Mellen Chamberlain Autograph Collection; [WHP], "Cui Bono?" *The United States Literary Gazette,* 1, no. 13 (October 15, 1824): 200–203. The quotations which follow immediately are from *ibid.*

of fact really enjoyed an advantage over writers of fiction. Canvassing numerous historical errors and some omissions—wherein he complained, "the name of Prescott has been hardly noticed"—he entertained doubts. Homer, he was sure, had exerted a stronger influence than any historian. And in his own day he felt that the impact of Scott's Waverley novels exceeded that of "any one, or two, or any dozen regular historians." On another occasion he would elaborate upon his estimate of Scott.

Meanwhile, trying to vindicate the utility of any profession, he stressed the importance of an author's capacity to communicate. Although he soon turned, in his own writing, from belles-lettres to history, Prescott, interestingly enough, never renounced his allegiance to readability and enjoyability, in conjunction with veracity.

Ten months later Prescott's "Romance in the Heroic and Middle Ages" appeared in two successive issues of *The United States Literary Gazette*. This article, according to Prescott's calculations, approximated nine pages of the *North American Review*.[17] Experience with the page size of that journal made easy William's converting his noctographic pages of manuscript into printed pages, a calculation which he performed throughout his life. In a journal chiefly concerned with contemporary America, Prescott presented a relaxed personal reaction to the literature of many lands. Rich and reliable pictures of society and manners attracted him. Of Scott he said, "future ages will gather more of this information from the novels of the author of Waverley, than from all the histories in the language."[18] Partly out of his love of such writing, Prescott came to stress the incorporation of social content in historical writing. Theop's editorship of *The United States Literary Gazette* did not last long, and as his identification with it faded so did that of Prescott.

When Theop, financially embarrassed, tried to interest his friend in certain securities, Prescott had to confess, "I cannnot buy the shares

---

[17] [WHP], "Romance in the Heroic and Middle Ages," *The United States Literary Gazette*, 2, no. 9 (August 1, 1825), 343–347; no. 10 (August 15, 1825), 386–389; and Gardiner, ed., *Literary Memoranda*, 1: 62. This article, likewise, has previously been unidentified.

[18] [WHP], "Romance in the Heroic and Middle Ages," *The United States Literary Gazette*, 2, no. 9 (August 1, 1825), 343.

for the same reason you cannot keep them." After unsuccessfully peddling his friend's securities, William added, "You are obliged to offer them to the County at the market price, you know, in preference to any other purchaser, and if they decline, you had better put them in the hands of a broker."[19] Accustomed to acquainting himself with the fine print of contracts and stock certificates as well as with the beauties of Homer and Dante and Scott, William never was the isolated scholar of ivy-towered unreality.

## 4

His Italian studies behind him, Prescott dawdled away three months before writing, "I never stand in need of such repose." "To the end of my life," he added, "I trust I shall be more avaricious of time and *never* put up with a smaller average than 7 *hours* intellectual occupation *per diem*."[20] It was one thing to jolt a lazy nature with a heavy work schedule; but it was something else to determine what that work should be. By November 20, 1824, the guidepost to study was at hand, a lengthy chronological listing of Spanish authors to be studied. Ticknor, having read his lectures on Spanish literature to William, helped to compile the reading list. Heavy with both poetry and prose, it featured romances, chronicles, dramas, lyrics, epics, and history. As he eyed a literature which he had not included in his original course of study, William also avoided a language, German, which he previously had planned to learn. This shift from central Europe to the Iberian peninsula proved to be of momentous significance.

Appropriately, he soon recorded, "I began the study of Spanish December 1, 1824." Pessimism initially marked this venture, as when he told George Bancroft, "I am battling with the Spaniards this winter but I have not the heart for it, I had for the Italian. I doubt whether there are many valuable things, that the keys of knowledge will unlock in that language."[21] His daily routine called for thorough study of A. L. Josse's *Grammar,* the writing of exercises, the study of his-

[19] Gardiner, ed., *Papers,* pp. 44–45.
[20] Gardiner, ed., *Literary Memoranda,* 1: 52. For this section see also Morison, *Three Centuries of Harvard,* p. 236.
[21] Gardiner, ed., *Literary Memoranda,* 1: 55; Ticknor, *Prescott,* p. 71; and WHP to G. Bancroft, December 25, 1824, Bancroft papers.

torical surveys of Spanish literature, and the reading of individual titles.

Of all the works which received his attention in the months immediately ahead, three titles were particularly significant in relation to his later career. Alonso de Ercilla's *La Araucana* enabled Prescott to indulge further his love of the epic, while acquainting himself with sixteenth-century South America. Antonio de Solís' *Conquista de México* alerted him to the majestic proportions of the conquest of Mexico, as well as challenging him on the scores of validity and literary style. The third title, Juan de Mariana's history of Spain, afforded the wider perspective on Spanish history so necessary as a preliminary to Prescott's concentration on special periods and themes.

In what is perhaps the earliest extant Spanish from his hand, William soon admonished himself, "Yo he leydo *menos* de en proporción de cuatro horas a cada día de la semana pasada; la causa era el perder del tiempo en el *soñar* sobre mis libros." After a scant five months, Prescott declared, "I have now studied all most essential in the Spanish literature. . . . There yet remain some works *relating to* Spain &c. which I shall read."[22] This short study of the long list hints at the most cursory consideration of most of the titles.

Perhaps Prescott terminated the Spanish studies at this time, the better to give attention to a literary dispute opened by one interested 1eader of his essay on Italian narrative poetry, Lorenzo da Ponte. The lisping seventy-five-year-old Venetian protested the assessment of Italian narrative poetry which one editor had termed "a learned and beautifully written essay."[23] Da Ponte challenged Prescott's estimate of the Italian influence on English literature and charged him with ignoring merits and magnifying defects. Attacking the American's remarks regarding the inordinate length of many epics, the Italian scored the interminable proportions of Scott's novels. He aimed other barbed words at Prescott's observations about the want of philosophical content and the overemphasis on sound in Italian poetry and accused him of being under the influence of French critics.

[22] Gardiner, ed., *Literary Memoranda,* 1: 59, 60.
[23] [Anon.], "North American Review," *The United States Literary Gazette,* 1, no. 13 (October 15, 1824), 203.

Initially baffled at having a small volume of dissent leveled at his article, Prescott loaded his guns in defense. His published reply to Da Ponte, replete with footnotes, is more important as an indication of intellectual method than as a proof of command of Italian literature.[24] "Looking up facts, authorities &c.," he wrote, "I have not managed this well. I should have copied the whole piece, correcting each error, of style or fact, supplying each deficiency &c. in the text as I went along. Then I should examine for the Notes, writing them down in their order, at the bottom of the pages, &c."[25] Although he never wrote another reply to a critic, Prescott, nonetheless, picked up some tenets of sound historical method in this introspective moment. Many more such moments would come as he educated himself in historical method and literary style.

On dry, dusty August 31, 1825, the Prescotts crossed to Cambridge for the Harvard commencement that counted Edward Goldsborough Prescott among the graduates. Ned soon turned to law, studying in his father's office. But he found it difficult to settle upon a life's work, and politics, journalism, soldiering, and the pulpit attracted him in quick succession.[26]

That autumn William initiated a search for "a suitable subject for historical composition."[27] Slowly and diligently he restricted and focused his attention. When Spanish history came under review, he examined the holdings of the libraries at Harvard and the Athenaeum. Mariana's history sharpened the Spanish focus; and Abbé Gabriel

---

[24] Lorenzo da Ponte, *Alcune Osservazioni sull' Articulo Quarto publicato nel North American Review, il Mese d'Ottobre dell' Anno 1824* (New York, 1825); [WHP], "Da Ponte's Observations," *North American Review,* 21 (July, 1825): 189–217; and April Fitzlyon, *The Libertine Librettist: a Biography of Mozart's Librettist, Lorenzo da Ponte* (New York, 1957).

[25] Gardiner, ed., *Literary Memoranda,* 1: 61.

[26] [Harvard] *Quinquennial Catalogue,* pp. 147–148; "The Order of Exercises for Commencement XXXI August, MDCCCXXV," Archives, Harvard College; Oliver Ayer Roberts, *History of the Military Company of the Massachusetts,* 4 vols. (Boston, 1822–1865), 3: 92–93; and Pierce, ed., Smith, "Some Notes on the Harvard Commencements, 1803–1848," Massachusetts Historical Society *Proceedings,* 2nd ser., 5 (1889, 1890): 167–263.

[27] Gardiner, ed., *Literary Memoranda,* 1: 64. The remaining quotations in this chapter are in *ibid.,* pp. 62–69 *passim.*

Bonnot de Mably's rules strengthened William's conceptions of historical method. He was aware of his three needs: historical method, literary style, and a proper theme.

Groping, Prescott came up with three likely historical themes: Spain from the days of the Moorish invasion to the era of Charles V; the Roman revolution which converted republic into empire; and a critical biographical study of eminent geniuses and their contributions. Even before the last subject took clear shape in his mind, William dropped it. The next to go was the Roman theme, in part because the level of related European scholarship in general and that of Barthold Georg Niebuhr in particular overwhelmed him.

Two of the themes discarded, the third did not win automatic endorsement. Instead, a new idea emerged, an analytical work related to Italian literature. Arguing on behalf of it, Prescott asserted, "I should be spared what I detest, hunting up latent barren antiquities." A week later he wrote, "The Italian subject has some advantages over the Spanish. It will save me at least one year's introductory labor. It is in the regular course of my studies, and I am comparatively at home in literary history, particularly the Italian." On the other hand, he knew that such a project, in the wake of Sismondi, would lack novelty. In addition, literary history, he felt, lacked some of the appeals inherent in civil history.

As the Italian theme receded, Prescott began to refine the Spanish subject, wondering, "What new and interesting topics may be admitted, not forced, into the reigns of Ferdinand and Isabel?" At random he savored a few: the Moorish dynasty, the conquest of Granada, the Inquisition, the Great Captain in Italy, and the discovery of the New World. By confining himself to the limits of biography, he would be responsible only for a restricted time interval. Furthermore, that kind of study would permit the narration that promotes the development of strong characters. The age of Ferdinand and Isabella additionally commanded respect for its contribution to the modern European system of national states. Thinking of the study, its outline and significance, Prescott paused, saying, "I will chew upon this matter."

While doing so, he again had to fight off the attractions of the Italian theme before concluding that the Spanish subject was "pregnant with rich and interesting materials." "The residence of an American envoy, a man of letters, and a friend [Alexander H. Everett], at the court at Madrid affords me another fortunate facility for the promotion of my Spanish enterprise," he added. Gradually the mounting advantages of the Spanish project eliminated the Italian subject. The field clear and resolution strong, he announced, "I subscribe to the History of the reigns of Ferdinand and Isabella.—January 19, 1826."

V

*Finally for the hundredth time I confirm*
*my preference and choice . . .*

HOST TO FIRM RESOLVE, the new year appeared propitious for historical scholarship. Dyspepsia and eye trouble of the previous summer had been forgotten. However, as his studies increasingly involved materials in foreign languages, Prescott overreached the abilities of a generous sister and a loving wife. Need and desire brought George Lunt to the post of reader-secretary.[1] A twenty-one-year-old graduate of Harvard in the class of 1824, Lunt initiated Prescott's practice of turning to recent graduates of that institution for bright young men to serve his purpose for short terms, usually while preparing for their own professional careers. As William's aide, Lunt spent certain designated hours with him six days a week—reading to him,

---

[1] The term "reader-secretary," despite its cumbersomeness, is singularly appropriate. The ordinary connotation of "secretary" does not feature, if indeed it includes, certain significant duties that WHP exacted of his aides: the reading aloud of newspapers and books, the reading aloud of incoming correspondence in order that replies could be written, and so forth. Because his aides invariably spent more time reading than performing more regular secretarial duties, and because that reading was preliminary to the other activities, the term "reader-secretary" more accurately describes those aides.

making notes, constructing bibliographies, transcribing correspondence, and so on.[2]

A letter to Minister A. H. Everett at Madrid,[3] accompanied by a fat catalogue of books desired by the would-be historian, tapped another advantage enjoyed by the young Bostonian. Everett was the first of a number of diplomats to serve his scholarly purposes.

The household at Twenty-two Bedford Street was possessed of an atmosphere favorable to scholarship. Although William was pampering his infant daughter—variously called little Kitty and Katie—she did not violate the quiet of his study. Susan, the Judge, and mother Prescott, all friends of literature, acknowledged William's need for quiet and isolation. Above and beyond all the other family assists was Judge Prescott's enthusiastic underwriting of his son's career at letters. However, some of William H. Prescott's advantages were of his own making. His was the ranging curiosity, the love of truth and beauty, the linguistic capacity, the sense of historical method, the concern about literary style. His, too, was the disciplining experience of more than a half decade of literary effort, of conceiving and executing small projects.

Then, just when everything seemed right, the man of decision became indecisive. Once again the Italian theme won favor, and months passed before he concluded, "I have again reviewed the grounds of my decision in favour of Spanish History and have confirmed it."[4] Early in the autumn he repudiated this decision, insisting, "I have determined to postpone my Spanish subject, and to occupy myself for some years to come with an Historical survey of English Literature." After five weeks of dilatory research cast the English theme into disfavor, his enthusiasm again swung toward Spain. In the spring of 1827 he clung to the Spanish theme, despite a deep interest in the age of Dante, Petrarch, and Boccaccio as a substitute project; but in November of that

----

[2] Concerning Lunt, see WHP to J. Sparks, August 26, 1826, Sparks papers and [Lawrence S. Mayo], "George Lunt," *Dictionary of American Biography,* 11: 507–508. The time interval of this chapter is treated in Gardiner, ed., *Literary Memoranda,* 1: 70–135, 241–243.

[3] Gardiner, ed., *Papers,* pp. 49–50.

[4] Gardiner, ed., *Literary Memoranda,* 1: 78. The quotations which immediately follow are in *ibid.,* pp. 79–90 *passim.*

year he threatened another inquiry into Italian literature. In June 1828, he concluded, "I shall rest permanently contented and steadily pursue, to the end, the history of Ferdinand and Isabella." Summer heat, instead of dissipating this resolution, reinforced it. "Finally for the hundredth time," he said with exaggeration and irritation, "I confirm my preference and choice of the Spanish subject." He had lost two and one-half years. Why?

2

Basically William's intellectual wavering was ascribable to his eyes. The preparation of the want list for A. H. Everett had overtaxed the good right eye. At first a stiffness set in. When it persisted, he concluded—and by this time he possibly was the best diagnostician of his own vision—that a nerve had been injured. Trying to be firm in the face of unpredictable work schedules, William asserted, "I may yet hope in 5 or 6 years to reach the goal. I have ordered my Spanish books from Madrid." Scores of authors crowded that list. Meanwhile, Lunt's reading of titles by Xenophon, Plato, Aristotle, Cicero, and Seneca hints forcibly that no titles significantly related to his project were initially available to him. Occasionally, even after due allowance for the state of his vision, William condemned his work habits. Presumably good for his soul, and possibly effective in correcting his tendencies, were such memoranda as those of October 15, 1826, and June 22, 1828: "I have been very dilatory and idle" and "Shame on my doubtings, delays, and idleness."

Prescott's vision fluctuated, but not as some writers suggest. Back and forth, across the years, William's sight generally ranged from good to fair to poor, not from poor to nonexistent. Sentimentalists, prostrating themselves before man's conquest of physical adversity, have commonly selected, as though it were the only evidence, that which exaggerates Prescott's problem with his vision. Illustrating his fluctuating sight are these entries, recorded within a period of weeks. "I have to depend upon my ears rather than my eyes" and "Examined maps a day and half." At times the man who understandably had considerable sympathy lavished upon him sympathized with himself to the point of overstating his disability. Behind any magnification of his physical ailment, however, is the undeniable truth of William's limited vision. Examining the first shipment of Spanish books, he rejoiced to find "two thirds of this number printed in such a manner as to be perfectly legible by me." As a reader, he appreciated large type sizes and well-leaded lines. As an author he saw to it that his own books likewise were easy on the eye. Vision was not completely responsible for his dilatory months in 1826, 1827, and 1828.

The arrival of a second child helps to explain why conditions favorable to work turned unfavorable. On Friday, January 27, 1826, Susan gave birth to their first son. For the father, he had exulted over little Kitty, the advent of a son called for celebration of the first magnitude, at the expense of historical studies. Infant William Gardiner Prescott, honoring Judge Prescott and William's closest friend, clearly distracted his father.

In this period the reader-secretaries also disrupted and discouraged his intellectual pursuits. A research project that spanned at least a half decade was poorly served by the annual coming and going of assistants. Prescott customarily contracted for a young man at the end of summer, after the Harvard commencement and his own stay at Pepperell. Usually the Pepperell period so invigorated him that he returned to town in the midst of scholarly matters and with plans and momentum for the winter. Immediately, however, the necessity of orienting a new man in the duties of reader-secretary upset those happy prospects. Conscious of the disadvantages of the short-term aide, he tried to avoid them when he sought Lunt's successor. Hearing that a young man named Walker, an instructor at the school operated by Bancroft and Joseph Green Cogswell, desired to study law, Prescott became interested in him and proposed that six days a week for three or four years Walker read six hours daily for him, in return for $250 cash per year, professional training in Judge Prescott's office, and access to a fine law library. Unfortunately the arrangement did not materialize, and William, obtaining the services of Hamilton Parker, had to settle for another one-year aide.

Once the Spanish theme suggested the desirability of readers equipped with that language, Ticknor made helpful recommendations. James Lloyd English, bearing George's blessing, was doubly important to Prescott, for the longer period of his service and the special talent he brought to his job. A Harvard graduate in the class of 1827, young English served Prescott between five and six hours daily for the next four years. Ordinarily those hours, 10 A.M. to 2 P.M. and 6 to 8 P.M. were spent in William's study, a room which the Judge had added at the rear of the house on the second floor. The green screen which Prescott faced while writing darkened the room on the east side. On the west a succession of light-blue muslin curtains covered the only window, permitting a tempering of light in response to outdoor conditions. Seated at his writing table in the middle of the room, William had the controlled light from the west window over his shoulders. Usually he occupied a rocking chair. Sometimes he wore a green eyeshade. While reading aloud, English sat behind him, close by an uncurtained window in the northeast corner of the room.

During a reading session, the taking of notes proceeded in two ways. For those passages that William wanted to refer to directly, he called out, "Mark that," and English penciled parallel lines in the margin. For other materials, only the gist of which was desired, Prescott, with ivory stylus in hand, sat with his noctograph before him on the writing table.[5]

Like his vision, William's noctographic writing was a variable. Half-joking, he himself often termed it hieroglyphics. Others, occasionally the same maudlin individuals who equate limited vision with blindness, have generalized by describing all his noctographic writing as baffling—as true hieroglyphics. Because of Prescott's humorous references and to the embellishments of others, the legibility of that writing has been undeservedly categorized and abused. Yet even though much of the noctographic writing was highly legible, the notes hastily scribbled as he listened to his aide were easily the least legible. Consequently English and subsequent reader-secretaries hurried to transcribe notes while their own recollection of the subject facilitated that labor. These transcriptions, intended for Prescott's use as he mulled over materials preparatory to composition, he required in big round letters.

[5] Gardiner, ed., *Papers*, pp. 46–48; and Ticknor, *Prescott*, pp. 86–87.

Another obstacle to the historian's progress was his near addiction to review writing. Of the poems in a volume he reviewed for Jared Sparks, he confided, "They are of that mediocre kind, that I could not find in my heart to praise, and yet so amiable that I can still less find in my heart to abuse them, so I have contented myself with something negative or neutral, which I hope the self love of the author will mistake for praise, but which I am sure no body else will."[6] As a reviewer William wasted on poetry and novels time he might better have bestowed on historical works. Also, Prescott, the reviewer who never published a truly adverse criticism of any writer or work, was postponing the acquisition of the critical judgment so necessary to the historian. Later he realized that he should review fewer works, and eventually he concluded that all reviewing was sheer waste of time.

Meanwhile the issue of the "Old North" which followed the one carrying the review of the mediocre American poetry contained a longer Prescott review, on Scottish poetry. In the Prescott manner it offered a long consideration of the traits of Scottish poetry at large and a short consideration of the work immediately at hand.[7] Next, as he reviewed two novels, he readily admitted, "The reading of the books aloud requires a great sacrifice of time." However, he tried to salvage something from the experience by assessing his methods of composition.[8]

In mid-1828 William, trying to harmonize reviewing and research, determined to go all out on the historical project "except only for a fortnight every year, in which I will write an article of some 20 or 25 pages at most, for Sparks only." To this he soon added, "Exercise myself when writing reviews on topics connected with my Spanish subject."[9] His next review, undertaken within the month, indicated that he still was better at formulating rules than he was at observing them. Unrelated to both history and Spain, William's review of Jules Tas-

---

[6] [WHP], "Leisure Hours at Sea," *North American Review*, 12 (April, 1826): 453–455; and Gardiner, ed., *Papers*, pp. 45–46.

[7] [WHP], "Scottish Song," *North American Review*, 22 (July, 1826): 124–142.

[8] Gardiner, ed., *Literary Memoranda*, 1: 86; and [WHP], "Novel Writing," *North American Review*, 25 (July, 1827): 183–203.

[9] Gardiner, ed., *Literary Memoranda*, 1: 89–90, 92.

chereau's *Histoire de la Vie et des Ouvrages de Molière* was, nonetheless, one of the finest things he had written.[10] More essay than review, it was more Prescott and less a patchquilt of quotations than had been numerous earlier reviews.

3

During these years of intellectual flitting from one quarter of Europe to another, William, in his own living, was very much a stay-at-home. He routinely joined his parents on their trips to Pepperell, and quite probably his sincere affection for the "philosophic shades" and "the old Manse" at The Highlands, and the perfection that they called to mind, discouraged wider travel.[11] At any rate, year after year he lived in a world bounded by Salem and Pepperell on the north, Hartford and the Connecticut Valley on the west, Taunton on the south, and the salt water to the east of Boston.

To Jared Sparks, off to European archives on the first leg of his project to collect and publish basic documents related to American history, William, with the enthusiasm of a small boy, announced, in the spring of 1828, "Where do you think I am going?—To Washington! . . . I am really bent upon this corporal feat, which is much more for me, than your voyage across the Atlantic for you."[12] Traveling with him was George Ticknor.

Moving southward rapidly, and returning more leisurely by the same route, George and William traveled by coach between Boston and Providence, by steamboat from Providence to New York, by coach between New York and Philadelphia. After steamboating down the Delaware to New Castle, they took a coach to a shipping point near Elkton on the headwaters of Chesapeake Bay, whence steamboat transferred them to Baltimore. Between that city and Washington they reverted to coach. On the Chesapeake Bay leg of the trip, William com-

---

[10] [WHP], "The Life and Writings of Moliere," *North American Review,* 27 (October, 1828): 372–402; and Gardiner, ed., *Papers,* pp. 62–63.

[11] WHP to J. Sparks, August 26, 1826, Sparks papers; and Gardiner, ed., *Papers,* pp. 63–65.

[12] WHP to J. Sparks, December 5, 1827, April 13, 1828, Sparks papers.

plained, "We had orators, Jacksonites and Adamsites aboard the boat who kept us awake spouting speeches till near midnight."[13]

For the well-recommended Bostonians, their whirlwind week in Washington was a rich experience. Assisting both, but more especially the friend of Ticknor, was Daniel Webster. William renewed his acquaintance with President Adams, found Henry Clay haggard but amiable, and declared British minister Charles Richard Vaughan well-bred and informed. John C. Calhoun possessed a striking physiognomy, Martin Van Buren was "a smooth, easy speaker," and a certain Miss Livingstone, elegant, languishing, somewhat affected, witty, and charming, was the Southern belle on whom Prescott passed himself "for a day or two for a single gentleman."[14]

Of his first visit to the White House William remarked, "I called to see Mr. Adams, in his princely residence, which forms somewhat of a contrast to the occupant. He was dressed in checked waistcoat, blue trowsers, yarn socks, and clod hopper shoes." On Friday, April 25, in a party of sixteen male guests, he and Ticknor dined with the Adamses. Earlier, on April 22, George and William had visited Congress. A land bill was being debated in the Senate, "and the everlasting Tariff in the House." William considered the senators quite respectable in appearance but the House members, one of whom was "blowing his nose with his fingers," he termed "somewhat mottled."[15]

The next day William was among the twenty-eight persons attending "the most splendid affair given at Washington in the course of the year," Minister Vaughan's dinner. The bachelor diplomat was well known for dedicating every shilling of his substantial salary to the maintenance of his social position. That evening doormen in white liveries and red facings ushered in the guests. Their host wore a blue coat covered with gold embroidery of oak leaf figures. Other diplomats lent additional color to the occasion. The wine, never overlooked by Wil-

[13] Gardiner, ed., *Papers,* p. 57.

[14] George Ticknor Curtis, *Life of Daniel Webster,* 2nd ed. 2 vols. (New York, 1870), 1: 323; and WHP to S. A. Prescott, April 22, 25, 1828, Prescott papers.

[15] *Id.* to *id.,* April 22, 1828, Prescott papers; and John Quincy Adams, Diary, Reel 40 (November 11, 1825–June 24, 1828), p. 510, Adams papers.

liam, was in eight silver urns on a three-by-twelve-foot plateau on the table. Twenty different dishes were served by candlelight; the green peas were from Norfolk, the lobsters and halibut, from New York, the truffles, from France, the olives, from Seville. A six-foot halibut occupied a serving table which required four men to carry it. Later William dined with both the French and Prussian ministers, but the splendor of the English evening, plus his pro-British disposition, placed the Continentals at a disadvantage.[16]

As in Europe, earlier, the stay in Washington included a pilgrimage to the home of a great man. As he crossed the Potomac to Mount Vernon, Prescott made his southernmost penetration of the United States. When the carriage broke down, he slogged four muddy miles afoot before Mount Vernon evoked mixed sentiments. He found it "in the finest situation in the world—but . . . in the most shocking state of dilapidation and ruin."[17]

Despite his crowded schedule, William repeatedly found time to be homesick. "As I told a lady today," he wrote from Philadelphia, "never will I set out upon such another expedition without five certain persons whom I could name, to keep me company."[18] The indispensables included his wife Susan, daughter Kitty, son Will, and his parents. Love of family, combined with the reportorial skill developed on his European trip and the knowledge that he was traveling, as it were, for the entire family, caused William to draft eleven letters on his noctograph, some of them lengthy, in the course of a three-week trip. Crowded with affection were such lines as: "Kiss little Kitty and William," "Kiss Katie and Will," "Kiss the darlings," and "write me dear Susan of the little chicks." Once he printed in bold letters, obviously for three-and-one-half-year-old Catherine to ponder, "I love little Kitty, and will buy her a work-box in New York, if she is a good girl."[19] She received the workbox, and Will, promised a whip, likewise suffered no disappointment.

[16] WHP to S. A. Prescott, April 24, 25, 1828, Prescott papers.
[17] *Id.* to *id.,* April 24, 1828, Prescott papers.
[18] *Id.* to *id.,* May 1, 1828, Prescott papers; and Hillard, ed., *Life, Letters, and Journals,* 1: 381, 382.
[19] WHP to S. A. Prescott, April 15, 28, 30, 1828, Prescott papers; and Gardiner, ed., *Papers,* pp. 56–60.

On the return trip a short stay in Baltimore was enlivened by attendance at a meeting of a phrenological society. The phrenologists
studied Prescott's skull and quickly concluded that his two most
dominant traits were firmness and a low measure of parental affection.
"I told them," he wrote Susan, "they were never more mistaken in
their lives: That I was totally destitute of *firmness*, being remarkably
weak of purpose, on most occasions; and that I never kept a secret in
my life. . . . There were lying upon the table—the sculls of five or six
pirates—who had been executed at Norfolk—who had certain developments not unlike mine."[20]

Philadelphia, like Baltimore, delighted the returning travelers. Relished most, one suspects, was editor Robert Walsh's delightful dinner,
which assembled seven or eight witty men of the community. Quick
with joke and pun, William remembered the occasion as the jolliest
time he had known since leaving Boston. A succession of dinners reinforced the favorable estimate he formed of the "cultivated and liberal tastes" of Philadelphia society. Summing up his stay there, he remarked, "I have 17 visits to return."[21]

Anticipating his return to Bedford Street, William remarked,
"Nothing short of life and death, shall ever send me upon such another tremendous journey and exile. The more I see of tavern life and
stages, and steamboats, and strangers, the more I long to be at home—
home—however Pepperell is a journey quite distant eno' for my time
of life."[22] At thirty-two, Prescott was not quite that near his dotage,
but years did pass before he again extended the limits of his world.

While William playfully posed in Washington as "a single gentleman," Susan was carrying their third child. On July 27, 1828, a second
daughter was born. Named Elizabeth, the infant honored her father's
sister. Needless to say, Lizzie's advent affected the summer routine.
In late August of this unusual year the father of the three spent ten
days at Nahant, an experience which greatly influenced the future.

Already the Prescotts had noticed Nahant, a cool, windswept mag-

[20] WHP to S. A. Prescott, April 28, 1828, Prescott papers; and Gardiner,
ed., *Papers*, pp. 58–60.
[21] WHP to S. A. Prescott, May 1, 1828, Prescott papers.
[22] *Id.* to *id.*, April 28, 1828, Prescott papers.

net to increasing numbers of Bostonians in the summer season. Picnics, dinners at the hotel, day trips, and the like had acquainted various Prescotts with the attractions of the resort. Now, however, William's desire to avoid the summer heat of the city reinforced a new surge of Judge Prescott's preference for rural and natural settings. The Judge, sixty-six years of age and in delicate health, had announced his professional retirement. His means, leisure, and tastes increased his interest in Nahant as the likely site for a summer residence. The decision in favor of Nahant was reached in 1828, and the plans which permitted them their first full summer there the following year quickly materialized.

Crystal-clear on many counts, the year 1828 represents unrivaled confusion concerning Prescott the writer. Immediately before his trip to Washington he had spent an indeterminate interval on an article about Italian literature. He estimated its length at approximately fifty printed pages of either the *Edinburgh Review* or the *Quarterly Review,* in one or the other of which he hoped to see it published. Sending the bulky manuscript to Jared Sparks, in London, he counted on his friend to put it in the hands of editor Francis Jeffrey of the *Edinburgh,* and then, if refusal necessitated, into the hands of editor John Gibson Lockhart of the *Quarterly.* Behind this effort and desire to be published in a major British literary review lay an accumulation of respect for those publications. As a reader of English literature and a close student of the British reviews, William admired their standards so much that he sought publication in at least one of them as proof of his own expanding achievement. Even as he admired the leading British journals collectively, his preference inclined toward the *Edinburgh Review.* For assistance in that quarter, he turned to Ticknor, who generously wrote Robert Southey about the Prescott article in Sparks's hands, hoping, even suggesting, that Southey mention it to Jeffrey.

Keenly aware of the different outlooks of the two British publications, William accommodated himself and his article to them. He instructed Sparks, should the *Edinburgh* reject it, to use two substitute pages which were intended to render it more palatable to the *Quarterly.* Apparently, however, neither journal accepted the article on Italian literature. Meanwhile, as he awaited word, he shuttled other articles, via Sparks, to the same editors, with generally similar results. One item, however, sufficiently struck Lockhart's fancy that he kept it. But when months elapsed without its appearance in print, Prescott, accustomed to the early, if not immediate, publication of his article in America, requested its return.[23] In the closely guarded silence which somewhat obscures this quest for transatlantic acceptance, he bore his British disappointment.

The autumn of 1828, for William H. Prescott, was more than mildly tinged with the politics of changing leadership. In the presidential race many persons with the economic, geographical, and intellectual orientations shared by the Prescotts viewed with alarm the victory of the Jacksonites. As though national politics were not enough that season, the selection of a successor to President Kirkland at Harvard provoked local speculation. William thought there were about fifty candidates, among whom Edward Everett and George Ticknor were counted prominent but unlikely ones. The Judge, no longer serving Alma Mater in any official capacity, knew little more than did his son about the circumstances which eventually led to the choice of Josiah Quincy.

4

Except for the physical injury to his eye and the related problem of health, Prescott had suffered little. Good fortune had almost smothered him with undisguised blessings—understanding and generous parents, warm, faithful friends, a sweet and adoring wife, and three small children: newborn Elizabeth, a mere infant; Will, nearing his third birthday; and Kitty, as his words and acts attested, the apple of his eye. When Kitty, well beyond her fourth birthday, died suddenly, William was plunged into deep grief. For weeks after that fateful February 1 he was less a social than a spiritual being. Finding it difficult to reconcile himself to the loss, he wondered, amid his tears, if the future offered a prospect of reunion for the living and the dead. Unable to immerse himself in historical studies, he read and reflected about Christianity. It was not the first time he had systematically and

[23] WHP to J. Sparks, March 24, April 13, 1828, Sparks papers; and Gardiner, ed., *Papers,* p. 64.

conscientiously explored Christian literature, but his close study of Christian revelation for more than a month was unusual.

Book after book, readily available on shelves of the family library, drew him: David Hume's *Essays on Miracles and a Future State,* Richard Watson's *Apology for Christianity,* Joseph Butler's *The Analogy of Religion,* William Paley's *Evidences of Christianity,* Conyers Middleton's *A Free Inquiry into the Miraculous Powers,* and Soame Jenyns' *Internal Evidences,* among others. They represented, as William insisted in his critical study, the views of the skeptic and the believer. In the leisure of his retirement, William Prescott joined his son in this inquiry. "Shall I add," the younger man wrote, "that an examination of miraculous testimony with an old and cautious lawyer, like my Father, is a sufficient pledge of the severity of my scrutiny?"[24] Many conclusions, cautiously reached, stubbornly persisted. Helped especially by Butler, he concluded, "that a habit of levity or sarcasm on topics connected with Christianity or its evidences, must be criminal and unwise, as tending, without reason, to shake the foundations on which my belief rests." Later, as historian, William wrote often and at length regarding religious practices which he personally found uncongenial but, adhering to this conclusion, he avoided light or sarcastic treatment of Roman Catholicism.

"As any conclusion as to the truth of the revelation, founded on its evidences," William insisted, "must be the deduction of pure reason, so it can never oblige or authorize me to receive a doctrine which may be manifestly contrary to reason." Concerning the prospect of a future life, he concluded, "that the doctrine of eternal damnation . . . is not authorised by the phrases and various epithets in Scripture to have been literally intended by our Saviour." Some conclusions demonstrated his Unitarian outlook. "The doctrine [of the Trinity]," he stated, "rests for its support on a few obscure texts of the Apostles, who, moreover, in the general tenor of their discourse, assert the unity and supremacy of the Deity in unequivocal terms."

His grief assuaged, his religious conviction strengthened by reason, William never turned evangelist. "The word of God, as delivered by

[24] Gardiner, ed., *Literary Memoranda,* 1: 109. The quotations which immediately follow are in *ibid.,* pp. 110–114, *passim.*

our Saviour himself so intelligibly that he who runs may read," he concluded, "will furnish us with the surest guide both of faith and of practice."

In late spring William returned to his scholarly labors. Then it was that he finished his reviews of two historical works, José Antonio Conde's *Historia de la dominación de los Arabes en España* and Washington Irving's *Conquest of Granada.* Sensing that it might fit into his projected history, Prescott did not send the article on Conde to a journal. And so it did, two years later, when it took its place in his developing manuscript as Chapter Eight, "Review of the Political and Intellectual Condition of the Spanish Arabs previous to the War of Granada."

The review of Irving's *Conquest of Granada,* on the other hand, revealed another facet of the nascent historian.[25] In this, the first of just two reviews on historical subjects—the second of which did not appear for another twelve years—William bared publicly his awareness of historiographical patterns, as well as his conception of the responsibilities of the historian. Like certain other reviews, this was more essay on related theme than critique of particular work. After impressively listing many qualifications of the nonexistent perfect historian—wherein he leaned heavily on Mably—he quickly reviewed the nature of history in ancient days, as written by Herodotus, Livy, Tacitus, Thucydides, and Xenophon. Turning to modern historians and stressing both changing method and product, William insisted that the historian "was no longer to concoct his narrative . . . . Libraries were to be ransacked; medals and monuments to be studied; obsolete manuscripts to be deciphered. Every assertion was to be fortified by an authority." In the modern era he addressed himself especially to Voltaire and Gibbon, only incidental attention going to Hallam and Amable Barante. Voltaire deserved reproach for his inaccuracies, but the structure of his work merited the highest praise. (Later, Prescott, learning much from Voltaire's *Essai sur les Moeurs,* developed a similar framework for his first history.) Gibbon's defects received more attention

[25] [WHP], "Irving's Conquest of Granada," *North American Review,* 29 (October, 1829): 293–314. The quotations which follow are in *ibid.,* pp. 297, 303, 314.

than did his virtues. Most blistering, possibly, was William's charge that Gibbon's "most elaborate efforts exhibit too often the perversion of learning and ingenuity to the vindication of preconceived hypotheses." The writings of neither Voltaire nor Gibbon were "warmed with a generous moral sentiment."

When, at last, William touched Irving, it was not his work so much as his theme that won attention. Prescott, himself, trying to depict the full reign of Ferdinand and Isabella, saw breadth, grandeur, and significance in the related theme. The fourth and final portion of the review, a consideration of the sources employed by Irving, directly and indirectly reproved the New Yorker for his limited sources. All in all, the Bostonian revealed much of himself in reference to historiography, method, theme, and sources. Just about his only word concerning Irving's work as such was the concluding statement which, in part, read: "Notwithstanding the romantic forms . . . we may honestly recommend it as substantially an authentic record of one of the most interesting, and, as far as English scholars are concerned, one of the most untravelled portions of Spanish history."

This book review turned essay enabled William to turn in upon himself the problem of the historian's responsibilities and methods. The writing of this review-essay in eleven days convinced him that by concentrating thought and study, mastering a given block of materials, and writing generally without recourse to notes—except where he needed a variety of illustrative detail—he could maintain a respectable rate of progress. Significant in his proposed method was the procedure whereby he revolved, organized, and revised his materials four or five times in his mind before picking up his stylus. He wanted to avoid tameness; he desired a rich, colorful style. As yet he had not accepted the necessity of rejecting the superfluous, the irrelevant, and multiplied detail. It was time to overcome his fastidiousness, in regard to both words and exhaustiveness. For the better flow of his writing, he hoped to adopt Sismondi's plan of reference to his authorities en masse at the end of the paragraph, except when a direct quotation was employed. To enliven the product of his stylus, William planned to include dialogue and anecdote.

Dedicated to a biographical focus on the reign of Ferdinand and

Isabella, he next studied the structure of biography, analyzing the strengths and weaknesses of five works: Lucy Aikin's *Memoirs of the Court of Queen Elizabeth,* Voltaire's *The History of Charles XII of Sweden,* William Roscoe's *The Life of Lorenzo de' Medici,* Amable Barante's *Histoire des Ducs de Bourgoyne de la maison de Valois,* and Augustin Thierry's *Histoire de la conquête de l'Angleterre par les Normands.*[26] Aikin's work, he concluded, was of no help and that by Voltaire of but limited utility. His most significant reaction to the latter was his conclusion that it possessed "the interest of a novel." From Roscoe he adopted in his own work that writer's "fashion of giving *general views and particular criticisms retrospective and prospective* of the state of culture &c."

Barante's work impressed Prescott on several counts. The author never intruded upon the narrative. His basic ingredients included conversation, correspondence, public documents, and anecdotes illustrative of the manners of the time. Rallying his themes as much as possible around one or two prominent characters in a continuous chronological account rich with detail, Barante gave his reader "all the interest of a romance with the solid instruction of history." William also remembered the parallel between Charles the Bold and Louis XI as a model of "easy, interesting and vigorous delineation." The last author, Thierry, he admired for his capacity to take both "wide and intimate views of every part of his subject," and for the extreme simplicity of his narrative. Four biographers, in varying degree, had helped Prescott more than he then realized.

Among the general conclusions he reached were these: write direct narrative without intruding upon the reader; transport the reader to the scene of the historical action; and have the notes serve to illustrate, criticize, qualify, display discrepancies, and quote original versions. Additionally, even as he planned to avoid too many incidents, he intended to establish a constant focus on political intrigue. "So not affect much learning—research &c.," he insisted, "it will not pay for it, and will disgust me." His gentlemanly nature further demanded, "Give no disgusting details—bad taste." Challenging himself to brevity and

---

[26] Gardiner, ed., *Literary Memoranda,* 1: 117–120. The remaining quotations in this section are in *ibid.,* pp. 114–121 *passim.*

reader appeal, he added, "Do not be afraid of being too brief. Those details are most interesting which affect the passions."

Again ready to wade into the record of his chosen monarchs, William declared, "I can think in one place as well as another, and in company as well as alone." At once he had an opportunity to test this declaration. The residence at Nahant was ready for occupancy by three generations of Prescotts.

5

To the northeast, halfway between Boston and Salem, lay Nahant.[27] Despite man's efforts, its charms were inherently natural ones. Precisely put, Nahant is an L-shaped peninsula dangling southward from the town of Lynn toward the approaches to Boston harbor. More romantically, Nahant is a pendant of rock and sand hung upon moody Atlantic waters. Embracing about five hundred acres, it stretches two miles from west to east and possibly one-half mile from north to south. Its predominant feature is its rugged, rocky nature. Along much of its coastline, steep cliffs rise abruptly twenty to sixty feet. Its rocks of gray and purple, of red and white, of green and blue and black, bathe in changing light and surging wave. Deep fissures and caverns dot the shoreline. Within the coves, especially at the eastern tip and along much of the southern shore, stretch silvery beaches of fine sand. Nahant had its special attractions: Swallows' Cave on a southeastern tip, Irene's Grotto somewhat to the west, and Pulpit Rock not far to the east. Natural Bridge, Cauldron Cliff, Castle Rock, Spouting Horn, and John's Peril also quickened romantic natures. Seals, porpoises, sandpipers, plovers, coots, loons, and white gulls awaited the lover of nature. But foremost of all its assets were Nahant's tempering breezes.

[27] Concerning Nahant, see Alonzo Lewis, *The History of Lynn, including Nahant* (Boston, 1844); Hillard, "Prescott," in *Little Journeys*; John G. Hales, *A Survey of Boston and Its Vicinity* (Boston, 1821), pp. 24, 89, 92; Willard de Lue, "Heroic Work on Wild, Windy Fitful Head," *The Boston Daily Globe*, December 5, 1956, p. 54; Gardiner, ed., *Papers*, pp. 63, 65; Abel Bowen, *Bowen's Picture of Boston*, 3rd ed. (Boston, 1838), p. 256; Walter Scott, *The Pirate*, 2 vols. (Philadelphia, 1866). Cleveland Amory insists that "Nahant grew to be a sort of symbol of Boston Society's idea of low-scaled high living" (*The Proper Bostonians* [New York, 1947], p. 198).

Moderated by winds from the Atlantic—some of which turned into squalls—Nahant was much cooler than Boston.

In the summer of 1829 William Prescott, his wife, and William and Susan and their two children moved into the new cottage. On occasion, Ned Prescott and Frank and Lizzie Dexter and their children augmented that family circle. Like every other Prescott residence outside Boston, the one at Nahant received a special name. Honoring one of Scott's Waverley novels, it became "Fitful Head," a place name lifted from the Shetland Islands and associated with insane Norna, a leading character in *The Pirate*. The name ideally suited the house.

On Swallows' Cave Point, at the southeastern tip of Nahant, the rambling, two-storied frame residence, rich in wide verandas, enjoyed a measure of relative isolation. A short distance to the northwest lay the wharf to which the boat from Boston delivered many of the residents and their guests. Some distance off to the northeast, just inland from East Point, stood the luxurious Nahant Hotel. On the east a promontory dropped fifty feet to the sea. At low tide the wooden staircase from the lower lawn lured one to the narrow strand at the base of the cliff. Fitful Head was wedded to the sea and any long-time resident came to enjoy those moody waters.

To promote his working that first season at Nahant, Prescott resolved that the year ending July 4, 1830, would mark the production of at least 250 pages, and if eyes permitted, 400 pages of his history. Unfortunately he was careless—possibly looking upon the Atlantic in sunny morning hours—and he soon complained of impaired vision. Denied work, and thoroughly dispirited, he registered disgust. "Never attempt to stay here again," he said, "or to make a longer visit than two days at most."[28] Soon he reversed himself—the setting had benefited his father's bad cough—but in 1829 he entertained a low opinion of Nahant.

6

Returned to Boston, the ambitious invalid constructed a chronological synopsis of the events which he planned to discuss in his history.

---

[28] Gardiner, ed., *Literary Memoranda*, 1: 124. The remaining quotations in this chapter are in *ibid.*, pp. 131–135 *passim*.

Somewhat to be expected in a day of three-decker novels and multi-volume histories, he never entertained the idea of a single-volume work. At this stage he conceived it as "not to exceed two volumes of 500 pages each, of 240 or 50 words to the page, broken up into chapters varying from 20 to 50 pages each, and where I can make it equally convenient, of about 30 or 35 pages." Chronologically the first volume would span the period between 1454 and 1492; topically it would emphasize the domestic policy of the Spanish monarchs; and biographically it would feature Isabella. Moving chronologically from 1492 to 1516, volume two chiefly would emphasize Spanish foreign policy, featuring Ferdinand biographically. Except that the history ran to three volumes, Prescott successfully adhered to these plans.

Struggling with the synopsis, he also gained the perspective which designated certain themes as primary. Among the subjects which required detailed treatment because of their permanent influence on Spain or on Europe were these: the constitutional liberties of Castile and Aragon, the Inquisition, the Spanish Arabs, the Jews, maritime discoveries, and Castilian literature.

In view of the fact that Prescott aimed at general and popular presentations of historical episodes, avoiding research as much as he possibly could, it appears that the accident of his fluctuating vision, far from bad in its total effect, forced him, at moments when he could do little else, to state and restate, with consequent improvement, the basic patterns of his histories. However, plan as he might, no book would result unless he faced up to the necessity of sitting down with his materials and working them into shape, sentence by sentence, chapter by chapter. Backing down from the idealized complete work to a thoughtful construction of his opening sentence, William wrote, in his literary memoranda, "Began to write on the first Chapter of my history of Ferdinand and Isabella on Tuesday October 6."

VI

*Twenty noctographs I can read for and . . .*

THE DISCIPLINE WHICH ENABLED Prescott to put the first word of his history on paper was related to many other intellectual problems then plaguing him. The process of his self-education as scholar and his lengthy and simultaneous search for truth and beauty—historical fact and literary style—reveal much of Prescott the man. As with literature, and life at large, William approached history with a desire to reduce it to rules. Mably helped greatly, but some regulations reflect his own physical nature and intellectual temperament. The state of his eyes, combined with desire to write unrestrainedly, inspired his dictum: "Never take up my pen until I have travelled over the subject so often as to be able to write almost from memory, not from invention as I go along."[1]

Another basic problem was his inordinate capacity for killing time. Beyond the fact that the servants opened the door to too many visitors, William was himself an accomplished daydreamer. To prod himself he gave this bond to English: either he would achieve a stated amount

[1] Gardiner, ed., *Literary Memoranda,* 1: 135. For general background for the interval treated in this chapter, see *ibid.,* 93, 135–195, 243–257. The quotations which follow immediately are in *ibid.,* pp. 135–142 *passim.*

of work in a specified time or he would pay his aide one thousand dollars.

"Finished the text of my first chapter," he wrote eight days after beginning it, "written at the rate of two sheets a day. If I had thought on the subject continuously and closely—especially over night and early in the mornings—I might easily have written three sheets per day, at least. I must get along with my notes faster." Consuming four weeks, the notes of that chapter came even more slowly. Approximating two-thirds the wordage of the related text, they posed a problem for which he needed more discipline, possibly additional rules.

"I must approach as near to biographical interest as possible," he insisted. "I must endeavor to exhibit as amply as possible the state of public feeling, civilization, personal comfort &c of the period, borrowing the language, and reflecting the manners of the age in the same manner as if I had been a contemporary."

"Could not the war of Granada be much vivified by drawing the popular opinions, attachments, sufferings &c, &c of the Moors, from the old ballads?" he asked himself. "Poetry itself becomes unexceptionable testimony in regard to these circumstances." Keenly concerned about characterization and every source that might breathe life into the past, William merged the man of letters and the historian.

In December 1829 and the following month he read, took notes, and "at the rate of two and a quarter sheets per day," wrote his second and third chapters. Looking over the 130 pages in the first 3 chapters, he realized that he was 50 per cent in excess of his space allotment. He devised more rules.

"On commencing to read for a chapter," he insisted, in his quest for faster writing, "I will look through the events in some one author; then fix on the *few* leading points to develop." To avoid writing too much, he added, "I must fix inviolably and exactly the limits of the chapter according to my MS. sheets, before commencing it." To these problems of speed and amount of writing, he adjusted certain matters related to his own temperament. "My taste and ability best fit me for generalization, and for treating subjects of moment, rather than petty details . . . Enlarge therefore on these general chapters—and select only the prominent features, the battles, capital negotiations, in short, conspicuous events and characters in the narrative."

Studying and refining his chapter outlines in the light of changing outlook, William went once more to Mably for guidance. In the writings of that "perspicuous, severe, shrewd and sensible writer," he marked passages for future reference. "I like particularly," he noted, "his notion of the necessity of giving an interest as well as utility to history by letting events tend to some obvious point or moral. In short in paying such attention to the development of events tending to this leading result as one would in the construction of a romance or drama." Pondering the great events and emphases in his project, he reaffirmed his biographical approach.

To this strong focus on historical concepts Prescott added an assessment of his style. In those opening chapters he found too many adjectives, paired substantives, and sentences from the same mold. "One strong adjective," he concluded, "more effect than adverb and adjective, e.g. propitious instead of highly favorable." He should replace some emphatic pronouns with articles; delete some expletives; and introduce his own reflections less ceremoniously. Less fastidious writing, he was certain, would be better writing. To achieve brevity and effect, he must curb his tendency toward repetition. That which smacked of the pedantic, inverted, irrelevant, obscure, abrupt, and petty required different handling.

The overlapping spheres of Prescott's intellectual life call to mind the competing spheres of his social world. One area related to his continuing identification with Club and numerous all-male dinner parties. Recalling the William H. Prescott encountered at Ticknor's dinners, George T. Curtis remembered William "talking with a joyous *abandon,* laughing at his own inconsequences, recovering himself gayly, and going on again in a graver strain, which soon gave way to some new joke or brilliant sally. Wherever *he* came there was always a 'fillip' to the discourse, be it of books, or society, or reminiscences of foreign travel, or the news of the day."[2] In these activities the social and intellectual interests merged sufficiently that this part of his social

---

[2] Hillard, ed., *Life, Letters, and Journals,* I: 39.

life actually stimulated William's scholarship. Not so, however, those aspects which found him husband of Susan and son of Judge and Mrs. Prescott. Both as husband and son, he participated in social activities which he enjoyed but increasingly resented because of the havoc they played with his historical labors.

As he piled up formulas for scholarship—for his history, its parts, chapters, paragraphs, and sentences—Prescott rather naturally added a capstone to the lot, a timetable. "Consider it," he said, "as a work to be achieved in *three years, say by January 1st 1833.*" Sad experience would alter this timetable many times, but its early formulation pressed added self-discipline upon him.

"I am persuaded," he mused, "that to write well and rapidly I must break the investigation of the subject into masses requiring about 10 nocto-graphic sheets. I must think over my ground, say five sheets at a time four or five times."[3] That summer Fitful Head was host to both physical well-being and scholarly progress, which surprised and pleased him. One sad moment was occasioned, however, by the death of Dr. John Sylvester John Gardiner, his ablest teacher. Prescott was inspired to write his first memoir. Gardiner, William recalled, had "adopted Pliny's maxim, to read much rather than many books, *multum non multa.*"[4] In succeeding years, the young historian repeatedly reflected his own acceptance of that maxim. Prescott later wrote and published other memoirs, but in no instance did the person concerned touch him so meaningfully as had Dr. J. S. J. Gardiner. Sorrow, love, admiration— these and other sentiments urged him to honor the deceased rector of Trinity Church.

2

In early years of the second quarter of the nineteenth century, the Prescotts were among the social and economic elite of Boston in identifying themselves with charitable and humanitarian undertakings. For a long time, while Catherine continued to be a mainstay of the Female Asylum, the Judge's services to the University had overshadowed the

[3] Gardiner, ed., *Literary Memoranda,* I, 143, 144.
[4] [WHP], "Obituary Notice of the Rev. Dr. Gardiner," *Columbian Centinel,* September 11, 1830, p. 1.

generosity with which he routinely contributed to numerous local causes. A child of such parents merely was taking the stand expected of his social set and his family when he, too, demonstrated his humanitarianism. William's troublesome vision inspired one of his contributions.

"Can you accommodate me with ten or twelve pages in the next number of the *North American* (your last, I understand?)" he wrote editor Sparks. "I want to recommend to the public an Asylum for the Blind, which we are organizing in this town." Far from writing a thin item of "appealing" journalism, William had thoroughly researched and meditated the matter.[5]

The New-England Asylum for the Blind, incorporated by an act of the Massachusetts legislature on March 2, 1829, and needing public support, inspired Prescott's article. To explode mistaken ideas concerning the blind, he sketched the achievements of mathematicians Nicholas Saunderson and Leonhard Euler and poets Homer and Milton. In some detail, he discussed the objectives and techniques of the educational programs in Edinburgh, Paris, and elsewhere. Turning from the achievements of Europe, and their implicit challenge for America, he next summarized succinctly what Boston was attempting to do for the blind. There, finances were not the only problem because the new asylum still had to determine whether its educational program would be basically intellectual or mechanical. Prescott insisted, regardless of that educational emphasis, "We want not to maintain the blind, but to put them in the way of contributing to their own maintenance."[6]

This article neither initiated nor concluded Prescott's identification with the movement. The original incorporators of the Asylum numbered thirty-one, including Dr. John D. Fisher, Thomas H. Perkins, Robert Rantoul, Israel and William Thorndike, Amos and Abbott Lawrence, William and William H. Prescott, and such intimates of the last-named as Franklin Dexter and John C. Gray. Even while

[5] Gardiner, ed., *Papers,* pp. 71–72. General accounts of the theme of this section are in Winsor, ed., *Memorial History of Boston,* 4: 271–272; Harold Schwartz, *Samuel Gridley Howe, Social Reformer 1801–1876* (Cambridge, 1956), pp. 42, 49–53. Prescott's article is "Asylum for the Blind," *North American Review,* 31 (July, 1830): 66–85.

[6] *Ibid.,* p. 84.

writing the article for Sparks, William had occupied himself with another problem of the new institution, the procurement of teaching
personnel.[7]

The quest for a director for the new institution took Dr. John D.
Fisher and William, representing the Board of Trustees of the Asylum,
to Hartford, Connecticut, to confer with the Reverend T. H. Gallaudet, soon to surrender his duties at the asylum for the deaf and
dumb which he had founded and served for thirteen years. Even as
he declined the superintendency of the new Boston institution, Gallaudet did offer helpful suggestions.[8] Soon, in the person of twenty-nine-
year-old Samuel Gridley Howe, the desired man was found. Drama-
tically and imaginatively, Howe and the institution for the blind
were on their way. Behind them, as one of the trustees, stood William
H. Prescott.

3

Concerned about the welfare of the sightless, the developing historian also had reason to reflect on his own faulty vision. In a moment
of deep depression, he set to planning his future in the event that
his eyes failed completely or he had to forego using them for long
intervals. Certain that review writing alone never could content him,
he planned to continue his history regardless of the obstacles. While
Prescott was thus moodily experiencing his highs and lows, English
continued to serve him, as, too, did Susan. "I nowhere reckon her
half hours for herself,"[9] declared the pampered husband to whom
she had presented a second son, William Amory, in January 1830.

The illness which confined William to his bed for a fortnight and to
the house another two weeks in the spring of 1831, while interrupting
his historical research, did encourage other things. In a letter to Nor-

---

[7] [New-England Institution for the Education of the Blind], *By-Laws, Rules,
and Regulations of the New-England Institution for the Education of the Blind,
incorporated 1829*, 6th ed. (n.p., n.d.), p. 3; and Gardiner, ed., *Papers*, pp.
72–73.

[8] Heman Humphrey, *The Life and Labors of the Rev. T. H. Gallaudet,
LL.D.*, (New York, 1857), pp. 237–244; and WHP to T. H. Gallaudet, January 3, 1831, Miscellaneous papers, New York Public Library.

[9] Gardiner, ed., *Literary Memoranda*, 1: 147.

thampton, he fell upon George Bancroft's politics. Unrelated to his dislike of Bancroft's identification with Jacksonian democracy, however,
was the displeasure which prompted the remark, "I perceive you are
. . . quitting the sweets of letters for the thorny path of politics."[10]
George heard this more than once from the friend whose indisposition
also invited thought regarding his annual contribution to his favorite
quarterly.

4

At first glance the article "Poetry and Romance of the Italians"[11]
would merely seem to be the 1831 crop of literary peppercorn which
Prescott, with extreme regularity in recent years, had planted in
pages of either the July or October issues of the *North American Review*. On closer inspection, however, the article supplies answers for
one of the few literary question marks in Prescott's life.

On circumstantial grounds, the present writer believes that "Poetry
and Romance of the Italians" was not written in 1831 but was instead the article of 1828 which had been tendered unsuccessfully by
Sparks to the two leading British reviews. The reasoning, in general, is
as follows: (a) both the article of 1831 and that of 1828 treated
Italian literature in broad perspective; (b) like the item of 1828,
William called that of 1831 an article, not a review; (c) both articles
deserved to be called fifty-page items; (d) like that of 1828, in his
admissions to Sparks, this article repeated numerous ideas expressed
in previous published writings; and (e) this article, lacking any
meaningful relationship to materials published after 1828, might have
been written then as easily as in 1831.

Closely related to 1831, these more specific factors buttress the above
conclusion:

(1) The article is out of character in that Prescott had not published
on an Italian theme since 1825. In 1831 he not only was dedicated to
his historical project, but he had put Italian literature, as a theme for
research and writing, behind him. This was not true in 1828, how-

---

[10] Gardiner, ed., *Papers*, pp. 76–77.
[11] [WHP], "Poetry and Romance of the Italians," *North American Review,*
33 (July, 1831): 28–81.

ever, when, in fumbling fashion, he still was unsuccessfully striving to dedicate his full energies to history.

(2) Ill for eight weeks in the spring of 1831—and his historical study interrupted—he quite possibly was also behind schedule with the preparation of his annual contribution to the *North American Review.* Such a combination of circumstances might have inspired his turning to the file which contained the unused item of 1828.

(3) Whereas the literary memoranda usually carried, in reference to any Prescott article, a statement of the number of pages written, the number of days consumed—plus some lament or resolution—this item was referred to with cryptic brevity: "I prepared an article for the July Number of the North American."[12]

(4) In 1831 A. H. Everett was the editor of the *North American Review*, having succeeded Sparks in 1830. The change of editor is significant in that whereas Prescott, prior to 1830, could not, in his humiliation, have submitted the article to his favorite American review because Sparks knew its British past, no such restraint operated upon him in view of Everett's ignorance of the prior history of the item.

To the circumstantial evidence which reduces the articles of 1828 and 1831 to a single manuscript might be added the intangible that was Prescott's pride. Long accustomed to having his every offering published, he might have been goaded into seeing that the manuscript eventually won publication.

5

"Journey to Niagara," a terse fragment in the memoranda, would be meaningless were it not for Prescott the letter writer.[13] Early in June 1831 William, recovering from illness, set out in search of better health. For five and one-half weeks, as one of a miscellaneous but congenial party of approximately ten Bostonians, he toured the Hudson and Mohawk valleys, marveled at Niagara Falls, sailed lakes Ontario,

---

[12] Gardiner, ed., *Literary Memoranda,* 1: 149.

[13] *Ibid.* During the trip Prescott addressed nine letters to Susan and one to his mother.

Champlain, and George as well as the St. Lawrence River, and visited Montreal and Quebec. William was the only Prescott in the party.

West of Albany, all of which was new to William, the party traveled between thirty and forty miles daily, rising at 4 A.M. and stopping about 4 or 5 P.M. As they drove to Schenectady, Amsterdam, Palatine, and beyond, the wheat fields and clover inspired the remark, "The land is every where dripping with fatness." The rich landscape and silvery Mohawk pricked William's romantic nature, but he curbed the urge to reduce the scenery to words. "My health continues mending," he reported. "My eyes, marvellous to tell, are about the strongest in the party. My spectacles I have never put on . . ." About the time the party reached Utica, William, who in a moment of daring had set out without a servant, was beginning to consider himself "adept at packing, not taking more than twice as much [space] as any body else."[14]

Trenton Falls was the first of several highlights the trip afforded William. "The falls are incomparably finer than any I have seen in Europe," he wrote.[15] Frequently rising and breakfasting two hours before the others, William was the picture of health, gaining weight—in spite of wind, rain, sun, and much else that discomfited him. Two and one-half weeks from home he reported, "what pleases me most is that my spectacles, of which I have brought two pairs, are on every body's nose but my own."[16]

While the party was sailing down the St. Lawrence, passing this way and that among the Thousand Islands, Prescott's romantic vein finally burst forth, as he wrote, ". . . the long bateaus of the Canadians moving over the water in the moonlight evening with their broad sails catching the feeble breeze, and the fires lighted in their sterns—have the air of spectre-ships gliding over the deep." The influence of more than one novelist sailed the St. Lawrence with him. But no such romantic chord was struck when, sighting Prescott, Ontario, he complained, "The town does no credit to the name."[17] To the vacationing

[14] WHP to S. A. Prescott, June 11, 1831, Prescott papers.
[15] *Id.* to *id.,* June 15, 1831, Prescott papers.
[16] WHP to C. G. Prescott, June 21, 1831, Prescott papers.
[17] WHP to S. A. Prescott, June 29, 1831, Prescott papers.

historian Montreal was just a second-rate French city, but Quebec was a "lion." Of the latter place he could say, "The *coup d-oeil* is on the whole finer in its way than anything I recollect perhaps except the bay of Naples." The fortifications and the Plains of Abraham sparked his romantic nature. As he departed the land, he observed, "I am very glad that I have penetrated into Canada—it has opened to me a new world—both of man and nature . . . But I am weary of this vagabond life—and long to become once more a fixture in Bedford—or rather Nahant, where you are all now I suppose."[18] On one occasion Prescott's cabinmate, brother-in-law William Amory, added a revealing picture of Susan's husband to one of the letters addressed to her:

quite sentimental and homesick, talks of nothing but his wife and Betty and knows as little how to take care of himself as his son the Colonel. He changes his pantaloons and coat every time the wind changes and wears from five to ten pair of drawers according to the thermometer. He finds his trunk enormous and unwieldy, can find nothing but what is on top and grooms every time he opens it.[19]

6

Returned in excellent health, William resolved, "I now propose to resume my labors systematically and industriously and to pursue them unbroken, without the intervention of so much as a review for a year to come." One chapter he remembered writing at the rural retreat "at the rate of about 10½ pages noctograph per day." Giving credit of a kind that the place frequently received in the future, he said, "The air of Pepperell, as usual, proves favorable for study."[20]

Re-established in Boston, he closed out the year by listing his published writings and sending yet another item off to an editor, the first of three pieces for his brother Ned's publication, *The New-England Galaxy*. In the thirteen months immediately prior to mid-January 1833, three articles by Prescott appeared in that Boston publication. None contributed to his becoming an historian. Two of the items,

---

[18] Gardiner, ed., *Papers,* pp. 77–78.
[19] *Ibid.*, p. 79.
[20] Gardiner, ed., *Literary Memoranda,* 1: 149, 151.

however, offer valuable insights into his mind and all illustrate his cooperative nature.

Twenty-eight-year-old Edward Goldsborough Prescott, the shadowy member of the family who was still trying to find his life's work, had become, early in November 1831, proprietor and editor of the *Galaxy*, a four-page weekly. Ned was less interested in and less prepared for the literary life than was his elder brother, making his acquisition of the paper primarily a financial investment. Simultaneously, Edward was pursuing his career as lawyer.[21]

Looked to, for many reasons, for an occasional contribution to the *Galaxy*, William never failed his brother. In view of the nature of his first contribution, one can almost hear Ned saying, about Christmas Day, 1831, "Will, I'm about a column and a half short for Saturday's paper—will you help me?" "Edinburgh Review," the piece published in the issue of December 31, 1831, simply summarized the contents of the September 1831, number of that quarterly.[22] The hack nature of the item was relieved only in two senses: it permitted a demonstration of his knowledge of the inner working of British criticism in the leading quarterlies and it induced an appraisal of several eminent figures in British literature.

The second and more thoughtful article for Ned found William, inspired by the publication of the seventy-fifth number of the *North American Review*, crisply summarizing the seventeen-year history of that publication.[23] Of the "Old North" in its opening years, he said:

The work in its infancy aspired to nothing more than the rank of a literary magazine, made up of essays, poetical effusions, criticism sparsely, and ample selections of foreign matter. The Journal . . . had the appearance of being made up too much with the scissors, with no great depth of learning,

---

[21] Joseph T. Buckingham, *Personal Memoirs and Recollections of Editorial Life*, 2 vols. (Boston, 1852), 1: 105–121 *passim*, 256; Frank Luther Mott, *A History of American Magazines, 1741–1850* (New York, 1930), p. 127 n. 33; and *The New-England Galaxy*, December 31, 1831, and April 28, 1832.

[22] [WHP], "Edinburgh Review," *The New-England Galaxy*, December 31, 1831, p. [2].

[23] [WHP], "North American Review," *The New-England Galaxy*, April 7, 1832, p. [3]. The quotations immediately following are in *ibid*.

and little of the authority and vigorous tone of a half assured and original
work.

Of the publication under E. T. Channing's brief editorship, he said,

Its miscellaneous department was gradually abridged, and its critical notices
expanded and more carefully elaborated. The writers, however, were comparatively unpractised, and criticism was mostly confined to popular works
in our own language. The work [William declared, beginning his assessment of the achievements of editor Edward Everett] now assumed the tone
as well as external form of a regular quarterly review. Miscellaneous effusions were discarded. The circle of criticism was greatly widened, embracing
foreign literature, and the most recondite subjects in our own. The productions of learned continental writers were examined before they had
passed the ordeal of the English press, and the journal gradually acquired a
weight of authority in criticism, paramount to every other in our own
country . . . .

In all this, the editorial influence was strongly perceptible, but much is
to be imputed to the improved state of scholarship in our community, and
the increased familiarity with composition which this very Journal had opened to young writers. A distinguished feature of the work under its new
editor, was its tone of nationality, of American feeling.

During this period Prescott initially had contributed to the *North
American Review.*

The new editor [Jared Sparks] was supported in the conduct of the Journal
by a better drilled and more scientific corps, than had been organised under
any of its predecessors. Contributions of elaborate length and preparation,
not hastily concocted for the nonce, but the comprehensive results of habit-
ual and patient application in various departments of letters and science,
were supplied by our ripest scholars. . . . The spirit of charity overflowed a
little too freely in the estimate of our native productions, whose authors instead of laurel, might often have been more properly visited with birch.
This bonhommie of criticism, gave rather a tameness to the Journal.

Of the labors of Alexander Hill Everett, in whose hands the editorship had not rested long as yet, Prescott could but speculate.

In the aggregate, he concluded that the most salutary influence of
the review lay in its contribution to the emergence of an American

school of classical writers "who might here try the strength of their wings before venturing on a bolder flight." William was himself guilty of generous estimates of native literary products; and he was one of those writers whose pen had been strengthened by the experience gained on the pages of the *North American Review*. For one so intimately related to the "Old North" and its editors, he appraised the opening years of the leading American literary review quite fairly.

As his first contribution appeared shortly after Ned become its editor, so his final contribution appeared shortly before his brother severed his ties with the *Galaxy*. Unlike either of the earlier pieces—and untitled in its published form—the essay might be termed, as it is in Prescott's literary memoranda, "On Identity and Diversity of Language."[24]

Inspired by a recent oration, in which the speaker had insisted that a common world language would accelerate greatly the circulation of knowledge and refinement, William presented a case for diversity, rather than identity, of language.[25] First he attacked the idea that ancient learning had been buried for centuries by the corruption and variety of language. Diversity of language, he asserted, "may on the whole prove favorable to the cause of literature and morality; since the translator, naturally rejecting those crude and impotent productions which have had no success in their own country, will employ himself upon such only as will justify the translation." Salient features of Italian, French, and English literatures, he insisted, derived from national characteristics, making it impossible for a common tongue to exhibit the characteristic genius of individual nations.

While stating his case for diversity, William demolished that of identity by asserting that, even if attainable, it could not be retained. Citing the increasing numbers of Americanisms in the English language, he recognized the influence of nationalism upon language. Satisfied that his arguments had carried the day, Prescott signed this article "Q. E. D." Brother Ned also thought highly of this contribution and made it the subject of a commendatory editorial in the same issue of the

[24] Gardiner, ed., *Literary Memoranda,* 1: 151.
[25] [WHP], "For the New-England Galaxy," *The New-England Galaxy,* January 12, 1833, p. [2]. The quotations immediately following are in *ibid.*

paper. This anonymous brother act was a suitable finale for Ned's and William's identification with the *Galaxy*.

### 7

In the early 1830's, as he found himself writing for his brother's paper and for A. H. Everett's *North American Review* and serving the expanding interests of the asylum for the blind—as well as pursuing the theme in Spanish history which presumably called for all his intellectual powers—Prescott entered into yet another relationship—with Boston's leading proprietary library, the Athenaeum.

Designated a trustee, he initiated, in 1832, a long period of official identification with the Athenaeum.[26] At home in the company of all eight of his fellow trustees, he knew a special sense of camaraderie with Ticknor and Franklin Dexter. Earlier, in 1827, the year that Judge Prescott had transferred proprietary certificate No. 76 to William, the Boston Athenaeum had held its first great art exhibition. The portrait of Judge Prescott, quite possibly the last such work by Gilbert Stuart— and one of eight portraits by Stuart on exhibition—was proudly loaned by its owner, William H. Prescott, for the exhibition of 1828.[27] Some time would elapse before William H. Prescott, at his father's behest, would be consigned to canvas.

Meanwhile, the Boston Athenaeum, having drawn the Prescotts to its art program, was engaging in an activity of potential importance to the historian. The days were yet to come when he gave serious attention to the quality of the illustrations gracing his histories, but one thing is clear: the love of portraits and the insistence upon fine works of art as well as historically accurate representations which led him to spend unusual sums of money for the illustrations that enriched his books derived, in part, from his identification with the Boston Athenaeum.

### 8

In the spring of 1832 the second, third, and fourth volumes of *English Literature of the Nineteenth Century—American Library of Use-*

[26] Quincy, *Boston Athenaeum*, pp. 86–134 notes, *passim*.
[27] Mabel Munson Swan, *The Athenaeum Gallery 1827–1873* (Boston, 1940), pp. 18–41 *passim*.

*ful Knowledge* inspired yet another annual contribution to the *North American Review.*[28] William's focus on "some of the characteristic features of elegant literature" embraced writers who had contributed notably to various literary forms. Among poets, he considered Scott, Wordsworth, and Byron the best. The novel, which should "be taken as the significant feature of the literature of the age," induced discussion of the works of Maria Edgeworth and Sir Walter Scott. To Prescott, "Scott's greatest glory . . . arises from the superior dignity to which he has raised the novel, not by its historic, but its moral character, so that . . . it is now made to furnish a pure and delectable repast for all the members of the assembled family."

Trying, as always, to profit from his own experience as well as that of others, the reviewer read his article again when it appeared in the *North American Review,*[29] but apparently William was so pleased with his writing that his inclusion of irrelevant materials and his bewildering organization did not attract his attention. The time had come for Prescott to break the rhythm of his annual stint for his favorite quarterly, to forsake the literary gymnasium of the review.

Nahant again proved favorable to work and, in addition to completing several more chapters, William worked out the system he planned to use when ready to subject his writing to a final review prior to publication. Meanwhile, he planned to allow sizable intervals of time —a year or more—to elapse before reviewing his work. By rapid reading of large sections of the work, he hoped to judge the general effect upon the reader, acquainting himself with the fatiguing parts which needed rewriting or abridgment. Forced to choices between verbal perfection and general effect, he would elect the latter.

In early October, writing at the rate of three and one-half noctographs per day, he completed his twenty-first chapter and, assessing his method, concluded, "Twenty noctographs I can read for and write without division."[30] Marring the tempo at which the history was

---

[28] [WHP], "English Literature of the Nineteenth Century," *North American Review,* 35 (July, 1832): 165–195. The quotations immediately following are in *ibid.*

[29] Gardiner, ed., *Literary Memoranda,* 1: 153.

[30] *Ibid.,* pp. 154–155. The quotations immediately following are in *ibid.,* pp. 155–161 *passim.*

emerging under encouraging breezes at Nahant and equally beneficial
shade at Pepperell was the fact that he never had all his materials at
either place. This meant that while away from Bedford Street his writing often was pockmarked by gaps that required attention upon his
return to the city. By the Christmas season of 1832, he had accomplished Part I of his two-part history. Reaching a point from which he
desired to survey his future operation, he interrupted his routine and
once more raked his writing over coals of self-criticism.

The only rule [he insisted] is to write with freedom and nature, with di-
rectness and simplicity, even homeliness of expression occasionally, with
alternation of long and short sentences, for such variety is essential to harmony. But after all, it is not the construction of the sentence, but the tone
of the *coloring* which produces the effect. . . . A book may be made up of
perfect sentences, and yet the general impression be very imperfect.

To guide his future work and to promote concise writing, Prescott
developed a detailed synopsis. Within his chronological-topical approach, he established the page limits for the themes and jotted down
some of the references which they called to mind. While outlining the
remainder of his first book, William began to look toward a second
major project. "This is probably the only civil history I shall ever
attempt," he concluded, adding, ". . . literary history is more consonant
with my taste, my turn of mind, and all my previous studies. The sooner
I complete the present work, the sooner I shall be enabled to enter on
it, so *festina*." Some of this outlook stemmed from earlier inclination
and some from the pleasure lately experienced while composing the
two chapters on Castilian literature which closed the first part of his
history.

Failure to conclude the history by January 1, 1833, the deadline established in 1830, prompted increased self-discipline. To motivate
himself, he planned to note more regularly in his memoranda the dates
when he began and completed chapters and related notes. The best
rules and most exciting themes, however, could not wed Prescott to
the history for long. The first of three interruptions in the spring of
1833 concerned the asylum for the blind.

With a condition attached which demanded widespread support,

Colonel Thomas H. Perkins had signified his willingness to deed his Pearl Street house to the institution for the blind. Boston and environs turned to raising funds, staging fairs which were supported by leaders of society.

The last ten days [William wrote Jared Sparks on May 8] I have been spinning round like a teetotum in consequence of a donation, which Colonel Perkins took it into his head to present to the Blind, of whom I am an unworthy guardian (*unoculus inter caecos*) on conditions which have given us work eno' I assure to comply with. These were to raise 50,000 dollars, and such is the public spirit of the good town, that, in little more than a week, we have raised within five or six thousand of the whole amount.[31]

On occasion trustee Prescott's continuing association with the institution destined to become the Perkins School for the Blind called for attention to legal details. "I informed Mr. Perkins of the form of the vote sent to you," he wrote S. G. Howe later that year," and requested his order for the amount, as I thought on the whole that would be the most regular way of doing the business. I enclose you his answer . . . . With regard to the tax on the Mansion House, it seems it is not paid."[32] William's levelheadedness in regard to business affairs also touched his history as he determined to convert the finished half of his manuscript to printed page.

"Taking Hallam volume I . . . as model of size, number of pages &c.," printer Dickinson agreed to run off four copies at a cost of twenty cents per page for text and twenty-one cents per page for notes.[33] For Part First of the history, amounting to 831 printed pages, William paid Dickinson $187.84. Before completing this four-copy printing, Prescott found it as pointless as it was expensive. The business details related to converting a manuscript to book, he learned rapidly.

In a season of expenses, William also was intent upon making

[31] Gardiner, ed., *Papers*, p. 90; Schwartz, *Samuel Gridley Howe*, pp. 53–54. Thomas G. Cary's *Memoir of Thomas Handasyd Perkins* (Boston, 1856) says little of this philanthropy.

[32] WHP to S. G. Howe, December 9, [1833], Letters, 1828–1835, Perkins School for the Blind.

[33] Gardiner, ed., *Literary Memoranda*, 1: 163. The work referred to is Henry Hallam's *View of the State of Europe during the Middle Ages*, 2nd ed. (London, 1819).

money. He and his father were interested in buying stock in one of the new western banks, in Louisville or Cincinnati. Knowing nothing of the region, he turned to Bancroft for his estimate of those new operations. In addition, William once again nudged the historian in George:

One thing more for which you will be damned, I beg you to understand, (at least in this world,) that is, if you do not render ample justice to the memory of my grandfather—who scarcely got bread during his lifetime, and it seems, is not likely to get a stone after his death—and who has had half his honors filched from him, by gulls of historians whose eyes have been fascinated by the apparition of General Warren, because he had the good luck of being shot on the battlefield. Excuse this little burst of patriotism.[34]

Another interruption to historical labors came when Sparks made a request he could not decline.

## 9

"I must now make a hiatus," he wrote, "while engaged on the biography of Brown, for Sparks' miscellany—probably two months."[35] In so doing, at the conclusion of Part II, chapter 3 of his history, William closed out an old routine, the writing of an annual article for the *North American Review,* and ventured into an untried field, American literature.

Editor of other multivolume projects, the energetic Jared Sparks possibly surprised none of his intimates when, early in 1833, he sought contributors to a projected series on American biography. For several reasons, however, William hesitated when asked to write a short biography of novelist Charles Brockden Brown. In the first place, his mind was fixed on Spain; and, furthermore, the biography meant hard work "for the dog days, when the height of a man's ambition is to draw a long breath in quiet."[36]

"I don't like to say nay to any request of yours," he told Jared as he

[34] Gardiner, ed., *Literary Memoranda,* 1: 214; and Gardiner, ed., *Papers,* pp. 88–89.
[35] Gardiner, ed., *Literary Memoranda,* 1: 162.
[36] Gardiner, ed., *Papers,* p. 90.

accepted the invitation and promised the fifty pages which he delivered in mid-summer. "I am very sorry to send you such sorry trash," he wrote Sparks. "But it was not written *con amore* . . . I have praised him twice as much as I think he deserves." Appalled at the dullness of his writing, he sought Sparks's candid opinion of it, adding, "Don't print it, or at least put my name to it, if it will discredit me."[37] Prescott's kind undertaking of a project so uncongenial to him was matched by Sparks's generosity. He accepted the work as submitted, paid Prescott $44.80 (64 pages @ $.70), and placed the contribution well forward in the first volume of the series.

Severe in his assertion that he had written trash, Prescott nonetheless rightly belittled his study of Charles Brockden Brown. Unlike his rich awareness of the English novel, his background in American literature was thin. The rapidity with which he produced the brief biography suggested that he had accomplished little reading of Brown during that interval. One is led to suspect that Prescott's evaluation of the novelist derived more from current writings, especially the selection- and letter-laden biography by Dunlap, than from direct study of Brown's works.[38] If this be true, and more than a little internal evidence in his writing points in this direction, Prescott's treatment of Brown was doubly secondhand, both as critic and as biographer. Instead of writing biography, he essentially reviewed William Dunlap's biography and other critiques of Brown.

Today Brown is hailed as "Gothic Novelist" and "Pioneer Voice of America" in numerous studies, and the sources and influences of his novels are studied in detail. Historical surveys of the American novel commonly begin with his works.[39] In Brown, Sparks had a fine sub-

[37] *Ibid.*, pp. 91–92.

[38] Adams, *Jared Sparks*, 2: 196; William Dunlap, *The Life of Charles Brockden Brown*, 2 vols. (Philadelphia, 1815); William H. Prescott, "Life of Charles Brockden Brown," in Jared Sparks, ed., *The Library of American Biography*, 25 vols. (New York, 1834–1848), 1: 117–180.

[39] Harry R. Warfel, *Charles Brockden Brown—American Gothic Novelist* (Gainesville, Fla., 1949); David Lee Clark, *Charles Brockden Brown—Pioneer Voice of America* (Durham, 1952); Lulu Rumsey Wiley, *The Sources and Influence of the Novels of Charles Brockden Brown* (New York, 1950); and Edward Wagenknecht, *Cavalcade of the American Novel* (New York, 1952).

ject for his series, but in Prescott he did not find the needed biographer. William was right when he told Jared, "The truth is, Brown should be worked up by some one that *feels* him."[40] Brown was a romantic verging toward realism, Prescott a die-hard romantic. Brown was revolutionary on many fronts, Prescott conservative on most.

This labor that drew William to Charles Brockden Brown came in the season during which he normally would have written yet another annual piece for the *North American*. So even as he, in the longer perspective of his own historical purposes and literary fame, should have eschewed the biography, it represented the ill wind that broke the rhythm of periodical writing which had interrupted and hindered his historical labors too long.

10

"Engage in nothing else," he observed as he concluded the biography, "not even a periodical stint till my History is finished."[41] At first glance only so many words, this effort at self-discipline was of sterner stuff than most of his rules. On one important theme, however, a shortage of sources made writing impossible until he could say, "I have received a copy of Marmol's History from Rich." He referred to Massachusetts-born Obadiah Rich who had based in London the bookselling business which generally found him on the prowl on the Continent. For years he had served Prescott's interests, along with those of other Americans and American institutions. Of Rich he asked anything that popped into his head. Couching his requests in statements such as "I shall be much disappointed if you cannot get them for me," William guaranteed the bookseller's maximum effort on his behalf. In due course Prescott did write, "The arrival of . . . Marmol's Moriscos came as quick upon the trigger as if I owned Aladdin's lamp. You are certainly a prince of Genii in the Bibliopolical way."[42] His need of helpers to secure materials for him later involved many per-

[40] Gardiner, ed., *Papers,* p. 91.

[41] Gardiner, ed., *Literary Memoranda,* 1: 164. Unless otherwise identified, the quotations in this section are in *ibid.,* pp. 165–172 *passim.*

[42] Wolcott, ed., *Correspondence,* pp. 1, 3; and Adrian W. Knepper, "Obadiah Rich: Bibliopole," *The Papers of the Bibliographical Society of America,* 49 (Second Quarter, 1955): 112–130.

sons, but William could not have had a better initial aide than Obadiah Rich.

In the Christmas season of 1833 Jared Sparks faced financial embarrassment, the first of a series of troubles to engulf him in quick succession. In his distress he turned to William. Sparks surely was surprised when his friend wrote, "I have neither credit nor cash in hand, the former being used up to get a note for five thousand dollars renewed which falls due on the first of January, and the last being required for manufacturing assessments for the 15th of January, to meet which I have put my last bank shares in the broker's hands."[43] Nevertheless he found a way to help his friend, and reported, "I have two thousand dollars in the Firemen's Insurance Company, and I will transfer five hundred dollars of it to you and you shall agree to replace the same six months or a year hence, as most convenient. This is the only disposable stock that I have." On Monday, January 13, the five hundred dollars was available to Sparks.[44]

Meanwhile, inspired by a rich theme and abundant sources, Prescott was working on his history in a manner that evoked self-congratulation, even exultation. "My eyes," he mused, "with the blessing of Heaven, in very good trim." The exceptional progress notwithstanding, he explored ways and means of bettering it, especially the preparatory reading and note-taking.

His new attack on the old problem embraced a six-point procedure: (1) notable passages would be marked and notes dictated from two leading authorities as they were read; (2) passages would be marked and notes dictated from the reading of incidental contemporary works; (3) passages would be marked and notes dictated from reflective passages of modern writers; (4) particular authors would be consulted for highly specialized material; (5) a mere glance would suffice for any other materials; and (6) additional reading of memoranda for the construction of notes would be eliminated by the marking, at the time of initial note-taking, of data intended for footnotes.[45] Because many

---

[43] Gardiner, ed., *Papers,* p. 96.

[44] *Ibid.*; and WHP to J. Sparks, January 9, 1834, Sparks papers.

[45] Gardiner, ed., *Literary Memoranda,* 1: 167, 169. The quotations that follow in this section are in *ibid.,* pp. 169, 171, 172.

of the earliest chapters would require abridgment, if not rewriting, Prescott gave thought to his final review of his manuscript. Also his desire to have the work published abroad suggested the desirability of having Rich as his literary agent in Britain. Nearer home a job for some good friends in Boston also came to mind. "Show it to half a dozen friends of various tastes whose opinion may be worth having, and who will have candor eno' to give it, and regard eno' for me to read the book conscientiously," he told himself.

When his thirty-eighth birthday came and went without the completion of a promised portion of his history, Prescott goaded himself with the thought, "Remember I have no time to lose, as my ground is likely to be poached on, in one way or another, by the best English writers." Neither groundless nor solidly factual, William's fear centered particularly on Southey.

In mid-June he experienced one of his old inflammations, "the first of the kind for nearly seven years." For a couple of weeks his aide led him "blindfold through a course of Latin, Spanish, French, Italian, and English authors." He learned anew how much depended upon the intelligence and ability of reader-secretary Henry Cheever Simonds. Fortunately he soon could say, "Since my last attack of old fashioned inflammation my eye has recovered unusual vigor . . ." For the first time in fifteen years, he had let twelve months pass without writing a piece for a periodical.

11

Happily the design for scholarship shaped in 1833–1834 remained the pattern for the following two years, the time required to complete the *magnum opus*. In the spring of 1835, as they had in 1834 and would in 1836, the Prescotts closed the house on Bedford Street and journeyed north the second week in May. Those years they also routinely departed from Pepperell during the third week of July, giving them eight or nine weeks in the country. Repeatedly Pepperell served Prescott's historical purposes in remarkable measure, evoking from him expressions of extreme satisfaction. At Pepperell in 1835, when his daily hours with Simonds were ten–twelve, one–two, five–seven, he mused, "The older I grow, the more I feel the country is suited to my tastes and habits." A year later the return to Pepperell inspired him to say, "The country in its delicious green, the leaves out on every tree, and the air loaded with perfumes from a wilderness of blossoms. How poetical it makes one, to get out of the prison of brick and mortar."

The Highlands, as the historian called the ancestral place at Pepperell, was forty miles from Boston, several times more distant from that city than was Fitful Head. Whereas any casual acquaintance, even stranger, at the Nahant Hotel, could set foot on the Prescott piazza at Fitful Head in a matter of minutes, only invited guests made the long trek to Pepperell. The growing family, as well as William's need of quiet work space, had dictated alterations on the original homestead of Colonel Prescott. To the modest two-story frame structure close upon the north side of the tree-shaded road which wound off toward the town of Pepperell, the Judge already had made some additions. They extended northward from the rear, toward higher ground. In time the T-shaped structure could stow away as many Prescotts, Dexters, Amorys, and Ticknors as might descend upon it.

One room in the rear wing, with windows unlike those in the remainder of the house, was designed for the historian. It commanded a view eastward, across the garden of fruits and vegetables, to a large pond and a clump of lordly oaks. Farther off was the woodland of elms and butternuts. Close to the study was the door through which he passed for outdoor meditation.

Prescott's favorite area for the quiet ordering of his thoughts—that ordering which helped his readings and notes fall into place for easier and more natural composition—lay behind the rambling white house. There, on higher ground, he walked with a regularity that produced paths. At times he sat on the piazza which enveloped a portion of the house at the southwest corner.

Out front, to the south, the land rolled gently down toward neighborhood streams. The Prescotts kept a small boat upon the Nissitisset, a clear little ribbon of water made all the more attractive by the willow and alder shading its banks and its moody exchanges of quiet pools for rippling shallows. Sometimes the long walks that they both enjoyed brought the historian and his father to the Nissitisset; sometimes the historian alone, on a morning canter, headed his horse in that direction.

At times, when neither striding the path near the pond nor following the meandering Nissitisset, William enjoyed a special, distant treat. Looking to the northwest, he could see the three-thousand-foot-plus peak of Monadnock in neighboring New Hampshire. Prescott often scanned Monadnock's outline to rest his eyes from things near at hand; sometimes he did so because he was writing of mountains in Spain and sought inspiration from one at hand.

The Highlands always had meaning for William, at first as the homestead of his Revolutionary hero grandfather, then as the object of the annual pilgrimages by Judge Prescott and his family. In his own rambles there over the 250 acres, he had fashioned delightful memories; but it was during those years of his maturity, when he sought calm settings for intellectual endeavor, that Pepperell took on the special meaning that never could fade. In town and city he had moved from house to house—and in time the seashore residence also would change—but Pepperell was a constant. Already in the mid-1830's, it was approached with anticipation, experienced with deep satisfaction, and left with regret tinged with pride of accomplishment.[46]

Like Pepperell, the annual stay at Nahant also assumed a fixed pattern in this period. The mid-July return to Bedford Street from Pepperell meant less than a week in the city before the exodus for Fitful Head. Arriving at Nahant during the third week of July, the Prescotts stayed two months, mid-September signaling departure. Despite the nearness of Nahant to Boston and the holiday air which prevailed at the summer resort, William found it congenial to his intellectual pursuits. However, the house overlooking the sea was much smaller than that in the country, and when guests descended upon Fitful Head, he was hard pressed to find proper conditions for his work. Despite the

[46] *Ibid.*, pp. 178, 180, 189, 194. Also see Hillard, "Prescott," in *Little Journeys,* pp. 104–105, 113–120; WHP to G. P. Putnam, May 12, 1852, in George Haven Putnam, *George Palmer Putnam—A Memoir* (New York, 1912), pp. 392–394. Prescott would have enjoyed these lines from Edwin Arlington Robinson's "Monadnock Through the Trees" (c. 1921):

You loomed above ancestral evergreens
Before there were the first of us around.

interruptions and the noises, Prescott routinely advanced his historical work further in two months at Nahant than in any equivalent period in town. "The tonic influence of the atmosphere here," he wrote of Fitful Head, "produces a sensible effect on my whole frame, and enables me to work more unremittingly than any other place."[47] Once, analyzing his work record in Boston, he confessed, "On looking over my card case find I dined out last winter between 50 and 60 times besides suppers &c."

The necessity of replacing reader-secretary Simonds in September 1835 occasioned an assessment of that aide's four-year service. The years 1831–1835 marked the most productive period the historian had yet known. Simonds not only had brought unusual linguistic capabilities to his job, he also had a sense of historical organization which resulted in helpful suggestions. Much of his progress, William readily admitted, stemmed from Simond's "industry, knowledge, and cheerful interests in my labors."

The new aide, Elijah Dwight Williams, would serve during the next five years. Like the physical transitions from residence to residence, the shifting of reader-secretaries hazarded William's physical well-being in addition to delaying his research. In those early weeks when a new man was learning his duties, Prescott tended to expend too much of his own eyesight on small print, notes, manuscripts, and the like. In this manner a brief laming of the eyes occurred in the autumn of 1835.[48]

Well-meaning friends posed other obstacles. To Sparks, who wanted another biography for his series, he indicated that once his history was behind him, "I will be at your service for any life you are disposed to lay at my door."[49] To John Gorham Palfrey, about to succeed A. H. Everett as editor of the *North American Review*, went a similar reply when William was asked to write an article.[50]

[47] Gardiner, ed., *Literary Memoranda*, 1: 194. The quotations which immediately follow are in *ibid.*, pp. 184, 195.

[48] *Ibid.*, p. 184; and WHP to C. Folsom, March 10, [1835], Folsom papers, Massachusetts Historical Society.

[49] WHP to J. Sparks, December 7, 1835, Sparks papers.

[50] Gardiner, ed., *Literary Memoranda*, 1: 186; and [James Truslow Adams], "John Gorham Palfrey," *Dictionary of American Biography*, 14: 169–170.

However much he controlled his intellectual life, it of course did not divorce him from those activities which stamped him a citizen of Boston. His service to community continued to pivot on the Athenaeum and the Institution for the Blind, both of which he was serving as trustee. For the latter institution, William ably advised Samuel Gridley Howe on minor matters which promoted good public relations.[51]

Time and experience led him to consider additional improvements in his writing. Listing expletives, periphrasis, and euphonious epithets among his literary sins, he concluded, "Cultivate a shorter, more antithetical form of expression—and remember a prominent idea or hint is worth an acre of detail, for the effect."[52] On occasion, as when he belatedly encountered the works of Bartolomé de las Casas, he reworked earlier chapters. Fighting the unending battle to stay within established page limits, he decided that "the story loses so much of its interest from the queen's death, although many of the transactions are of moment, that it would be impolitic to protract the work."[53]

Health and vision account for much of Prescott's timetable of achievement. For short intervals he was troubled by the digestive organs which apparently had never wholly regained the tone which they had known before being subjected to a continuing procession of pills and liquid medicines in the 1810's. Loss of appetite, nausea, heartburn, an unhappy sense of fullness, and the presence of gas generally warned him to adhere to certain precautions. One aid was the licorice tablet which relieved his constipation. He often plucked several from his pocket and shared them with youthful visitors. Aside from brief moments of dyspeptic discomfort, his general health in this period was excellent. Throughout the extremely productive last two years of labor on the history, the right eye stood him in good stead—often up to as many as three hours daily.[54] His memoranda teemed with words of the

[51] Quincy, *Boston Athenaeum*, p. 138; Swan, *Athenaeum Gallery*, pp. 144–147; Samuel Gridley Howe, Letterbook for 1833–1834–1835–1836, p. 80, Perkins School for the Blind; WHP to S. G. Howe, October 24, 1835, Letters, 1828–1835, Perkins School for the Blind; and S. G. Howe to WHP, February 12, 1836, Letterbook for 1836–1837, no. 22, Perkins School for the Blind.

[52] Gardiner, ed., *Literary Memoranda*, 1: 184.

[53] *Ibid.*, pp. 177, 187, 189.

[54] *Ibid.*, pp. 178, 180, 182, 184, 188, 190; and Wolcott, *Jottings*, p. 78.

happy state of his vision: "my eyes have been in excellent trim [September 1834];" and "My eyes served me well [January 1835]." "Eyes continue in very good order [July 1835]." "My eyes have served me on an average three hours a day for my own wear and tear [January 1836]." In August 1836 he said, "My eyes have been uniformly in excellent condition, permitting a free use of them from four to five hours, indeed as much time as I desired every day."[55]

When, on June 26, 1836, there was no more to read and no more to write, he noted, "Finished yesterday the last Note of the last chapter of the Reign of Ferdinand and Isabella."[56]

[55] Gardiner, ed., *Literary Memoranda,* 1: 174, 175, 186, 187, 190, 194.
[56] *Ibid.,* p. 190.

VII

*Mr. Prescott's work is one of the most successful . . .*

JUST AS THE COMPLETED MANUSCRIPT was unlike the searching endeavor which had launched it a decade earlier, so, too, historian
Prescott had changed. Some of his maturity of 1836 belonged to any
normal forty-year-old. Some of it, however, reflected a variety of dis-
ciplines: the regularity of hours and the dietary care which maintained
the physical equilibrium so important to his powers of concentration,
his ignoring some of the demands of society, as well as the intellectual
shift from reviewer-essayist to historian. The great difference between
Prescott of 1826, searching for a subject, and Prescott of 1836, about
to search for a publisher, lay in the realm of self-discipline.

His own awareness of positive forces in his life foretold much of
his future. "On the whole," he confided to his memoranda in mid-
1835, "there is no happiness so great, as that of a permanent and lively
interest in some intellectual labor. I, at least, never could be tolerably
contented without this. . . . As this must be my principal material for
happiness, I should cultivate those habits and amusements most congenial with it . . ."

Despite the basically intellectual side of his nature, Prescott scarcely
needed to prod himself with the reminder, "do some good to society

by an interest in obviously useful or benevolent objects."[1] He intended to face the problems of life with a calm, moral, philosophical outlook reflective of his reliance on God. He expected to lay aside much of the levity of earlier and less purposeful years without diminishing his social nature. Three growing children, an expanding circle of friends, and the activities of three generations of Prescotts demanded it. Even as he recognized the primacy of his intellectual life, he sought no ivory-towered detachment. Having disciplined his intellectual endeavors and regulated his social life, he was the happy, complete man.

2

To convert his bulky manuscript into a book, William again turned to Dickinson, who agreed to complete the work begun in 1833 "in the same style as the previous portion, at the rate of twenty-five cents per page, text and notes. He revises the first proofs." For the complete printing, Prescott paid $456.10. At the moment he considered it "*valeat tantum,*" two years later "an expense *I shall never incur again.*"[2] For his money he received, in addition to an initial proof which Dickinson corrected, three clean copies of the complete work.

At least five reasons prompted the Dickinson printing of the *History of the Reign of Ferdinand and Isabella, the Catholic*:

(1) It enhanced the prospects of publication in England by facilitating publisher evaluation. (2) It aided the author's revision of his work and minimized the likelihood of eye strain. (3) It facilitated critical evaluation by Prescott's friends. (4) The desired simultaneous publication in Britain and America, impossible from one penned fair copy, would be served by the multiple printed copies. (5) The multiple copies represented a security factor that spelled peace of mind for the author.

No rampant optimism attended the author's estimate of the product of his decade of labor. He sensed that the work was not very profound; and he feared it would not be popular. He did believe, however, that his honest record of a significant historical theme previously

[1] Gardiner, ed., *Literary Memoranda,* 1: 180–181. For general background for the interval treated in this chapter, see *ibid.,* pp. 181–231, 257, and 2: 3–11.
[2] *Ibid.,* 1: 188, 190.

untreated in English constituted, until a better statement of it came along, a contribution to learning and literature, whether or not it brought fame or fortune to its author. "Come to the worst—and suppose the thing a dead failure, and the book born only to be damned," he wrote. "Still it will not be all in vain, since it has encouraged me in forming systematic habits of intellectual occupation."[3]

Expecting very little of his manuscript, he was downright reluctant to publish it, until pressured to do so. Discussing this matter with his father, as indeed he discussed everything of consequence, William got it straight from the Judge when the latter declared that "the man who writes a book which he is afraid to publish is a coward."[4]

Publication plans advanced rapidly as a result of discussions at an all-male dinner party at the Bedford Street residence late in February 1836. The small circle included Jared Sparks and Colonel Thomas Aspinwall, the latter briefly home on leave. Ten years Prescott's senior, Aspinwall, son of a well-known Brookline family, graduate of Harvard and trained for the law, was a veteran of the War of 1812, during which he had lost his left arm to an enemy musket shot during the assault on Fort Erie. In 1836 he had twenty years of experience behind him as United States consul at London, where he had served Washington Irving and other Americans as literary agent.[5] Two men whose opinions Prescott honored, Obadiah Rich and George Ticknor, had expressed high regard for Aspinwall. For help with the publication of his history in England, William initially had approached Rich who, loath to shift from bookseller to literary agent, had recommended Aspinwall. The Colonel obligingly agreed to shepherd William's work in London publishing circles. His role as Prescott's agent in Britain would span almost two decades.

In November William wrote, "The volumes . . . in the packet of November 1, being sent by Mr. Goodhue to the house of Barings,

[3] *Ibid.,* p. 193. No copy of the Dickinson printing can be located.

[4] Ticknor, *Prescott,* p. 102.

[5] WHP to J. Sparks, February 24, [1836], Sparks papers; Curtis, *Brookline,* pp. 102–103; Adams, *Jared Sparks,* 2: 66; Charles C. Smith, "Memoir of Col. Thomas Aspinwall, A.M.," Massachusetts Historical Society *Proceedings,* 2nd ser., 7 (1891–1892): 32–38; Carl L. Cannon, *American Book Collectors and Collecting from Colonial Times to the Present* (New York, 1941), p. 103.

Liverpool." Earlier a deluge of instructions had gone from author to agent. He desired his book in well-illustrated octavo with double-column notes, preferably from the press of Murray. Informing Aspinwall that he had "taken no steps for its publication here, and shall take none till I have heard from you, since I would do nothing which can interfere with securing a copyright in England," he confessed his overwhelming desire for publication in Britain.[6] The Colonel dutifully put the history into the hands of one publisher after another. Weeks dragged into months, slow transatlantic communication feeding the author's gnawing anxiety.

At a 3 P.M. dinner on Tuesday, February 28, 1837, a small group that included Jared Sparks, William Amory, and Henry Wadsworth Longfellow discussed publication in America. Sparks, having read the work, had already written, "The book will be successful,—bought, read and praised." To make the most of Jared's knowledge of publishing, his host urged him to come early, adding, "I count on you for all the information relative to the mysteries of the trade."[7] Longfellow, a comparative newcomer to Boston, was the youngest man present, having celebrated his thirtieth birthday the day previous. The background of European travel and literary tastes that the amiable poet brought to the professorship resigned by Ticknor embraced Prescott's theme.[8]

Encouraged not only to publish his book in America but also to employ stereotype, William quickly leaned toward suggestions emanating chiefly from Sparks, one of whose publishing agreements he studied. Tapping George Bancroft's experience, he asked, "Will you have the goodness to let me know, in a few words, what your stereotyping costs you, and what agreement you have made with Bowen?"[9]

In the meantime, Aspinwall, having had refusals from both Murray and Longmans, had carried the manuscript to Richard Bentley in New Burlington Street. On March 20, 1837, Aspinwall and Bentley signed

---

[6] Wolcott, ed., *Correspondence,* pp. 4–6, 8–11 *passim.*

[7] Gardiner, ed., *Papers,* p. 107.

[8] [W. C. Bronson], "Henry Wadsworth Longfellow," *Dictionary of American Biography,* 11: 382–387.

[9] Gardiner, ed., *Papers,* pp. 108–109.

the contract by which the latter promised to publish at his expense an edition of unstated size.[10] Author and publisher would share net profits on a fifty–fifty basis, with English publication preceding that in America, the better to insure the English market to the English publisher in the absence of international copyright between the two countries.

While this agreement was en route to Boston, Prescott settled on the stereotyping process for the printing and the American Stationers' Company for the publishing. As a loyal Bostonian, he had known where his book would be published. Again aided by Sparks, he signed on April 10, 1837, the contract which promised 1,250 copies of his work from stereotype plates which he would furnish. Absorbing the cost of those plates, while the company met all other publishing expenses, he would receive one thousand dollars.

Stereotype plates enabled the historian to insinuate many of his preferences into the eventual book: fixed type size; few, if any, instances of broken type; uncrowded lines; generous leading between lines; and the style and location of the notes accompanying the text. The manufacture of the plates he entrusted to Folsom, Wells and Thurston of Cambridge. Renowned for printing many of America's finest books in that period, that house also manufactured stereotype plates for Prescott's later books.

The stereotyping also developed close ties between Charles Folsom and the author. Folsom marked the proofs at the press and forwarded them to the historian, who, after studying and revising them, returned them to Cambridge. Prescott's high regard for Folsom is evident in the request for criticism of his idea regarding the style of the biographical notices in the history: "I should not take any decision in this point," he wrote, "till I have had your counsel, who are my Magnus Apollo in these perilous concerns." Counting on Folsom to detect typographical errors, he wrote, "I rely on your lynx-eye-ed-ness."[11]

[10] The text of this contract is in Gardiner, *Prescott and Publishers*, p. 283; both the British and American agreements are discussed in *ibid.*, pp. 50, 52–53. One view of Prescott's English publisher is in Royal A. Gettmann, *A Victorian Publisher, A Study of the Bentley Papers* (Cambridge, Mass., 1960).

[11] Gardiner, ed., *Papers*, p. 110; and WHP to C. Folsom, [c. April, 1837], Folsom papers.

Matching his dependence upon others was Prescott's own generosity. Learning that a townsman, Thomas G. Bradford, desired to borrow a certain Latin book from his library, the historian wrote, "If you will take the trouble to mount up into my Attic, you will find him [Peter Martyr], snugly ensconced among some old Spaniards, on the lower shelf, middle compartment of the bookcase, western side of the room. That or any other book, which I have, is entirely at your service."[12] Like other borrowers, Bradford was expected to leave a note with one of the servants.

Negotiations with publisher and printer and the demands of proof reading did not claim all of William's attention in 1837. Reading Francis Sales's edition of Cervantes' *Don Quixote*, he wrote the review which Palfrey used as the lead article in his mid-summer issue.[13] His first item in five years for the "Old North," it also was his first piece for his friend Palfrey. Cervantes brought him into the Spanish arena in which he had long been working. In a sense his public appearance in mid-1837 on a Spanish theme was a preliminary to the emergence of his own book six months later. The review pleased Sales, an instructor at Harvard, who read it "with ineffable pleasure," adding, "I do not recollect to have perused in any language so lucid, elegant and instructive views of the Spanish character and literature within so narrow limits."[14] And that in turn pleased the reviewer.

In mid-1837 Prescott once more explored certain religious tenets,[15] this time in the season that saw his brother enter the clergy. Thirty-three-year-old Edward Goldsborough Prescott, taking the last step in his search for a satisfying career, had been admitted to the Order of Deacons of the Protestant Episcopal Church. An able speaker, with an oratorical flair that led to frequent demand for his services, Edward had orated in Pepperell and Boston. For the Bunker Hill celebration on June 17, 1835, he had stood amid patriotic emblems in the church at Pepperell to address the Prescott Guards. His brother, in attend-

[12] Gardiner, ed., *Papers,* p. 113.

[13] [WHP], "Sales's Don Quixote," *North American Review,* 45 (July, 1837): 1–34.

[14] F. Sales to WHP, July 7, 1837, Prescott papers.

[15] Gardiner, ed., *Literary Memoranda,* 1: 196–212.

ance, proudly declared, "the audience were brought into the Niobe vein by the patriotic reminiscences of the orator."[16] But through it all —business, the bar, editing, politicking, soldiering, and orating—there must have been an aching emptiness that even increasing activity and tempo could not fill. The day had come when, turning his back on everything and everyone, he left the family on Bedford Street, left the city which since the age of four had been home to him, and went to New Jersey to prepare himself for the clergy under the guidance of Bishop George Washington Doane.[17] Prescott, as he engaged in his spiritual inquiry of June and July 1837, must have done so, in part, thinking of Ned.

3

Miscellaneous activities of late 1837 illustrate the emergent literary generalissimo in Prescott. As he pressured Folsom for a perfect set of stereotype plates, he bombarded the "Cambridge Aldus" with reasons for their prompt execution, adding, "I can not conceive of one for twaddling along as if we had peas in our shoes, which we have been doing for the last fortnight."[18]

Letter after letter attested his concern about the total book: wanting good black ink, demanding the finest paper, approving the style of the title page, criticizing the leading of lines and the frequency of broken type, urging that errata lists be sent to his London publisher, pressing for a speedier conclusion of John Langdon Sibley's index, and desiring copies for eager reviewers.[19]

---

[16] Colonel Edward G. Prescott, *An Oration: delivered before the Officers of the Militia, and Members of the Volunteer Companies of Boston* . . . (Boston, 1832), p. 3; Edward G. Prescott, *An Oration: delivered before the Citizens of Boston* . . . (Boston, 1833), pp. 4, 20; Gardiner, ed., *Papers,* p. 102; Roberts, *Military Company of the Massachusetts,* 3: 91, 92–93, 102, 111, 116–117; George Washington Warren, *The History of the Bunker Hill Monument Association during the First Century of the United States of America* (Boston, 1877), p. 414.

[17] George Burgess, *List of Persons admitted to the Order of Deacons in the Protestant Episcopal Church* . . . (Boston, 1875), p. 22.

[18] Gardiner, ed., *Papers,* pp. 113–114.

[19] Gardiner, *Prescott and Publishers,* pp. 135–166 *passim*; and WHP to

A long-time reviewer, Prescott sensed the relation of reviews to the successful launching of a book and accordingly gave the matter close attention.[20] Knowing that his friend William H. Gardiner was to review his history for the *North American*, he pushed his printer in order to get more and more of the work into Will's hands. A related solicitude he directed to Bentley in London when he wrote, "My friend, Mr. Ticknor, now in France, will be in London in the winter, and will take eighteen or twenty copies to distribute among persons whose opinions would be desirable."[21] At home, Prescott's friends rose to the occasion, Gardiner, John Pickering, Sparks, and Bancroft promising to assist the literary launching. Pickering, a native of Salem, was another who had read and liked the manuscript. William's own contacts and those of most of his friends assured access to the Whig press, but the Democratic press well might have ignored the book if it had not been for the politically powerful Bancroft. To George he admitted, "For the great Jackson editor I must look to a word from you." Marshaling his friends as carefully for reviewing as he had his facts for his history, Prescott admitted, prior to publication, "If the book does not go well before the wind, it will not be from want of a favorable breath from my friends."[22]

For some, as Sparks and Bancroft, these assists were a reciprocating action. Indeed, that same hectic autumn Prescott wrote for his favorite local newspaper, Nathan Hale's *Boston Daily Advertiser*, a critique of the first volume of Sparks's *The Writings of George Washington*. When that review proved somewhat tedious, he counseled at length with Folsom, concluding, "Now is not this a mighty comboberation about a penny trumpet twaddle in the Newspaper! But . . . I had rather

---

C. Folsom, eleven letters between August 24 and December 20, 1837, Folsom papers, six of which are in Gardiner, ed., *Papers*, pp. 114–117, 119–122.

[20] Gardiner, *Prescott and Publishers*, pp. 167–201 *passim;* C. Harvey Gardiner, "William Hickling Prescott: Launching a Bark," *The Americas*, 15 (January, 1959): 221–234; C. Harvey Gardiner, ed., "Promoting a Book: Prescott to Bancroft, December 20, 1837," *The Papers of the Bibliographical Society of America*, 51 (Fourth Quarter, 1957): 335–339; and WHP to W. H. Gardiner, September 4, 1837, Gardiner papers.

[21] Gardiner, ed., *Papers*, pp. 117–118.

[22] WHP to G. Bancroft, December 16, 1837, Bancroft papers.

write a quire in MS. than print a word that should harm or displease a friend."[23]

The historian also reflected on his own career. In so doing, he entertained an idea which, as a big new project, might combine literature and biography. Why not, he mused, so treat the life and works of Molière as to produce "an agreeable book for the parlor table"?[24] Exploiting Ticknor's presence in Paris, he asked him to assemble a collection related to Molière. Faithful George did so, turning for advice to Jules Taschereau, whose writing on Molière William had reviewed ten years earlier. In the autumn of 1837 William's love of literature was ascendant once more, but that enthusiasm had lessened perceptibly even before the shipment of approximately fifty volumes concerning Molière reached Boston.

Although he seemed to be doing a bit of everything in those prepublication weeks, one thing credited to William H. Prescott he did not do. It was Judge William Prescott, not the historian, who spiritedly endorsed Channing's views in a letter full of opposition to the annexation of Texas and the extension of slavery in the United States.[25]

On Christmas Day the *History of the Reign of Ferdinand and Isabella, the Catholic* was published in three volumes by the American Stationers' Company. The exultant author wrote that very day to Sparks, Bancroft, and Folsom. With a presentation copy went a request that Sparks supply the publisher a list of editors between New York and Charleston to whom review copies should be sent. To the indispensable Charles Folsom, William declared, "The book may safely stand along side the best English productions of this class—in all that relates to the typography and paper and general effect."[26]

[23] Gardiner, ed., *Papers*, pp. 116, 118; and [WHP], "A Close Parallel," *Boston Daily Advertiser*, October 4, 1837, p. 2 (another previously unidentified published item by Prescott).

[24] Ticknor, *Prescott*, p. 161.

[25] W. Prescott to Dr. Channing, September 5, 1837, in Fulmer Mood and Granville Hicks, eds., "Letters to Dr. Channing on Slavery and the Annexation of Texas, 1837," *New England Quarterly*, 5 (July, 1932): 600–601, is mistakenly assigned to William H. Prescott; and Arthur W. Brown, *Always Young for Liberty* (Syracuse, 1956), p. 233.

[26] Gardiner, ed., *Papers*, pp. 122–124.

All the Prescotts rejoiced with the elated author, but for the Judge it was not only a moment of intense pride, it was one of honor, the *magnum opus* having been dedicated to him. To anyone ignorant of the father-son relationship, the words might have appeared maudlin but not so to those who knew.

> To the
> Honorable William Prescott, LL.D.,
> the guide of my youth,
> my best friend in riper years,
> These Volumes,
> with the warmest feelings of filial affection,
> are respectfully inscribed.

With the new year came the issue of the *North American Review* in which *Ferdinand and Isabella* made its bow to the public via Gardiner's long review. Eighty-nine pages long, it at once was facetiously dubbed "the fourth volume of the History."[27] In a long comparison of Irving and Prescott on Spanish subjects, the latter came off much the better. Prescott's organization of his themes as well as the literary execution of his work drew encomium and illustration. Hard put to find a few peccadilloes, Gardiner chided his friend for his excessive use of foreign-language terms. This most significant American appraisal of the book was speedily joined by equally anonymous and favorable assessments in newspapers and magazines. In Boston the author's friends deluged the editors with a carefully planned shower of reviews. Such draughts of friendly commendation might have intoxicated a less temperate author, but Prescott soberly assessed the situation.[28]

---

[27] Ticknor, *Prescott,* p. 115; and [William H. Gardiner], "History of the Reign of Ferdinand and Isabella, the Catholic," *North American Review,* 46 (January, 1838): 203–291. To lessen his friend's labor, Prescott had sent Gardiner a twenty-two-page letter, accompanied by an eight-page bibliography. The former opened, "I am to tell you what I have done—or rather tried to do." Toward the end of the letter he remarked, "There—I think your ears must have tingled long enough with this trumpet-blast about myself." See WHP to W. H. Gardiner, September 4, 1837, Gardiner papers.

[28] *Boston Daily Advertiser,* December 27, 1837; *Boston Weekly Messenger,* December 28, 1837; *Boston Courier,* January 4, 1838; [Francis William Pitt Greenwood], "History of the Reign of Ferdinand and Isabella, the Catholic,"

The same issue of the "Old North" which reviewed *Ferdinand and Isabella* carried Prescott's short review of the two-volume *Tales from the German*. The only item related to German literature ever penned by him, he executed this review for several reasons. The translator was a fellow townsman, and William never failed to lend a helping hand to local literary talent. Secondly, the review found him assisting his own publisher, for this work, too, bore the imprint of the American Stationers' Company.[29]

Unlike his short and uninspired review of *The German Tales*, Prescott's consideration of the studies of Sir Walter Scott by Lockhart and Robert P. Gillies evoked a lengthy piece which he wrote *con amore*.[30] Treating the nineteenth-century literary figure that he most admired, this was Prescott's most thoroughly sympathetic essay. In view of Scott's influences on Prescott—his sense of the dramatic, his use of color in language, his patterns of characterization, his addiction to the romantic, plus many others—one hopes for insights that are not revealed. The high place accorded Scott is evident in his assessment of "Waverley." "Its appearance," William insisted, "marks a more distinct epoch in English literature than that of the poetry of its author. All previous attempts in the same school of fiction,—a school of English growth,—had been cramped by the limited information or talent

---

*The Christian Examiner and General Review,* 24 (March, 1838): 99; and Gardiner, ed., *Literary Memoranda,* 1: 223.

[29] [WHP], "Tales from the German," *North American Review,* 46 (January 1838): 156–161. In addition, those who term indefensible the ascription of this article to Prescott (William Charvat and Michael Kraus, *William Hickling Prescott: Representative Selections, with Introduction, Bibliography, and Notes* [New York, 1943], p. lxxxviii n. 274) should consider the following: Prescott had numerous intimates, among them Sparks, Ticknor, Amory, and Bancroft, to assist him with the little German employed behind this brief review; indeed Bancroft had translated extended passages from that language for him on other occasions.

Among those with sizable financial stakes in the American Stationers' Company was W. H. Gardiner; see Notice of American Bank to W. H. Gardiner, March 28, 1838, Gardiner papers.

[30] [WHP], "Memoirs of Sir Walter Scott," *North American Review,* 46 (April, 1838): 431–474. This essay is honored, by being included and placed first, in Allen Thorndike Rice, ed., *Essays from the North American Review* (New York, 1879)), pp. 3–63.

of the writers." After citing the limitations of Tobias Smollett, Henry Fielding, Samuel Richardson, Ann Radcliffe, and Fanny Burney, Prescott remarked, "But a work now appeared, in which the author swept over the whole range of character with entire freedom, as well as fidelity, ennobling the whole by high historic associations, and in a style, varying with his theme, but whose pure and classic flow was tinctured with just so much of poetic coloring, as suited the purposes of romance. It was Shakespeare in prose."[31]

While Prescott focused on literature beyond the sea, critics in that quarter were directing attention to *Ferdinand and Isabella.* In the *Edinburgh Review* the scholarly Spanish exile Pascual de Gayangos closed his forty-page consideration of it with the judgment, "Mr. Prescott's work is one of the most successful historical productions of our time." Commending the historian for many things, and particularly for his impartiality, Gayangos tagged *Ferdinand and Isabella* "a most valuable addition to our historical literature." In the rival *Quarterly Review* the ultra-British Richard Ford balanced his jibes of cultural condescension with the admission, "Mr. Prescott's is by much the first historical work which British America has as yet produced, and one that need hardly fear a comparison with any that has issued from the European press since this century began."[32] Unlike the warm friends who reviewed his history at home, these reviewers were complete strangers to Prescott at this time. Later, however, Gayangos became Prescott's most indispensable aide; and Ford, through correspondence and personal contact, won a place in the growing international circle of his literary friends.

In Britain no other first book by a nineteenth-century American au-

---

[31] [WHP], "Memoirs of Sir Walter Scott," *North American Review*, 46 (April, 1938): 445–446. One appraisal of Scott's influence on Prescott and historical writing is in Harry Hayden Clark, ed., *Transitions in American Literary History* (Durham, 1953), pp. 132, 144, 158, 202 n., 203 n., 211.

[32] [Pascual de Gayangos], "The History of the Reign of Ferdinand and Isabella the Catholic of Spain," *Edinburgh Review*, 48 (January, 1839): 376–405; and [Richard Ford], "History of the Reign of Ferdinand and Isabella the Catholic of Spain," *Quarterly Review*, 44 (June, 1839): 1–58. See Rowland E. Prothero, ed., *The Letters of Richard Ford 1797–1858* (New York, 1905), p. 166, wherein Ford pronounced *Ferdinand and Isabella* "an admirable book . . . the *best* book ever written by a Yankee."

thor had received as much unstinted acclaim. Behind that early success
stood many things. First of all, credit was due Prescott because of the
inherent value of the product of his labors. Without George Ticknor,
however, that value might have been unnoticed in Britain. "Among
some other places I went to afterwards was John Murray's—the publisher's—where I fell in with Lockhart," Ticknor wrote in his journal
entry of March 29, 1838. "I wanted to talk with him about Prescott's
Ferdinand and Isabella; and by a sort of violence due to myself as well
as to him, I did so. . . . I gave him one, with little ceremony." Four
weeks later, in Edinburgh, George, reporting his visit with Macvey
Napier, the editor of the *Edinburgh Review*, wrote, "before I had
been with him half an hour it was fully agreed, that there should be an
Edinburgh Review of Ferdinand and Isabella."[33]

The significance of Prescott's essentially European theme helped to
ingratiate him with British and Continental readers. Had William's
first title been his *Conquest of Mexico*, instead of *Ferdinand and Isabella*, his initial British reception, like that later accorded Francis
Parkman's first book, might have bordered on disaster. Twelve years
would pass before Prescott visited Britain, years which added two extremely popular titles to his name, but there he always remained "the
historian of Ferdinand and Isabella."

On the Continent, meanwhile, Ticknor placed presentation copies
of Bentley's edition in influential hands, among them those of Charles
Fauriel, Count Adolphe de Circourt, François Guizot, Friedrich von
Raumer, Nicolaus Heinrich Julius, Henri Ternaux-Compans, and
Martín Fernández de Navarrete. Better-informed scholars of France,
Germany, and Spain it would be difficult to name, yet all might have
long remained ignorant of Prescott except for Ticknor's activity.
Among those who early helped Prescott to recognition in Continental
literary circles, none contributed more than Circourt. In a five-
instalment French-language appraisal of *Ferdinand and Isabella* published in Geneva the Count produced what, like Gardiner's review,
has been jokingly referred to as a fourth volume of the history.[34] In

---

[33] George Ticknor, Journal, 9 (March 19–July 15, 1838): 13–14, 77–78,
Ticknor collection.
[34] Gardiner, ed., *Papers*, p. 130; Adolphe de Circourt, "Histoire du règne

less than two years Britain and Western Europe, along with America, had hailed Prescott's first history as masterwork. What, we may ask, is today's verdict?

Scholarly myopia attends most judgments of Prescott's histories. The specialists in the era of Ferdinand and Isabella, like those in Mexican history, in Peruvian history, and in the era of Philip II, have their choices preordained for them. For one who, instead of being a student of a segment of Prescott's subject matter, is rather a student of Prescott, the answer is neither so automatic nor so prejudiced.

Among Prescott's histories uniqueness attaches itself to *Ferdinand and Isabella* on several counts. More than any other complete work, it is an institutional study; conversely it is less biographical. Accordingly, it presented more problems of organization. Instead of having an obvious point of origin, *Ferdinand and Isabella* forced the historian to summarize the complexities of medieval Spanish life as his point of departure. Furthermore, this initial work posed the greatest demands ever faced by Prescott in reference to the time and space dimensions of his subject matter.

*Ferdinand and Isabella* contributed many of the precedents related to Prescott's over-all reputation. In it he established for American historians new standards of objectivity and impartiality. In it he set higher standards of documented authenticity. The most cursory comparison of Prescott and Bancroft on the scores of impartiality and documentation indicates the measure of Prescott's contribution. In *Ferdinand and Isabella* he originated, and jokingly said he should patent, the idea of critical biobibliographical notes which knows wide acceptance today. As in these matters Prescott's later works simply adhered to precedents launched in *Ferdinand and Isabella,* so his subsequent histories also took cues from the first one in regard to characterization, colorful description of settings, the high drama of vigorous military conflict, and the moral tone surrounding Christian-pagan relations.

---

de Ferdinand et d'Isabelle la catholique, souverains de l'Espagne," *Bibliotheque universelle de Geneve,* n.s. 16 (July, 1838): 5–30; (August, 1838): 233–252, 23 (September, 1839): 31–59; (October, 1839): 251–275, 25 (January, 1840): 5–44.

To the exemplary aspects of *Ferdinand and Isabella,* add the following considerations: (1) This, the biggest and most complex history, was the product of an untrained historian, an amateur feeling his way, hammering out method as he penned pages; (2) without its success, Prescott, ever inclined to literature and seriously considering a major project therein, might never have produced his other histories; (3) it established such balanced and thorough consideration of the era of the Catholic Kings that all subsequent research in the field has adhered to the basic proportions established by Prescott, an idea expressed by the Spanish historian José Cepeda Adán in these words: "Realizada así su obra, el cuadro general del reinado se ha hecho clásico y ha sido aceptado por todos los que pretenden dar una idea general de este período";[35] and (4) the corrections and additions made in subsequent editions of *Ferdinand and Isabella* hinted at a pursuit of perfection by Prescott which he never exhibited in reference to any other history.

Greatness and popularity are often quite different things. With *Ferdinand and Isabella,* Prescott earned his reputation; with his *Conquest of Mexico* and his *Conquest of Peru,* he won his popularity. Ironically the novel-like *Conquests* are always available, usually in competing editions, but not so the full text of *Ferdinand and Isabella.*[36]

[35] José Cepeda Adán, "Prescott y la 'Historia del Reinado de los Reyes Católicos," *Inter-American Review of Bibliography,* 9 (March, 1959): 45. Somewhat earlier Roger Bigelow Merriman had said, "Prescott's work still remains the standard authority on the reign of the Catholic Kings" (*The Rise of the Spanish Empire in the Old World and in the New,* 4 vols. [New York, 1918–1934], 1: xii). Judging all of Prescott's writings, Merriman termed *Ferdinand and Isabella* "Unquestionably the masterpiece of one of America's greatest historians" (George Matthew Dutcher *et al.,* eds., *A Guide to Historical Literature* [New York, 1931], p. 647. Another historiographer, evaluating Prescott's first history, said, "Though not the most brilliant, it is certainly the most solid achievement of its author" (G. P. Gooch, *History and Historians in the Nineteenth Century* [London, 1913], p. 413).

[36] William H. Prescott, ed., C. Harvey Gardiner, *History of the Reign of Ferdinand and Isabella, the Catholic* (London and Carbondale, 1962) abridges the work along lines established by Prescott in 1841. Translated into at least five languages, *Ferdinand and Isabella* has been published approximately 150 times; see C. Harvey Gardiner, *William Hickling Prescott—An Annotated Bibliography of Published Works* (Washington, 1958), pp. 3–56.

Early and late the work received and deserved adverse criticism. Applicable to *Ferdinand and Isabella*, although written about Prescott's collective work, is Henry Steele Commager's remark,

> Prescott's defects as a historian lie not in method or in scholarship, but in a certain superficiality of mind and exclusiveness of approach. His history was narrative rather than analytical, descriptive rather than philosophical, and the brilliance of the coloring conceals a lack of depth. His concern was with politics, war and diplomacy rather than with social or economic institutions; his Spain was the Spain of the court and nobility and not of the common people.[37]

This criticism derives, in part from Prescott's unchanging nature, and in part from history's changing nature.

For many reasons, related both to the work and the author, *Ferdinand and Isabella* is distinctly Prescott's masterwork.

4

A century and a third after the initial publication of *Ferdinand and Isabella*, Prescott's niche is secure, but those weeks and months immediately following its publication found him exceedingly nervous. Susan, an authority on the man to whom she had been married almost eighteen years, remarked that she had not known William "so out of spirits as since the book has come out." Adding to his uncertainty was the mix-up between Bentley and Aspinwall that denied the author a copy of the London edition for many months.[38]

Preparations for a second American edition soon occupied the author, the first having been exhausted in a matter of weeks. When friends supplied errata lists, he dispatched scores of corrections to his printer. Late in April the second and last edition required to fulfill the contract with the American Stationers' Company appeared. Despite the success of Prescott's book, that house, a victim of the spreading financial panic which had begun the previous year, became bankrupt.[39]

[37] Henry Steele Commager, "William Hickling Prescott," in Edwin R. A. Seligman *et al.,* eds., *Encyclopaedia of the Social Sciences,* 15 vols. (London, 1930–1935), 12: 324.

[38] Ticknor, *Prescott,* p. 115; and Gardiner, ed., *Papers,* pp. 128–129.

[39] *Ibid.,* pp. 125–126; and WHP to C. Folsom, January 30, February 3,

On May 14 Prescott signed with James Brown and Charles C. Little a contract which allowed them five years to publish 1,700 copies, for which the author would receive $2,975 and furnish his plates. Little and Brown issued their initial edition of the work in August 1838.[40]

The combined lure of history, appeal of Spanish themes, and reception of his book, which encouraged Prescott to shelve the study of Molière, also led him to shy away from an invitation to write a second piece for Sparks's *American Biography*. Instead, hitting upon Cortés' conquest of Mexico as a possible theme for another project, he wrote to James Rich in London, wondering if James's father, the redoubtable Obadiah, could make a book-collecting expedition to Spain to serve Prescott's purposes. Although willing to appropriate "twelve or even fifteen hundred dollars to it," he felt it would be a waste of time to dedicate himself to the Mexican theme prior to being assured he could acquire basic Spanish materials.[41] Before Rich could reply or act, the historian found in Ángel Calderón de la Barca the kind of entree he needed in Spanish intellectual circles.

Upon reading *Ferdinand and Isabella*, the idle former Spanish minister to the United States, then in New York, became an instant admirer of historian Prescott. The author, in turn, was beside himself when he learned that Calderón was sending copies of his book to the queen of Spain and to the Real Academia de la Historia, that nation's most important historical body. Climaxing all, Calderón spoke of personally translating the work into the Castilian. Prescott eagerly awaited an opportunity to seal this newborn friendship by a face to face meeting.[42] More than anything or anyone else, Calderón de la Barca affirmed Prescott's dedication to the Spanish conquest of America. With courtly grace the Spaniard phrased his desire to be of assistance: "I think it the duty of every Spanish lover of literature to show his

---

March 14, 16, 21, c. April 27, [2], 1838, Folsom papers. On occasion the corrections, too wordy for his stereotype plates, were not incorporated in the book. See WHP to C. Folsom, June 15, 1838. Folsom papers.

[40] The text of this contract is in Gardiner, *Prescott and Publishers*, pp. 284–288; and Gardiner, *Prescott—Bibliography*, pp. 5–6.

[41] WHP to J. Sparks, April 13, 1838, Sparks papers; and Wolcott, ed., *Correspondence*, p. 22.

[42] WHP to J. Goodhue, March 19, 1838, Goodhue papers..

gratitude to one who like yourself has expended so much time and money to perpetuate for posterity, with the mastery that you have shown, the memory of the most glorious and interesting period in the history of Spain." In the last week of March 1838 William hurried to New York to meet his newest aide.[43] Next he urged speedy completion of a new printing of the history, desiring to put a half dozen copies into Calderón's hands for distribution among Spanish intellectuals. Nudging perfectionist Folsom, he asserted, "they are to be my credentials for getting what I am now sending for to Madrid."[44]

Presentation copies of *Ferdinand and Isabella* repeatedly became entering wedges for Prescott's second project. To Tomás González, keeper of the archives of Simancas and a recipient of the history, he indicated, "I now propose to assume a narration of the conquest of Mexico and Peru," adding thereto his hope ". . . to obtain your permission to copy such manuscripts in the archives as would further the objects I have in view." To Martín Fernández de Navarrete, senior historian of Spain and president of her Real Academia de la Historia, he reiterated the indebtedness which he had expressed on more than one occasion in notes in his book. From that scholar he now sought permission "to allow a copy to be made for me of such manuscripts in your possession as relate to the Discovery and Conquest of Mexico and Peru."[45] In the shower of presentation copies rained upon European scholars by Prescott, Ticknor, Calderón, and others, those to non-Spaniards possibly helped Prescott most to international acclaim, while those to Spaniards were peculiarly productive in regard to his subsequent titles.[46] In the letters to González, Fernández de Navarrete, and others, Prescott mentioned Arthur Middleton as his agent in Spain.

In Madrid in diplomatic service, Arthur Middleton was expected to

---

[43] Wolcott, ed., *Correspondence,* p. 24; Gardiner, ed., *Papers,* pp. 127–128; WHP to J. Goodhue, March 7, 1838, Goodhue papers; and WHP to C. Folsom, March 31, [April 2], 1838, Folsom papers.

[44] *Id.* to *id.,* [April 6, 1838], Folsom papers; and Gardiner, ed., *Papers,* p. 128.

[45] Wolcott, ed., *Correspondence,* pp. 25, 31.

[46] A fuller discussion of the role of Prescott's presentation copies is in C. Harvey Gardiner, "Prescott obsequia sus libros," *Historia Mexicana,* 8 (January–March, 1959): 301–324.

play a prominent role in the second project. Never so much as offering his Harvard classmate an opportunity to decline the assignment, Prescott named him his agent in Spain and sent him full instructions. First, a sound scholar, one who could approach Spanish scholars and archivists and who could ferret out the pertinent documents, should be found. That scholar in turn should secure amanuenses to produce transcripts legible enough for Prescott's personal use. Middleton would have to settle the rates of payment for both supervisor and copyists; Prescott would furnish instructions regarding the published titles to be bought and the manuscripts to be copied. To cover expenses, he authorized Middleton to present drafts on him through Barings of London.

"You, my old friend, are on the very spot and situation which can lay this career open to me," William declared, brushing aside any qualm entertained by Arthur. Middleton speedily set to work, signifying later, "I regard the commission as a labor of love."[47]

Both in his inner social nature and in his public and intellectual life, William H. Prescott cannot be understood without an awareness of what friendship meant to him. As April increased his friends in Europe, May highlighted two friends on the home front. George Bancroft, much influenced by suggestions made by William, had penned a review of *Ferdinand and Isabella* for one of the politically oriented reviews to which Prescott did not have ready access. In addition, George purposely had held his article so that at a comparatively late date it could sustain the swell of approbation of earlier weeks. Thanking him, William labeled it "one of the most delightful tributes ever paid by friendship to authorship."[48] Later in May Prescott was giving rather than receiving an expression of friendship. Jared Sparks, shaken in his publishing ventures by national depression and uncertain about

[47] Wolcott, ed., *Correspondence*, pp. 28, 38; Clara Louisa Penney, ed., *Prescott; Unpublished Letters to Gayangos in the Library of the Hispanic Society of America* (New York, 1927), pp. 1–2.

[48] [George Bancroft], "Prescott's Ferdinand and Isabella," *The United States Magazine and Democratic Review*, 2 (May, 1838): 160–166; WHP to G. Bancroft, May 5, 1838, Bancroft papers; Ticknor, *Prescott*, p. 362; Gardiner, "Promoting a Book," *The Papers of the Bibliographical Society of America*, 51 (Fourth Quarter, 1957), 335–339.

his future prospects, drew the thoughtful attention of some of his moneyed friends, among them the Prescotts. The historian wrote Jared, "My father will join me in a loan of 2000 dollars to you in the way most convenient to you."[49]

Sizing up his combined Mexican and Peruvian plans, Prescott believed they represented about four or five years of work—three years for the former, in two volumes, and between one and two years for the latter, in a single volume. As usual these estimates proved optimistic; slightly more than nine years elapsed before the publication of both works, and that in five volumes approximating five hundred pages each rather than three volumes of three hundred pages each.

Doubts attended Prescott's endorsement of the conquest themes. "The daring achievements of these bold adventurers is a striking subject to the imagination. But I confess I do not relish the annals or the conquests of barbarians, so much as those of civilized people."[50] However, settling on Mexico and Peru, his plans progressed even one step further. "Should I succeed in my present [Mexican-Peruvian] collection, who knows what facilities I may find for making one relative to Philip IIds reign—a fruitful theme." Thus, late in May 1838, Prescott outlined his intellectual activity for the remainder of his life.

On the fringes of his Mexican theme, he was reading Peter Stephen DuPonceau's "Essay on Indian Languages," two works by Alexander von Humboldt: *Researches concerning the Institutions of the Ancient Inhabitants of America* and his *New Spain*, and a title by Irving. DuPonceau, inquisitive and acute, had recently sponsored Prescott for membership in the American Philosophical Society. Of the German scholar, read in translation, William remarked, "Humboldt's works are full of facts and observations indispensable to a thorough knowledge of the history, whether physical, political, or moral,—of Mexico —Ancient and modern." At the moment he was simply browsing, but the time would come when notes in his second history echoed this continuing high regard for Humboldt. Of Irving he held a different opinion, witness his estimate of *Companions of Columbus*—"prettily

[49] WHP to J. Sparks, May 23, 1838, Sparks papers.
[50] Gardiner, ed., *Literary Memoranda*, 1: 229. The quotations which immediately follow are in *ibid.*, pp. 230–231.

told, without much expense of thought or research." Pondering, in late spring, an English translation of Francisco Xavier Clavigero's *Historia antigua de México*, he sensed, for the first time, the dimensions and complexity of the pre-Hispanic native civilization so important to any history of the Mexican conquest. He entertained and later reaffirmed a favorable opinion of Clavigero.[51]

During the last week of June, when the Prescotts were closing the Pepperell household preparatory to moving to Fitful Head, Catherine Hickling Prescott suffered an inflammation of the brain. Lethargy overtook the vigorous lady who was approaching her seventy-first birthday. Her reason departed, and all in attendance thought death was near. To William, who had spent almost all of his forty-two years within range of his mother's voice, it was a time of indescribable distress. Fortunately she weathered an early crisis and turned for the better. However, her long road to recovery dictated that the family spend the summer in Boston.[52]

There the historian tackled Juan de Torquemada's multivolume *Monarquía Indiana*, "dictating copious notes so that the work will not in these parts, one or two chapters excepted, require reperusal." Less rewarding was the English translation of José de Acosta's *Naturall and Morall Historie of the East & West Indies*. Before the summer expired, Prescott faltered. The second half of 1838 he worried, trifled, and waited. Worried about his mother's health and waiting to hear of his prospects in Spain, he was sufficiently unnerved that even if the creative urge had been upon him, it is unlikely that he would have accomplished much. As it was, however, he indulged his social inclinations, relishing at the same time the widening acclaim that settled upon his name.[53]

When the English edition of *Ferdinand and Isabella*, published in

[51] *Ibid.*, 2: 3; and William H. Prescott, *History of the Conquest of Mexico, with a preliminary view of the Ancient Mexican Civilization, and the Life of the Conqueror, Hernando Cortes*, 3 vols. (New York, 1843), 1: 52–53.

[52] WHP to J. Sparks, June 30, 1838, Sparks papers.

[53] Gardiner, ed., *Literary Memoranda*, 2: 7, 10; and WHP to C. Folsom, July 9, 11, December 3, 1838, Folsom papers; and William H. Prescott, *History of the Reign of Ferdinand and Isabella, the Catholic*, 3rd ed., 3 vols. (Boston, 1838), 1: xv.

January, finally reached Prescott in July, he studied it closely. Particularly desirous that his history be enriched by fine illustrations, the author had spent $475.00 on the engravings and printing of the portraits in the American edition. Realizing that some of the American illustrations, as those of Ferdinand and Isabella, should appear in future English editions, and that future American editions could be enriched by the magnificent Columbus which Bentley had used, Prescott encouraged the exchange of illustrations between London and Boston.[54]

To the perfection of his text and the improvement of the illustrations he joined lively concern about sales. Joyfully informing Bentley that the four American editions represented 2,300 copies of the expensive ($7.50) work within ten months, William added with evident glee, "It shows that Brother Jonathan, with all his democracy, has a certain relish for kings and queens—at least on paper."[55]

The widening acceptance of *Ferdinand and Isabella*, facilitated by the generous bestowal of presentation copies, prompted a wider horizon and a mushrooming correspondence for William H. Prescott. Historian Henry Hallam of London penned the prophetic words, "I expect your book to acquire by degrees a classical reputation," and thereby opened a friendly correspondence which spanned decades. In America, one of the many presentation copies had gone to the intellectually vigorous Francis Lieber, then professor of history and political economy in South Carolina College. As with Hallam, it cemented a firm friendship, a rich correspondence, and an interchange of writings.[56] In time, too, Lieber spearheaded one of the moves resulting in honorary degrees for Prescott.

By late autumn the uncertainty surrounding Prescott's future historical activity had largely dissipated. Middleton already was shipping some of the desiderata. Meanwhile, Friedrich Wilhelm Lembke, the German-born agent in whose hands Middleton had placed the supervision

[54] Wolcott, ed., *Correspondence*, pp. 37–38, 40–41; and WHP to C. Little, September 7, 1838, Historical Society of Pennsylvania.

[55] Wolcott, ed., *Correspondence*, p. 41.

[56] *Ibid.*, p. 36; WHP to F. Lieber, July 22, 1838, Lieber papers; and Gardiner, ed., *Papers*, pp. 131–132. For fuller appreciation of Lieber, see Frank Friedel, *Francis Lieber, Nineteenth-Century Liberal* (Baton Rouge, 1947).

of Prescott's affairs in Spain, was himself reporting to the historian. Having obtained access to the holdings of Fernández de Navarrete and to the Juan Bautista Muñoz collection, among others, Lembke had hired four copyists to fulfill Prescott's needs. By late November 1838 Lembke felt that he had completed the search for materials related to Cortés. He continued to search for records of the Peruvian conquest. The completeness of his report to Prescott, touching as it did on printed materials, manuscript sources, and portraits, pleased the eager Bostonian.[57]

While matters progressed so favorably in Spain, Prescott pressed the Riches into service, instructing them to obtain copies of works by Giovanni Battista Ramusio and Andrés González Barcia. About another title, Lord Kingsborough's richly illustrated oversize work on ancient Mexico, the historian had trouble making up his mind. Not long before this the trustees of the Boston Athenaeum had voted to acquire a set of Kingsborough's *Antiquities of Mexico.* "Provided the whole cost should not exceed $400."[58] The growing certainty of his Mexican project induced the historian to write Obadiah Rich, "as to Ld. Kingsborough's great work I should like to have a copy sent to me as soon as one can be got." The simultaneous serving of Prescott's purposes and the Athenaeum's desires is evident in his additional word, "I wish you would direct the volumes to the Boston Athenaeum and I will arrange to have the books in my possession. I propose to give the Athenaeum the copy subject to my control during my life time."[59]

As 1838 faded, the final obstacle to Prescott's pursuit of the Mexican and Peruvian themes—namely, the likelihood that Washington Irving had pre-empted them for himself—dissolved into thin air. Irving had published on numerous Spanish themes, occasionally to William's discomfiture. In addition, Irving's popularity and speed made of him a kind of competitor that Prescott did not relish. Toying first with the idea of writing directly to Irving, William changed his

[57] Wolcott, ed., *Correspondence,* pp. 41–46.

[58] WHP to James Rich, draft, [autumn, 1838], Prescott papers; and Quincy, *Boston Athenaeum,* pp. 139 n., 143.

[59] WHP to O. Rich, draft, November 25, 1838, Prescott papers.

mind and entrusted the matter to Joseph Cogswell, who spoke with Irving at length about Prescott's Mexican intentions. Cogswell was told to inform Prescott that Irving, though interested in the same subject, was relinquishing it in favor of the Boston historian.

Appraised of this happy turn of events on the last day of the year, Prescott wrote the letter that initiated a friendly correspondence with Irving. Thanking him for his magnanimity, he added, "It will be conferring a still further favor on me, if you will allow me occasionally, when I may find the want of it, to ask your advice in the progress of the work."[60] These words typify Prescott the diplomat, the truth being that, given the differences between their concepts of history and their employment of substantial research, there was no likelihood that Prescott ever would need, much less ask, Irving's advice. At best, Irving was an indifferent historian, and the generosity with which he yielded the conquest of Mexico to Prescott was possibly his greatest contribution to history.

The first year following publication of *Ferdinand and Isabella* had been a mosaic of growing reputation, mounting correspondence, social activity, family crisis, and intellectual loafing. On Christmas Day, 1838, the anniversary of the appearance of "their Catholic Highnesses," the historian joyfully recapitulated his success. Lest that success foster complacency, he also converted the anniversary into a goad. Seizing upon the Reverend Dr. Channing's assessment of *Ferdinand and Isabella,* "It has been received by acclamation," he told himself, "yet I am not such an ass as not to know that fires which blaze up the quickest are soonest out."[61]

[60] Ticknor, *Prescott,* p. 168.
[61] Gardiner, ed., *Literary Memoranda,* 2: 10.

## VIII

*My journal is paved, like some other places . . .*

T HE HIGH RESOLVE and favorable prospects with which Prescott
greeted 1839 suggested he would plunge into his Mexican project
with singleness of purpose, which he did not do. Fearful that revolution might absent from Mexico City the Count Cortina and Manuel
Eduardo de Gorostiza, scholars recommended by Calderón, Prescott
opened correspondence with Joel R. Poinsett, at the suggestion of
Bancroft. More correspondence than aid resulted, the former American minister to Mexico having left numerous enemies south of the
border.[1] To Middleton and Lembke, his aides in Madrid, went one
long letter after another, teeming with chitchat, requests, orders, and
increasing awareness of his bibliographical needs. To establish the
best channels between Madrid and Boston, the historian informed
Jonathan Goodhue of New York of his plans and enlisted him to
handle correspondence, shipments, and the remission of funds. To the
New Yorker he wrote, "I suppose the channel of communication may
be sometimes Cádiz; and I find that the U. S. Consul there, Mr. Alex-

[1] Gardiner, ed., *Papers,* pp. 133–137; and J. R. Poinsett to WHP, January
15, 1939, Prescott papers. For the general background of the interval treated
in this chapter, see Gardiner, ed., *Literary Memoranda,* 2: 11–79.

ander Burton, is a cousin of my mother. So I have written to him, to interest him in the matter."[2] Friendship and blood added Goodhue and Burton to the growing corps of Prescott's aides.

Enlarging the search for materials for the Mexican and Peruvian projects, the historian sent Henri Ternaux-Compans, along with a presentation copy of *Ferdinand and Isabella*, a request for transcriptions of any relevant documents which the Frenchman did not intend to translate and print. Foreseeing a visit to Europe by Prescott, Ternaux-Compans replied, "My entire library would be at your service."[3]

In early spring the anxiously awaited first shipment of Spanish transcriptions arrived. Their extreme legibility permitted their owner to scrutinize them personally. Unaware of the untapped riches of various Spanish archives, he fondled his 2,500 pages of transcripts with extreme satisfaction, declaring, "Of course I have all the solid basis for prosecuting my labors." Looking to the future while he had such excellent facilities in Madrid, he reminded Middleton of his interest in another theme. "I should like to make a collection of materials for the reign of Philip II and . . . I should be glad to have Dr. Lembke superintend it when he has accomplished the Peruvian."[4]

The socially "dizzy-pated winter" of 1838–1839 left the historian "with less to show, in any other way, than any past winter for these ten years—nay twenty."[5] Favorable critiques of *Ferdinand and Isabella* from Germany and Switzerland and the Marquis Gino Capponi's desire to translate it into Italian also distracted him. The forthcoming fifth American edition encouraged Prescott to write Little and Brown, "Pray be particular." "The paper [of the fourth edition] is too *cottonish* . . . and in fact it is a paper that I don't *cotton* to myself at all."[6]

Meanwhile London often vied successfully for Prescott's attention. There Charles Sumner, in early 1839, was aiding the American author

[2] Wolcott, ed., *Correspondence,* pp. 47–54, 57–59, 61–64; WHP to J. Goodhue, January 19, March 7, 1839, Goodhue papers.

[3] Wolcott, ed., *Correspondence,* pp. 60–61, 75.

[4] *Ibid.,* pp. 62, 65; and Gardiner, ed., *Literary Memoranda,* 2: 13.

[5] *Ibid.,* pp. 14–15.

[6] WHP to G. W. Greene, draft, January 28, 1839, Prescott papers; WHP to G. E. Ellis, February 4, 1839, Ellis papers; WHP to Little & Brown, [c. January, 1839], Ford collection; and Gardiner, ed., *Papers,* p. 137.

much as Ticknor had the previous year. In anticipation of a second English edition, Bentley was sent more than a hundred alterations in the text. To reviewer Pascual de Gayangos, also in the English capital, Prescott was writing, "Mr. Ticknor has mentioned to me that he understood you had some letters, or other MSS, relating to this period, not familiarly known. . . . Will you also allow me to ask if, among your papers, you have any which can throw light on the history of Cortés or Pizarro?" Tying past performance to present project, this letter inaugurated decades of assistance.[7]

Another Prescott contribution to the nothingness of early 1839 was the review written for the "Old North." Treating John Kenyon's writing as the work of a friend's friend—Ticknor had known the dilettantish Englishman for many years—he heaped undeserved compliments upon the philanthropist's poetry. Of the same verse a later writer said, "These productions hardly pass muster as poetry."[8]

2

Eventually the Mexican theme competed successfully with the distractions, and Prescott delved into successive authors to sharpen his understanding of preconquest Mexico, his first order of business. Appalled by the perplexing aspects of ancient Mexico, he concluded, "I shall step gingerly over them." Further study altered his estimate. "What alarmed me at a distance, under the appearance of curious erudition," he wrote one week later, "turns out for the most part mere mist—moonshine speculation,—a boundless region into which my duties as a writer of fact will not carry me."

The essentially raw, often brutish pattern of the Mexican record,

[7] Gardiner, ed., *Literary Memoranda,* 2: 12; WHP to C. Sumner, April 18, 1839, Sumner papers; WHP to R. Bentley, February 8, 1839, Bentley papers; Wolcott, ed., *Correspondence,* pp. 55–57; and Penney, ed., *Letters to Gayangos,* pp. 2–4. Mentioned in various places in the present work, Gayangos' aid is given unified treatment in Gardiner, "Prescott's Most Indispensable Aide," *Hispanic American Historical Review,* 39 (February, 1959): 81–115.

[8] [WHP], "Kenyon's Poems," *North American Review,* 48 (April, 1839): 401–415; Hillard, ed., *Life, Letters, and Journals,* 1: 411 n., 418; 2: 144, 145, 149; [J. M. Rigg], "John Kenyon," in Leslie Stephens *et al.,* eds., *Dictionary of National Biography,* 21 vols. (London, 1908–1909), 11: 30.

unlike either the literate, moral historian or his first historical theme, so clashed with William's inner nature as to lead him to observe, "I hope my readers will take more satisfaction than I do in the annals of barbarians."[9] He welcomed, consequently, the brief respites for the correspondence which swelled in volume.

To Paris went a copy of *Ferdinand and Isabella* to facilitate a French translation. In Germany a presentation copy went to Nicolaus Heinrich Julius, whom Prescott had met in Boston. And despite the Spanish sources which led him to believe that Mexico had little to offer, Prescott sought additional aides there.[10]

Straining the accounts of preconquest Mexico, he moved toward a few firm conclusions and a welter of unanswered questions. "Read somewhat in old Bernal Díaz—a jewel of a chronicler," he penned into his memoranda.[11] Early and late Díaz influenced Prescott's handling of his Mexican theme. Any eagerness to begin writing was tempered by the fact that he still had not seen Lord Kingsborough's massive work. After marking time for a while, he renewed his intellectual determination at Nahant and studied Humboldt, Solís, and Clavigero.

Pondering the pattern into which his new theme seemed to fall, William outlined his second book. In view of the fact that he had not written a word, and had four years of labor ahead of him, he established a remarkably firm outline. In fact, he published six of its seven parts—he termed them books—under the exact headings assigned in July 1839.

The detailed manner in which Prescott outlined his projects, a little-known facet of his genius, deserves comment. Along with his selection and division of materials, he assigned the number of pages for individual chapters as well as for complete sections of the work. On physical dimensions, however, he guessed badly, because the two-volume history swelled to three. Wordy in his histories, in his letters, and in conversation, he wasted on himself the borrowed admonition,

---

[9] Gardiner, ed., *Literary Memoranda*, 2: 15, 16, 17.

[10] Wolcott, ed., *Correspondence*, pp. 70, 76; WHP to Manning & Marshall, draft, May 21, 1839, and WHP to P. Ellis, draft, May 21, 1839, Prescott papers.

[11] Gardiner, ed., *Literary Memoranda*, 2: 21. The quotations which immediately follow are in *ibid.*, pp. 26, 29, 30, 31, 32, 36, 39.

Brevity is very good
When we are or are not understood.

Later the book published in 1843 demonstrated repeatedly the author's adherence to the plans and hopes of 1839: employment of de-
scriptive detail capable of "transporting the reader to the country,
and to the age"; "omit no trait which can display the character of
Cortés, the *hero* of *the piece*"; "the other, subordinate characters, . . .
are not without interest"; "vary the tissue of blood and battle, which
is to form the staple of the story, with other circumstances of milder
complexions"; "the true way of conceiving the subject is, not as a
philosophical theme, but as an *epic in prose,* a romance of chivalry; as
romantic and as chivalrous as any which Boiardo or Ariosto ever
fabled." "The Conquest of Mexico," he continued, "was the greatest
miracle in an age of miracles. . . . It is, without doubt, the most poetic
subject ever offered to the pen of the historian." Prescott thus forecast the strengths and weaknesses of his second history, his prose response to a continuing love of Italian epic poetry.

Despite his clear conception of this second book, William allowed
many distractions to invade Nahant. Then, regretting he had wandered
afield, he resolved to avoid tangential interests, "save only my annual
peppercorn for the Old North." His memoranda, fat with trifles, he
would restrict "to the hebdomedal notices of my studies, and to the
criticisms on the subjects of them,—strictly. For all the rest is—
'leather and prunella.' " Some of the latter cropped up in the very
next entry, when he rejoiced in the news of his election to the Royal
Academy of History in Madrid.

On Commencement Day the historian crossed to Cambridge to join
twenty-five to thirty classmates on the twenty-fifth anniversary of their
graduation. Names and faces eluded him:

I greeted one companion-in-arms [he recalled] by the name of another, who
he told me with some dissatisfaction had been dead these ten years. Old
Time had played the devil with most of their physiognomies, grizzling most
of the moustaches and headgear, or what is worse, thinning them off sadly.
. . . It was a queer sort of meeting, and as we looked at one another's
grizzled, weather-beaten visages, and heard the old remembered tones so

long silent, it was looking through the mists of many years, and called up feelings that had as much of the melancholy as the mirthful in them.[12]

Dignity and false gravity mingled with bad puns and jokes. Among fellow Porcellians the historian surely contributed his share of the humor.

Good humor, however, did not attend his reception of Colonel Aspinwall's first report of his transatlantic earnings. Bentley's accounting, replete with sums assigned to advertising, bad debts, and so forth, invited Prescott's curiosity, doubts, and suspicions.[13]

At shady Pepperell the initiation of George Frederick Ware as reader-secretary delayed his pulling notes together preparatory to writing an introduction to the Aztec civilization. In mid-October he again undertook to organize that introduction. Once more masterly outlining put geography, peoples, government, religion, science, arts, and every other subject into place. With restraint and pride, he declared, "Wrote the first page of the *'History of the Conquest of Mexico'*—October 14th."[14]

3

The month that Prescott initiated the writing of his new history also marked the appearance of his nineteenth article in the "Old North," his lengthy critique of François René Chateaubriand's *Sketches of English Literature.*[15] Liking the theme and disliking the treatment of it, he wrote with greater vigor than usually characterized his periodical pieces. In another rush to the side of Sir Walter Scott, he wrote, "He had given new value to romance, by building it on history, and new charms to history, by embellishing it with the graces of romance." All of Prescott's historical writing consciously adhered to the second part of that statement. More of Scott's influence streams from his state-

---

[12] Wolcott, ed., *Correspondence,* p. 97.

[13] T. Aspinwall to WHP, September 2, 1839, Prescott papers; Gardiner, ed., *Literary Memoranda,* 2: 40–42; and Gardiner, *Prescott and Publishers,* pp. 227–228.

[14] Gardiner, ed., *Literary Memoranda,* 2: 46.

[15] [WHP], "Chateaubriand's Sketches of English Literature," *North American Review,* 49 (October, 1839): 317–348. The quotations which follow immediately are in *ibid.,* pp. 339, 342.

ment, "Scott was, in truth, master of the picturesque. He understood, better than any historian since the time of Livy, how to dispose his lights and shades so as to produce the most striking result." In this essay on Chateaubriand, Prescott published a partial prospectus, as it were, of the outlook and method he was applying to the Mexican conquest.

As his research lost hours to reviewing, so, too, the time allotted to leisure pursuits and society often yielded to his continuing identification with the New England Institution for the Blind. Still a trustee, he contributed to its financial support, endorsed its printing program, and suggested ways of winning additional public support. Realizing, however, that his lengthy annual stays at Nahant and Pepperell, plus accidental absences, had prevented his attending in recent years to his duties as trustee, he determined to resign that post. Furthermore, he was confident that the once-struggling institution was on the road to continuing success. Accordingly he wrote, "I beg leave to communicate through you my intention to decline being a candidate for reelection as a Trustee, at the next annual meeting." To Howe's remonstrance he was unyielding.[16]

While dissolving his official tie to the Boston movement in behalf of the blind, William was associating himself with a national effort to improve the American copyright law. But he had not always been so minded. During the copyright activity of 1837–1838, he had been a passive bystander, supporting neither the British-inspired memorial of February 1837 nor Henry Clay's bill of mid-December 1837. However, in October 1839 Professor Francis Lieber, trying in advance of the opening of the next session of Congress to enlist support for action promised by Senator William C. Preston, requested and won Prescott's assistance in the preparation of a memorial. "Touching the movement for the introduction of a copyright law," Prescott wrote, "I can truly say, I feel sincerely interested in it; as well I may, now that I enter my fillies for the plate."[17]

---

[16] WHP to S. G. Howe, August 6, December 16, 26, 1839, Perkins School for the Blind; and Gardiner, ed., *Papers,* pp. 142–143, 145–146.

[17] *Ibid.,* pp. 147–148. For Prescott's total relation to the copyright issue, see Gardiner, *Prescott and Publishers,* chap. 4; for Lieber, see Frank Friedel,

Beyond identifying himself with the desire for a more just law he would not go, declining to shepherd a memorial to Washington and once there standing ready to explain and defend it. That same abhorrence of the political arena he had exhibited earlier that year to Arthur Middleton, when he said, "I never meddle with the dirty trade of politics." Never one to make public addresses, he now informed Lieber, "I am a dull hand in action."[18] Excusing himself, he named Irving as the logical leader of the movement which Lieber desired. "If any thing be done," Prescott wrote Irving, "there can be no doubt that you are the one, who, from your literary position in the country should take the lead in it." Reaffirming his support for a new copyright law, Prescott added, "if you will prepare a paper, I shall be very glad, when it has been signed in your city, to do all in my power, to get such signatures to it here, as will give it most weight."[19] Prescott next turned to Webster, who promised to support the measure if it reached the floor of the Senate. Economically and politically cynical, William wrote his liberal friend in South Carolina:

I fear nothing is to be passed, this session, nor have I much hope in any other. The *apparent* interests of the public are too much in the same seals with those of the publishers . . . As to appealing to higher motives, one must have more faith in the stuff that statesmen are made of, than I have, to think they will weigh against the little calculations of selfishness.[20]

Meanwhile the American copyright law of February 3, 1831, remained the law of the land.

### 4

Prescott's efforts to improve his research prospects by curtailing and fending off outside activities involved even his household. He resolved that in the future the children must neither invade his library nor receive so much of his attention in the country. In 1839, William Gardiner was thirteen, Elizabeth, eleven, and William Amory, nine—

---

"Lieber's Contribution to the International Copyright Movement," *The Huntington Library Quarterly,* 8 (February, 1945): 200–206.

[18] Wolcott, ed., *Correspondence,* p. 54; and Gardiner, ed., *Papers,* p. 147.

[19] *Ibid.,* p. 152; and Ticknor, *Prescott,* pp. 176–177.

[20] Gardiner, ed., *Papers,* pp. 154–155; and WHP to F. Lieber, April 13, 1840, Lieber papers.

an energetic trio at high tide. In addition to their interruptions, their recitations had consumed too much of his time.[21] Pepperell required schedules and discipline for the children as well as for the historian. An accompanying resolution to plunge at once into his writing went awry. After five months on the coast and in the country, it was another verse of an old refrain: the interval between the return from The Highlands and the opening of the new year was misused.

Failing to dedicate sizable intervals to history, Prescott spent many small ones on his correspondence. Indeed some of his voluminous correspondence, in addition to a love of letter writing, seemed to derive from a desire to employ his time and that of his reader-secretary, even when a major project was not the order of business. Letters went to historian Hallam, agent Lembke, crusader Lieber, and Washington Irving. Balancing this indoor activity, he rode out daily some four miles from home to watch the sun rise on Jamaica Plains. Such exercise, he insisted, "winds up the machinery for four and twenty hours."[22]

Firm resolution gradually took hold and, in January, 1840, he laboriously produced the texts and notes of successive chapters. But he soon announced, "Very much retarded by a very bungling and perplexed *modus operandi*."[23] He was trying to embrace more than he could hold in his mind at one time. In addition, his notes were in too many forms. To the other problems he added verbosity, for he had written twice the desired amount.

By mid-winter his new reader-secretary's greater experience and his own disciplined social life—he seldom dined out more than once a week—encouraged greater momentum. Also he used his eyes between two and three hours daily. In the fourth chapter, concerning Aztec culture, he nervously tackled science and mathematics, subjects about which he knew little and cared less.

Meanwhile, he cared more and more about his international correspondence. Gayangos' offer of services and books and manuscripts

[21] Gardiner, ed., *Literary Memoranda*, 2: 47. Excerpts of many letters of this period are in Wolcott, ed., *Correspondence*, pp. 100–133.

[22] *Ibid.*, pp. 100–102; Gardiner, ed., *Papers*, pp. 147–148, 152–154; and WHP to J. Goodhue, January 28, 1840, Goodhue papers.

[23] Gardiner, ed., *Literary Memoranda*, 2: 49.

was accepted; and manuscripts were sought from the Duke of Monte-
leone. Aspinwall agreed to a commission of 10 per cent on the historian's English earnings. From Thomas Stewart, a Catholic monk at
Palermo, came a detailed critique of *Ferdinand and Isabella,* a helpful
criticism which influenced and improved Prescott's subsequent writing. Letters between Prescott and the Calderóns, then in Mexico City,
put the diplomat and his lady at the historian's service. Declining their
invitation to visit them there, he wrote, among other things, about the
depressed American economy, a subject of supreme interest to investor
Calderón. "I have my share of the bubbles . . . ," Prescott told them,
"having invested three years since eighteen thousand dollars in what
were called *fancy* stocks—I suppose because nobody fancies them—
for I cannot now sell them at more than seven thousand. But *pazienza
—meliora speremus.*"[24] Another hope centered upon Edward Everett
who, soon to embark for Europe, was asked to ascertain whether the
French archives administered by François A. M. Mignet contained
documents concerning the reign of Philip II.

Not every letter related to distant lands, witness one to the librarian
at Harvard: "I still have Cogolludo's 'Yucatan' which I take the liberty to retain—under the presumption that this will be permitted me.
It is the only authority relating to my subject—not in my own library."[25]

5

When lank twenty-nine-year-old Charles Sumner returned to Boston in the spring of 1840 from his two-and-one-half-year stay in
Europe, he quickly took a place in social circles that included Story,
Longfellow, Howe, Bancroft, and Prescott.[26] Although fifteen years
older than Charles, William fashioned a special intimacy with him.

[24] WHP to J. Sparks, June 20, 1840, Sparks papers; Wolcott, ed., *Correspondence,* pp. 111, 114; Gardiner, ed., *Papers,* pp. 156–158; WHP to T.
Aspinwall, draft, March 27, 1840, and T. Stewart to WHP, Feb. [blank],
1840, Prescott papers.

[25] Ticknor, *Prescott,* pp. 365–366; and Gardiner, ed., *Papers,* p. 159.

[26] Concerning Sumner's personality and European trip, see David Donald,
*Charles Sumner and the Coming of the Civil War* (New York, 1960), pp.
45–69.

All the rest of the historian's years counted Sumner in the select category reserved for William Gardiner, George Ticknor, and William
Amory. Possessed of little imagination and less wit, Charles, devoid
of a sense of humor, was considerably unlike William. They shared,
however, ranging literary interests, delightful memories of England
and the Continent, and lively social instincts. The lively friendship between the Prescotts (the Judge must be included) and Sumner is
demonstrated in their casual, unguarded notes, those by the historian
often being undated, brief, and crowded with abbreviations. At a moment when he was unsuccessfully trying to arrange a dinner party for
actor William Charles Macready, Prescott wrote of the English
tragedian, "He has nothing of the flash and orange-peel." To Sumner's office at Four Court Street he addressed invitations and plans,
such as, "Will you do me the favor to dine with me at the *Tremont*
on Saturday at 5 ock?" and "I will call at your office this forenoon—
between one and two."[27] (Like lunch, the "forenoon" came late for
Prescott.)

That season at Nahant Prescott hoped to complete the troublesome
Introduction. Fitful Head again worked miracles, strengthening the
vision that had been indifferent upon arrival there. But still he was
disappointed. "Have had more company this season than ever—here
i.e. in this house," he observed in mid-summer.[28] Yet not all the visitors were either unwanted or uninvited. The historian and Samuel A.
Eliot, constituting the committee in charge of the meeting of Club on
Tuesday, July 21, decided upon a 2 P.M. dinner at the Nahant Hotel.
The invitations to their "Brothers in Arms" closed with the admonition, "You are requested to send a notice whether you will attend—
to Brother Loring's Office—Court St."[29]

One summer visitor, General William Miller, an English participant in the South American wars of independence, helped William
with military matters. Studying the inaccuracies in the military por-

[27] WHP to C. Sumner, [c. November–December, 1843], Wellesley College;
*id.* to *id.,* [n.d.], American Antiquarian Society; and *id.* to *id.,* [n.d.], Sumner
papers.
[28] Gardiner, ed., *Literary Memoranda,* 2: 54.
[29] WHP to C. Folsom, July 13, 1840, Folsom papers; and WHP to T. Parsons, July 13, 1840, Chamberlain autograph collection.

tions of *Ferdinand and Isabella,* the general constructed the list of recommendations which the historian incorporated into his memoranda, saying, "which I will set down for a future guide in military details."[30] A stranger upon arrival, Miller departed an esteemed friend and willing correspondent.

At Fitful Head the interruptions, as usual, inclined the historian toward correspondence, a prominent portion of which concerned the Calderóns in Mexico. One of Scotch-born Fanny's letters, rich in colorful detail, inspired him to enlist her eyes and pen. To the Spanish minister, Fanny's husband Ángel, went long letters on myriad subjects related to the Mexican project. "You say I can have a copy of the portrait of Cortés for $200," he wrote. "Could I not get the head and shoulders at half the price?"[31] As helpful contacts in Mexico increased, they took an opposite turn in Spain. Middleton wrote him, "I regret that my departure from this place in the course of August, will prevent my taking part in the researches after Philip."[32] Meanwhile Edward Everett, losing no time in Paris, had found archival officials most cooperative. Even as he learned of 284 bundles of documents at the Hotel Soubise of potential interest to him, the eager historian added, "Should you visit Berlin . . . I shall be obliged by your looking at the collection in the library there."[33]

Exceeding both Calderón and Everett in productive effort, Gayangos reported that some eighteen hundred pages in English, Spanish, and French had been copied, that he planned to visit England's pre-eminent collector of manuscripts, Sir Thomas Phillipps, that soon a trip to Paris, Madrid, the Escorial, and Simancas could be undertaken on Prescott's behalf.

Locally, on occasion, short notes conveyed invitations. From Nahant he wrote bachelor Sumner, "If you cannot do better with the *fair* at a Hotel we will treat you with chowder and Dr. Parkman at two o'clock —and if you are godly you will find a seat in my pew at Church this

[30] Gardiner, ed., *Literary Memoranda,* 2: 56–58; WHP to C. Folsom, August 3, 1840, Folsom papers; and Gardiner, *Prescott and Publishers,* pp. 288, 289.
[31] Wolcott, ed., *Correspondence,* pp. 128–133, 136–139, 146–151.
[32] *Ibid.,* p. 141.
[33] Ticknor, *Prescott,* pp. 366–367, 367–368; and Wolcott, ed., *Correspondence,* p. 161.

morning."[34] Often, however, those who crossed the piazza at Nahant to visit represented the intrusion that prompted resolves: issue and accept fewer invitations; remain upstairs at Fitful Head behind a closed door; do not look out of the window. "I will devise some way another year," he insisted, "or Nahant can be *nae haunt* of mine—as old Stewart used to say."[35] A punning nature surely dissipated some of his irritation.

For years the Prescotts—all of them—had been helping to devise means of completing the Bunker Hill Monument project. In years past the Judge had served as president of the Bunker Hill Monument Association. On occasion Catherine Prescott served on the six-woman Executive Committee of the Ladies' Fair at Quincy Hall which netted thirty thousand dollars for the completion of the monument in 1842. Naturally the historian actively supported the project which so complemented his desire to see his grandfather appropriately honored.

From military affairs of the past to literary affairs of the present, the historian shifted his reflections on Anglo-American relations. Of the latter he wrote Sumner, "It is a hard case for letters here. We are obliged to write a language, which is not spoken around us, are brought before foreign tribunals, tried by foreign laws, while even the venerable authority of British precedent is over-ruled. We have achieved only half our independence."[36]

6

The presidential contest of 1840 between Democratic incumbent Martin Van Buren and Whig general William Henry Harrison affords one of the best glimpses of the political nature of William H. Prescott. Reared in the heady atmosphere of Federalist doctrines, political and economic, William was politically at sea when that party disintegrated. Dead nationally by the early 1820's, Federalism lingered a while longer in Massachusetts, thus postponing the inevitable for the Prescotts. But

[34] *Ibid.,* pp. 145–146; and WHP to C. Sumner, July 31, August 30, 1840, Sumner papers.

[35] Gardiner, ed., *Literary Memoranda,* 2: 59.

[36] Warren, *Bunker Hill Monument Association,* pp. 298, 305, 307, 309, 413, 418; and Gardiner, ed., *Papers,* p. 165.

the close of that decade enabled the Prescotts to know, at least nationally, what they opposed. Andrew Jackson was a bitter pill for the Judge, William, and all other Prescotts. Background and nature stamped the general a radical departure from the traditional gentility and urbanity of his predecessors. Furthermore, his victory elevated the brash young West, a region which both the Judge and his son refused to include in their thinking; indeed, neither ever traveled west of Niagara Falls. Aristocrats, the Prescotts viewed with hostility the sources of Jackson's popularity and power. Add Old Hickory's fiscal policies, and it became natural for the Prescotts to take their places among the opposition. Jackson's battle with the Second Bank of the United States, his designation of Van Buren as his political heir, and the national depression which had enveloped most of Van Buren's presidency focused unusual interest upon the election of 1840.

On September 10, two days before decamping for Pepperell, the historian saw Boston turned topsy-turvy by a procession of approximately 25,000 Whigs, "all full of loyalty to the good cause, and as decorous and orderly as a conventicle of Quakers could have been." In high glee, he continued, "Whiggery is triumphing everywhere." "There is no one who has a stronger claim than Mr. Webster," he wrote Edward Everett. "No one has taken a more active part in the electioneering canvass. It is said he does not want a foreign mission, but would prefer the Secretary of Stateship."[37] Months before the election, William correctly forecast the Whig victory and Webster's appointment. Politics might disgust Prescott, but they did not baffle him.

To Sparks, in Europe, William continued his reportage on American politics, ". . . it is a glorious victory. Though I agree with you a log cabin and hard cider are indifferent qualifications for the presidency."[38]

---

[37] Wolcott, ed., *Correspondence,* p. 162. A unified treatment of Prescott's political outlook, derived solely from published materials, is in William Charvat, "Prescott's Political and Social Attitudes," *American Literature,* 13: (January, 1942): 320–330; and Michael Kraus's "Political Ideas," in Charvat and Kraus, *Prescott: Representative Selections,* pp. ci-cxiii, is similarly restricted in reference to sources.

[38] WHP to J. Sparks, November 25, 1840, Sparks papers.

A quarter of a century after their stanch Federalist outlook of 1815, William and both the older and younger generations of Prescotts were equally stanch Whigs.

Like his affection for the Whigs, the historian's love of children extended far beyond his own household. One special object of his affection was Anna Eliot Ticknor, daughter of George and Anna. Young Anna early came to call him "uncle," and he, to eliminate confusion between Anna the mother and Anna the daughter, called the youngster Anika. More than two years older than Prescott's eldest surviving child, Anika won some affection from him because she was quite close to the age of his deceased Katie. The autumn of the great Whig victory initiated a correspondence with Anika, then seventeen.[39] "My dear Anika," he wrote, "You said you should like to try to make out my writing with my noctograph; so I will give you a specimen of it, and believe, if you can decipher it, you will be qualified to read Egyptian papyri or the monuments of Palmyra."

"But to change the subject," he rambled on, "and take up one which we were speculating upon this morning at breakfast table,— Lord Byron. I think one is very apt to talk extravagantly of his poetry; for it is the poetry of passion, and carries away the sober judgment." Exhausting his views on Byron, Prescott concluded, "When you have made this out, burn it, as a lady would say *Addio*!" Anika deciphered this first letter and Prescott, pleased, wrote another. She and her parents had just returned to Boston from a trip to The Highlands, and his letter brimmed with love of Pepperell:

The bright colors have faded, the naked trees stare around wildly, and, as the cold wind whistles through them, the shrivelled leaves that still hold out rattle like the bones of a felon hung in chains. The autumn seems to be dying, and wants only the cold winding-sheet of winter to close the scene. In fact, she is getting some shreds of this winding-sheet before the time, for, while I am writing, the snow-flakes are dancing before the window. There's a mess of romance for you, all done up in hieroglyphics. When you read Mrs. Radcliffe, or Miss Porter, or Miss ——— any other mumbler of scenery and sentiment, you'll find it all there.

[39] The following picture of Prescott is based upon Ticknor, *Prescott,* pp. 183–185, 187–188.

"I hope your respected father," the forty-four-year-old historian wrote of his forty-nine-year-old friend, "gets on yet without his wig, ear-trumpet, and glasses! By the by, my mother lost her spectacles yesterday. All the town has been ransacked for them in vain. They were a gold pair. Do you think your father carried them off?" He who from boyhood had indulged high humor now set a teenage lady to tittering and giggling.

The successive tests of Anika's ability to read his noctographic writing quickly passed, but Prescott's affection for her never ceased. He evidenced it again the next summer when he wrote to her at Woods Hole. "Has the spirit of improvement," he asked, "beset you in your solitude, . . . or have you been meandering among romances and poeticals? You have read Irving's 'Memoirs of Miss Davidson,' I believe. Did you ever meet with any novel half so touching? It is the most painful book I ever listened to. I hear it from the children, and we all cry over it together." Informing all the Ticknors, through Anika, of the scheduled arrival of certain Prescotts at the Ticknor summer home a week later, he said, "Well, we descend on 'The Hole' on Tuesday next, William Prescott 1st, 2d, and 3d will make the party. Three persons and one name,—just the opposite of my friends the Spaniards, who each have a dozen names at least." Beneath the formal manners and impeccable attire of William H. Prescott, gentleman, was a nature forever young, one that captured and held the affections of children and young people.

### 7

Prescott repaid Bancroft in kind by reviewing the third volume of George's *History of the United States.* Twelve years had elapsed since Prescott's first review of an historical work; and never after this second effort did his diminishing labors as reviewer include another historical title. Whereas the earlier history, Irving's *Conquest of Granada,* drew from him the jealous concern of another laborer in the same vineyard, this second one was purely a generous act of friendship. Bancroft had helped Prescott to the pages of a Democratic publication, so William now helped George onto the Whiggish pages of the *North American*

*Review.* Published shortly after the bitter struggle between Harrison and Van Buren, the volume voted Democratic in a community which, heavily Whig, was toasting the winners, not the losers. Upon concluding his article, Prescott wrote, "As the author of the book and the editor of the journal are at loggerheads, it was rather a ticklish business . . . An even chance—at least—the article—never sees daylight."[40]

To Sparks, mousing out documents in Europe, he confided, "I have written a notice of it for the North, wishing to do Bancroft a good turn, tho somewhat at my own expense for I know as little as may be of the topic. However, I have dealt liberally with the scissors . . . I suppose nobody else here would have done it for an author, who is not in the odour of sanctity among Whigs. But the historian should not be confounded with the politician,—and a friend is a friend."[41]

In the review, as in his correspondence, Prescott praised George's "Many brilliant and spirited sketches."[42] With evident enjoyment, he quoted pages of his friend's treatment of the discovery of the Mississippi by Marquette. Bancroft and Prescott were kindred souls in their delight in spirited passages. Having commended Bancroft's writing unstintingly, he freely expressed his displeasure with the defective presentation of the authorities upon which that writing rested. Neither man ever changed his nature, and Prescott strongly reflected his when he demanded, "We want to see the grounds of his conclusions, the scaffolding by which he has raised his structure; to estimate the true value of his authorities."

One theme which he discussed, the Indians of the eastern United States, possibly appealed to William because of his own concern about Indians, those of pre-Columbian Mexico. Conscious of his limited competence to review Bancroft's volume, he did as many reviewers

---

[40] [WHP], "History of the United States from the Discovery of the American Continent," *North American Review,* 52 (January, 1841): 75–103; and Gardiner, ed., *Literary Memoranda,* 2: 60.

[41] WHP to J. Sparks, November 25, 1840, Sparks papers. For differences between fair copy and noctographic draft, see Wolcott, ed., *Correspondence,* pp. 178–179.

[42] WHP to F. Lieber, November 20, 1840, Lieber papers; and [WHP], "History of the United States," *North American Review,* 52 (January, 1841): 90. The quotations which follow immediately are in *ibid.,* pp. 85, 95.

before and since, he seized upon themes related, however remotely, to his own research. Emphasizing Bancroft's personal relationship to his subject, Prescott could not have meant exactly what he said when he queried, "Who would think of looking to a Frenchman for a history of England; to an Englishman for the best history of France?" After all, this was the period during which the American author of *Ferdinand and Isabella* was increasingly acclaimed in critical and popular circles as "the" historian of Spain.

Likewise insistent upon becoming the historian of Mexico, he resolved, "I *will not furnish another article to the Dean* [Palfrey]— *before 1842.*" Unfortunately this determination did not hasten historical composition, and when the year expired the vexing Introduction was still unfinished. Greeting the new year, he admitted, "My journal is paved, like some other places, with good resolutions."[43] In desperation he nearly revived the idea of working against a forfeit, the goad which he had employed successfully years earlier. Without that incentive, however, he did buckle down and finish the tedious Introduction before the snow melted.

"Corresponding is no sinecure," he reminded himself on March 1, "received last week letters (several) from London—also from Paris—Florence and Mexico, all requiring answers." At the end of April, Jared, returned to America, joined Longfellow, Cornelius Conway Felton, Ticknor, and Palfrey at Prescott's dinner table. The host's note of April 27, reinforcing his earlier invitation, implored Sparks, "Can't you get in by 4—or half past—as I have much to say to you— which would not come so well at table."[44]

In Spain, Middleton had stayed on longer than anticipated and Gayangos likewise in England, both to Prescott's advantage. Learning of the American's interest in Philip II, Gayangos congratulated him and proffered his assistance. From Mexico, Fanny Calderón was penning colorful answers to Prescott's questions. Meanwhile Ángel Calderón de la Barca, still the key to Prescott's Mexican prospects, had

[43] Gardiner, ed., *Literary Memoranda*, 2: 61, 63.
[44] *Ibid.*, p. 65; Wolcott, ed., *Correspondence*, p. 177; and WHP to J. Sparks, April 23, 27, 1841, Sparks papers.

written off the procrastinating Count Cortina and had turned to Lucas Alamán for aid. By this time William, possessor of five thousand pages of manuscript material, cared little about additional basic sources. He was delighted, however, to receive a full-length portrait of Cortés and that conquistador's autograph signature.[45]

On a nonscholarly front, Prescott attuned himself to the booming welcome accorded the arrival of the first British steamer at Boston:

This age [he asserted] may as well be called that of the march of body as of mind. Its true characteristic is the power shown, in making the *material* promote the great interests, moral and intellectual, of humanity. . . . This is the go-ahead age certainly, and the genius of our own people and institutions is remarkably well suited to that of the times; all looking forward, none behind, hoping every thing, believing every thing.

One more American intellectual thus identified himself with the philosophy of automatic progress. William, however, was somewhat ill at ease in changing times:

The exciting conditions of things in a new and changing community like ours, impels us forward [he told Lieber] we have no time to reflect—little to study,—except as this last prepares us to act. Go ahead, is the motto—a confounded uncomfortable one for a quiet, sedentary body, who likes repose in an armchair.[46]

With one correspondent, the historian forewent projects and philosophy for simple friendly exchanges. In mid-winter he wrote Charles Sumner, "I was thrown last week on the ruts, by my horse falling— but got off with a few bruises. This fall has been due some time, as it is more than a year since my last."[47] Many letters, in his own hand, testified to the state of his vision.

In time, the historian established his *modus operandi* for the story of Cortés. Toward that end he had studied accounts of great personal enterprises, including Voltaire's *Charles XII,* Livy's treatment of Han-

[45] C. Harvey Gardiner, "Prescott's Ties with Mexico," *Journal of Inter-American Studies,* 1 (January, 1959): 13–15.

[46] WHP to F. Lieber, November 20, 1840, Lieber papers; and Gardiner, ed., *Papers,* pp. 170–171.

[47] WHP to C. Sumner, January 25, 1841, Sumner papers.

nibal, and Irving's *Columbus*. From all he derived assurance that the historian must be a great painter of pictures of natural scenery. Irving's book, he observed, contained too much material beyond the climax. Taking this to heart, he wrote, "On my plan, I go on with Cortés to his death. But I must take care not to make this tail piece too long, like Irving's."[48] On April 1, 1841, scarcely the day for such seriousness, he projected a timetable: "complete the work in two years and a quarter—*say in July, 1843.*" This promise he fulfilled.

Assessing his historical method, he decided to mark long passages in the materials themselves, thereby restricting his note-taking to short and heterogeneous items. He planned to base his work on two or three principal authorities, garnishing it with collateral and incidental touches from materials drawn from travelers, especially Humboldt. Aiming at probable truth rather than research, and wasting no time on matters of style, he intended to push ahead, always keeping his hero in view. On the subject of footnotes he declared, "The proper object of them and one to which I shall try to confine them is statement of discrepancies in authors, criticism on their manner, remarks illustrating their character and credibility, examination of the *per* and *contra* of a debatable point, explanation of a term in the text, *a citation from an original to corroborate the text.*" Again he intended to register in his memoranda the initiation and conclusion of his work on the text and notes of each chapter.

The first week of April he began to compose the opening chapter of his narrative of the conquest. For weeks all went smoothly, and then he was beset by a haunting fear that he must abridge *Ferdinand and Isabella.*[49]

The same spring that death abridged Harrison's term in the White House witnessed Prescott's one intentional effort to abridge a book. Initially that part of the fifth clause of his contract of May 14, 1838, with Little, Brown and Company which reserved to the historian the right to abridge his first book was just another of those safeguards which neither party to the contract desired or intended to use. Ten

48 Gardiner, ed., *Literary Memoranda*, 2: 67–69; and Wolcott, ed., *Correspondence*, p. 69.

49 Gardiner, ed., *Literary Memoranda*, 2: 69, 70, 71–73.

days later, restudying that agreement and looking to the future, William entertained two ideas. When ultimately the market was saturated with the expensive edition, he might permit, first, an edition of inferior quality for yet another segment of the reading public, and secondly he might abridge the three-volume work. Formulating his thought, he wrote, "It will be worth while, too, to keep my eye on an Abridgment; which may be obtained partly by amputation of notes, introduction, &c. &c., as in the case of the late duodecimo edition of Roscoe's *Lorenzo de Medici.* Irving's abridgment of *Columbus* is managed on another principle, by a condensation; which I suspect I must also, in some degree, resort to."[50] As time demonstrated that Prescott's elegant tastes precluded his reducing the book to the inferior binding, poor print, and shoddy paper of a cheap edition, so time also converted the idea of the abridgment into something more than idle speculation.

In May, 1841, in a manner which remains obscure, he had learned that the very success of *Ferdinand and Isabella* threatened to bring an abridgment of it upon the market from the pen of some hack literary adventurer. To forestall that dismal prospect, he quickly executed another agreement with Little and Brown.

The contract of May 27, 1841, provided for a one-volume abridgment of not less than four hundred pages. Prescott was to provide stereotype plates of the text and three engraved plates, one for a portrait and two for maps. Little and Brown would publish four thousand copies within five years.[51] For the maintenance of standards, a recent Bancroft abridgment served as model in reference to size, paper, and so on. At twenty cents per copy, Prescott's royalties would total eight hundred dollars.

The full measure of his dislike for his task he poured forth to his South Carolina correspondent. "I have undertaken the . . . task, for youth and schools . . .—an infernal job, to pare off the nose and ears and toes of one's own and only begotten, to sweat down the muscles and sinews to a mere skeleton,—an unsightly little abortion of one

---

[50] Gardiner, *Prescott and Publishers,* p. 287; and Gardiner, ed., *Literary Memoranda,* 1: 225.

[51] The text of this contract is in Gardiner, *Prescott and Publishers,* pp. 290–292.

tome 12mo—stunting and dwarfing ideas as well as paragraphs."[52] "Nothing but dire necessity of protecting myself from piracy—as the laws cannot protect me—induces me to do this unnatural work—sweating down my full grown offspring to the size of a pigmy—dwarfing my own conceptions from a manly stature—I trust—to the compass of a nursery capacity!"[53]

While Prescott labored on the abridgment, Aspinwall and Bentley arranged for an English edition of it. As in the earlier London agreement, this one provided for Bentley's assumption of all risks and a fifty-fifty division of profits between publisher and author.[54] Working furiously, Prescott continued his unpleasant job. On July 19, just three and one-half weeks after starting it, the abridgment was finished. Of his method he said, "About one tenth of the volume written *de novo,*— the rest docked, scissored, sweated, headed and tailed. I shied —like a skittish horse at a leap—and find it's a mud puddle only— dirty work however, and I wish the publishers would let it sleep—till some one starts up with a rival abridgment."[55]

In his eagerness to conclude the despised labor, he had overworked. His vision faltered, his body felt weary, and his spirits out of sorts. Quite obviously the man who often loafed so thoroughly that he could drive himself to work only with great difficulty had fallen into another pitfall, too much uninterrupted sedentary labor. He would speedily remedy his overworked state by renewing his social life. Meanwhile, in consultation with Charles C. Little, he reached one firm decision: the abridgment would never be printed until a poacher actually moved into the market. If and when that occurred, Prescott could obtain stereotype plates for his abridgment and get the work out within three weeks. The poacher never appeared and neither did Prescott's abridgment.[56]

---

[52] Gardiner, ed., *Papers,* p. 176.

[53] Gardiner, ed., *Literary Memoranda,* 2: 73.

[54] The text of this contract is in Gardiner, *Prescott and Publishers,* p. 293; and R. Bentley to WHP, August 7, 1841, Prescott papers.

[55] Gardiner, ed., *Literary Memoranda,* 2: 74–75.

[56] Gardiner, *Prescott and Publishers,* p. 292; and also see chap. VII, n. 36.

8

Nahant and the abridgment led Prescott to Woods Hole and the Ticknors. Intellectually exhausted and socially starved, he keenly anticipated the visit. But first, on Sunday, August 1—George Ticknor's fiftieth birthday—Catherine Prescott celebrated her seventy-fourth birthday at Fitful Head. The following morning from windy Nahant to equally airy Woods Hole, seventy-five miles south of Boston—down where the land runs out between Vineyard Sound and Buzzard's Bay —went three male Prescotts: the Judge, hale at seventy-nine, the forty-five-year-old historian, and William Gardiner Prescott, then between fifteen and sixteen and, like his father at that age, ready for Harvard.

Rustic and secluded—just as Prescott intended The Highlands and Fitful Head—Woods Hole contributed a delightful interlude to an otherwise hot and hectic summer. Teenagers Will and Anika played and loafed together; William strolled and conversed with his father and George and chatted with Anna—nothing spectacular, merely that refreshing harmony of kindred spirits, like interests, and common aspirations, however uncommon the Ticknor-Prescott way of life. The short visit admirably fulfilled Prescott's resolve, "I mean to date health and spirits and renovated industry from the visit to 'Wood's Hole.' "[57]

Upon his return to Nahant, he determined to stave off any threatened deluge of visitors, the better to resume his Mexican project. "Emulate April and May" became his slogan, and he produced two chapters before leaving Fitful Head the first week in September.

At Pepperell he tackled the last chapter of Book II with a new modus operandi. To reduce the taking of notes and thereby save time, he proposed to read and mark his staple authority, Bernal Díaz, and to establish a scale of reference to other authorities for prominent events, taking notes only on passages that differed from or added to Díaz' account. As he lessened his research and leaned heavily on a single source, William freely admitted, "The above modus operandi will answer only for direct narrative." Applying this technique, he wrote a

[57] Ticknor, Prescott, p. 188.

chapter in less than a week. As he warmed to his work, he sensed that his book was swelling from two to three volumes.[58]

This rapid progress continued. The following week he composed the first chapter of Book III, which he described as "full of the picturesqu*ee*—reads very like Miss Porter—rather boarding-schoolish finery I am afraid. But the *tierra caliente* without flowers would be—a garden without roses." That chapter points up his heavy dependence upon Díaz, the rich details offered by Fanny Calderón, collateral tidbits drawn from travel accounts, and his awareness of the general histories treating the subject. Seeking to improve a successful method, William declared, "I can save labor equally well however—by taking *no notes* from the *one or two leading authorities,* which only mark, and note the *discrepancies &c &c.* in the *others."*

The second week of October the Ticknors made their annual trek to The Highlands, and despite the attention and time given them, William logged another chapter during their visit. Maintaining a remarkable tempo, he observed, "have *read, written and corrected 27 pages print in 7½ days* exactly . . . The *mere composition* of the Text of these two chapters occupied *2½ days* exactly, or *about 10 pages print per diem."*[59] Never had he worked so rapidly.

That summer and autumn, at the shore and in the country, Prescott, in addition to curbing his social activity, gained better control over his mountainous correspondence. For the Calderóns in Mexico, destitute and scheduled to be superseded diplomatically, it was nearly the end of the line. Ángel toyed with the idea of translating Prescott's unfinished work. William, citing the lack of a Spanish edition of his first book, wrote, "I should be glad indeed if you had leisure and inclination to put their Catholic Highnesses into a Castilian costume."[60] As a translator, however, Ángel never produced anything. To Fanny, William continued the epistolary flow of social trivia and questions related to his work. "Could you not specify a bird or two, with their effect on the

[58] Gardiner, ed., *Literary Memoranda,* 2: 76, 78; and Wolcott, ed., *Correspondence,* p. 245.

[59] Gardiner, ed., *Literary Memoranda,* 2: 78, 79.

[60] Wolcott, ed., *Correspondence,* p. 230, 240.

eye? You see I want to dip my pencil in your colours—the colours of truth, gently touched with fancy, at least feeling." Edward Everett, soon to serve as the American minister to the Court of St. James, continued in Prescott's service.

When Francis C. Gray, the historian's friend and brother of John, with whom William had journeyed in Europe a quarter of a century earlier, went abroad, he, too, searched out materials, especially portraits suitable for illustrations. The generous Pascual de Gayangos, besides ferreting out more documents, was planning an extended trip to North Africa. "I have decided to put in a safe place certain of my more important valuable manuscripts," he wrote, "and as I think that they can be no safer anywhere than in your hands, I have decided to send them to you (whether you like it or not) to keep for me until I ask for their return." However, Gayangos' idea of going to North Africa, motivated partly by his unfortunate finances, was countered by Prescott, who requested the Spanish scholar to superintend the collection of materials in Paris, Brussels, London, and Spain, for his Philip II project. Pascual acquiesced.[61]

In America, meanwhile, the publication of John Lloyd Stephens' *Incidents of Travel in Central America, Chiapas and Yucatan* meant two things to Prescott: increased respect for pre-Columbian civilizations in America and the establishment of another meaningful friendship.

As autumn waned and packing loomed at Pepperell, William rejoiced in his achievement. At The Highlands he had written material equal to about 120 printed pages. His joy was tempered, however, by the prospect which he phrased, "But *Boston*—the word includes a thousand obstacles."[62]

---

[61] WHP to E. Everett, December 29, 1841, E. Everett papers; and Wolcott, ed., *Correspondence*, pp. 231–232, 254–255, 256, 257–258, 259–261, 268.

[62] *Ibid.*, pp. 240–243, 257; and Gardiner, ed., *Literary Memoranda*, 2: 79.

IX

*Y con mis ojos oygo hablar los muertos . . .*

THEY INVADED HIS TIME, especially increasing his correspondence, but the numerous honors tendered Prescott greatly pleased him. Significant and trifling, from far and near, they attested his expanding popularity and reputation. When, on April 20, 1838, the American Philosophical Society elected him to membership, he received one of the earliest and most important of his American honors. As became a habit, he acknowledged it by sending a copy of his history to the Society. The first local honor, election to membership in the Massachusetts Historical Society, also came in 1838. Then and later that scholarly body included many of his cronies, and although he seldom attended meetings during the ensuing decades, he always treasured his identification with the Society. The lasting proof of that regard was the portion of his will which bequeathed one of his most treasured mementos to the Society.[1] Many other state historical societies quickly

[1] American Philosophical Society, *Proceedings of the American Philosophical Society* (Philadelphia, 1840), 1: 11–13. A partial view of Prescott's relations with the Massachusetts Historical Society may be seen in Massachusetts Historical Society *Proceedings,* 2 (1835–1855); 110, 112, 113–115, 117, 129, 132, 147, 182, 245, 265, 312, 347–348, 368, 372, 375, and 3 (1855–1858): 33, 63, 154; and Gardiner, ed., *Papers,* p. 403. For general background for the interval treated in this chapter, see Gardiner, ed., *Literary Memoranda,* 2: 79–120.

honored Prescott with honorary memberships, among them Rhode-Island Historical Society, New-York Historical Society, New-Hampshire Historical Society, and the Georgia Historical Society.[2] Another Massachusetts honor came when the American Antiquarian Society elected William to membership. Soon the librarian's report on recent acquisitions carried the note "Prescott's beautiful History of the Reign of Ferdinand and Isabella, deposited by that gentleman himself."[3]

After recounting some of his honors, Prescott confided to Arthur Middleton, "There is one academic honour however which I do covet, and of which I should avail myself. I mean that of being a Member of the Royal Academy of History of Madrid. This would obviously be of great advantage in facilitating my access to its literary stores." Six weeks later Navarrete informed Calderón of the American's election to the Academy. Couching this success and honor in his memoranda, he wrote, "It secures to me, I am informed, the *right* of access to any and all MSS. in its possession."[4] A citizen of a region which long had fought over the diplomatic distinction between right and privilege in reference to the North Atlantic fisheries, Prescott was understandably happy to exchange privilege for right in reference to his use of certain manuscript riches in Madrid.

Next to Spain, Italy had constituted a basic theme in *Ferdinand and Isabella* and next to the Spanish honor, in this period, Prescott treasured his diploma from the Royal Academy of Sciences of Naples. Reveling in Count Camaldoli's statement that *Ferdinand and Isabella* had placed "Signor Prescott nel primo rango de piu grandi istorici," William added, "This will do for *pulcherisma Italia.*"[5]

From literary societies on the American collegiate scene came more recognition. The Gorthean Literary Society of Marshall College, Mer-

[2] Notifications of these honors, dated October 12, 1838, March 12, June 29, and July 9, 1839, are in the Prescott papers.

[3] American Antiquarian Society, *Proceedings of the American Antiquarian Society, 1812–1849* (Worcester, 1912), pp. 367–385.

[4] The pattern of Prescott's presentation copies in Spain is developed in Gardiner, "Prescott obsequia sus libros," *Historia Mexicana,* 8 (January-March, 1959): 305–308. See also Wolcott, ed., *Correspondence,* p. 63; and Gardiner, ed., *Literary Memoranda,* 2: 39.

[5] *Ibid.,* p. 50.

cersburg, Pennsylvania, enrolled Prescott as an honorary member because he had "done so much to elevate the character of American literature." At Rutgers the Peithessophian Society elected him to honorary membership. The American Whig Society of the College of New Jersey, at Princeton, added Prescott's name to its roll.[6]

In addition to memberships in societies and academies, the historian received several honorary degrees. Columbia College of New York conferred the first one, a doctorate of laws, in the autumn of 1840. The College of William and Mary likewise honored him with an LL.D., in July 1841. At South Carolina College, Francis Lieber initiated the movement which, six months later, on December 20, 1841, yielded an honorary degree of LL.D. to the absent author.[7]

Under mounting honors Prescott wavered and then repudiated his insistence that none would ever be employed by him. Concerning his membership in the Royal Academy of History in Spain, he said to Bentley, "If it would help the sale of the book, you can stick it on my name. Otherwise not."[8] Bentley employed that and other honors; and soon Prescott, ever in pursuit of uniformity in his English and American editions, also saw them on American title pages.

2

In Boston, Prescott had Cortés and his men marching briskly into the interior of Mexico—"39 pages in 15 days, not bad for the giddy town where I have been spinning about in dances and dinners, *plus quam suf.*" Never satisfied for long with his research methods, he observed, "My way has been lately to go over a large mass in my mind—over and over—till ready to throw it on paper—*then* an

[6] The Gorthean Literary Society of Marshall College to WHP, June 26, 1840, Prescott papers; and notifications of the New Jersey honors, dated October 29, 1840, and September 30, 1841, respectively, in the Prescott papers.

[7] Trustees Minutes, September 7, and October 5, 1840, Columbia College, Columbiana Library, Columbia University; H. L. Ganter to C. H. Gardiner, July 11, 1960, contains information derived from the Faculty Minutes of the College of William and Mary; WHP to C. Folsom, March 22, 1842, Folsom papers; F. Lieber to College Board of Trustees, November 23, 1840, The South Caroliniana Library, University of South Carolina; Gardiner, ed., *Papers*, pp. 176, 183–184; and E. L. Inabinett to C. H. Gardiner, September 16, 1960.

[8] Gardiner, ed., *Papers*, p. 182.

effort rather of memory than creation." This technique sped his writing and reduced the demands upon his eyes.

Soon the society which he had hoped to avoid absorbed him. Lord Morpeth impressed the historian as "a beautiful specimen of British aristocracy, in mind and manners."[9] Likewise welcome as elegant representatives of Britain were the Lyells. Charles Lyell, the geologist, was offering a series of lectures for the Lowell Institute; his beautiful wife Mary was conquering Boston society with her charm and grace. Among her conquests was William H. Prescott. The nobleman, the geologist, and the geologist's wife—all quickly became correspondents and later Prescott would visit them in England.

The dawning new year brought from bookdealer Obadiah Rich an unpublished sonnet by Francisco Gómez de Quevedo y Villegas which Prescott copied into his memoranda. The opening lines read:

> Retirado en la paz destos desiertos
> Con pocos pero doctos libros juntos
> Vivo con el comercio de difuntos
> Y con mis ojos oygo hablar los muertos.[10]

After bestowing attention upon Charles Dickens, his dinner guest on February 5, the historian resolved to stick to his work, at least until May 4, his birthday. The first month he wrote two chapters, totaling forty-seven pages. Early spring was brightened by a letter from novelist Maria Edgeworth which the Ticknors shared with him. "It [*Ferdinand and Isabella*] is of great consequence both to the public and private class of readers,—and he will surely have readers of all classes . . . The work will last," Edgeworth wrote. To this Prescott added, "I never worked for the dirty lucre. Am I not right in treasuring up such golden opinions from such a source?"[11]

Never one to visit archives in person, Prescott was brought closest to the basic sinews of history by the unique records that Gayangos

[9] Gardiner, ed., *Literary Memoranda,* 2: 80, 81.

[10] Wolcott, ed., *Correspondence,* p. 278; and Gardiner, ed., *Literary Memoranda,* 2: 82.

[11] *Ibid.*, pp. 82, 84–85, 86. An earlier estimate of *Ferdinand and Isabella* by Edgewood is in Augustus J. C. Hare, ed., *The Life and Letters of Maria Edgeworth,* 2 vols. (Boston and New York, 1895), 2: 632.

loaned him. Yet nothing whetted his interest more than the prospect of chronicles and memoirs. Characteristically he wrote Gayangos, "I have always found a good gossiping chronicle or memoir the very best and the most fruitful material for the historian."[12] Meanwhile several of his aides were no longer in their accustomed places: Fanny and Ángel Calderón de la Barca had sailed from Mexico, Arthur Middleton had finally left Madrid, and Friederich Wilhelm Lembke, *persona non grata* to Spanish authorities, had been forced out of Spain. Most active then in Spain on Prescott's behalf was Valentín Carderera, who occupied himself with illustrative materials.

After reading Longfellow's most recent publication, the historian wrote his friend, "I am too much your debtor for the beautiful poems you have just published not to express my pleasure to you." He considered the hexameters least impressive, adding, "our language is not nicely enough modulated for them." Highest praise he meted out to several ballads, including "Skeleton" and "Hesperus," in which he enjoyed the antique coloring.[13]

His New Year's Day note to Sumner was as sincere as it was short. "I reciprocate your kind wishes, my dear Sumner, with all my heart; and sincerely hope that every New Year may add new strength to our Friendship." Heterogeneous interests drew William and Charles together. In the manner of backyard gossips they kept abreast of the American travels of Lord Morpeth and Charles Dickens; and Prescott became one of many solicitous about Sumner's health. Short, personal, and wholly in his own hand, William's notes to Charles illumine the effervescent and casual in his nature.[14]

### 3

Two reasons inspired as many trips to New York City in the spring of 1842. Historical labors and Washington Irving's imminent departure as minister to Spain prompted the first trip; resort to Dr.

---

[12] Wolcott, ed., *Correspondence,* p. 307.

[13] *Ibid.,* pp. 264–276, 283–284; Samuel Longfellow, ed., *Life of Henry Wadsworth Longfellow,* 3 vols. (Boston, 1893), 1: 412; and [Anon.], "Ballads and other Poems," *North American Review,* 55 (July, 1842): 114–144.

[14] WHP to C. Sumner, January [blank], March [blank], May [blank], 1842, Sumner papers.

Samuel Mackenzie Elliott, the oculist, accounted for the second journey. While administering to intellectual tastes and physical disability, the historian was agreeably engulfed in a sea of social activity.

Early in April Prescott hurried to Manhattan to meet and chat with Irving and to ask his aid in Spain. The two writers, one long famous and the other recently acclaimed, met at the home of their mutual acquaintance, the Reverend Jonathan Wainwright. Three years William's senior, Wainwright had graduated from Harvard in 1812. College and postcollege years had welded a fast friendship, as Porcellians and as members of Club. Between 1834 and 1837 William, when worshiping with Susan at Trinity Church, had heard his friend in that Boston pulpit. Wainwright's hospitality enabled Prescott to have six hours one evening with Irving. Conversation embraced many things, but it pivoted on the projects of the moment, Prescott's studies in Spanish history and Irving's pursuit of materials for a biography of Washington. The New Englander enjoyed the New Yorker immensely, declaring, "Found him delightful, and what is rare—they say— *wide awake*. He promises to aid me in my applications."[15] His purpose served so admirably, Prescott hurried back to Boston, but not before Wainwright effected a brief meeting between him and Dr. Elliott. The popular Scots oculist, then slightly more than thirty years of age, confidently insisted that he could help the historian's vision.

In Boston, Prescott pondered Dr. Elliott's sanguine words. He inquired widely about the oculist and, curiosity countering doubt, he packed for a second trip to New York.

On April 26, between 12:30 and 1:45, Prescott submitted to a thorough eye examination. Studying the left eye, the one injured at Harvard, Dr. Elliott concluded that it suffered from "a paralysis of the nerve which covers much of the retina with a deposit of "lymph," complicated by the affected state of the vitreous humour about the iris. Believing that the paralysis resulted from interrupted circulation, not decay of the organ, he said that he could counteract it with six months of treatment, the first six weeks of which must be directly under his

---

[15] Gardiner, ed., *Literary Memoranda*, 2: 87; and Gardiner, ed., *Papers,* pp. 187–189. The quotations that follow closely are in *ibid.*

hands. Such treatment, he believed, would result in stronger and clearer vision from that eye—enough that Prescott might see words but not sufficient to permit regular reading. To the historian, any benefit that fell short of use of the eye in his studies was not worth the time and effort.

The right eye, Elliott's examination disclosed, suffered from both iritis and retinitis, inflammation of both the iris and the retina. Retinitis, the more serious of the complaints, must be carefully guarded against because it might lead to blindness. Rheumatism, colds, excessive use, a trio of William's oldest enemies, contributed to retinitis, which, through successive attacks, would gradually undermine his vision. As with every other doctor, Boston's Dr. Jackson and London's Sir William Adams included, this examination coupled vision with general health.

Dr. Elliott's hope to strengthen Prescott's right eye included treatments by him and a full-year regimen of internal medicines and external unguents. If the historian successfully completed this program, the oculist believed that the right eye would better withstand light and could even serve for reading in the evening. Under no circumstance, however, did he believe that Prescott could obtain five to six hours daily use from it. In fine, a year of successful treatment might obtain some evening study time. This scarcely appealed to William, who reminded himself, "The loss of the evening is, perhaps, a benefit, as a check on my over-use." He thus reinforced his love of family reading, Club, and all else that evenings meant to him with the truth that his living had to be balanced to maintain the general health so important to his vision.

Dinner at Wainwright's that evening, presumably a finale to New York, proved prelude to a delayed departure and his thorough immersion in New York society. Among those who met Prescott at Wainwright's party were Henry Brevoort, George Griffen, John C. Hamilton, Henry Carey, and Philip Hone. Diarist Hone, describing the Prescott of that evening, wrote, "a handsome man . . . of intellectual appearance, good manners, agreeable conversation, and much vivacity."[16] To the historian's room at the Carlton House the following morning came five invitations to dinner.

Committed to additional days in New York, Prescott dutifully reported all to Susan. "The city," he wrote, "is a dirty-fied London. If it were not for the rains and the pigs there would be no stirring."[17] Yet even as he struck this condescending pose of the proper Bostonian, he was meeting New Yorkers whose friendship he treasured. If the frequency and fulness of his letters constituted reasons why Susan stayed contentedly at home while her husband traveled, she was not disappointed. "Shall I give you an account of how the time goes?" he wrote. Rising about 8 A.M.—very late for him—he breakfasted, wrote his wife, and about 10 A.M. ventured forth to see the city for about an hour and a half. During the afternoons, until about 4 P.M., he made visits. Then, after dressing, he dined out, sometimes going on to another party the same evening. Usually he returned to the Carlton House about midnight—also very late for him. Lavish tables demanded the utmost self-discipline. But in this interval which required no reading and little writing, he indicated, "My eyes stand it beautifully."

One treasured experience was a call upon eighty-year-old Albert Gallatin. Prescott remembered having visited him a quarter century earlier in Paris when the great man was the American minister to France. After chatting amiably with the guest whom Wainwright had brought and introduced, Gallatin abruptly exclaimed. "What Mr. Prescott is it?" When the clergyman identified the historian, Gallatin bounded from his chair, hurried across the room, and pumped his visitor's hand. "I shan't tell you," he wrote Susan, "what things he said about that immortal work of ours." Gallatin and Prescott talked of Toltecs, Aztecs, and other Mexican subjects, establishing the tie which later correspondence maintained.

In time, his experience mounting, Prescott summarized his impressions of New York society, comparing it with that of Boston. "There is a good deal of difference in New York and Boston society and in the appearance of the houses," he wrote. "The rooms are larger, much

[16] Allan Nevins, ed., *The Diary of Philip Hone 1828–1851,* 2 vols. (New York, 1927), p. 597.

[17] WHP to S. A. Prescott, April 27, 1842, Prescott papers.

higher, and showily furnished. The dinners more elaborately got up. I have heard little or no politics at table. The talk chiefly anecdotical— in the literary way below us, certainly. The men very attentive to costume—quite troublesomely so." He considered both the men and women of New York overdressed. Ever one to notice pretty feminine faces, he found some to his liking. At the same time he termed the manner of New York women "more free and easy than ours." Of another segment of society he remarked, "The young men are rather too brusque and conceited for my tastes." In summary, he told Susan, "Indeed as characteristic defects of Boston and New York manners— the one are too prim, the other too pert."[18]

Before New York, the demands of friendship had cost the historian days. High regard for political exile Antonio Gallenga (alias Luigi Mariotti), whose lectures he had enjoyed, had led Prescott to review the Italian's *Italy—General Views of Its History and Literature in Reference to Its Present State.* In yet another testimonial to his love of Dante, Petrarch, and Boccaccio, Prescott wrote gracefully rather than critically.[19] Assessing the five-day product, he declared, "thin porridge. Such writing—job writing—can do no credit to the Journal, nor me. I do not find other writers, who find a ready market for their works thus putting on the reviewer's harness. Why should I? I have furnished now six articles—some quite long and elaborate, for Palfrey—who in meantime has sold half his interest in the work. I believe this will do." Jealous of his time, and possibly envious of those years in the mid-1830's when he had done no such writing, Prescott concluded, "In my present mind, I *will never be guilty of another*—except for a friend who has reviewed—*in extenso*—me, and has the folly himself to print a *book*,—and except—one to whom I am under deep obligation,— and I know but one such likely to become an author."[20]

After New York, while cranking himself up for scholarly endeavor,

[18] *Id.* to *id.,* [April 29, 1842], Prescott papers.

[19] WHP to L. Mariotti, April 22, 1839, July 28, October 9, 1840, Ann Mary Brown Library, Brown University; *id.* to *id.,* November 15, 1841, New York Public Library; Wolcott, ed., *Correspondence,* p. 134; and[WHP], "Mariotti's Italy," *North American Review,* 54 (April, 1842) : 339–356.

[20] Gardiner, ed., *Literary Memoranda,* 2: 85.

he found to his surprise that his total of 450 pages for parts II, III, and IV "corresponds to a page with the estimate made before I began the work."[21]

4

Fitful Head was cooler and Prescott, unusually free of dyspepsia, was healthier than usual, but he nonetheless fell into a dawdling mood, or, as he termed it, "one of my imbecile fits of the *far niente*." His will weakening, his resolutions increased. The one that promised the equivalent of three hundred printed pages before his autumn return to Bedford Street hurried him back to his noctograph. Of Cortés and his men he wrote a succession of colorful chapters: of the Spaniards besieged in Tenochtitlán, of Montezuma wounded and dying, of the bloody Spanish retreat of the Sad Night, of the climactic battle of Otumba, of the march to Tlaxcala, and of the reception there of the Spaniards. "And after one day of chewing the cud," he declared, "I should be ready to write."[22] Some of that meditation occurred early in the morning, before arising. At odd hours, as when walking, he tried to fashion and limit the notes which invariably were too long and too numerous. In less than twice as many weeks, he wrote more than six chapters. Good vision, a strong stomach, and the cool air at Nahant were undisguised blessings. His only complaint, a rheumatic pain in his back, stifled neither his intellectual nor his social activity. On August 2, pursuant to an earlier vote, Prescott laid aside his work and entertained Club at dinner. Firm handclasps, tinkling wineglasses, clouds of cigar smoke, rich food, heady conversation—they were worth a day.

To Charles Sumner, that same summer season, he revealed his intention of sidestepping service on the examining committee for history at Harvard, an appointment which President Quincy had made without prior consultation with the historian. "I mourn for the Historic Muse," he told Charles, "But I do not design to be part or parcel of that in Committee—beg—by my Modern Language Committee shot—exempt from all others."[23] The historian plainly did not allow himself to be drawn into Harvard's official business as much as had his father.

[21] *Ibid.*, pp. 88, 89.    [22] *Ibid.*, pp. 89, 90.
[23] WHP to C. Folsom, July 26, 1842, Folsom papers; WHP to J. Sparks,

During the closing days at Nahant, a deluge of visitors, however welcome individually, represented the collective obstacle which led Prescott to rage,

Company—company—company. It will make me a misanthrope. And yet there is something very interesting—and instructive in the conversation of travellers—from distant regions. Last week we had Calderón—just from Mexico,—Stephens from Central America and Yucatan,—Gen. Harlan, from Afghanistan—where he commanded the native troops for many years. But what has it all to do with the "Conquest of Mexico"? I have had the pleasure to make a bargain with the publisher for Madame *Calderón's* Travels—and to afford *Stephens* some facilities for his, in the way of books. We are all labourers in the same soil.[24]

Reflecting a smooth transition to The Highlands, Prescott soon was writing, "As I charge valiantly over hill and dale in my morning rides, I fight over in fancy many a stout battle with the Aztecs." At Pepperell he established a new record of three and one-half pages per day, reading and writing included. Nahant had been good but not that good. "An acre of grass and old trees is worth a wilderness of ocean," was the historian's way of distinguishing between them. After putting down a chapter at the rate of three and one-fifth pages daily, he mused, "A country life would enable me to turn off as much as any regular bookwright."[25] The achievement at Pepperell led him to toy with the idea of lengthening his season there. "Shall I not some time or other make it cover from April to Thanksgiving season?"[26] But Prescott, a creature of habit, never did extend the season at The Highlands.

## 5

Late in the summer of 1842 William Gardiner Prescott—"Will" to

---

July 26, 1842, Sparks papers; and Gardiner, ed., *Papers,* p. 194. For years Prescott had served on the Examining Committee for Modern Languages, and he continued to do so.

[24] Gardiner, ed., *Literary Memoranda,* 2: 93–94.

[25] WHP to Lord Morpeth, September 19, 1842, Lord Carlisle papers, Castle Howard, Yorkshire; Gardiner, ed., *Literary Memoranda,* 2: 95; and WHP to C. Sumner, September 11, 17, 1842, Sumner papers.

[26] Gardiner, ed., *Literary Memoranda,* 2: 95–96.

family and friends—was returning for his second year at Harvard, under his father's surveillance. During his first year in Cambridge Will had fallen in with collegians whose carefree natures and unstudious dispositions matched his own. Some of his behavior might be catalogued as chip off the old block, because it smacked of his father's early collegiate career. Will returned to Cambridge, accompanied by firm, full regulations, copies of which both father and son had for ready reference. That ruinous first year inspired the underscored injunction, *"I never will pay a bill for any object, necessary or not, in Cambridge or Boston without it is contracted with my previous knowledge and approbation."* Lest uncertainty invite Will's misuse of discretion, his father left little to his imagination. "I am willing to pay for your *shoe shining, fire-making, your washing, your oil*; also, for *your clothes when I am asked about them first.* For all else, I make you what I intend to be an adequate allowance." To encourage method and responsibility in his not-yet-seventeen-year-old son, he continued, "I would advise you by all means to keep a cash book, in which you may set down *every cent* you expend and for what. I have done it for a great many years."[27]

Weeks passed, and Will's unaccustomed punctuality and method again yielded to indolence and academic troubles. By February 1843 he had been suspended. Disappointed and grieving, the historian was again firm. To win re-entry into his class, Will was sent to Boylston, near Worcester, to study under Reverend Sanford. "During your suspension," father wrote son, "your allowance will be 50 cents a week, and I shall pay no bills of any description."[28] From Reverend Sanford the historian expected fortnightly reports on Will's studies and conduct.

The elder son's banishment provoked correspondence. Elizabeth, then nearing fifteen and variously called Lizzie and Bessie by intimates, showered Will with social tidbits: the parties which she attended along with her guest Martha Peabody; the fact that "Father has just snatched his pen out of my hand"; the bright memory of blind-

[27] Gardiner, ed., *Papers,* pp. 194–195.

[28] WHP to W. G. Prescott, November 14, 1842, and February 20, 1843, Prescott papers; and Gardiner, ed., *Papers,* pp. 197–199.

man's buff at a recent party; a dinner at Aunt and Uncle Ticknor's; and her box seat at the circus.[29] A typical male, thirteen-year-old Amory hated to write letters. When driven to it, he filled most of his short communications with the lament that the others had already written all the news. Possessed of news of his own making on one occasion, Amory sadly reported, "The other day as I was shooting with my bowgun, I smashed a window . . . and I am deprived of my bow-gun whilst I am in town, so much for braking [*sic*] windows." When Will, given to serious contemplation of his future, announced that he intended to become a lawyer, grandfather and father surely rejoiced. Amory was alone in his phrasing, "I hope you will not turn before you come back."[30]

Upon receipt of a good initial report from Will's tutor, the historian wrote his son, "Do not omit the literary journal, with remarks and criticisms of your own. Exercise your critical powers freely and independently . . . In short, get knowledge. A man may skim through a library and yet get no knowledge, from want of thorough reflection and research." William was leading Will down the path he had blazed for himself in the 1820's.

When melting snow and the promise of spring encouraged their taking the train to Worcester, the historian, Susan, and young Amory visited Will. Indulging one of the appetites which Will possibly had acquired at home, the father had promised, "I shall bring some cigars for you."[31]

6

In the late autumn of 1842, while sternly disciplining a son, Prescott played a special kind of literary godfather for a friend's book, Madame Calderón de la Barca's *Life in Mexico during a Residence of Two Years in that Country.* Years earlier, the historian had sensed that Fanny's colorful accounts of her ranging interests—compounded

[29] E. and W. A. Prescott to W. G. Prescott, February 26, 1843, Prescott papers.

[30] W. A. Prescott to W. G. Prescott, April 17, 1843, Prescott papers.

[31] Gardiner, ed., *Papers,* p. 199; and WHP to W. G. Prescott, April 27, 1843, Prescott papers.

of history and geography as well as contemporary society—might enrich his own undertaking. The diplomat's lady had risen to the occasion, matching Prescott long letter for long letter. Among other things, she described the terrain and enumerated forms of vegetation, adding, "As for the appearance of the country in the *tierra caliente*, you may boldly dip your pen in the most glowing colours."[32] "Many thanks to you, my dear Madame Calderón," he replied, ". . . for the rich description . . . It was what I wanted." Sharing Fanny's love of the colorful, the romantic, and the picturesque, Prescott enriched numerous passages of his *Conquest of Mexico* with materials which she supplied.

Fanny's letters mounted in number and were dispatched to her family in the United States as well as to Prescott. Conjecturing that what had amused and instructed a few might be put before the general public, he induced her to consider publication in book form. Consenting, she deleted numerous derogatory sentiments and reduced the names of persons to mere initials, to comply with her husband's sense of diplomatic propriety.

Prescott then sought publishers for her, at home and abroad. In Boston, Little and Brown gladly undertook the task. In Britain, through Charles Dickens, he contracted with Chapman and Hall, who sent Fanny, via Prescott, £25 for the advance American sheets. Even as they hoped she might produce another book, they also expressed a desire to publish Prescott's next history.[33]

Reviewing Fanny's book, Prescott employed his scissors-and-paste method, crowding half his pages with lengthy quotations which exhibited towns, personalities, scenery, and religious and social activities. "And we may safely assert," he concluded, "that for spirited portraiture of society, . . . for picturesque delineation of scenery, for richness of illustration and anecdote, and even for the fascinating graces of style, no one of them [previous travel books] is to be compared

[32] Wolcott, ed., *Correspondence,* pp. 150, 169. The quotation that follows immediately is in *ibid.*, p. 186.

[33] Gardiner, ed., *Papers,* p. 196; Wolcott, ed., *Correspondence,* p. 329; and Chapman & Hall to WHP, March 3, 1843, Prescott papers.

with 'Life in Mexico.' "[34] To his memoranda, meanwhile, he confided, "Finished yesterday article on Madame de Calderón's *'Life in Mexico,'* —words—words—words—i.e. my article—they fill up however the same space as ideas . . . ."[35]

In his eagerness to insure favorable American reception of the book, Prescott wrote Sumner, "So Madame de Calderón de la Barca is afloat —can't you fill her sails with a gentle puff—in the Courier—a ten liner with an extract or two?"[36]

*Life in Mexico* was on its way to undying fame. Frequently reprinted, translated, and abridged during the century since initial publication, it still possesses an appeal unrivaled by any other travel account of independent Mexico. Doing a bit of everything for the book, Prescott, in large measure, had caused it to be written; had encouraged its formulation as a book; had found publishers for it both in America and England; had penned a brief introduction to it; had encouraged others to review it; and had himself reviewed it—a remarkable demonstration of the lengths to which he could go in the name of friendship. Prescott repeatedly played the role of author's agent for friends, but no other instance ever challenged the completeness of his identification with *Life in Mexico.*[37]

The trifling sum received by Fanny from an English publisher for advance sheets from the American edition of her book reawakened Prescott's concern about copyright. Early in 1843 polite concern yielded to consternation. "I don't understand, by the bye," he wrote Dickens, "how the circumstance of a work appearing here just before it does in London can affect the price of the copyright there. Doesn't

34 [WHP], "Madame Calderon's Life in Mexico," *North American Review,* 56 (January, 1843): 137–170. The quotation that follows immediately is in *ibid.,* p. 170.

35 Gardiner, ed., *Literary Memoranda,* 2: 97.

36 WHP to C. Sumner, [December 23, 1842], Sumner papers.

37 For a unified treatment of Prescott's role as literary agent, see C. Harvey Gardiner, "William Hickling Prescott: Authors' Agent," *Mid-America,* 41 (April, 1959): 67–87; Gardiner, *Prescott and Publishers,* pp. 112, 269–273. Prescott's unsigned preface is in Madame Calderón de la Barca, *Life of Mexico* (Boston, 1843), 1: ii–iv.

the purchase of a copyright protect the English publisher? . . . I am in somewhat of a puzzle."[38]

Dickens carried Prescott's query to Chapman and Hall, from whom the historian received words that shattered both his ignorance and his sense of security. "We beg to say," the publishers wrote, "that we think you will find on enquiry, that no copyright can be maintained here, legally, for a book first printed in America; and that any English publishers may print any work so published."

The importance of the legal position of his works in England quickly mounted, because the very day on which he had exhibited his ignorance to Dickens, Prescott had informed Colonel Aspinwall that his second work was sufficiently advanced that it probably could be offered to an English publisher by June.[39]

7

"I can't write a short one," the historian declared, speaking of letters, "though it were on my death-bed."[40] Beyond the natural loquacity which easily converted a brilliant conversationalist into a wordy correspondent, several other circumstances contributed to their length. For one thing, as in letters to Gayangos, Greene, Aspinwall, Bentley, Sparks, Everett, Middleton, and others, he often introduced a multiplicity of subjects into a single letter—family affairs, Boston society, and American politics as well as matters related to his intellectual pursuits. A second factor derived from the means of conveyance: letters incurring no postage charges in diplomatic pouches encouraged writing at length; and when he paid postage, his economical nature dictated the use of all available space.

Adjusting to Boston, "this whirligig place," as he worked off his correspondence, he gradually slipped into his historical harness. The week before Christmas, as he concluded Cortés' gory siege operation, he wrote more rapidly than ever before, composing the equivalent of nine printed pages daily.[41] Early in the new year he must write the

[38] Wolcott, ed., *Correspondence*, pp. 316, 323, 329–330.

[39] Chapman & Hall to WHP, March 3, 1843, Prescott papers; and Wolcott, ed., *Correspondence*, p. 330.

[40] Gardiner, ed., *Literary Memoranda*, 2: 96.

[41] *Ibid.*, p. 97.

post-1521 career of Cortés, arrange the Appendix, compose bibliographical notes, revise the entire manuscript before turning it over to
the printer, and execute a printing contract. The better to pursue various portions of this labor simultaneously, he renounced the "wining,
and hot-watering—gadding—gossiping" with which he had ushered
in 1843.[42]

The experienced publisher at Eight New Burlington Street, London, knew a good thing and desired another from his successful
American author. The third English edition of *Ferdinand and Isabella*
was selling in the steady fashion that forecast a fourth edition. The
history was becoming a classic, and, in addition to making money, it
lent artistic and scholarly luster to the publishing house of Richard
Bentley. In the autumn of 1842, Bentley had sent the historian a copy
of one of his latest publications, J. S. St. John's *The Manners and
Customs of the Ancient Greeks*, a title that meant nothing to Prescott's
research. For the publisher, however, it served as an entree, permitting
the letter in which he asked about the new history. Among publishers
the technique of the gift-query was an old one, one which Bentley
would employ many times in his relations with Prescott. Although he
held Bentley at arm's length by insisting that his project would drag
on for months, the historian also whetted the publisher's desire.

"The story is so full of marvels, perilous adventures, curious manners, scenery etc. that it is more like a romance than a history," he
wrote, "and yet every page is substantiated by abundance of original
testimony. If I have not done it in a very bungling style it ought to be
taking with children as well as grown people."[43]

Eloquent proof of Prescott's diligence in January 1843 was his fore-
going the pleasure of Club, to which, nonetheless, he contributed
"half a dozen bottles of Sherry—some I received from Ticknor twenty
years since when it was nearly twenty years old—so it is high time it
should receive the *coup de grace*."[44]

---

[42] WHP to C. Sumner, [December 26, 1842], Sumner papers; and Gardiner, ed., *Literary Memoranda*, 2: 98.

[43] R. Bentley to WHP, November 29, 1842, Prescott papers; and Wolcott,
ed., *Correspondence*, p. 328.

[44] Gardiner, ed., *Papers*, p. 197.

Serious thought concerning the publication of his second history produced a torrent of questions for Aspinwall. Deepening doubt about the wisdom of doing business with Bentley led to a willingness to consider any publisher and either outright sale or a half-profits agreement. Months passed before contract negotiations got seriously underway. Meanwhile Prescott, leaving Book VII untouched, wrote numerous bibliographical notes and corrected, with generous assists from the Ticknors, books I–VI inclusive. Sumner also cast a critical eye over the thick manuscript.

To calculate more accurately the stereotyping, another appraisal took place. The physical make-up of *Ferdinand and Isabella* understandably represented the model to be matched. Satisfied with binding, paper, length of line, and much else, Prescott nonetheless made some alterations in the specifications of his second history. For example, he now planned thirty-one rather than thirty-two lines of text per page, and increased the leading between lines in the notes. Since it carried his first appendices, this history received special attention on that score. To all this, Edmund Burke Otis, Prescott's reader-secretary since the autumn of 1842, contributed greatly. High regard from the Cambridge establishment prompted another contract for stereotyping by Metcalf, Keith & Nichols.

As the historian arranged for publication in America, John Lloyd Stephens was most responsible for his shift from Little and Brown to Harpers. Stephens' book on Central America, published in 1841, had been physically attractive, intellectually exciting, and financially successful. When his two-volume *Incidents of Travel in Yucatan* made its bow from the Harpers' press, the author sent a copy to Prescott and regaled him with the advantages of the big New York house. Stephens struck even deeper and more responsive chords when he mentioned Harpers' superior distributive capacity. To Stephens, playing go-between, the Boston author detailed his desires. Plumbing the market potential of the *Conquest of Mexico*, its author felt it could be "published in both a handsome and a cheaper form at the same time." "I think also," he told Stephens, "the Abridgment of the work hereafter will make a popular book for schools, Etc." Hopeful that the three-volume work might retail at six dollars, Prescott sought one dollar and fifty cents per copy for himself. Coupled with that basic figure was his hope that the Harpers publish eight thousand to ten thousand copies within four years. He promised stereotype plates resembling those for *Ferdinand and Isabella.* The better to know how to treat with Little and Brown, to whom he felt an honorable obligation, Prescott desired to obtain any proposition that the Harpers cared to make.[45] Once Stephens relayed Prescott's thinking to the Harpers, he stepped aside while publisher and author dealt directly with each other.

"We shall be happy to publish your 'Conquest of Mexico,' and pay you one dollar and fifty cents per copy, on all that we may sell, for the use of the stereotype plates, engravings, and copyright," the Harpers quickly wrote. Accepting also the author's ideas on format and price, they indicated an anticipated sale of twelve to fifteen thousand copies in four years. Little and Brown could not match, much less exceed, these terms. One month after Stephens had opened the matter, the historian mailed a signed contract, dated April 25, to New York. "The terms," Prescott declared, "are princely—such as no other house could afford."[46] For a Bostonian contemptuous of New York City, it was no snap decision.

While thus coming to terms with one publisher and continuing to read ten sheets of proof daily from the new stereotype plates, the historian reached an understanding with his agent in England. He and Aspinwall preferred either Murray or Longmans to Bentley; but they also sensed that a switch from Bentley would jeopardize future income from *Ferdinand and Isabella.* An angry Bentley might even publish a competitive edition of the new book. Suspicions and preferences to the contrary, everything dictated that Bentley be given first consid-

---

[45] Wolcott, ed., *Correspondence,* pp. 330–331, 341–343; and WHP to C. Sumner, January [1843], Sumner papers.

[46] Gardiner, ed., *Papers,* pp. 200–201; WHP to Harpers, draft, April 25, 1843, Prescott papers; and Gardiner, ed., *Literary Memoranda,* 2: 99. The text of this contract, initially thought lost in the Harper fire of 1853, has been located in the company's files by vice-president Eugene Exman. His cooperation, which has included photographic copies of this and other agreements with Prescott, is gratefully acknowledged. This negotiation, like every other Prescott contract in America, contradicts the statement, "Every major publisher in the country bid for Prescott's works ..." (William Charvat, *Literary Publishing in America 1790–1850* [Philadelphia, 1959], p. 74).

eration. If he refused to offer to buy the new work outright, Aspinwall would turn to other houses.

"If you expect five or six hundred pounds," the Colonel advised, "you must begin by asking a thousand or more." Hoping to realize between £450 and £600 on the outright sale of the work, Prescott realistically faced the copyright confusion. "I ought if I could give a good copyright to get £1000," he told Aspinwall. The historian continued to express his ideas to the Colonel, but he put his affairs completely in the hands of his agent, writing, "I wish you . . . to act in the matter as you would for yourself."[47]

Busy though he was with agent, printer, and publishers, Prescott had time for other men and matters. His failure to see Sumner for some weeks led him to write, "What the devil has become of you? Are you buried in that musty office like a toad in a hole? You will be disinterred some future day—stiff and stark—and geologists will speculate on your withered remains—as they do sometimes on those of a toad found in the middle of a rock." Headier matters crowded the letters to and from Gayangos.[48] Liberally mixing work and play, Prescott, meanwhile, was often in society.

Even as he immersed himself in plans for the concluding section of his history, he wrote, "I hope this biographical sketch of the Conqueror will not appear tame after the grand battle crash of the Conquest itself." Two chapters of it were on paper when he hurried to New York where, on June 13, he met the Harpers in force for the first time. Previously he had known only Fletcher Harper, the brother who had come to Boston to discuss matters with him.

The meeting at the Harpers' establishment, which was mammoth enough to impress anyone, resulted in a publishing timetable. To get the work out by November, they needed everything before October 15, a date which seemed neither unreasonable nor inconvenient. Tempering his admiration of Harpers' forthrightness and daring, Prescott early adopted a measure of caution. "I must be careful," he wrote in

[47] Gardiner, ed., *Papers,* pp. 201–202; and Wolcott, ed., *Correspondence,* pp. 337, 344.

[48] WHP to C. Sumner, March 1. 1843, Sumner papers; and Wolcott, ed., *Correspondence,* p. 334.

his memoranda, "to set down all carefully in black and white—and I anticipate then no misunderstanding."[49] Prompting this course were many factors: his own meticulous nature in business affairs, his awareness via his father of proper legal safeguards, and his knowledge that a variety of charges had been hurled at the Harpers—some by authors.

Amid all the rest, letters went to many men in Europe, but none was a greater pleasure to write than that to H. Eberty, the retired German banker whom historian von Raumer had induced to translate *Ferdinand and Isabella.* While one translation after another had been noised across the Atlantic from Florence, Madrid, and Paris—without the completion of any as yet—this German had quietly performed that task. The author's letter of appreciation also looked to the future. "As to the 'Conquest of Mexico'," he said, "I shall esteem myself very fortunate if you can find it convenient to give that work to the German public."[50]

In London, meanwhile, the publishing pot was boiling. Bentley, quickly learning what Prescott hoped to receive for the new work, announced he would match any other publisher's offer and so urged Aspinwall to canvass other houses. Furious about the ethics of that proposal, Aspinwall engaged in a bitter exchange of notes with the Englishman. Bentley's suggested course of action, if adopted, not only insured him this book but possibly all subsequent works by Prescott as well, because surely no publisher who found himself once used for Bentley's purposes would even make an offer for any future manuscript. In addition to trying to create an unabridgeable chasm between the other houses and Prescott, Bentley also attempted to drive a wedge between author and agent, as when he asked Aspinwall to refer certain matters to the historian. As bitter deadlock set in between publisher and agent, Bentley indicated that he would not pay £1,000 for the work.[51]

Aspinwall quickly turned to other publishers. John Murray proved a

[49] Gardiner, ed., *Literary Memoranda,* 2: 100, 101.

[50] Wolcott, ed., *Correspondence,* pp. 361–362, 365–368; Gardiner, *Prescott —Bibliography,* p. 9.

[51] Gardiner, *Prescott and Publishers,* pp. 65–67; related correspondence is in Wolcott, ed., *Correspondence,* pp. 351–354, 355–356, 357–359.

disappointment, offering to publish only on a half-profits basis. Several days later the Longmans' offer, eagerly tendered, also proved disappointing. Completing the circuit of preferred houses, Aspinwall returned to Bentley.

"I will now beg to inform you," the agent wrote Bentley, "that I am prepared to conclude arrangements with another publisher for the publication of Mr. Prescott's work; and shall do so the day after tomorrow, unless in the meantime, it should suit your views to take the work at six hundred and fifty pounds."[52] Uncertain is the ratio of truth to bluff in the Colonel's words. Rising to the bait, Bentley hurriedly concluded an agreement, promising £650 for the *Conquest of Mexico,* provided that his publication of it preceded the American edition by a fortnight.

8

The season of 1843 at the shore began with resolves about guests, dinners, correspondence, and other distractions. Juggling his problems as historian, Prescott alternately wrote concluding chapters, advanced the stereotyping, worried about a publishing arrangement in London, and reminded himself that he had erred in making the American one prior to completing his manuscript. Making matters worse, he was below par physically, suffering from what proper Bostonians termed the New York grippe. "It has left me feeble—catch-coldy, rheumatick-y, dyspepticalish, altogether below par," he complained. "I will rally now. *Deo volente.*"[53] And rally he did.

Late in July he readied the last pages of Book VII for stereotyping and sought criticism of the entire manuscript. Inviting Will Gardiner's reaction, he wrote, "Should you see any *blunders,* pray note them down. Defects of taste, bad writing &c., &c., must run for luck. The iron law of stereotype forbids change for lighter causes."[54] Gardiner's reading of stereotype rather than raw manuscript severely limited his critical usefulness.

[52] *Ibid.,* p. 365.
[53] Gardiner, ed., *Literary Memoranda,* 2: 102.
[54] Wolcott, ed., *Correspondence,* pp. 363–365, 371–372; Gardiner, *Prescott and Publishers,* pp. 67–69 (the text of this contract is in *ibid.,* pp. 294–297); and Gardiner, ed., *Papers,* p. 206.

"Finished Preface—which since *all* the Text, Notes, Appendix, finished—may be said to end the 'History of the Conquest of Mexico'— my second historical work," he wrote in his memorandum of August 2, 1843.[55] Some stereotyping, as well as the maps, portraits, and index, still required his attention.

While struggling to tidy up these loose ends, Prescott worried about the legal status of the forthcoming book as property. Bentley's insistence upon priority of British publication caused him to wonder whether such an arrangement endangered American copyright. The Judge, though keen of mind and abreast of many legal matters, feared that his removal from practice for a decade and a half did not enable him to resolve his son's dilemma. Accordingly William turned to Sumner.

"Now I should like very much to know what Judge Story thinks in this matter," he wrote. "Whether he supposes that a priority of publication by two or three weeks would shake the copyright of a work here. Could you not ascertain his views—not as a direct opinion—but as it may now strike him—without break of propriety—as a light to guide me?" Story's opinion put William's mind at ease.[56]

That season at Nahant the historian had reduced, but not eliminated, his social activities. One pleasant dinner party brought Consul George Washington Greene, returned from Rome, Lieber, up from South Carolina, and Sumner and his law partner George S. Hillard to the table at Fitful Head. Hillard soon would review the *Conquest of Mexico.*

Before the close of the stay at Nahant, a summary of certain activities prompted new rules. Pleased by his rate of progress in recent months, Prescott pointed to the fact that he had written two and one-half volumes in approximately the same amount of time required by the troublesome Introduction on the Aztec civilization. That newly achieved facility for getting things on paper he wanted to perpetuate. On the subject of contracts, however, he established a massive DON'T for all time. Never again would he contract for the publication of a work

[55] Gardiner, ed., *Literary Memoranda,* 2: 103.
[56] WHP to C. Sumner, July 6, 11, 1843, Sumner papers.

before he had completed the manuscript. It was impossible to estimate the time required for completing projects, and he planned to avoid the wearying pressures to which his second book had subjected him. Before leaving Nahant he prescribed for himself, "3 months of literary loafing." [57]

Mopping up on still another front before retiring to the shades of The Highlands, he sent a check for $150 to Charles Folsom for editorial services. "I beg leave to assure you, however," he wrote the Cambridge Aldus, "that I do not think that a compensation can be made in money for the services of friendship—as I consider yours." Prescott's secret estimate of Folsom's services was less flattering. "Though I have not taken more than one in five of his corrections," he wrote in his memoranda, "I think they are worth the money. If I had taken them all *or nearly all, it would have ruined the book.* For he is hyper-critical, very apt to efface the poetical coloring of the style, for in his severe system, prose should be the antipode of poetry."[58]

The Harvard Commencement of 1843, although not attended by Prescott, had special significance for him. Included among the honorary degrees was his LL.D. It was a season for honoring historians, Sparks and Bancroft receiving the same degree.

Pursued a little more leisurely during his *villeggiatura* at The Highlands, Prescott's correspondence continued as miscellaneous as ever in reference to correspondents, destinations, and subjects. To the Harpers went a copy of *Ferdinand and Isabella,* to serve as model. Discussing maps, plates, and much else, Prescott, in deference to home-town taste, added, "I must request you not to cut the leaves of the copies sent to Boston."[59] To Sumner he spelled out his literary loafing.

As with his first book, he facilitated and awaited the reviews. One set of proofs went to Sumner late in September. "I believe that I mentioned to you, that the Preface and the critique of Solís, at the end of Book the sixth, contain my views on the manner of treating the sub-

---

[57] *Id.* to *id.,* [August, 1843], Sumner papers; and Gardiner, ed., *Literary Memoranda,* 2: 104.

[58] Gardiner, ed., *Papers,* p. 207; and Gardiner, ed., *Literary Memoranda,* 2: 105.

[59] WHP to Harpers, draft, September 17, 1843, Prescott papers.

ject," he wrote. Six years earlier Prescott had written an equally busy George Bancroft a similar letter in which the author, to help a busy friend save time, had pointed out possible approaches to writing the review which he expected from him. Sumner, in turn, convinced William that Theodore Sedgwick Fay might assist him in German archives. Prescott began by asking, "Will Mr. Fay allow one who is personally unknown to him to ask a favour of him?"[60] Once more the historian's charm, scholarship, and contacts added an aide to his roster.

Further thought about his forthcoming book led Prescott to request, through bookdealer James Rich of London, two copies of every English publication carrying a review of the *Conquest of Mexico*. "I wish them for my publisher here," he wrote, "as the opinions of the British press have a considerable influence on the sale of a work."[61] In addition, he asked Rich to dispose of his author's copies of the English edition. Ten presentation copies, for owners of manuscripts, historians, aides, and literary acquaintances, went to Sir Thomas Phillipps, Lady Holland, Samuel Rogers, Lord Morpeth, Henry Hallam, P. F. Tytler, Colonel Aspinwall, Charles Dickens, Edward Everett, and Pascual de Gayangos.

Early in October business interests took the historian and Judge Prescott to Manchester, New Hampshire, to pass a day with William Amory. There the historian's brother-in-law was identified with the textile industry. Although Amory never practiced the law which he had studied in the office of Franklin Dexter and William H. Gardiner, his legal knowledge, coupled with administrative talent and natural charm, marked him for business success. Now the three men combined business and pleasure while surveying the Amoskeag operation.

Gloom overwhelmed The Highlands the morning of October 28, when eighty-one-year-old Judge Prescott suffered a paralytic stroke. Most of the effects, however, soon passed away, but the forty-seven-year-old historian had occasion to reflect, "He has been always a part of myself, to whom I have confided every matter of any moment—on

[60] WHP to C. Sumner, September 14, 25, [Oct. 5], 1843, Sumner papers; Massachusetts Historical Society *Proceedings,* 4 (1858–1860): 415–416; Wolcott, ed., *Correspondence,* p. 398; and Gardiner, ed., *Papers,* p. 212.

[61] Wolcott, ed., *Correspondence,* p. 400.

whose superior judgement I have relied in all affairs of the least consequence . . . I have never read a book of any merit without discussing it
with him; and his noble example has been a light to my steps in all the
chances and perplexities of life." Sumner, knowing nothing of the
gloomy atmosphere, wrote brightly of his reaction to the *Conquest of
Mexico*. "Since I first devoured the Waverley Novels," he told William, "I have read nothing by which I have been so entirely *entraîné;*
sitting at my desk for hours, then trimming my lamp and still sitting
on, and finally with the book under my arm adjourning home, where I
read on until after midnight."[62]

9

The Judge liked to walk. The re-establishment of his health of paramount concern, he walked with greater regularity than usual. At his
side was the historian, enjoying his father's company, the exercise, and
the literary loafing. Accompanied by an occasional lament, days and
weeks were whiled away.

The historian's lethargy scarcely lessened when an English copy of
the *Mexico* arrived. After all, he still awaited the reviews. Mere mention of the *Edinburgh* and the *Quarterly* caused him to wonder and
worry. "Do you think the English Aristarchs will visit the sins of re-
pudiation on a Yankee author?" he wrote T. J. Phillips. "I don't mean
the small craft of critics, who generally sail with the *trade* winds, but
heavy metal gentry."[63] Prescott referred to the hostility against all aspects of American life which had recently crowded English publications. To the caustic views of English travelers who had written books
and to the battle of words among the quarterlies, a new factor had been
added. In the course of the Panic of 1837 English investors had
learned, for the first time, that all was not profit beyond the Atlantic.
When a state such as Pennsylvania repudiated its bonds for a canal

[62] Gardiner, ed., *Literary Memoranda,* 2: 108; Wolcott, ed., *Correspondence,* p. 401. Sumner's praise was not the exaggeration that sometimes passes
between friends, for he expressed himself similarly in a letter to Lord Morpeth,
October 31, 1843, Lord Carlisle papers, Howard Castle, Yorkshire.

[63] Wolcott, ed., *Correspondence,* pp. 406, 413; and Gardiner, ed., *Literary
Memoranda,* 2: 110.

construction program, hard-hit English investors squealed loudly. Witty Sydney Smith's petition to the American Congress on the subject of Pennsylvania's fiscal irresponsibility had received wide publicity in the London *Chronicle* and equally wide support among the English public. William wondered whether such unrelated matters would color English criticism of his book.

In idle and anxious moments he also fondled his collection of materials related to Philip II. "In truth," he wrote don Pascual, "I cannot lay my hand on any particularly weak spot in the collection. But I would get whatever is of real historical value, and all contemporary *narrative,* including letters which narrate actions or the motives of them."[64]

Interested though he was in the vague future heavily freighted with the affairs of Philip II, Prescott sharply returned to the present when the first volume of the American edition of the *Conquest of Mexico* appeared, on December 6, 1843. To win wide acceptance of an expensive book, the Harpers had planned to issue the three volumes in as many weeks. "I don't like this *disjecta membra* operation," Prescott insisted. "But as the burden falls on them, and as they will pay the whole copy-right money on the day of first publication—I have not thought it right to object."[65]

December in 1843 was much like that of 1837, the historian awaiting the shower of approbation which his friends promised via Boston newspapers. To Sumner, he wrote, "Bien obligé, mon ami—if Felton is so kind as to take care of the 'Courier'—the 'Daily' will be the best field for you. Ticknor prepares his piece today. He will furnish little but excerpts from English Journals. I shall send all to the Harpers' mill, to make the most of." One of five undated notes written to Sumner in December closed, "Are you not rejoiced that unlike most animals, my period of gestation runs years instead of months, and that I am not likely to be delivered again in a hurry."[66]

To the Harpers, meanwhile, the author expressed his estimate of

[64] Wolcott, ed., *Correspondence,* p. 414; and Gardiner, "Prescott's Most Indispensable Aide," *Hispanic American Historical Review,* 39 (February, 1959): 99–101.

[65] Gardiner, ed., *Literary Memoranda,* 2: 112.

[66] WHP to C. Sumner, two letters [December, 1843], Sumner papers.

their edition. He liked its general execution, but his love of color repudiated their black binding. Deep in a letter laden with suggestions,
the historian added, "You may smile at the idea of my pretending to
give you any assistance in your own business."[67]

By this time the Harpers had rushed copies of reviews to their author. One day he received seven, six from New York City newspapers.
All were "high in the wind" in their praise of the book. "One," he
continued, "says the author is stone blind."[68] He soon read more on
that theme, and eventually it irritated him. Welcome, on the other
hand, was Harpers' payment, shortly before Christmas, in the amount
of $7,500.

Neither Ticknor nor Sumner was in England to help him this season, and, in consequence, Prescott sought help elsewhere. Edward
Everett, having sent reviews, made easy the request, "If you are thrown
into the society of any of the critical brotherhood, could you not do me
the favour to recommend the book to a *fair notice?*" The historian's
desire for English approbation fought his resentment of the degree of
American deference to English opinion.

As on an earlier occasion, certain presentation copies constituted en-
trees for favors sought. One went to Baron Alexander von Humboldt,
whose approval Prescott sought as an open sesame to archives in Berlin
and Gotha. To the able Eberty, from whom he expected a German
translation, went another copy.[69]

From near and far came the swelling acclaim. Joseph G. Cogswell,
in New York City, wrote, "It comes up entirely to my idea of a perfect
history, uniting all the charms of a beautiful spirited narrative with
the authenticity of documentary history." In London, illustrator Frederick Catherwood wrote, "I like it better than Ferdinand and Isabella . . . . I devoured it as I have formerly done a new and interesting
novel, not leaving off until I had finished it."[70] Some encomiums,

[67] WHP to Harpers, drafts, December 5, 11, 1843, Prescott papers.

[68] WHP to C. Sumner, [December, 1843], Sumner papers; also see William
Charvat, "James T. Fields and the Beginnings of Book Promotion, 1840–1855,"
*The Huntington Library Quarterly,* 8 (November, 1944): 80, 89.

[69] Wolcott, ed., *Correspondence,* pp. 420, 422–423.

[70] *Ibid.,* pp. 425, 426.

equally flattering, went into private diaries upon which Prescott never
cast an eye. Diarist Philip Hone declared, "Higher praise need not be
bestowed upon this work than that it is worthy of the author of 'Ferdinand and Isabella'." Fanny Appleton Longfellow wrote in her diary,
"It has the fascination of a romance and cannot be left . . . Mr. Prescott
seems to have seen it all with his own eyes as he makes his reader."[71]

The major reviews, at home and abroad, substantially echoed the
sentiments expressed earlier by lesser organs. In the *Quarterly Review*
historian and critic Henry Hart Milman asserted, "Mr. Prescott may
take his place among the really good English writers of history of
modern times; and will be received, we are persuaded, into that small
community, with every feeling of friendly and fraternal respect." The
*Edinburgh Review* was also ecstatic, S. M. Phillips comparing Prescott's sketches of scenery to Scott, his battlepieces to Napier, his views
of disaster to those of Thucydides. On the Continent, Michel Chevalier
and Count Circourt lauded *Mexico* in multi-instalment reviews. At
home, meanwhile, in the *North American Review*, George S. Hillard
had termed it "a noble work; judiciously planned, and admirably executed . . . We can confidently predict for it an extensive and permanent
popularity. . . . it will take its place among those enduring productions
of the human mind."[72]

Prescott's second history has endured. In the century and a quarter
since initial publication, the *Conquest of Mexico* has been issued more
than two hundred times, more often than any other Prescott title. Likewise, it has been his most frequently translated work.[73] Admittedly it
possesses the most balanced story proportions of any Prescott history.
In certain ways, quite obviously, it is stylistically superior to his first

[71] Nevins, ed., *Diary of Philip Hone,* p. 684; and Wagenknecht, ed., *Mrs.
Longfellow: Letters and Journals,* pp. 103, 104.

[72] [H. H. Milman], "History of the Conquest of Mexico,"*Quarterly Review,*
73 (December, 1843): 235; [S. M. Phillips], "History of the Conquest of
Mexico," *Edinburgh Review,* 81 (April, 1845): 434–473; Gardiner, ed., *Papers,*
p. 221; Wolcott, ed., *Correspondence,* pp. 441–443; [George S. Hillard], "History of the Conquest of Mexico," *North American Review,* 58 (January, 1844):
209–210. For Hillard's admiration of the historian, see Gardiner, ed., *Papers,*
pp. 213–214.

[73] Gardiner, *Prescott—Bibliography,* pp. x, 59–128.

book. Students of literary style have directed more attention to the *Conquest of Mexico* than to any other Prescott title.

Early in the present century, considerably more than a half century after the publication of that work, Harry Thurston Peck directed his attention to its literary style. Peck concluded that "from the standpoint of literary criticism, the *Conquest of Mexico* is Prescott's masterpiece"; "the style is Prescott's at its best . . . free, flowing, and often stately"; "in this book Prescott shows a power of depicting character that is far beyond his wont"; "one secret of its effectiveness lies in its artistic unity"; in certain episodes Prescott "has risen to a height of true greatness as a story-teller and masterful word-painter."[74]

More recent criticism, basically in agreement with Peck, has been set forth in great detail. Writing in the early 1940's, William Charvat emphasized that "his style was in harmony with his material . . . In general, Prescott's style represents a modification of traditional prose rather than any radical departure from it. His syntax and diction, and his use of alliteration and metaphor seem a little old-fashioned, even for his time, but they give his prose dignity and an air of deliberate art."[75]

In his discussion of the artistry of Prescott's *Conquest of Mexico,* Donald A. Ringe has focused on two interrelationships, that between theme and form and that between theme and character. Contrasts between characters, the employment of anecdote, and the creation of suspense also mark Prescott's artistry. The flexible, often rhythmic style, the piling up of sharp detail, and evocative description are other significant characteristics of the writing which succeeds, literarily, in part because of Prescott's ability "to achieve a variety of moods and tones." "The *Conquest of Mexico,*" the critic concludes, "is that rare type of book which satisfies fully the demands of both history and art."[76]

[74] Harry Thurston Peck, *William Hickling Prescott* (New York, 1905), pp. 133–136 *passim.*
[75] William Charvat, "Prescott's Style," in Charvat and Kraus, *Prescott; Representative Selections,* pp. lxxviii–lxxxvii *passim.*
[76] Donald A. Ringe, "The Artistry of Prescott's 'The Conquest of Mexico'," *New England Quarterly,* 26 (1953), 454–476 *passim.* Ringe's view that Prescott derived his telling of the conquest from a nineteenth-century attitude regarding Christian-pagan conflict ignores the fact that Spain of the sixteenth-

Writing at greater length than any previous modern critic, but occasionally forcing Prescott into categories because he is considered along with three other romantic historians, David Levin assessed the *Conquest of Mexico* from the standpoint of structure, characterization, and style. Of the first he says, "The great virtue of *The Conquest of Mexico* is its brilliant design." Prescott's characterization, on the other hand, is criticized for its frequent distortion, shallowness, and lack of sharp detail. "The triumph of excellent design over faulty detail is nowhere clearer than in Prescott's prose style." On the score of style, Levin says, "In *The Conquest of Mexico* it is often his organization, his control of the narrative, or his conception of a scene—rather than brilliant rhetoric or precise description—which contributes most to the effectiveness of a passage." "The main virtues of Prescott's style are its graceful balance, its frequently stately cadences, and its clarity." "The rhythms of this prose also require attention. Phrase, clause, and sentence consistently end with a firmly stressed word, emphasizing the almost orotund symmetry."

"The central weakness is inadequate attention to detail, a surprising insensitivity to precise meaning." His imagery is overworked, even monotonously repetitious in reference to battles. Among his flaws of language, Levin cites "cliché, abstract, unnecessary simile, and repetitious or unnecessary telling." "Prescott's most remarkable achievements in the history are the general scenes." "Prescott's style is better adapted to the tableau than to vigorous action."[77]

Frank Goodwyn, searching for the stylistic secrets of Prescott's astonishing success, focused, more so than most critics, upon individual

---

century was obsessed by this crusading zeal. In other words, Prescott's outlook in this connection derived as easily from sixteenth-century fact as from nineteenth-century feeling.

[77] David Levin, "History as Romantic Art: Structure, Characterization, and Style in *The Conquest of Mexico,*" *Hispanic American Historical Review,* 39 (February, 1959), 20–45 *passim.* This is also in Levin, *History as Romantic Art,* chap. VII. Levin's criticism is noteworthy for its balanced consideration of merits and flaws; because so many critics had overemphasized the former, he tends to emphasize the latter. Between the critic and the historian this difference emerges: whereas Prescott made artistry the handmaid of history, Levin and other literary critics incline to make history the handmaid of artistry.

literary techniques. "Perhaps the most powerful—certainly the most apparent—propellant of the Prescott style is the broad generalization." Analyzing the clarity, grace, and "constant forward impetus," Goodwyn richly illustrates the historian's use of simile, metaphor, alliteration, semifigurative expressions, and rhythmic recurrence of stressed syllables. So considerable and so effective is the end result of Prescott's stylistic labor that one concludes that "he certainly gave much conscious thought to the potentialities of both the sonic and the thematic content of language."[78]

However diverse in time and outlook the criticisms by Peck, Charvat, Ringe, Levin, and Goodwyn, a representative swath of the twentieth-century literary critics of Prescott's *Conquest of Mexico,* one common conclusion emerges: the historian's second book was, from the standpoint of literary artistry, his masterpiece.[79]

The appeals of the *Conquest of Mexico* have been numerous and varied: almost immediately the book went to Mexico with American servicemen, while early and late it has persistently influenced the historical novel, from Edward Maturin and Joseph H. Ingraham, contemporaries of Prescott, through Lewis Wallace and G. A. Henty to Samuel Shellabarger and Alexander Baron in our own day. All wrote vividly about Mexico because, in part, they leaned heavily on Prescott.[80]

The historian's second book also contributed greatly to the myth that he was blind. In his long, rambling preface he had written, "Owing to the state of my eyes, I have been obliged to use a writing-

[78] Frank Goodwyn, "The Literary Style of William Hickling Prescott," *Inter-American Review of Bibliography,* 9 (March, 1959): 16–39 *passim.*

[79] Because of the basic similarity between the *Conquest of Mexico* and the *Conquest of Peru,* a single modern evaluation is made of them as history; see *infra,* pp. 266–269.

[80] "The appearance in 1843 of William H. Prescott's *History of the Conquest of Mexico* was an important stimulus to the composition of novels about Mexico. Within two years the tales of Ingraham and Maturin had appeared." (J. T. Flannagan and R. L. Grismer, "Mexico in American Fiction Prior to 1850," *Hispania,* 23 [1940], 312–313.) Maturin's *Montezuma: the Last of the Aztecs. A Romance,* 2 vols. (New York, 1845) was dedicated to Prescott. Poetry and drama likewise have received inspiration from Prescott, witness Archibald Macleish's prize-winning epic, *Conquistadores,* and Lewis F. Thomas' *Cortez the Conqueror. A Tragedy in Five Acts* (Washington, 1857).

case made for the blind, which does not permit the writer to see his own manuscript. Nor have I ever corrected, or even read, my own original draft."[81] These words, on close reading, did not insist Prescott was blind; but many persons, reading cursorily, concluded that he was. The New York reviewer who termed him stone-blind was only one of many who put that idea into print. Eventually the historian took up his noctograph to combat the untruth. He lost that battle, and the myth of his blindness, to which he had himself contributed, persists.[82]

Somehow Prescott's admirers never have been satisfied with his intellectual, artistic, and literary achievement. There must be a physical triumph as well. And indeed there was such a triumph, but it was a triumph over indolence, over social appetites, not blindness. But a triumph over blindness is a more romantic conquest than is self-discipline of one's dawdling, dreamy nature, of one's love of night life, rich food, and wine. Consequently romance has spun a web about the romantic historian which is not to be broken. A further word, partially conjectural and partially derivative in the light of William H. Prescott's nature, may be advanced about his vision.

To a degree, Prescott seems to have "enjoyed" limited vision—in the sense that ulcers or backaches have enlivened the existence of many

---

[81] WHP, *Conquest of Mexico*, 1: xiv.

[82] Arranged chronologically, the following items are representative of those which, across a century, have perpetuated the myth regarding Prescott's vision: J. McKinstry, "To Wm. H. Prescott, the Blind Historian," *Moore's Rural New-York* (Rochester, N.Y.), December 13, 1856; William Henry Milburn, "Mr. Prescott," in *The Rifle, Axe, and Saddlebags, and Other Lectures* (New York, 1857); [Anon.], "Literary Blind Men," *Frank Leslie's Illustrated Newspaper* (New York), August 27, 1859; Kenyon West, "William Hickling Prescott," *Outlook*, 53 (April 25, 1896): 745–750; Ella M. Fowkes, "William Hickling Prescott," *The Ohio Harp*, January 1905, pp. 52–54; E. W. Gosse, "Two Blind Historians," in *More Books on the Table* (New York, 1923), pp. 275–284; "A Tribute to Prescott the Historian," *Boston Transcript*, March 24, 1924; [Robert] Ripley, "Believe It or Not," Bridgeport (Conn.) *Telegram*, February 5, 1938; L. M. Angus-Butterworth, "William Hickling Prescott," *The South Atlantic Quarterly*, 44 (April, 1945): 217–226; Thomas F. McGann, "Prescott's Conquests," *American Heritage*, 8 (October, 1957): 4–9, 109–111; Samuel Eliot Morison, "Prescott: the American Thucydides," *The Atlantic Monthly*, 200 (November, 1957): 165–168, 170, 172. No evidence supports Morison's statement that "one of his eyes was artificial," *ibid.*, p. 165.

individuals, furnishing theme for endless conversation and reason for
continuing sympathy, furnishing that factor which places one at the
center of a circle of concerned relatives and friends. Pampered by parents, wife, and friends, Prescott often exhibited a childlike nature
which reveled in the attention focused upon it. His vision was bad, but
he caused it to appear worse than it was. Scores of lines in letters and
memoranda attest this overstatement of his disability. In early 1839
Fanny Appleton, discussing the historian as well as his first history,
wrote in her diary of Prescott's "certainty of utter blindness in two
years."[83] She voiced the view commonly held by Prescott's friends. Yet
no doctor, in England, France, or America, ever doomed him to darkness. His worst fears were so confirmed in his own mind that he voiced
them in tones of finality that others accepted and passed on. As pampered boy and injured man, Prescott was as complex as he was likable,
and the shades of distinction between the psychological and the physical about which we wonder are forever beyond us.

10

For a time, early in 1844, the literary loafer played social lion. "We
have been merry enough within doors—soirees, levees, routs and balls,
and I have been uncommonly carpet-knightish for me," he admitted.[84]

A sidewise glance at his Peruvian materials led him to conclude,
"The subject is by no means so rich a one, so poetical and picturesque
as Mexico." For the second conquest study the first one would serve
as model. Accordingly he would base the new work on manuscripts,
would begin by studying the geography and resources of the land.
"Alas!" he sighed, "for a Humboldt to guide me. He stopped short of
Peru."[85]

Unable to give himself seriously to the Peruvian project, he evalu-
ated his *Conquest of Mexico* and resolved three doubts. Of the materials in the Introduction and Appendix he decided, "I did not spend
my time injudiciously on them." Here emerged his willingness to include similar items in the next history. A serious doubt, concerning the

---

[83] Wagenknecht, ed., *Mrs. Longfellow: Letters and Journals,* p. 55.
[84] Wolcott, ed., *Correspondence,* p. 447.
[85] Gardiner, ed., *Literary Memoranda,* 2: 113.

postconquest career of Cortés, disappeared amid the reviews which stamped it necessary and interesting. As for the style of the work— "richer, freer, more animated and graceful—than that of *Ferdinand and Isabel,*" its success invited more in the same vein.[86]

Still shying from historical labors, he did put his noctograph to good use—thanking Milman for his generous review, discussing Mexican codices with Gallatin, asking favors of cousin Alexander Burton in Cádiz, and declining B. F. French's invitation to turn his attention to Louisiana history.[87]

From mid-February to late March, Prescott occasionally killed time a new way, sitting as subject for both painter and sculptor. The canvas by Boston's Joseph Ames was Susan's idea. The marble bust was done at the request of the sculptor, Richard S. Greenough. By the end of March, Prescott was asking Catherwood to ascertain how much it would cost in London to have an engraving and some prints made from the portrait.[88]

This season of triumph for the historian was one in which his clergyman brother was searching desperately for renewed health. Leaving his New Jersey parish, the forty-year-old clergyman briefly visited family and friends in Boston. On April 8, he sailed for the Azores. What could be better for pale cheeks and melancholy than the Azores and the Hicklings! The third day out of Boston, however, Edward died and was buried at sea.[89]

Ignorant then of this event, the historian journeyed to New York on April 15 to confer with the Harpers. From them he learned that they had sold four thousand copies of the *Mexico,* and that the fifth and last thousand purchased was on the presses, a bare market awaiting.

[86] *Ibid.,* p. 114.

[87] Wolcott, ed., *Correspondence,* p. 438; Gardiner, ed., *Papers,* p. 216; Ticknor, *Prescott,* p. 213; WHP to Gallatin, January 29, February 8, 1844, The New-York Historical Society; WHP to A. Burton, January 10, 1844, Wilkinson collection.

[88] WHP to C. Sumner, March, 1844, Sumner papers; Wolcott, ed., *Correspondence,* pp. 455 n.3, 456; and Quincy, *Boston Athenaeum,* pp. 159–160. Judge Prescott presented this bust of his son to the Athenaeum.

[89] James Spear Loring, *The Hundred Boston Orators* (Boston, 1852), pp. 502, 503.

This possibly represented the largest sale of an historical work in the United States in an interval of four months.

Instead of returning home immediately as planned, Prescott once more enjoyed the pleasantries of New York society. In many respects it was the spring of 1842 all over again—a round of dinners and parties, of rich food and late hours, of conversation and congratulation. He so enjoyed himself that a two-day stay stretched to twelve. "Not a day on which I rose before 9, dined before 5 or 6—went to bed before 12!" he later recorded in his memoranda. One new acquaintance, Roman Catholic bishop Hughes, commended and thanked the historian for his liberal treatment of Catholicism.[90] In the face of more than one criticism that his histories voted Protestant, this sentiment gratified him whose historical method included objectivity as a cardinal tenet of his approach to the past.

Additional honors also helped to sabotage the historian's resolve to dedicate steady effort to Peru. One, honorary membership in the Maryland Historical Society, came via Brantz Mayer.[91] From the National Institute for the Promotion of Science came a request for Prescott to read a paper at its April meeting in Washington, D. C. That body learned, as did any and every other that expected him to attend and perform, that he was not that kind of historian. Highly erratic in his attendance at meetings of the Massachusetts Historical Society, a hometown organization for which he had considerable respect and affection, he was not gallivanting about the country to attend meetings. As for reading a paper, the idea was preposterous! His refusal did not dampen the admiration of the Washington body for him; it duly elected him a corresponding member.

Buying, copying, lending, recommending—in every manner historical materials occupied Prescott as he strove to get back to history. To aid the venerable Gallatin, he shipped four bulky volumes of Lord Kingsborough's *Mexican Antiquities* to Fifty-seven Bleecker Street, New York City. "I well believe there is no man in the world who can

[90] Gardiner, ed., *Literary Memoranda*, 2: 117–118.
[91] Maryland Historical Society to WHP, April 5, 1844, Prescott papers; WHP to B. Mayer, April 28, 1844, Archives, Maryland Historical Society. That same year Mayer published his *Mexico as It Was and as It Is*.

so well profit by these materials as yourself; and I am most happy to have it in my power to supply you with them," he told the ethnologist.[92] A week later Prescott recommended to Senator Rufus Choate the purchase of certain Spanish manuscripts by the Library of Congress. Bookdealer Rich, having trouble in interesting the United States government in twenty volumes of unpublished manuscripts from the Kingsborough estate, had solicited Prescott's opinion of them.[93]

From London came good and bad news. Believing that the English market was being invaded by American copies of Prescott's titles, Bentley sought and obtained two affidavits concerning the publication of the books. When the New Burlington Street publisher indicated that a second English edition of the *Conquest of Mexico* was forthcoming, its author rejoiced, despite the fact that the swelling demand did not put coin into his pocketbook.

The Peruvian theme, meanwhile, prompted the reading of Pedro Cieza de León, Diego Fernández, Fernando de Montesinos, and others. Once more a pre-Hispanic civilization commanded the historian's attention, and he again found it misty, confusing, tedious. The parallel between Mexico and Peru continued.

"It will not be near as laborious an investigation as that of Mexico"; Prescott insisted, "the materials are more scanty." The South American conquest disturbed the storyteller in the historian, as when he mused, "the astonishing contrast presented by the Mexicans in the extremes of civilization and barbarism produced a striking and picturesque effect, which I shall not get from the uniform, tame, and *mould-like* character and institutions of the Incas. How many pages shall I allow for the Introduction? A hundred?"[94]

While calculating the initial proportions of his third book, he also tried to serve up his first history in a different fashion. After his New

[92] WHP to National Institute for the Promotion of Science, drafts, February 21, May 17, 1844, Prescott papers; and Gardiner, ed., *Papers*, pp. 217–218.

[93] Wolcott, ed., *Correspondence*, pp. 466–467; WHP to C. Sumner, [May, 1844], Sumner papers.

[94] R. Bentley to WHP, May 3, 1844, and WHP to T. Aspinwall, draft, May 30, 1844, Prescott papers; WHP to R. Bentley, May 30, 1844, Bentley papers; Wolcott, ed., *Correspondence*, pp. 469–471; and Gardiner, ed., *Literary Memoranda*, 2: 118–120.

York visit, during which the subject apparently had been broached, he corresponded with the Harpers on the subject of issuing *Ferdinand and Isabella* in numbers. This practice, common among American publishers, would permit the invasion of another sector of the American market. After all, *Ferdinand and Isabella*, at seven dollars and fifty cents per copy, had been prohibitively high for most of his countrymen. The idea was to issue it in twenty-four numbers, at twenty-five cents each, using the old plates and increasing the number of illustrations. Prescott would receive one dollar per complete copy. When author and publisher failed to agree, the Harpers shifted their tack.

"If however the number plan is not deemed mutually advantageous before another edition is called for, we propose taking the work upon the same terms as your *Mexico*," the publisher wrote, "and paying you for 1500 copies for the control of the work for one year and in case an additional quantity is required, to pay you at the same rate per copy within the year and thereafter."[95]

The new idea appealed to Prescott; but this proposition and his Peruvian research—indeed all intellectual activity—suffered suspension early in June. The man who hated to travel was packing his bags.

[95] Gardiner, ed., *Papers,* pp. 216–217; and Harpers to WHP, June 7, 1844, Prescott papers.

X

*I have lost the greatest stimulus, and ...*

Mixed emotions attended the mid-June departure for Niagara Falls. Thirteen years after a trip there with brother-in-law William Amory and a host of others, the historian was returning with two of his children. William Gardiner Prescott, occupied with academic matters at Harvard prior to graduation in August, was the only child who did not make the trip. For Elizabeth, as she approached her sixteenth birthday, and William Amory, a bit beyond fourteen and possessed of so many characteristics of his grandfather that he was fondly called the Little Judge, the occasion was a memorable one. Until then they had lived almost completely in the Boston-Nahant-Pepperell triangle of family activity. Accompanying the three Prescotts were two of the Salem Peabodys, Francis—five years the historian's junior, and daughter Martha Endicott Peabody, two years Elizabeth's senior.

Everywhere sights called Pepperell to mind. Constant in his admiration of trees, the historian remarked the beauties of the ash, butternut, maple, white oak, elm, and beech. With the same facility with which he allotted duties to reader-secretaries, copyists, printers, and the like, Prescott had appointed fourteen-year-old Amory general superintendent of baggage. The youngster doggedly watched the bags as they were stowed aboard and removed from coaches and trains. Solemnly he distributed them to their owners.

At Niagara the five tourists tarried for days, their hotel within sight and sound of the tumbling waters. There, battling a touch of rheumatism, Prescott wrote complainingly, "The truth is, I am too old, or what is the same, too infirm, to set out on my travels. The sun and water blind me, the dampness gives me rheumatism, the half baked biscuit gives me the dyspepsia." Scarcely had he posted such bleak lines to Susan before he regretted writing while so despondent. Yet, on another occasion, he told her, "I find too I have lost my relish greatly for the picturesque."[1]

## 2

Prescott packed for Fitful Head even as he unpacked from Niagara. At Nahant, the previous August, he had done his last serious work. He counted on its invigorating breezes to whip him into action. "I now propose to pursue," began his latest resolution, "uninterrupted by any more loafing vagaries—my history of the Peruvian conquest—the gold of Peru is not to be won by idle hands." Two circumstances happily reinforced this determination: his recent receipt of eight hundred folio pages of manuscript material from Berlin and Gotha, and excellent health. For the former, Humboldt's good offices and the diligence of diplomat Theodore Sedgwick Fay deserved thanks. The good health possibly derived from the Niagara trip. Aware of his advantages, Prescott asked, "How can I be a sluggard?"[2]

Yet one thing after another crowded in upon him, defeating that singleness of purpose required for successful research. As Elizabeth and Amory grew older, the historian gave them more personal attention during the months at Nahant and Pepperell. Hearing their daily lessons probably consumed little time, but such interruptions wreaked havoc with his prospects of long, unbroken intervals of work. The motives which so identified father with daughter and son were, one suspects, multiple. Basically, parental affection eased their invasion of

---

[1] Wolcott, ed., *Correspondence*, pp. 472–481. For the general background for the interval treated in this chapter, see Gardiner, ed., *Literary Memoranda,* 2: 121–161.

[2] *Ibid.,* p. 121.

his privacy and guaranteed his wanting to be a part of their world. Beyond that, it follows that the man who was so conscious of discipline, though often ill-disciplined himself, thought it necessary to discipline the minds of Elizabeth and Amory during their carefree vacations. In addition, the case of Will surely stimulated the father's injection of more parental discipline into the lives of Lizzie and the Little Judge. By all means, they must not totter, as Will had, over the brink of academic failure and undisciplined social activity. Accordingly, love of family often transformed Prescott into historical sluggard.

To fan his dormant spark of historical endeavor, he looked once more to Italy for inspiration, this time to Alfieri's *Life.* He also tried to induce intellectual activity by reminding himself of the audience that awaited his next book. In not unusual fashion, he dreamt of ideal working and living conditions: how about six months in town and six months outside it?[3] Nahant always gave him his best over-all physical vigor, even though the dampness sometimes induced rheumatism. More inaccessible to visitors, Pepperell invited meditation, concentration, and writing, but its occasional heats disturbed the historian and somehow dyspepsia troubled him more frequently there. In the combination of Boston, Nahant, and Pepperell no perfect formula presented itself, and the search for ideal work conditions continued to be psychological and mental as well as physical.

Late in July Prescott was reading for the Introduction to his new work and distributing memoranda related thereto. With greater awareness of his theme, he crystallized plans and expectations. "The narrative of the Conquest," he forecast, "will not be as stirring in events, nor as *epical* in its conduct—as the Mexican." Assigning two volumes to the full work and four chapters to the introductory survey of the Inca civilization, Prescott designated February 1, 1845, as the target date for completion of the latter. On August 12 he wrote the first words of the opening chapter of the *Conquest of Peru.* The dreary business of breaking ground, now achieved, suggested that he learn certain lessons once and for all time.

---

[3] Wolcott, ed., *Correspondence,* p. 485; and Gardiner, ed., *Literary Memoranda,* 2: 123. The quotations that follow immediately are in *ibid.,* pp. 125, 127.

"When one work is finished," he told himself, "don't pause too long before another is begun—and so on till eyes, ears, and sense give way—then resignation!" The three months of literary loafing after the completion of his *Mexico* had lengthened to almost one year. And as the joys of the trips to New York and Niagara receded in memory, he asserted, "Locomotion riles up all the wits till they are as muddy as a dirt puddle, and they don't settle again in a hurry." Strangely the man whose nature, at its best, required varied activity—intellectual, physical, social, indeed all kinds—longed for phlegmatic serenity.

On Wednesday, August 28, the Prescotts went to Cambridge for Will's graduation exercises.[4] For the historian and the Judge the day quickened memories. Will's room in Hollis was the very one which his father had occupied in the 1810's and his grandfather in the early 1780's. Three generations of Prescotts proudly linked the names Hollis, Harvard, and William.

The fervor of American politics, shunned generally by the historian but then mounting to new heights of public interest as James K. Polk and Henry Clay contested the presidency, drew Prescott's attention in unusual fashion. When Calderón asked questions about the American political system, an answer was immediately forthcoming.

"I will answer you the best I can," the Spaniard read, "though to say truth I am most indifferently versed in the politics of my own country." Speaking of the electoral college, the two major parties, and the characters of ten presidents, the historian revealed much of his own political outlook. Of John Tyler he said, "The Presidency has never reached so low a degradation as under the present incumbent." Of the vote that he planned to cast in November, he left little doubt when he said, "A Conservative of our day is as much of a Liberal in his politics as a Democrat of the time of Jefferson, while a Democrat of the present day—Lord help us!"[5]

Swinging from politicians to books, Prescott's attention fell on an-

---

[4] "Order of Exercises for Commencement, XXVIII August, MDCCCXLIV," Archives, Harvard College; Gardiner, ed., *Literary Memoranda*, 2: 128–129; and Rollo Ogden, *William Hickling Prescott* (Boston, 1904), p. 22.

[5] WHP to J. Sparks, October 10, 1844, Sparks papers; and Wolcott, ed., *Correspondence*, pp. 499–503.

other incidental. An ardent admirer of Frederick Catherwood's drawings of pre-Columbian sites in Central America, he had corresponded with that artist, even hoping that their mutual interests could be served in a joint project. Aware of the publication, in London, of Catherwood's *Ancient Monuments of Yucatan*, Prescott hurriedly wrote a puff. In an unsigned article for an esteemed Boston newspaper, he termed the new work "of inestimable importance to the student of American antiquities." In addition, he urged his fellow townsmen to contribute to the subscription required to finance Catherwood's expensive publication.[6] Less wordy by far than his reviews of friends' books in the "Old North," the article constituted proof of his continuing loyalty to friends turned author.

Meanwhile Gayangos' loyalty to Prescott had led him to Simancas "astride of a mule like Gil Blas, since in keeping with everything else in Spain the General Archives of the Kingdom are in an almost inaccessible place." At the archive he encountered many prohibitions— no copy, extract, summary, or notes of any document could be made.[7] A hurried appeal to authorities in Madrid enabled the knowledgeable Pascual to sidestep certain regulations. In time he turned up documents which clearly demonstrated that the years spent at Yuste by Charles V were more significant than previously thought. In consequence he urged Prescott to append a study of that segment of the Emperor's life to the history by Robertson. On another theme, the imprisonment and death of Prince Charles, Gayangos made another significant find.

"The history of Philip II," the Spaniard declared, "is in a way a history of the world." Prescott, with eight thousand folio pages of manuscript on hand and rich prospects, was wont to agree. Except for archival regulations such as those at Simancas, his holdings might have grown by leaps and bounds. As it was, Gayangos lamented, "I was

[6] [WHP], "Catherwood's Ancient Monuments of Yucatan," *Boston Courier*, September 17, 1844, p. 2. This is another previously unidentified published item by Prescott.

[7] Wolcott, ed., *Correspondence*, pp. 471, 488; Gardiner, "Prescott's Most Indispensable Aide," *Hispanic American Historical Review*, 39 (February, 1959): 103–104. Also see Pascual de Gayangos, trans., *The History of the Mohammedan Dynasties in Spain*, 2 vols. (London, 1840–1843), 1: xviii–xix.

pressed for time and examined only 40 packages out of the 549 containing the papers of Philip II under the single heading of *State*, and I examined nothing under the headings of *Interior, War, Finance, Dealings with Rome, the Indies*, etc."[8] His intention of returning might have been strong, but he never made the trip on Prescott's behalf.

While autumn colors intensified the outdoor beauties of Pepperell, Prescott stayed indoors sufficiently to dig out the second chapter of his survey of the Incas. Hours and days routinely went into the reading of materials and the taking of notes, into mulling over materials and composing text, into reviewing and correcting text, into fashioning footnotes. The signs of dying nature were everywhere as he approached peak production.

Contrary to that resolve born of recent experience, he informed the Harpers of his progress on the Peruvian theme. At the same time he reported that since only fifty copies of the last Little and Brown edition of *Ferdinand and Isabella* remained unsold, he could now consider seriously the proposition which they had made earlier. At once the publishing house renewed its offer to publish fifteen hundred copies of the first history on the same terms as those for the *Conquest of Mexico*. In addition, the Harpers promised that the next edition of the *Mexico* would satisfy him. Again Little and Brown could not meet a New York offer. Severing completely his publishing ties with Boston, the historian had the stereotype plates of the first book shipped to Harpers. A full flourish of publicity followed, it having been decided that seventy to one hundred copies of the seven-year-old book should go as review copies to newspaper editors.

To Colonel Aspinwall, meanwhile, Prescott had broached another matter. Why not, he suggested, publish a volume of his selected *North American* articles in England? The agent replied, "the publication of the Essays shall have my best attention in conformity with your wishes and instructions."[9]

[8] Wolcott, ed., *Correspondence*, pp. 495, 503–504, 598; and Penney, ed., *Letters to Gayangos*, p. 58.

[9] Gardiner, ed., *Literary Memoranda*, 2: 131; WHP to Harpers, drafts, November 19, 1844, and Harpers to WHP, November 4, 1844, Prescott papers;

3

Occupied with non-Peruvian projects during the early weeks in Boston, Prescott ignored for three weeks the work which had progressed so favorably at Pepperell. To prod himself, he did establish a daily work schedule which, like resolutions, was easily ignored, and he accomplished little.

On Thanksgiving Day the Prescotts enjoyed another of their happy annual gatherings, with dinner at 4 P.M. This season Sumner was one of the outsiders who augmented the family. In addition to Judge Prescott, his wife Catherine, the historian, Susan, and their trio of Will, Lizzie, and the Little Judge, Franklin and Elizabeth Dexter brought their four boys from the house around the corner in Chauncy Place. There was young Franklin Gordon Dexter, handsome William Prescott Dexter, who had received his M.D. degree two years earlier, Edward Dexter, destined to graduate from Harvard in 1845, and Arthur Dexter, who was the Little Judge's junior. Singly and collectively the Prescotts had much for which to be thankful, though they did not count the Polk victory earlier in the month among their blessings.

Ten days later, at 7:30 A.M., Sunday, December 8, Judge Prescott, always an early riser, was in the library, among the books which meant so much to him. When Nathan Webster, his faithful servant of thirty years, noted that the Judge was faint, he ran at once for aid. After a moment of apparent recovery, the Judge suffered a relapse. Stretched out upon the floor, he was surrounded by loved ones who were apprehensive of another paralytic attack like that of October 1843. And yet it might be something else, for he had not been feeling well for about ten days, complaining of a pain in his left side. That, along with the inclement weather, had prohibited his walking about town. When the doctor arrived, the stricken one was carried upstairs to his bedroom, in a state bordering upon insensibility. Within fifteen minutes the eighty-two-year-old man died.

Boston and Massachusetts had lost a sterling citizen. At home the loss was catastrophic. Seventy-six-year-old Catherine Prescott was be-

---

Gardiner, ed., *Papers,* pp. 220, 222. A copy of the Prescott-Harper agreement of November 16, 1844, is in the Harper files.

reft of her partner of fifty-one years of married life. Susan lost a considerate father-in-law and her children the only grandfather they had known. But the greatest loss was the historian's.

The Judge's love of truth, his integrity, his love of books—these, among other factors, had molded William H. Prescott into what he was as man and historian. The Judge's love of learning, as much as his wealth, had encouraged the scholarly pursuits of his son. The Judge had delighted in William's periodical writing and had challenged him, when the historian was weary with the uncertainties of a decade of striving, to publish his first history. When acclaim came, the historian savored it as much for what it meant to his father as for himself. One less person figured in the circle for the reading of the evening novel, and life in the big house on Bedford Street could never be the same. Some of the man's greatness, and likewise a measure of the loss that his passing constituted, went into a memorandum which a friend requested from the historian. In part, William wrote, "As he had great sagacity, extensive learning, high principle, chivalrous honor, love of truth, reverence for the Diety most unaffected and remarkable, he had the qualities which command reverence without forfeiting love."[10]

For weeks the historian was so shaken that no thought of serious work entered his mind. Even when he resumed his correspondence, the Judge dominated his thoughts. "In losing him," he wrote Gayangos, "I have lost the greatest stimulus, and in his approbation the greatest reward of my labours."[11]

The size and complexity of Judge Prescott's estate placed new demands upon the historian.[12] Besides being the recipient of considerable property, he assumed two roles by virtue of his father's will. Fortunately his coexecutor, brother-in-law Franklin Dexter, was an

[10] Gardiner, ed., *Literary Memoranda*, 2: 135–140; and WHP to W. H. Gardiner, [c. December, 1844], Gardiner papers.

[11] Wolcott, ed., *Correspondence*, p. 522. Also see WHP to E. Everett, January 31, 1845, E. Everett papers.

[12] The discussion of the Judge's estate is derived from the following: W. Prescott, Last Will and Testament, July 29, 1844, Probate Court, Suffolk County, Massachusetts; Estate inventory, December 13, 1844, Prescott papers; and Gardiner, ed., *Papers*, 222–223.

able lawyer. In like fashion, in the management of the trust for his sister, William was fortunate that the cotrustee, his boyhood friend William H. Gardiner, also was a skilled lawyer. The legal skills of Dexter and Gardiner, however comforting, did not eliminate the demands upon the historian's own business acumen.

Some of the tasks derived from the size and nature of the estate. The Judge had held stocks in six railroads, twelve manufacturing companies, four banking institutions, and four insurance companies. Miscellaneous stocks in eight different operations related to libraries, canals, bridges, and so forth. In addition, there were ten promissory notes. Various houses and other properties rounded out the estate. Five days after the Judge's death, the total property value approximated $343,736.86.

Beyond the numerous monetary bequests—one of which, in the amount of eight thousand dollars, went to the historian "to aid him in hiring a reader, which the weakness of his eyes renders necessary,"—the lifetime trusts for the Judge's widow and Edward's widow, the residue of the estate, personal and real, was divided between the historian and his sister. Aside from the books which his mother might select from the library and the best copy of Hume's *History of England*, which went to Elizabeth, and the law books, the library belonged to the historian. In addition, everything at Pepperell—house, furniture, farm, and stock—went to William, "to hold to him and his heirs forever." Some real estate, as the house in Chauncy Street occupied by the Dexters, was near at hand; some, as the land in Maine which the Judge had acquired in partnership with David Sears—and of which 6,500 acres remained—was quite distant.

The trusts, as well as the cash bequests, prompted sales and conversions, all of which required time and thought. Indeed, the Judge had passed along quite a bit of his own investment philosophy in the form of suggestions concerning bonds, mortgages, and stocks. William H. Prescott needed every bit of the experience he had gained while handling smaller investments across a quarter of a century.

The new year had lost little of its newness when the Prescotts decided to move from Bedford Street. Exactly when and with whom the urge originated are not known. But the Prescotts, being the kind of people they were, were beset by too many memories of the Judge in the house which they had shared with him for more than twenty-five years. Familiar places were less pleasant because of the loss of the familiar face. By mid-February they had chosen the new residence. Owned by Augustus Thorndike, it stood on the northwest side of the Common, at Fifty-five Beacon Street. Prescott knew it well as the residence of his friend Francis Calley Gray. Paired architecturally, numbers Fifty-four and Fifty-five Beacon Street had been built in 1806 by merchant James Colburn. The Prescott's speedily executed the financial arrangements for the house but not so the extensive remodeling which they desired on the four-storey structure.[13]

4

Grief and business persisted, but the historian, who often had asserted that there was little real happiness and less meaning in his life without intellectual activity, kept returning to his historical studies. Mail from Aspinwall helped to guarantee that.

When the Colonel had put to Bentley the idea of publishing in book form selected essays by Prescott, the publisher's interest was advanced with some caution. Already having published three editions of *Ferdinand and Isabella* and two of the *Conquest of Mexico,* Bentley knew that Prescott's name possessed a magical quality in English reading circles. It was, however, one thing to publish great histories with prospects of widening popularity and a totally different thing to serve up, secondhand, articles which ranged in age from two to twenty-two years. In consequence, Bentley said he could publish the essays only on a half-profits basis, along which lines a contract was concluded.[14]

"They will be taken from the *'North American',*" the historian declared regarding the items for his proposed book. "As most of the

[13] Allen Chamberlain, *Beacon Hill, Its Ancient Pastures and Early Mansions* (Boston, 1925), p. 171; C. G. Prescott to F. Gordon Dexter, May 19, 1845, Dexter papers; Gardiner, ed., *Literary Memoranda,* 2: 141; Place, *Bulfinch,* p. 187. Wolcott errs in his statement that Prescott built the house at Fifty-five Beacon Street (*Jottings,* p. 85). The Bedford Street house was bought and razed by a Unitarian congregation.

[14] Wolcott, ed., *Correspondence,* p. 523; Gardiner, *Prescott and Publishers,* p. 298; the full text of the contract is in *ibid.,* pp. 297–298.

articles, which I shall send were written with some care, and show my attention to *literary* investigation—I am not sorry to have them put in a[n] independent and therefore more permanent form, than when strung at random with the other beads and porcupine quills of the North American wampum.

"My preparation of these papers may consume a week or so." Two weeks later, a memorandum noted, "Finished—doctoring my old articles in the *'North American'*—for Bentley. Have run them over very superficially. If they prove as hard reading to the public, as to me, I pity them. But to me they are an old tale. Now set about completing my Introduction."[15]

In February, while selecting and buying the house and choosing and retouching his essays, Prescott concluded the chapter in his history which he had laid aside at the time of his father's death. One more chapter, he hoped, would finish the Introduction. His January deadline unrealized, he did conclude the tedious Introduction in mid-April.

Then he assessed the themes and techniques to be used in the dramatic narrative of the conquest. Despite its lack of unity, the story must be striking and picturesque. Because he must treat considerable Spanish dissension after the collapse of Inca authority, he faced Irving's problem with Columbus, that of maintaining interest far beyond the climax. He could manage it, thanks to certain ingredients: character sketches, high adventure, gold, heroism, cruelty, passion. Furthermore, the sublime character of Pedro de la Gasca offered intense contrast to the many evil figures. Lacking the epic proportions which enabled his *Mexico* to resemble the *Iliad,* the *Conquest of Peru* must approximate the rambling *Odyssey.*

To invigorate his writing, he listed many devices which would be re-employed. "Variety, variety is the secret of interest," he reminded himself. "Expectation is another. Development of passion and personal character another. Scenes of excitement are obvious ones. Portraiture of remarkable character." Stern candor would attend the deeds and misdeeds of the Spaniards.

[15] T. Aspinwall to WHP, two letters, February 3, 1845, Prescott papers; and Gardiner, ed., *Literary Memoranda,* 2: 141.

"The introduction may be for students," Prescott asserted, "but the narrative for intelligent loungers. The elbow grease has been worked out in the Introduction, so do not aim at erudition." So saying, he derived a synopsis of events and dates from Manuel José Quintana, Irving, and Robertson.[16] Upon this skeleton the flesh of breathing men must hang.

If Prescott needed additional encouragement, he received it in the form of signal honors. In Paris, in mid-January, Mignet had reported to the Academy of Moral and Political Science of the French Institute, on behalf of the Section of History, the names of those proposed for the place made vacant by the death of the Spaniard Fernández de Navarrete. In the ensuing election, Prescott received eighteen out of twenty votes. This membership he considered his greatest honor.

On the heels of the French honor came a German one, election to the Royal Academy of Berlin. One suspects that President Humboldt, a frank admirer of Prescott's second history, sparked this honor. "Such testimonies—from a distant land," the historian wrote in his memoranda, "are the real rewards of the scholar. What pleasure would they have given to my dear Father!"[17]

Another kind of honor also cropped up in this period. When Edward Maturin wrote of his projected romance on Mexico, the obliging historian offered to read several chapters and to recommend it to the Harpers. "With regard to the dedication with which you propose to compliment me," Prescott wrote the fiction writer, "I need not say that it gives me great pleasure that you should think me deserving of it."[18]

In the same season Rufus W. Griswold, who had published the very popular work *The Poets and Poetry of America*, was planning a volume of prose selections. He turned to Prescott with a request. "I beg permission to make selections from your historical and critical writings," Griswold wrote, "and shall be grateful for a list of such articles

[16] *Ibid.,* pp. 143–148.
[17] *Ibid.,* p. 149; and Gardiner, ed., *Papers,* 224–225; and Ticknor, *Prescott,* pp. 239–240.
[18] Gardiner, ed., *Papers*, p. 223.

by you in the periodicals, as you would suffer to be quoted." In *The Prose Writers of America,* which Griswold published, Prescott's co-operation was evident. Indeed, some of the material in the five-page biographical sketch had to come from Prescott. Of eight pages of his writings, more than seven came from the two histories.[19] William's generosity possibly stemmed, in part, from his persistent belief that published extracts constituted effective advertising.

While competing Spanish translations of the first history faltered in Spain, competing Mexican translations of the second history quickly put that work before Mexicans in two editions. To the scholarly statesman Lucas Alamán, the historian early had sent a copy of the *Conquest of Mexico.* Alamán impressively annotated the González de la Vega translation, which Vicente García Torres published in 1844. Shortly thereafter the Ignacio Cumplido edition, enriched by annotation and illustration, also appeared in Mexico City.[20] These volumes caused Prescott to re-evaluate contemporary Mexico. His previous awareness of its instability, revolutions, and apparent purposelessness had engendered an attitude of mild ridicule and humorous indifference. But now its scholars and publishers had erected monuments of intellectual worth. On the score of politics, and particularly in regard to Texas, his views paralleled Alamán's.

"The Texas project is very distasteful to most of the North," he wrote, "and the party to which I belong view it with unqualified detestation." Four weeks earlier John Tyler had signed the joint resolution which annexed Texas to the United States. Continuing the Texas theme in a later letter, Prescott told Alamán, "I consider the manner that is likely to be acquired as even more pernicious than the acquisition itself and both together as striking the most serious blow ever yet given to our political fabric."[21]

[19] R. W. Griswold to WHP, January 10, 1845, Prescott papers; and Rufus Wilmot Griswold, "William H. Prescott," in *The Prose Writers of America,* 2nd ed. (Philadelphia, 1847), pp. 369–381.

[20] Gardiner, "Prescott's Ties with Mexico," *Journal of Inter-American Studies,* 1 (January, 1959): 16; and Gardiner, *Prescott—Bibliography,* pp. 62–63.

[21] Wolcott, ed., *Correspondence,* pp. 533–534; and WHP to L. Alamán, draft, June 5, 1845, Prescott papers.

While correspondence on dozens of themes moved in and out of Bedford Street, Prescott hit upon a brand new goad to keep him at his historical projects. "To be mainly occupied with my literary labours," he wrote, "better for my *happiness,* for my *character,* for my *property*—even in a general view—this last for without such more ennobling occupation, I am so figetty [*sic*], that I should be perpetually changing investments—like the boy who pulled up his plants to see how they were getting on."[22]

On May 4, 1845, his forty-ninth birthday and twenty-fifth wedding anniversary, Prescott counted his blessings: family, friends, fortune, fame, and work. Reminding himself that he was "getting on the shady side of the hill," he renewed his determination to win the gold of Peru with the Pizarros.

Despite the illness of reader-secretary Otis, which delayed the clean copies from which he corrected manuscript, Prescott dug in. After preliminary fussing and fuming—and momentary resort to the forfeit idea, his last resort for getting up literary steam—he composed the first two narrative chapters so rapidly that he automatically doubted their quality. The doubts subsided and he rejoiced once more that narrative passages flowed easily across his noctograph. Yet the theme continued to plague him.

"A hero that can't read!" he exclaimed. "I must look into some popular stories of highwaymen." He pushed on, his absorption bringing contentment he had not known for months.

As so often in times past, just when he had regained his literary momentum, interruptions came from all sides. Estate business required attention, as did those matters which normally occupied him before leaving for coast or country. Harpers' promise of another edition of the *Conquest of Mexico* was welcome news, as, too, were the notices in British papers concerning the forthcoming volume of essays. And, finally, the *Edinburgh Review* offered a magnificent review of *Mexico,* the heartiest endorsement of Prescott by any major British publication. High glee inspired the memorandum. "I begin to have a higher opinion of reviews." In that review, however, it was too much for him

---

[22] Gardiner, ed., *Literary Memoranda,* 2: 149. The quotations that follow immediately are in *ibid.,* pp. 150–152 *passim.*

to read S. M. Phillips' note, "Mr. Prescott has, for many years, been blind."[23]

"The next thing," he ejaculated, "I shall hear of a subscription set on foot for the blind Yankee author." Prescott never had bothered to write to the American papers which had said the same thing, but the great Scots quarterly must be set right. To Macvey Napier the historian related some of the story of his vision. "But of late years," he wrote, "my eye has acquired sufficient vigor to enable me, most of the time, to use it reasonably during the day in study, though in writing I am still obliged to make use of a Secretary, who deciphers a very illegible manuscript made by means of a writing-case used by the Blind."[24] The effort to remedy the British misconception about his vision failed, failed as badly as had the historian's Whig Party on the national scene in America.

"What a devil of a capsize we have got!" Prescott remarked to Sumner. "I think the Whigs may as well resolve themselves into their primitive elements and be mixed up with some other party. It is not agreeable to be always crawling on the shady side of the hedge."[25] Ever able to discuss politics, the historian never did more than that. Sumner, on the other hand, soon entered the political arena in memorable fashion.

Knowing that his essays would soon emerge in London, Prescott dropped a hint to the Harpers. "You may see in the English papers my 'Essays—Biographical and Literary' . . . by Bentley," he wrote. Continuing, he indicated the nature of the work—size, pagination, and so on. Grabbing the bait, the Harpers replied, "We should be proud to be the publishers of the work in this country." "Ponder well," he told them, "and come down with a gentlemanlike offer." The New York house quickly countered with a half-profits proposal, adding that it, too, would like to include the author's portrait in its edition. A contract was speedily concluded.[26]

---

[23] [S. M. Phillips], "History of the Conquest of Mexico," *Edinburgh Review,* 81 (April, 1845): 435 n.

[24] Gardiner, ed., *Literary Memoranda,* 2: 152; WHP to G. Ticknor, [n.d.], Ticknor papers; Ticknor, *Prescott,* p. 377; and Gardiner, ed., *Papers,* p. 225.

[25] WHP to C. Sumner, May 9, [1845], Sumner papers.

[26] WHP to Harpers, drafts, May 27, June 5, 24, 1845, memorandum of

Bentley, meanwhile, had not informed Prescott of the English publication date, nor had he sent the requested sheets. Prescott was irked, and he showed it. "You are a very bad Transatlantic correspondent," Bentley read, "and fancy you are dealing with some North country squire, whom you can answer by the next post, if too late for this." Such fire seldom blazed in Prescott's letters.[27]

5

The previous June the historian, favoring Pepperell, had wanted to skip Nahant, to which he dutifully went; this year he consulted his own wishes and went to The Highlands. For decades Judge Prescott had been head of the family in every respect, and the annual moves fitted into a timetable of his making. Now, for the first time, William H. Prescott, long head of a family, was the male head of the household. Perhaps the new role had helped to precipitate the move from Bedford Street; it definitely explained his going straight to Pepperell in June 1845.

Since infancy, except when he was abroad, William had spent part of every year at Pepperell with his father. His sorrow was renewed as he sat in the shade of trees which his father had planted. The morning rides and evening walks, in settings as lovely as ever, were made melancholy by the memory of his father's companionship on other occasions. He occupied his father's place at church; and every day he entered familiar rooms expecting the Judge. The place abounded with reminders so disturbing to his sensitive nature, and Prescott might have dawdled and mooned the days away in nothingness had not firm resolution led to action.

Plunging in, he wrote the third, fourth, and fifth narrative chapters.[28] Occasionally he groused: he was writing too much; it was done too rapidly; it must be inferior stuff. On the positive side, however, his health was in good order—eyes, stomach, everything.

WHP to Harpers, August 7, 1845, Harpers to WHP, June 2, 10, 1845, Prescott papers.

[27] WHP to R. Bentley, May 30, 1845, Bentley papers; and Wolcott, ed., *Correspondence*, p. 542.

[28] Gardiner, ed., *Literary Memoranda*, 2: 153.

When, on July 4–5, business pulled him into Boston, Prescott coupled it with a spree. It is unlikely that he heard Charles Sumner as City Orator—the role played by Edward G. Prescott twelve years earlier, as he spoke on "The True Grandeur of Nations." Charles later sent William a copy of his discourse. He enjoyed it, even though he strongly disagreed. William warmly admired his friend, six feet four inches of him, for saying what he thought, even though officers, soldiers, and militiamen occupied the front seats while Charles voiced his massive denunciation of war.

" 'There can be no War that is not dishonorable,'—I can't go along with this," Prescott wrote him. Citing those who fought at Marathon, Bannockburn, Bunker Hill, and other places, he continued, "In all those wars which have had—which are *yet to* have freedom for their object—I can't acquiesce in your sweeping denunciation—my good friend." Ridicule and admiration mingled in his words, "I may one day see you on a Crusade to persuade the great Autocrat to disband his million of fighting men—and little Queen Victoria lay up her steamships in lavender!

"You have scattered right and left the seeds of a sound and ennobling morality—which may spring up in a bountiful harvest, I trust —in the millenium—but I doubt."[29]

Sumner's speech that day—set against the problems of Texas and slavery—precipitated him into political life. And as Bancroft, a Democrat, was Prescott's friend, so Sumner, soon to turn his back on the Whigs in favor of the Free Soil Party, remained the historian's friend.

After the breather in Boston, Prescott returned to the Peruvian theme. Less meditation and more spur-of-the-moment writing characterized his manner of composition. Soon the sixth chapter lay behind him, and the seventh and eighth he achieved with equal ease. As though to stifle his customary insistence that fast work meant inferior work, he remarked, "I flatter myself—tho written fast—this animated portion of my subject has been treated *con amore*—and with thorough investigation of authorities."[30]

[29] WHP to C. Sumner, August 15, 1845, Sumner papers.
[30] Gardiner, ed., *Literary Memoranda,* 2: 155.

Contributing to his physical vigor and intellectual achievement was his daily outdoor regimen. Before breakfast he was in the saddle for an hour and a half; at noon he walked for thirty minutes in the shade of the orchard; and his evening drive—combined with a walk of a mile or so—occupied another hour and a half.

A mid-August inventory of seventy-five days of labor at Pepperell disclosed that he had written manuscript equal to 209 printed pages. Projecting on a yearly basis his two and three-quarter pages per day, he concluded that it amounted to more than one thousand pages, or two fat volumes, per year. Closing this speculation, he remarked, "Lucky for the world I am not starving."[31]

As publication of his essays neared, doubts mounted. "I am about to commit a folly," he wrote Edward Everett, "which you will think savours of mental blindness; that is, the publication of some of my periodical trumpery, whose value, or rather little value you know." He also wrote Gayangos, "I have just been guilty of the folly of allowing Bentley to publish some of my Periodical trumpery." On August 16 Bentley published the *Biographical and Critical Miscellanies*.[32]

Progress on the remodeling at Fifty-five Beacon Street, glimpsed occasionally by William that summer as he passed through Boston, was a regular concern of his mother. Hale and hearty seventy-eight-year-old Catherine Prescott, who had long throttled her dislike of rural life in deference to her husband's wishes, spent the summer in Boston. Twice as busy as most women half her age, Mrs. Prescott, still deeply involved in charitable activities, was remarkably regular in her attendance at meetings of the Asylum. In a long letter to Susan, one of many communications which hint that the historian got some of his wordiness and romantic outlook from his mother, she wrote, "Today is my Asylum meeting, and I feel as if I had got the seven Churches on my shoulders, children to put out, children to take in, arrange the expenditure of the Appleton Fund, decide upon what is best to be done with poor Theresa who is very unhappy at the Alms House, and many other matters." All the business in the world, however, could not have kept

[31] *Ibid.*, pp. 155–156.
[32] Wolcott, ed., *Correspondence*, p. 547; Penney, ed., *Letters to Gayangos*, p. 181; and Gardiner, *Prescott—Bibliography*, p. 131.

her from inspecting and reporting the activities at Fifty-five Beacon Street.

As the remodeling advanced and she repeatedly visited the new house, Catherine Prescott's affection for it grew. William's library she pronounced perfect. In late July the painters were beginning their work, starting in the attic and coming down, floor by floor, room by room. For Lizzie, then momentarily with her parents at Pepperell, grandmother had a feminine note. "Tell her," she wrote, "her dress closet contains 30 pegs for dresses, five drawers and three shelves, which I think will be enough." By late August some furnishings were moved into the new establishment. Early in September the carpets were laid and the furnace installed. The furnace fascinated elderly Mrs. Prescott, as her letter indicated. "I never saw so complicated a machine, it will be almost as well worth seeing, as William's Library."[33]

While the entire family looked forward to moving day, Will, back in old haunts at Harvard, drew the historian's attention. William crammed a letter to the beginning law student with fatherly concern. Commending him for passing his time recently at Newport "in the ballroom and in the society of ladies—and not in the bar-room among rowdies," the historian suggested that he plunge with equal completeness and enjoyment into his professional studies. At the same time he told Will, "I send you the balance of your Dividend on your Reading Rail Road Bonds."[34] Just as the Judge had transferred property to his son to inculcate in him at an early moment an added sense of responsibility and maturity, so the historian was doing the same for his elder boy.

One of the historian's new correspondents that season was Richard Ford, whose condescending review of *Ferdinand and Isabella* had long rankled the Bostonian. Ford wrote to Prescott as he sent him a copy of his *Handbook for Spain.* Of the note, he remarked, "The blackguard writes like a gentleman."[35] Prescott upheld his end of what developed

[33] C. G. Prescott to S. A. Prescott July 28, August 25, September 1, 1845, Prescott papers.

[34] Gardiner, ed., *Papers,* p. 229.

[35] *Ibid.,* pp. 227–228. Wolcott, ed., *Correspondence,* p. 553; and WHP to C. Sumner, September 11, 1845, Sumner papers.

into a warm, friendly correspondence. This season an unusual percentage of Prescott's correspondence was completely in his own hand, a
reminder that his vision was right for historical studies.

At Pepperell, meanwhile, the daily evening routine still included
the reading of some novel within the family circle. At the moment
Lizzie was the reader and the novel was Scott's *Fortunes of Nigel,* to be
followed by Mrs. Radcliffe's *The Mysteries of Udolpho.*[36]

Other demands and interests notwithstanding, the historian ham-
mered away at the Peruvian project. By mid-October his completed
work also included chapters twelve and thirteen. As he packed for an
earlier than usual return to Boston, in order to effect the transfer to
Beacon Street, he assessed this unusual season. In the first summer in
15 years spent wholly at Pepperell, he had written 11 chapters, approximating 330 printed pages, at the rate of 2½ pages per day. On
occasion the heat had been excessive, but the writer had learned that
hard work left less time for complaining.

Health, determination, isolation, and several other factors had contributed to this most productive season. Among the latter, the children
must be mentioned. Whereas a few years earlier all three, their lessons
to be heard, had been underfoot daily, they were not much in evidence
this year. Lizzie had spent considerable time with Grandmother Prescott; the Little Judge had favored Grandmother Amory in like fashion;
and Will had been here and there, including Newport and Cambridge.
The intrusions of the children and the time passed in conversation with
his mother being much reduced this summer, Prescott had the most
ideal working conditions he had ever experienced. Unusual opportunity
had elicited unusual achievement. With facetious understatement he
wrote, "I do not think I have wasted the summer."[37]

## 6

Every energy focused on the remodeled residence, but six weeks
passed before the Prescotts felt genuinely settled. Under the supervision of George M. Dexter, the big house had undergone extensive
alterations, the account for which totaled $13,973.25. Tastefully fur-

[36] Wolcott, ed., *Correspondence,* p. 556.
[37] Gardiner, ed., *Literary Memoranda,* 2: 159.

nished throughout, the mansion easily accommodated all to whom it was home. Each child had a room; mother Prescott enjoyed the measure of privacy she desired; the historian and Susan had a comfortable apartment; and high above all others the servants had quarters. The ample proportions of the parlors and dining room bespoke the sociable nature of the Prescotts. To the rear, on successive floors, were the historian's library and study.

Impressive on all counts, the library was Fifty-five Beacon Street at its elegant best. Rectangular, and finished in oak, it was richly carpeted and well lighted, in part by numerous well-draped windows, in part by small lamps and the single large chandelier which, in the center of the room, hung from a beautifully paneled ceiling. The marble fireplace, utilitarian as well as decorative, was garnished by andirons, poker, and tongs. Above it was space for a portrait, as well as the swords which grandfathers Prescott and Linzee, the latter on Susan's maternal side, had carried in American and British service, respectively, during the War of Independence. About the fireplace were grouped a number of large, comfortable armchairs. They were there, too, because of the light admitted by the window directly opposite the fireplace.

Except for space given to fireplace, doors, and windows, the walls of the thirty-five-foot long room were given over generally to cases and shelves. The wooden-doored cases were waist-high. Atop each was a single drawer. The top of the cases constituted a narrow shelf-like area above which rose recessed bookshelves. The surface which separated the cases and drawers from the shelves admirably supported small pictures and those books temporarily withdrawn from the shelves. The shelving stopped at a molding near the ceiling. The fourteen-foot ceiling permitted no fewer than seven levels of shelves.

Owner of four to five thousand volumes, the historian needed lots of time to order the library. He conceived, tried, and discarded various systems of arrangement, declaring, "The great point is to have a particular place for each work, and to know where that place is. I shall master this by degrees, and I shall not change,—and I trust I shall never have occasion to pull down and set up again."[38]

[38] Gardiner, ed., *Papers,* 234–236; Gardiner, ed., *Literary Memoranda,* 2: 160; Ticknor, *Prescott,* p. 320; Wolcott, ed., *Correspondence,* p. 560; and Hil-

The magnificent library was not a workroom. It belonged to the entire family, housing nineteenth-century novels as well as sixteenth-century histories. The library also was a social area. To it William retired after dinner with his cronies. There he chatted with Ticknor, Sumner, Sparks, Longfellow, Bancroft, Gardiner, Amory, and others. About them hung canvases of heroic figures identified with Prescott's books. There, too, stood busts of two men whom the historian admired, Scott and Irving. A superb setting for momentary browsing, for conversation, wine and cigars with friends, the library was supplemented by a study to serve William's everyday needs.

The study was immediately above the library, from which one went directly to a concealed stairway. This workroom measured approximately twenty feet square. The fireplace was small, and the bookshelves, also above storage space in the form of cases and drawers, accommodated several hundred volumes. Prescott's reader-secretary shuttled material back and forth between library and study. One side of the room, given over to a series of windows—possibly the first picture-window architecture in Boston—was designed to assist Prescott's vision. In bay fashion the successive windows admitted light from the north, northwest, and west, with shades controlling the intensity of that light. For similar control, a stout screen stood near the fireplace. Miscellaneous chairs and a sofa hinted that the study was not an inner sanctum forbidden to all visitors.

The middle of the study was the heart of the work area. There stood two desk-tables which the historian and his aide customarily used. On the one Prescott rested his noctograph as he composed manuscript. Behind the historian's desk was a massive leather chair. To the right stretched a red velvet sofa. Near the windows, the reader-secretary labored at the second desk. On it he propped up the materials which he read aloud, wrote the fair copies of many letters, and transcribed the original noctographic drafts of successive chapters of history.[39]

---

lard, "Prescott," in *Little Journeys*. Except for the house at Pepperell, the mansion on Beacon Street is the only Prescott residence still standing.

[39] Wolcott, ed., *Correspondence*, p. 565; Ticknor, *Prescott*, p. 277; Emilie Tavel, "Light Shed on History by Six Panes," *The Christian Science Monitor*, April 16, 1958; Emilie Tavel, "High Odds Failed to Stop Historian," *The Chris-*

In the parlor downstairs Prescott exhibited his social nature; in the library two sides of his nature met; in the study he pursued his intellectual activity.

Directly opposite the mansion lay the Mall, the column of elms, planted in 1816, having attained magnificent proportions. Beyond them stretched the Common. To one side lay the Frog Pond. At his doorstep Prescott, in quiet contemplation, friendly conversation, or vigorous exercise, could walk with enjoyment.

The Beacon Street address placed William in a neighborhood of friends. Next door, in No. Fifty-four, lived the William Appletons. A short distance up the slope toward the State House were the residences of David Sears II and the families of two of his married daughters. To one side of Sears lived his son-in-law William Amory. High on Beacon Street, where Park Street framed the northeast edge of the Common, stood George Ticknor's mansion.

The satisfactions of the new residence, however, did not reduce Prescott to a Beacon Street circle. Old neighbors and friends remained beyond the Common—in Bedford and Summer and Chauncy. A special friend, William Howard Gardiner, happily married to Caroline Perkins, daughter of the wealthy Colonel T. H. Perkins, lived in Temple Place, just off Tremont.[40]

The historian never had experienced a smooth transition for his historical labors between Pepperell and Boston, and this season was no exception. Having recently accomplished so much in the country, he was disappointed that he did nothing in town. Settling into the new house, he sensed anew that his role, as well as location, had changed. One day, as the anniversary of his father's death neared, he mused, "His death has given me a new position in life, a new way of life altogether, and a different view of it—from what I ever had before."

---

*tian Science Monitor,* April 17, 1958; Octavius Brooks Frothingham, *Recollections and Impressions, 1822–1890* (New York, 1892), pp. 20–21.

[40] M. A. DeWolfe Howe, *Boston Common, Scenes from Four Centuries* (Cambridge, 1910), p. 45; William Appleton, ed., Susan M. Loring, *Selections from the Diaries of William Appleton 1786–1862* (Boston, 1922), pp. 125, 136, 171, 198; Crawford, *Famous Families,* 1: 204; 2: 366–368; and Browne, *Amoskeag Manufacturing Co.,* p. 201.

Failing to respond to old goads to intellectual activity, he exclaimed, "What the deuce is the matter. Is it the lazy Beacon Street atmosphere. Fie on it!"[41]

Detailing the delights of his library to Pascual de Gayangos, he wrote of his holdings on Philip, "I have had the manuscripts already received arranged and bound up in green morocco, to the number of sixteen volumes in folio, a beautiful little picked corps of my Spanish battalion."[42]

Although he must still write one-third of his Peruvian study, Prescott, particularly in corresponding with Gayangos, thought ahead to Philip II. William termed that monarch the prudent one; Gayangos preferred to call him the timid one. "All that I have seen," William told his Spanish aide, "raises my ideas of his capacity for affairs, but not of his greatness of soul. I shall not find it easy to meet with an Isabella *la Católica* nor a Gonsalvo de Córdova in this bustling and most eventful reign. The events were great, but I fear there was not much true greatness of soul in those who conducted them. I am sorry for this, as one likes a noble character for his canvas." As Cortés was the conquistador that Pizarro could not measure up to, Isabella was the sovereign who dwarfed Philip in Prescott's mind.

In November the historian sent a copy of the English edition of the *Miscellanies* to editor Francis Bowen of the *North American Review.* If he hoped for its review, William suffered disappointment. Early the following month the Harpers published their edition. Aside from frowning upon the black binding, William considered it "very neat and pretty."[43]

A few reviewers said a few polite words about the collected essays. Little was said because there was little to say. In the *Miscellanies* Prescott offered a unified reprinting of thirteen pieces which he had published between 1824 and 1843. Initially twelve of them had appeared in the *North American Review.* The odd item was his contribution to

[41] Gardiner, ed., *Literary Memoranda,* 2: 160.

[42] Wolcott, ed., *Correspondence,* p. 561. The quotation that follows immediately is in *ibid.,* p. 565.

[43] WHP to F. Bowen, draft, November 10, 1845, Prescott papers; and Gardiner, ed., *Papers,* p. 231.

Sparks's *American Biography.* For many reasons—competence, interest, and time, among others—William's small pieces were of uneven quality. Not all merited reprinting, a truth which provokes the question: how and why did he select these particular items?

First of all, having decided to publish such a collection, he early concluded that the volume must be uniform in size with his histories. Accordingly he needed approximately six hundred pages of material. Thus a quantitative consideration rather than a qualitative one became paramount in the formulation of the *Miscellanies.*

An undated memorandum, which he submitted to Sumner for consideration, listed thirteen items from the "Old North" and toyed with the idea of adding the essay on Charles Brockden Brown.[44] Unknown is the influence exercised by Sumner, but the published volume differed from the memorandum in just two respects. Two articles were dropped to permit the definite inclusion of the biography of Brown and the substitution of another *North American* article. Secondly, the chronological arrangement, which William had suggested, was forsaken.

Some thematic balance was sought and obtained, witness the distribution of subjects: American (3), British (3), Italian (3), Spanish (2), French (1), and Mexican (1). Another conscious effort broadened the time span of Prescott's writings. Despite his own admission that some recent articles had been rushed, undigested, padded with quotations, and otherwise not up to his earlier standard, he included his most recent reviews, those of books by Fanny Calderón and George Bancroft. Loyalty to friends exceeded any desire to put the best only into the *Miscellanies.*

The almost exclusive use of articles from the *North American Review* hinted strongly at an exaggerated sense of importance attached to anything related to that journal. Admittedly it was the best literary review in America at the time, but that should not obscure the fact that certain of Prescott's pieces in lesser publications, for example his "Cui Bono?" in *The United States Literary Gazette,* were superior to many of his items in the "Old North." While going along with his

[44] WHP to C. Sumner, undated memorandum, Sumner papers.

friends, Prescott also accepted the public estimate of journals as a criterion for his selections.

A rehash of old essays was not necessarily a mistake, such volumes then being very common. Scott had done this; and an unauthorized American publisher had so treated Macaulay. In 1844 John Foster had published his collected essays, all of them previously published, and in a single periodical at that. Among Prescott's intimates, Alexander H. Everett had published one volume of critical and miscellaneous writings in 1845 and would publish a second one in 1846. In the latter year F. W. P. Greenwood also had published his miscellaneous writings. Prescott was indulging a literary fashion of the day.[45]

Although the thirteen pieces in the *Miscellanies* admirably demonstrated the breadth, and occasionally the depth, of Prescott's studies, the volume added nothing to his reputation.[46] Its poor sale in England and America attested the reading public's powers of discernment. The unnecessary volume did honor, however, a man who had been most necessary in the historian's life, George Ticknor. To him who was most responsible for drawing Prescott to themes of the Hispanic world, the volume was dedicated, in the hope that it would remind George "of studies pursued together in earlier years."[47] Whatever it was and was not, the *Miscellanies* lay behind Prescott.

As the year which had witnessed the birth of an unexpected volume closed, the historian sadly wrote Will of Grandmother Amory's death.

---

[45] Sir Walter Scott, *Miscellaneous Prose Works of Sir Walter Scott,* 6 vols. (Edinburgh, 1827); Thomas B. Macaulay, *Critical and Miscellaneous Essays,* 5 vols. (Philadelphia, 1841–1844); John Foster, *Biographical, Literary, and Philosophical Essays, contributed to the Eclectic Review* (New York, 1844); Alexander H. Everett, *Critical and Miscellaneous Essays* (Boston, 1845) and *Critical and Miscellaneous Essays, Second Series* (Boston, 1846); F. W. P. Greenwood, *The Miscellaneous Writings of F. W. P. Greenwood, D. D.* (Boston, 1846).

[46] The present writer has assessed these writings elsewhere in this study. For additional estimates of Prescott as literary critic, see William Charvat, *The Origins of American Critical Thought, 1810–1835* (Philadelphia, 1936); H. H. Clark, "Literary Criticism in the *North American Review,* 1815–1835," *Transactions of the Wisconsin Academy of Sciences, Arts, and Letters,* 30 (1940): 290–350 *passim;* and William Charvat, "Prescott as Literary Critic," in Charvat and Kraus, *Prescott; Representative Selections,* pp. lxxxviii–ci.

[47] WHP, *Biographical and Critical Miscellanies,* dedication.

For Susan, 1846 was ushered in by mourning. Her husband hoped to usher it in with work. By rekindling his determination and regaining his momentum, he could finish the book that year. The wild rumblings of the Oregon Question had so excited Anglo-American relations that it behooved him to complete his manuscript and settle for English publication before deteriorating international relations complicated that prospect. Reader-secretary Otis constituted another good reason for finishing the book. Otis would surrender his post in the autumn, an ideal time to end a major project.

Such thoughts prompted the memorandum, "I will—God willing— conclude the *'History of the Conquest of Peru'* by *December 31, 1846.*"[48]

[48] WHP to W. G. Prescott, December 30, 1845, Prescott papers; and Gardiner, ed., *Literary Memoranda,* 2: 161.

## XI

*The triumph of moral power over the physical ...*

THE NEW YEAR BROUGHT GIFTS, a heavy cold and a work delay for
William H. Prescott. For a time Dr. Jackson, guardian of the
health of the Prescotts for more than three decades, vetoed any idea of
literary labor. Unable to do more, the historian sat back and listened
to portions of Lord Brougham's works concerning English culture in
the eighteenth century. Throwing off the cold and laying aside Brougham, he enthusiastically turned to his work. Incident to getting up
steam, he once more reminded himself that the chief ingredient in his
recipe for happiness was literary activity.

In mid-January he resumed the history which had gathered dust for
three months. Although he could not give himself over completely to
history—rents, leases and other property interests crowded upon him
at that season—he stuck doggedly with it. By mid-February he was well
into that section which dealt with the civil wars among the victorious
Spaniards. Little interested in that unprofitable and repetitious military
confusion, he reduced the details, increased the generalizations, and
kept his narrative moving. To safeguard his momentum, he enunciated more rules.

"Be out to loungers—not go down to tea, in evening—and in short
keep up unbroken thought—till work of the day ended," he jotted in

his memoranda. Digging in the works of Joaquín T. Trueba y Cosío and Robertson, Prescott sized up the work ahead of him and arranged anew his principal topics. What Cosío treated in 70 pages and Robertson in 200, he allowed 250 pages.

"Business prospects are good, if the *war* question can be dropped," the Harpers wrote as they announced that another printing of the *Conquest of Mexico* would soon go to press. To their request for any corrections that he might care to send them, Prescott said little.[1] He was less interested in policing the perfection of his second book than he had been concerning the first one.

Budding authoress Mary Elizabeth Wormeley, in England, prompted a letter. In the course of peddling her first novel to publisher Bentley, young Miss Wormeley had dropped Prescott's name. Bentley seized upon it and suggested that the historian's name appear as editor of the Wormeley title.

"As to my appearing as Editor, it is a proposal to make money on my name," the historian wrote, "without giving you the advantage of the profits or the credit of the composition. And to be Editor of a work one has never seen, would as you say be funny enough—and not very fair. You answered Bentley just as I should suppose you would." Bentley, however, shifted his tack and succeeded in retaining some of Prescott's appeal.

"As to the Dedication, I need not say how much pleasure it gives me to have this mark of your affection and regard," Prescott informed Mary.[2] In essence, as with Fanny Calderón's book earlier, Prescott was helping a friend. Though living in England, Mary Elizabeth Wormeley was a daughter of one of the Preble girls of Watertown so highly esteemed by all the Prescotts.

Not every letter was so trifling, yet even those to Gayangos lacked the old significance. From Gayangos, on the other hand, came indi-

---

[1] Gardiner, ed., *Literary Memoranda*, 2: 162. The quotation that follows immediately is in *ibid.*, p. 164, and for background for the interval treated in this chapter, see *ibid.*, pp. 162–180. Harpers to WHP, January 17, 1846, and WHP to Harpers, draft, January 22, 1846, Prescott papers.

[2] Wolcott, ed., *Correspondence*, p. 579. The novel was *Forest Hill, A Tale of Social Life in 1830–31* (London, 1846).

cations that the Spaniard was pursuing Prescott's projects more regularly than was the historian himself. From bookdealer Rich, meanwhile, Prescott was requesting engravings of portraits which he intended to use as frontispieces for the two-volume work on Peru.[3]

Paralleling this concern about illustrations was more planning for the *Conquest of Peru*. Characterization would be emphasized: bold, cunning, unscrupulous, efficient Francisco Pizarro; brave, generous, handsome, sordid Gonzalo Pizarro. Francisco de Carbajal was the consummate soldier; and Gasca the good and great would serve as "an illustrious example to show that Spain could furnish the noblest as well as the worst specimens of human nature." Chapters seventeen and eighteen commanded his attention and then, early in March, it happened.

Perhaps it was entirely the physical strain of too close study of manuscripts. Possibly, too, nervous strain augmented the physical—desire to adhere to a timetable of which he was ever conscious. A sudden and severe strain of the nerve of his good right eye occurred. Of the fortnight following March 10, he wrote, in his own hand, "I have not read nor written in all—five minutes on my History—nor ten minutes on any thing else." Gone for a time, at least, were those rapid literary strides taken so often on *Peru* and *Mexico* in league with good vision. The clock turned back to the snail's pace characterized by dependence upon ear and reader, as in many long months when *Ferdinand and Isabella* lay unfinished and challenging. When his physical capacity for work had been best, Prescott's wasted opportunities often had glaringly exhibited an ill-disciplined nature. Now, in adversity, his disciplined side was ascendant. Many men with the touch of genius, dogged by physical limitation, would have cursed their lot. Prescott simply exclaimed, "*Eheu!—pazienza.*"[4]

Carrying on the correspondence which at times seemed to thrive on his limited vision, he addressed a particularly chatty letter to long-time correspondent Thomas J. Phillips. Once beyond his literary enterprises,

[3] Wolcott, ed., *Correspondence*, pp. 576–581; P. de Gayangos to WHP, February 20, 1846, and WHP to O. Rich, draft, January 30, 1846, Prescott papers; and Gardiner, *Prescott—Bibliography*, p. 65.

[4] Gardiner, ed., *Literary Memoranda*, 2: 167.

the historian launched into politics, American and British, with easy abandon. "We don't comprehend here the politics of President Polk," he told the English barrister. "It is probable he doesn't perfectly comprehend them himself. He seems to be playing at fast and loose, and I rather think it will prove a loosing game with him. He stands on two crutches, the South and the West, but they will not walk the same way it seems." Turning next to the English scene and Sir Robert Peel's policies, he continued, "I suppose when your Free Trade flag is fairly floating from your topmast you will be monstrous annoying in forcing your system on all the rest of the world. Master Bull is a canny chiel, and when he has climbed up to the top of the building has no objection to kicking away the scaffolding by which he has got up, and by which his younger brethren are trying to get up."[5] Of such was Prescott's economic and political outlook. Possessed of the interests of the investor in industry, he had no enthusiasm for territorial expansion that served agricultural interests. Prescott's dislike for the new British commercial attitude illustrated the truth that Britain and America, in the industrialization of their economies, were on different timetables. The American timetable, Prescott's, demanded continuance of protective tariffs. Never one to enter political arenas as a contestant, the Boston scholar was, nonetheless, a concerned citizen.

2

When Charles Sumner initially proposed the trip, the reluctant traveler hesitated. "You give me a cold sweat," William wrote. "You really take away one's breath . . . I can't go any how . . . but I will be at your office at eleven, and talk it over with you."[6] As an aftermath to conversation, Sumner cleared his desk of pressing legal matters, Prescott signed his latest batch of letters, and both packed for their trip to Washington, D. C.[7] By train and overnight boat, with the lawyer in the berth above the historian, they launched the expedition.

[5] Wolcott, ed., *Correspondence*, p. 586.
[6] WHP to C. Sumner, [March, 1846], Sumner papers.
[7] Unless otherwise indicated, this section, both generally and in direct quotations, derives from Wolcott, ed., *Correspondence*, pp. 587–592; and Gardiner, ed., *Literary Memoranda*, 2: 167–168.

In a chance meeting afloat, Dr. Elliott agreed that the trip should benefit William's vision.

Eager to proceed southward, the Boston pair breakfasted and spent only thirty minutes in Manhattan, just long enough for the Beacon Street resident to observe that New York was "the noisiest, filthiest and most crowded city that ever was built." Whisked across New Jersey by train, they reached Philadelphia in the early afternoon. After dinner, a stroll, renewal of acquaintances, and a night's sleep, the two men hurried toward Washington, last seen by William in the spring of 1828 in company with Ticknor.

In the capital Fanny Calderón, alerted to their coming but unable to house them in the Spanish minister's establishment, had arranged for rooms at Coleman's Hotel on Pennsylvania Avenue. At 7 P.M., Wednesday, April 1, the handsome thirty-seven-year-old Robert C. Winthrop, soon to become Speaker of the House, met his fellow Bostonians. Five years later Winthrop lost a United States Senate seat to the taller of the two visitors who rode to the hotel with him that evening.

That same night, Charles and William attended a party given by the Calderóns. "I circulated round among French, Prussians, Germans, English, etc. etc.," William wrote Susan, "till I fancied myself on the other side of the water." Fanny Calderón reveled in this moment which permitted her to entertain Prescott as good friend and famous author.

The following day Charles and William repaired to the Senate, enjoying seats obtained by Daniel Webster. As on so many other days, the Senate occupied itself with the trifling and the significant—commutation pay for deceased veterans of the Revolutionary War, a petition by the Tonawanda band of Seneca Indians, requests for lighthouses on Mississippi's Gulf coast. Professor Espy's wind-and-animal-powered ventilator for the Senate chamber drew attention, including hopes that it would be quiet and inexpensive. The major issue that day, however, was the Oregon question—how much land we claimed —what boundary would be acceptable. Lewis Cass urged adherence to 50° 40′ and Thomas H. Benton insisted upon the 49° line, with Massachusetts' godlike Daniel siding with Benton.[8] Politically opposed to

8 [Charles K. Bolton], "Robert Charles Winthrop," *Dictionary of American Biography*, 20: 416–417; and Blair and Rives, comps., *The Congressional Globe*

the annexation of Oregon, the historian was uncertain about one matter, "the quantities of tobacco which were worked up in a debate."

The next day introduced more names, faces, and activities. In the afternoon the venerable John C. Calhoun, "a very remarkable man, as you know," called upon Sumner and Prescott and chatted an hour with them. Whiskered George Bancroft, historian-politician now turned Secretary of the Navy, entertained his home-town friends.

At Bancroft's elaborate dinner, the story that Prescott enjoyed most came from John Y. Mason of Virginia. The former Secretary of the Navy who returned to it as soon as Bancroft evacuated it in favor of the diplomatic assignment in London, told the historian that when the sailors aboard the U.S.S. *Delaware* petitioned for a copy of the *Conquest of Mexico* in the ship's library, it was ordered that Prescott's history be included in the library of every American fighting ship. To William this was a pleasingly new dimension of his popularity.

Next came a soiree at the White House, an evening remembered variously by Polk and Prescott. "This being reception evening an hundred or more persons, ladies and gentlemen, called and were received in the parlours by Mrs. Polk and myself," the president wrote in his diary entry for Friday, April 3, 1846.[9] To his wife, the historian wrote two days later, "In the evening we went to a soiree at the President's, a mean looking individual enough, who gapes and chaws tobacco. Madame is much the more of a President in air and conversation."

Another social highlight in store for Prescott was the party at the home of Mr. and Mrs. Benjamin Ogle Tayloe. Their three-storied brick mansion, The Octagon, stood a short distance west of the White House. Greeting Prescott on the evening of April 4 was the master of The Octagon, Ogle Tayloe, an old friend. Thirty years had passed since those days at Cambridge, but their warm embrace invoked mem-

---

. . . *The First Session of the Twenty-Ninth Congress* (Washington, 1846), pp. 586–591.

[9] [William G. Bean], "John Young Mason," *Dictionary of American Biography,* 12: 369–370; and James K. Polk, ed., Milo Minton Quaife, *The Diary of James K. Polk during his Presidency, 1845 to 1849,* 4 vols. (Chicago, 1910), 1: 317.

ories of Porcellian fellowship. At Harvard, Ogle Tayloe was one class
behind William but not a whit behind him socially. At the White
House, Prescott had condescendingly appraised President Polk, but
here, close upon the Potomac, with planter Tayloe, he was as much
at ease as on Beacon Street. The Tayloes were some of Virginia's finest
moved to the north bank of the Potomac, their mansion a showplace
of gracious living. Like many other ladies earlier and later, Mrs. Tayloe
requested lines in her album. For her William wrote:

> To take the pen when there is naught to tell,
>     No deeds of human glory—
> Would prove me recreant to the Muse I serve,
>     The Muse of History.
> Yet if I venture with a hand so rash
>     To stain the page of beauty,
> 'Tis thou commandest, and I thus obey—
>     To obey is but my duty.[10]

Titillated by the reception accorded Sumner and himself, Prescott
never knew a quiet moment in Washington. Cabinet members, ranking diplomats, members of Congress, and high society planned his entertainment. Cards left by callers covered his table. At hand were
sufficient dinner invitations to occupy him indefinitely. Lady after lady
thrust albums before him, requesting signed lines. And who was Prescott to disappoint a lady! In addition to all else, he consented to sit
for a portrait by George P. A. Healy, who was then painting President
Polk. Prescott thrived on late hours and full days. Much stronger, his
eyes not only permitted his reading Susan's letters, they also allowed
him to write every word of every letter to her.

Before turning his back on Washington, he repeatedly assessed his
experiences there. Among public figures newly met, three particularly
pleased him, Calhoun, Benton, and John J. Crittenden, the last-named
despite his addiction to a habit detested by Prescott, tobacco chewing.
It was not strange that these sons of the South and West, regions that
the historian neither knew nor liked, politically or economically, ap-

---

[10] [Anon.], *The Octagon,* 3rd ed. (n.p., 1956) offers floor plans and photo-
graphs; and [Winslow Marston Watson], *In Memoriam: Benjamin Ogle
Tayloe* (Washington, 1872), pp. 3, 38.

pealed to him. Prescott was a complex man—a social being, an intellectual being, a political being, and more—and individuals who were anathema to him in some respects were irresistibly appealing in others.

In the diplomatic corps at Washington he especially relished Richard Pakenham, the bachelor British minister. Some of the favorable impression derived possibly from the brilliance of the dinner at which Pakenham honored the historian. Beyond that, however, and the fact that well-bred Englishmen always appealed to him, he could write to Susan, "We have much to talk on about Mexico." Few foreigners had enjoyed as lengthy an opportunity to comprehend modern Mexico as had the aristocratic diplomat.[11]

Will power and homesickness facilitated the Bostonians' departure from Washington. In New York City both travelers intended to see Dr. Elliott, among others.

Prescott decided to subject his eyes to treatment for five or six days. Sumner, suffering an inflammation of his eyelids, also visited the oculist. Based in Manhattan for a time and finding the Carlton House unspeakably dirty, Prescott set forth to find different quarters. Once in them, he had time for other than medical matters. New York society received some attention; and so did his publishers. Reports from the Harpers warmed his heart.

"They consider my copyright," he later recorded in his memoranda, "as worth no less than twenty five thousand dollars apiece. If I allow only half that sum, which I should be very loth to take for them, the amount, with about thirty thousand dollars I have already received on the two histories, will swell up to a very pretty little *honorarium* for my literary lumber."

Dr. Elliott, meanwhile, was trying to strengthen William's stronger eye by bloodletting and strong applications. Before he left New York, the historian felt that the circulation in the eye area had greatly improved.[12] Returning to Boston, he had reason to be pleased: Sumner had proved an excellent traveling companion; the trip had been a delight socially; his vision was strengthened and his spirits revived.

[11] Quaife, ed., *Diary of James K. Polk*, 1: 316, 318–319; and [Charles Alexander Harris], "Richard Pakenham," *Dictionary of National Biography*, 15: 85.

[12] Gardiner, ed., *Literary Memoranda*, 2: 168.

3

Easing once more into the worlds of Boston and Beacon Street, the historian, for weeks and weeks, was everything but historian. He did adhere to the regimen prescribed by Dr. Elliott. Although his vision was sensibly stronger, he was depressed. Unmistakable signs that his eyesight was weakening with advancing years disturbed him the more when he considered what that meant to his historical labors.

At a friend's request, Prescott sat for portrait painter William Edward West. He was highly cooperative because, to date, no portrait had pleased him. Inasmuch as these sittings for West came immediately before and after May 4, this portrait might have been conceived in connection with his fiftieth birthday, a milestone which evoked celebration and meditation.

To Gayangos, the cooperative Spaniard whom he had never seen, Prescott wrote of the recent trip to Washington. Two assessments mirrored clearly his nature. The House of Representatives, savoring of its popular origins, was wild and turbulent. The Senate, on the other hand, exhibiting ability, dignity, and decorum, had favorably impressed its visitor. A second observation concerned Americans at large. "The Southern and Western men have a free and open bearing that contrasts with the more prim and cautious manners of the North, which still retains a slight savour of the original Puritan stock, but with more really good stuff in its composition than is to be found in any other quarter of the country,—and much more mental cultivation."[13] He might have continued with sharp distinctions among Northerners. In fact, he could easily have stated his peculiar pride in Boston, and further demonstrated his own Brahminism.

As spring trailed away, Prescott was warring with himself. Should he accept the limitation of vision and pursue his Peruvian project at a slow pace, or should be continue to give himself almost completely to social affairs? "Eyes so poorly," he jotted into his confidential record, "that not able to use them half an hour a day—now not ten minutes."[14] Depressed, he prodded himself with the reminder that

13 *Ibid.*; and Wolcott, ed., *Correspondence,* p. 595.
14 Gardiner, ed., *Literary Memoranda,* 2: 169.

January 1, 1847, remained his deadline for the completion of *Peru*. Then, just as his resolve stiffened, he packed his bags for a gala social event.

The invitation indicated that Miss Cornelia P. Van Rensselaer, daughter of the Stephen Van Rensselaers of Albany would be united in marriage to Mr. Nathaniel Thayer of Boston. As the June wedding day approached, numerous friends of the thirty-eight-year-old banker rode west from Boston and nearby communities. David Sears, Harrison Gray Otis, some Ritchies, and several Peabodys were in the Massachusetts contingent which also included the historian, his daughter, and his younger son.[15]

On Wednesday, June 10, the guests—180 strong—descended upon the patroon's manor house. Elegant and grand, the shaded brick and stone mansion of more than twenty rooms bespoke the wealth and power of the family which once had owned all the land comprising the modern counties of Albany, Columbia, and Rensselaer. Prim and quiet, Elizabeth, the introvert, received her share of attention. Amory, the unquiet extrovert, drew more than his share. Immediately upon his arrival, he had begun a flirtation with one of the Livingston girls. At dinner, seated next to a married lady, he continued to exhibit his charm. The bride, the avowed center of attention, exclaimed to the historian about his son, "What a handsome little dog he is." The proud parent, himself a conscious female charmer in his own right, admitted to absent Susan, "He is quite a go!"

Pressing invitations from the Van Rensselaers occupied the Prescotts for days. Lover of delicious scenery—and so he termed this—the historian enjoyed himself immensely. Saturday brought packing, calls, good-bys.

Skimming down the breezy Hudson, the party arrived at West Point and stopped at Ryder's Hotel. Almost at once the Superintendent of the Academy and two staff officers waited upon Prescott, offering to guide him and his party about the establishment. This official attention was not desired by him, but Amory, Elizabeth, and others enjoyed it.

---

[15] Both generally and in specific quotations, this theme derives from Wolcott, ed., *Correspondence,* pp. 601–605; and Gardiner, ed., *Literary Memoranda,* 2: 170.

By the time he had reached New York, the historian, fast wearying, eagerly anticipated the sight of Boston.

4

During the few days between the return to Boston and the departure for Fitful Head, Prescott, refreshed and determined, dug into the Peruvian theme. Picking up the threads which he had dropped early in March, he wrote thirty-two pages of text and notes for his nineteenth chapter.

At Nahant better health reinforced his creative urge. In addition to giving tone to his system generally, the salty atmosphere notably strengthened the eye to which Prescott still regularly applied the medicines prescribed by the New York oculist. Utilizing every safeguard, he employed the eye about two hours daily in reading. He rapidly drafted more than a score of pages for the next chapter. Then, early in July, he shed his literary nature, picked up certain papers related to his estate, and set out for Maine.

The trip to Belfast, Maine, enters so slightly into extant records that we do not even know with whom the gregarious Prescott made the trip. Because his nature excluded the idea of traveling alone and because the investments in Maine originally involved David Sears, one suspects that neighbor Sears accompanied him. The object of the trip, as the historian alludes to it, was "to look over the accounts of my Eastern Lands."[16] The trip via Portland to Belfast, near the head of Penobscot Bay, was unremarkable and the round trip interrupted the historical labors for one week only.

Reaffirming his insistence upon concluding the history before the late autumn return to Beacon Street, he resumed his labors. Putting finishing touches to the twentieth chapter and looking ahead, he exclaimed, "I begin to see the end .... Yet without eyes—'It is a far cry to Loch Aw.' "[17] By the second week of August he had two more chapters behind him.

Now he was so close to completing his history that his mind occasionally moved to another matter, the finished book. Sad experience

[16] *Ibid.*
[17] *Ibid.,* p. 171; and Sir Walter Scott, *Rob Roy,* chap. 29 n.

cautioned him not to convert the work into stereotype prematurely. He began, however, to estimate the wordage of the individual page and the total number of pages in the book. These calculations reinvigorated his attack upon the remaining chapters. The stylus swept across the wires of the noctograph as he produced one chapter at the rate of eleven pages per day. Mingling intellectual achievement with physical limitation, he exclaimed, "I begin to see the winning post. *Tantum sine oculis!*"[18]

To effect these gains, William limited his social life and correspondence, but eliminated neither. Another box of books and transcripts from Gayangos arrived late in August. Among other things it included the four-volume translation of *Ferdinand and Isabella* by Pedro Sabau y Larroya. In every respect it pleased Prescott, who wrote don Pascual, "I prize a translation into the noble Castilian, more than any other tongue. For if my volumes are worthy of translation into it, it is the best proof that I have not wasted my time, and that I have contributed something in reference to the institutions and history of the country which the Spaniards themselves would not willingly let die."[19] To Mary Elizabeth Wormeley he wrote a pro-and-con appraisal of *Forest Hill,* the three-decker novel which she had dedicated to him. Full of praise and encouragement, Prescott also pointed out major blemishes in the novel: the excessive complexity of the story line, occasional obscurity which resulted from the author's taking too much for granted from her readers, and, lastly, its excessive moral emphasis. "No writer," he told her, "stops after a first successful effort."[20] Elated by kind words from the man whom she called Uncle William, Mary anticipated the day when she might fasten his name to the dedicatory page of a finer work.

Serious conversations about Will's future led the historian to help the embryo lawyer. During the winter vacation of his first year in law school, Will had studied in a Boston law office. Embarking on his second year at Cambridge, he now hoped to wind up his schooling there in half a year. That schedule made it desirable for him to begin

---

[18] Gardiner, ed., *Literary Memoranda,* 2: 172.

[19] Wolcott, ed., *Correspondence,* p. 611 n.; Penney, ed., *Letters to Gayangos,* p. 62; and Gardiner, *Prescott—Bibliography,* pp. 11–12.

[20] Wolcott, ed., *Correspondence,* p. 607.

the final phase of his professional training in some law office in January 1847. The historian wrote his friend C. G. Loring, who, graduating from Harvard two years before him, had always been his intimate in Club.[21]

The transfer from Nahant to Pepperell ushered in September. Deep love for the country place, coupled with recollections of its past contributions to his literary achievement, caused William to hope that he might conclude *Peru* while there. The theme in hand, the career of Viceroy Gasca, delighted him. "The triumph of moral power over the physical," Prescott phrased it. After the greed and blood of uncouth conquistadors, he welcomed the Gasca administration with unfeigned relief. Reading and pondering his material—and kept closer to the house than usual by the equinoctial weather—he organized in his mind the mass of data which, spread on fifty-seven pages of paper, became his twenty-fourth and twenty-fifth chapters. The organization of this amount of material—this being the first of two such performances in his entire career—has been cited as routine labor, to reinforce extreme statements about his genius.[22]

At Nahant he had accomplished four chapters, and a like number at Pepperell. Throughout all, his vision had permitted close work on an average of less than two hours daily. For once the brevity of his memoranda, and the gaps between dates, did not indicate inactivity. On the contrary, his neglect of that record was part of a plan to husband his eyesight for his work. "For I reckon time by eyesight as distances are now reckoned by railroads," he said. "There is about the same relative value of the two, in regard to speed."[23] The state of his vision considerably affected the speed of his writing at Pepperell, but many a morning gallop, as of old, had helped him organize his materials.

"Now after this is packed off," Prescott wrote Gayangos regarding the fourth shipment out of Spain, "do not, my dear Gayangos, spend any more time upon me. For my arsenal is well stored with ammunition

---

[21] WHP to C. G. Loring, August 13, 1846, Loring papers.

[22] Ticknor, *Prescott,* p. 150, asserts, "He frequently kept about sixty pages in his memory." Numerous subsequent writers, failing to study Prescott's papers, have accepted and perpetuated this exaggeration.

[23] Gardiner, ed., *Literary Memoranda,* 2: 173.

of all sorts, for carrying on a much more desperate paper war than that before me." Knowing several things that the historian did not know, the extent of the archives of Spain and the small portions which he had tapped, Gayangos found this hard to believe.[24]

Occupied with the last chapter of his *Peru,* he wrote his American publisher, "It may take me a few weeks more to run over the whole with the last coating of varnish." "Two stout octavos of historical stuff in 3 years, not bad for a blind man!"[25]

Excited by the prospect, he effected one of the quickest transitions ever between Pepperell and Boston and quickly completed his labors. On November 7 the elated historian wrote, "*Finis coronat opus. Wrote first page of the Introduction August 18, 1844.*"[26] A longer entry might have exulted over his adherence to the time table of 1845.

Only a few loose ends remained, including brief biographical notices of authors important to his research. Then, for reasons of style, some of the bulky manuscript received additional attention. Next would come the stereotyping, to be executed once more by the Cambridge printers. They received the initial portion of the manuscript in mid-December. A week later Prescott was reading the first proofs. Again he lived in the world of printer, printer's devil, messenger, and critic Charles Folsom. Observant and precise, Folsom was filling the role which he had essayed for each of the earlier histories. By returning the corrected proof directly to the printer, Prescott avoided the necessity of justifying his limited acceptance of Folsom's suggestions.

Because of weak vision, the historian gave only two thirty-minute periods daily to the proofs. Nonetheless, this routine, supplemented by the labors of his reader-secretary, permitted the handling of fourteen pages per day. That pace, agreed upon, continued with remarkable regularity.[27]

As the stereotyping proceeded, Prescott informed the Harpers that

[24] Penney, ed., *Letters to Gayangos,* p. 65; and Wolcott, ed., *Correspondence,* p. 612.

[25] WHP to Harpers, draft, October 10, 1846, Prescott papers.

[26] Gardiner, ed., *Literary Memoranda,* 2: 174.

[27] WHP to C. Folsom, March 4, 1847, Folsom papers; and Gardiner, ed., *Papers,* p. 240.

the stereotype plates, patterned after those of his previous works, would be available by April 1. He offered them *Peru* on the basis of the terms reached for *Mexico*—that is, at a royalty of fifty cents per volume. Inasmuch as the initial 5,000-copy edition of *Mexico* had brought him $7,500, the author, with that latter figure in mind, now suggested an initial edition of 7,500 copies for *Peru*. The Harpers quickly acquiesced, and the contract of December 18 was concluded. To the historian's proposal that he furnish them with a brief statement of the contents of the book for advertising purposes, the New York house replied, "It would probably not be expedient to disclose too much of the material . . . There is a great itching to travel over your ground, as is evident by the number of applications we receive to publish works on Mexican and Peruvian history, &c."

Months had passed when the historian shipped thirty-four boxes of stereotype plates to New York City. Included were plates for illustrations and maps, as well as the text—everything, in fact, except part of the appendix and the index. As the plates moved between printer and publisher, Prescott seized the opportunity to advance a favorite idea. "Do you not think that dark green or maroon color, for the bindings, would make an agreeable variety with the everlasting black?" he asked.

Meanwhile he had opened his transatlantic negotiation. Almost immediately after contracting with the Harpers, he had set forth his ideas to agent Aspinwall and asked, "Do you think it would be too much to *ask* for it as much as you did for the 'Mexico'?"[28] Again £1,000 was the asking price.

Without the confusion, delay, and ill will of 1843, Aspinwall reached an amicable agreement with Bentley. As with *Mexico,* Bentley bought *Peru* outright, paying £800 for it. In most respects the contract of January 19, 1847, resembled the Prescott-Bentley agreement of 1843. Before the stereotype plates started to the Harpers, proofs off them went to New Burlington Street via Aspinwall and the diplomatic pouch. Bentley planned to publish *Peru* in May.

[28] Harpers to WHP, December 15, 1846, and WHP to Harpers, draft, December 21, 1846, Prescott papers; Gardiner, ed., *Papers,* pp. 237–238, 239–240; and Wolcott, ed., *Correspondence,* p. 614. A copy of the agreement of December 18, 1846, is in the Harper files.

As some of the reserve which had punctuated their relations for a decade began to melt, the London publisher sent recent titles from his press to his author in Boston. With them came the admission, "of all the Works which I have yet been the humble medium of presenting to the World yours are those which will live."[29] Such words could have dissipated the suspicions of a less friendly person than William H. Prescott. For him it was easy to reciprocate Bentley's friendly overtures.

His contracts and plates in order, and a mid-year publishing schedule in prospect, he moved increasingly in society. This derived in part from his belief that literary loafing and social indulgence were in order upon the completion of any big project. This season, in addition, daughter Elizabeth accounted for much of his social activity. Nearing nineteen, Lizzie no longer was in the social world of young misses and masters on the edge of adult society. Freely admitted and expected to take a place in the adult community, she made her social bows this season on her father's arm. Although Boston society pressed a demanding schedule of balls, musicales, and other affairs upon him, the historian did not limit his social life to the Bay City. In April he escorted Lizzie and her friend Cora Lyman to New York.

In Manhattan Prescott enjoyed a round of dinners, soirees, and dances. Society was uppermost but not his sole concern. One day he journeyed to Tarrytown, to see Irving at Sunnyside. The sixty-four-year-old bachelor had returned to his homeland the previous September, via Boston, at a moment when Prescott was at Pepperell. As minister to Spain, Irving had served the historian's purposes on many occasions. When amiable and loquacious Prescott renewed his acquaintance with equally loquacious and amiable Irving, more than words of thanks were in order. Having never seen Spain, the historian must have phrased a torrent of questions—about archives, politics, and personalities. Warmed that day at Sunnyside was a common interest in the Spanish world which in the vivacious Irving meant

[29] T. Aspinwall to WHP, January 19, March 3, 1847, WHP to T. Aspinwall, draft, February 28, 1847, R. Bentley, to WHP, March 27, 1847, Prescott papers; Gardiner, ed., *Papers*, pp. 238–239; and Wolcott, ed., *Correspondence*, p. 618. The text of the contract is in Gardiner, *Prescott and Publishers*, pp. 299–301.

conversation garnished by dimpled smile and twinkling eye. Each frankly admired the work of the other. They had years of activity ahead of them, yet both were, in the spring of 1847, unknowingly on the brink of declining literary power.

Upon his return to Boston, the historian joined those who were giving more attention than usual to music. An Italian opera company, the best ever to visit Boston, had obviously captivated its audience. "The *prima donna* is excellent, the company numerous, and the whole got up in brilliant style," William reported. "We take seats by the month, so it furnishes an agreeable lounge for five evenings in the week to Boston fashion and beauty."[30]

Novelties notwithstanding, Prescott also had time for old friends. At 5 P.M., Thursday, March 18, his dinner party brought together Ticknor, Sparks, Gardiner, N. L. Frothingham, Sumner, Kent, Choate, Longfellow, Hillard, and Bowen. The historian counted the affair one of his celebrations of the completion of *Peru*.

Also, his correspondence quickened. A favorite correspondent was sister Elizabeth Dexter, traveling in Europe with her husband and their sixteen-year-old son Arthur. As a child of Judge and Catherine Prescott, Elizabeth knew more of the world of literature than did most women. Moreover, as frequent reader for her brother, she had additionally widened her horizons. And as wife of Franklin Dexter, a sensitive soul more inclined to art and literature than to law or business, she had continued the kind of life that made her European travel especially rewarding.

"Arty and I saw the sun go down last night from the arches of the Coliseum and a glorious view it is," she penned, continuing, "Can you not see it with your mind's eye?"[31] Thirty years had passed since William, in Rome, had written to her. Now her gentle prodding goaded the romantic in his nature and stirred anew his love of things Italian. For a time he seriously considered going to Europe in the spring of

[30] Stanley T. Williams, *The Life of Washington Irving*, 2 vols. (New York, 1935), 2: 201–203; and Wolcott, ed., *Correspondence*, p. 643.

[31] WHP to J. Sparks, March 14, 1847, Sparks papers; WHP to C. Sumner, March 15, 1847, Sumner papers; Longfellow, ed., *Life of Longfellow*, 2: 84; and E. Dexter to WHP, February 15, 1847, Prescott papers.

1847—in part, one suspects, because he anticipated the pleasures of traveling and returning in company with the Dexters. In April, however, he showed the white flag, surrendering to his dread of separation from family and his distaste for voyaging.

The autumn which had returned Irving from Spain had taken Bancroft to England as American minister. Despite his Jacksonian democratic political outlook and some anti-British historical outlook, Bancroft greatly enjoyed the social and cultural experience that London, his position, and his intellectuality fostered. "Historical breakfasts" found him in company with Charles Babbage, Sir Charles Lyell, John Kenyon, William Thackeray, Thomas Carlyle, Thomas Macaulay, and others. Savoring these joys, George soon shared them.

"Our brother Historians, here, I see very often," he told William. Penning thumbnail sketches of Hallam, Milman, Macaulay, and other unseen correspondents of Prescott, the diplomat added, "I find here your name as familiar as though you had been born here."

"The society in which you move now," Prescott replied, "is in many respects the most to be coveted in the world—so much wit, learning, high breeding; all that health, rank and education can give—the Corinthian capital, is it not!" Tempted, he continued, "I should like right well to accompany you in a visit to some of our fellow-labourers in the great historic field." In mid-May George, having seen the English edition of *Peru*, was full of praise of it. "Come next season," he wrote the author, promising a room in his house at Ninety Eaton Square. "Come out and dwell with us for a month," he insisted.[32]

To ask a favor of an old acquaintance, William addressed a letter to Caroline Preble Wormeley. Somewhat more than thirty years had passed since he, in the Azores and Europe, had asked in various letters to be remembered to Caroline Preble. Wife of Captain Ralph R. Wormeley and mother of three daughters, among whom was Mary Elizabeth, the young novelist, Caroline was the ideal person to carry out the historian's shopping commission. Having lately seen some plated ware which cost a mere fraction of what he had paid for silver articles, he desired one waiter and six vegetable dishes with covers.

[32] Russel B. Nye, *George Bancroft—Brahmin Rebel* (New York, 1945), pp. 159–167; and Wolcott, ed., *Correspondence*, pp. 625, 626, 627, 639.

For them he would spend up to £40. Trusting the matter of design to Caroline's good taste, he added, "I should like my coat of arms engraved in a *modest* way on the articles." Accordingly he sent a copy of the Prescott arms. Caroline carried out the commission.

Unlike the purposeful letters which asked favors, introduced travelers, and exchanged views with his publishers and his agent, those to the Lyells at Eleven Harley Street, London, as well as those from Mary Lyell, were almost pure gossip born of friendship and mutual admiration. To the Lyells, Prescott wrote at length concerning his social life and his leisure.

"Now that I have discharged Peru, I feel like an idle tar whose ship is laid up in ordinary," he told Mary Lyell. "But time is a bitter drug, and I feel I shall soon be afloat again, probably on board the good ship Philip the Second, of which you have heard me speak, though I am a blind pilot and have not half an eye to navigate her with."[33] Already time hung heavily but the state of his vision limited his enthusiasm for launching into another history. So he divided his days between chattering society and quiet correspondence.

When Prescott solicited Joseph G. Cogswell's aid in behalf of young Sam Eliot, many claims of friendship came into operation. Son of William Havard Eliot and nephew of Samuel Atkins Eliot, both of whom were members of Club and friends of Prescott since college days, young Eliot had published a work entitled *Passages from the History of Liberty*. Only half of the six-hundred-copy edition had sold in Boston. For wider circulation, the author had thought of the Harpers. Prescott had recommended the work to them; and he desired that Cogswell, in New York City, do the same.[34]

Early in the spring of 1847 reader-secretary George F. Ware, a former aide who had returned to Prescott's service in the autumn of 1846, signified that he must resign his duties. As he did so, he recommended Robert Carter to the historian. Prescott promptly interviewed him. Unlike his Harvardian predecessors, Robert Carter had gained

---

[33] *Ibid.*, pp. 619, 633.
[34] WHP to Harpers, draft, May 8, 1847, Prescott papers; and Gardiner, ed., *Papers*, pp. 240–241. Eliot's work is reviewed in the *North American Review*, 64 (April, 1847): 511–512.

his training in the school of experience. For nearly a decade the Irish-American from Albany had served in the world of writers, as journalist, with James Russell Lowell and the short-lived literary journal, *The Pioneer*, and as literary adviser to several Boston publishing houses.[35] Except for a notable capacity for shifting his interests, twenty-eight-year-old Carter seemed an excellent prospect. Only one ability remained to be acquired by him, a month's instruction in Spanish pronunciation, which he procured at Prescott's expense. Carter assumed his duties at the beginning of May, apparently on a trial basis.

A week after the English publication of *Peru*, the historian shipped the Harpers the last two boxes of plates for their edition. Having promised Bentley that the American edition would not appear until June 7, Prescott apparently guaranteed it by withholding some plates. At the close of May the historian employed the good excuse that came round every year. "We are in the botheration of taking up carpets, taking down curtains, &c. &c., for the summer campaign," he wrote Sumner by way of explaining his inability to entertain certain distinguished travelers.[36] Yet he was not too busy to share a promotion idea with his New York publisher.

"When the book is published would it not be well to advertise my nine volumes as Works, putting my Miscellanies, with the portrait, as the first volume?" he asked. "I think you might get rid of the complete batch occasionally in this way." Later utilized by many publishers of Prescott's writings, this was but the author's latest suggestion in support of his idea that a new title should jog the sales of the previous ones. Before June expired, the American edition of *Peru* had emerged.

From all, the friends to whom he had sent presentation copies, the critics, and the general public, he awaited judgment on his *Conquest of Peru*.[37]

[35] [Claude Moore Fuess], "Robert Carter," *Dictionary of American Biography*, 3: 542–543. Present and subsequent references to Carter's service are based upon Carter's "Recollections of W. H. Prescott," *Boston Journal*, February 15, 1859. The most recent reprinting, edited by S. E. Morison, is in the *New England Quarterly*, 32 (September, 1959): 372–388.

[36] WHP to Harpers, draft, May 24, 1847, Prescott papers; WHP to C. Sumner, May 28, 1847, Sumner papers.

[37] Gardiner, ed., *Papers*, pp. 242–244.

5

"I felt some distrust as to the success of the volumes," Prescott reminded himself long after it had dissolved.[38] The feeling that the Peruvian story was inferior to that of Mexico on the scores of interest, importance, and unity haunted him. Possibly these matters over which he did not have complete control did not trouble him so much as did another fear: had he written too rapidly? Remembering occasions on which he had composed sixteen printed pages of material in a single day, he feared that conscientious critics might detect inaccuracies incident to rapid composition. More imagined than real, these fears quickly evaporated before the barrage of acclaim from all sides. This time so many acquaintances rushed to review the new book that it was unnecessary for Prescott to buttonhole them for duty.

"Mr. Prescott has added to his well-merited reputation by his narrative of the Conquest of Peru," one British review asserted. Coupling the latest work with the earlier histories, the reviewer noted that the Yankee author had "produced three long and important historical works, conspicuous by their impartiality, research, and elegance; entitling him to an exceedingly honourable position amongst writers in the English tongue, and to one of the loftiest places in the as yet scantily filled gallery of American men of letters. The last of these works, of which Pizarro is the hero and Peru the scene, yields nothing in merit or interest to its predecessors." A second British journal insisted, "Spanish America is fortunate in her historian, and Mr. Prescott is fortunate in being the historian of Spanish America . . . Mr. Prescott's style and manner of composition are adapted with singular felicity to this half-poetic history."[39]

If any doubt lingered in Prescott's mind, the pattern of American criticism served to eradicate it. Francis Bowen said, "Predilection for his authorities . . . has acted upon his style, and reproduced in it the vivacity and freshness of the contemporary observer and narrator. . . .

[38] Gardiner, ed., *Literary Memoranda*, 2: 175.
[39] [Anon.] "'Prescott's Peru," *Blackwood's Edinburgh Magazine*, 62 (July, 1847): 1, 2; [Anon.], "History of the Conquest of Peru," *Quarterly Review*, 81 (September, 1847): 317, 318.

There is a witchery in Mr. Prescott's style."[40] Scores of reviews, in England and America, lavished praise upon Prescott's third history.

So similar stylistically to the *Conquest of Mexico* is the *Conquest of Peru,* that having discussed the former title, the average twentieth-century literary critic ignores or accords scant attention to the latter. After all, the two works are similar structurally, from title page to index. Characterization, description, battlepiece, metaphor, alliteration—all of the ingredients, large and small, of Prescott's style are in evidence again in the *Conquest of Peru.* A recent Peruvian evaluation insists, "The rapid, graceful, lucid style of Prescott is suffused with the reflected light of poetry and imbued with dramatic vigor." Continuing, Lohmann Villena says, "In sum, he sought truth sprinkled with the gold dust of imagination." The literary criticism most commonly aimed at the *Conquest of Peru,* its lack of epic proportions, was beyond the author's control. Yet Prescott's memoranda teem with his agonizing awareness that his hero was an unworthy individual and his denouement tortuously long.[41]

One peculiarly interesting criticism of Prescott's historical labor, during his lifetime, came from Theodore Parker. Having given some thought to the philosophy of history, as well as time to Prescott's themes, the Boston clergyman fired a double-barreled attack, at the historian and his histories. Convinced that American scholars should concern themselves with the propagation of democracy and the vindication of morality, Parker disapproved of Prescott's handling of his subjects. In the words of Parker's biographer, "His objections were characteristic and logical. Mr. Prescott's concept of history was narrow

[40] [Francis Bowen], "History of the Conquest of Peru," *North American Review,* 65 (October, 1847): 369, 399.

[41] Goodwyn, "The Literary Style of William Hickling Prescott," *Inter-American Review of Bibliography,* 9 (January–March, 1959): 16–38 *passim*; Guillermo Lohmann Villena, "Notes on Prescott's Interpretation of the Conquest of Peru," *Hispanic American Historical Review,* 39 (February, 1959): 47, 74; Peck, *Prescott,* pp. 160–162; M. Romera-Navarro, "Guillermo Hickling Prescott (1796–1859)," in *El hispanismo en Norte-América; exposición y crítica de su aspecto literario* (Madrid, 1917), pp. 27–42; Luis Aznar, "Prescott en el cuadro de la historiografía americanista," in *Historia de la conquista del Perú* (Buenos Aires, 1943), pp. 7–26.

and aristocratic, Mr. Prescott's interests were superficial and frivolous, Mr. Prescott's moral judgment was warped. In short, Mr. Prescott was no philosopher. And just for good measure, Parker threw in so many gratuitous slurs on Mr. Prescott's scholarship as to arouse a suspicion that Mr. Prescott was no historian."[42]

Whereas the liberal Theodore Parker, imbued with missionary zeal, was campaigning for the intellectual, moral, religious, and political education of a nation, Prescott, gentleman and scholar, established only two simple objectives for his writing: some instruction and considerable entertainment. The latter sufficiently outweighed the former so that, along with Prescott's conservative nature, it eliminated the prospect of the philosophic content which Parker would have considered significant.

Parker's criticism left Prescott unruffled. Years earlier, he had given critics of his style his closest attention. But as time passed and he felt that his style had been formed, such criticism meant very little to him. Meanwhile, he never had altered his concept of the history he intended to write: simple narrative history, that and little else. Having established and maintained in his own mind and practice the limits within which he planned to operate, Prescott was impervious to criticism, such as Parker's, which fell outside it.

A century later, most historians, because of changed conceptions of their field, share the belief that Prescott's "view of history was not profound." "The purpose of history for Prescott," says another historian, "may be reduced to a single element: to express the course of events in the most clear and simple way—but at the same time in a lively and charming way—without penetrating into causes or searching for ultimate meanings." Yet, even if he lived today and accepted its wider view of history, Prescott still could ignore that criticism which charges him with "aloofness from the sordid realities of America."[43]

[42] Theodore Parker, "The Character of Mr. Prescott as an Historian," *Massachusetts Quarterly Review*, 2 (March, 1849): 215–248; Theodore Parker, "Prescott's Conquest of Mexico," *Massachusetts Quarterly Review*, 2 (September, 1849): 437–470; and Henry Steele Commager, *Theodore Parker* (Boston, 1936), p. 142. Parker's essays have been reprinted many times.

[43] R. A. Humphreys, "William Hickling Prescott: The Man and the Historian," *Hispanic American Historical Review*, 39 (February, 1959): 16; Loh-

On three counts Prescott failed to establish rapport with the problems and men of the sixteenth-century era of conquest. His own republicanism so obtruded in his histories as to defy basic understanding of the monarchical idea, the Spanish state, and the Aztec and Inca political systems. Also, his religious nature "forbade his comprehension of the possibility of the miraculous or of the supernatural and induced him to reject everything tinctured with fanaticism and superstition." Thirdly, the humanitarian spirit Prescott imbibed and to which he subscribed rendered him automatically hostile to the conquistadors as a class.[44]

Nonetheless, within the limits that Prescott conceived and executed his *Conquest of Mexico* and *Conquest of Peru*, those accounts of the conquests merit and receive the commendation of modern historians. For his telling of both conquests, he utilized a much broader range of materials, published and manuscript, than had any previous writer. Very little that was significant and printed escaped his attention, but he sampled only a small fraction of the manuscript riches related to his subjects.

"The historian who intentionally avoided definitive pursuit of materials possessed an uncanny and apparently intuitive capacity for sizing up an historical theme and producing a balanced record of it. The genius of Prescott is not that of a physical giant wading through every document but rather that of one whose sensitive, critical faculties permitted him to produce whole cloth from a limited selection of historical threads."[45]

----

mann Villena, "Notes on Prescott's Conquest of Peru," *Hispanic American Historical Review*, 39 (February, 1959): 72; and Vernon L. Parrington, *The Romantic Revolution in America, 1800–1860* (New York, 1927), pp. 438–439.

[44] Lohmann Villena, "Notes on Prescott's Conquest of Peru," p. 77; also see Guillermo Lohmann Villena, "Prescott y la Historiografía Hispanoamericana," *Inter-American Review of Bibliography*, 9 (March, 1959): 1–15 *passim*.

An interesting and insufficiently explored area of Prescott's significance is contained in the statement, "Prescott has been neglected as a formative force in comparison with Mrs. Stowe. . . . the expansive concept of God, glory and gold, inseparable and indivisible, was as real in America in the first half of the nineteenth century as in the first half of the sixteenth." Jonathan Daniels, *Prince of Carpetbaggers* (Philadelphia, 1958), p. 30.

[45] Lohmann Villena, "Notes on Prescott's Conquest of Peru," p. 70; José

The most vulnerable areas of Prescott's *Conquest of Mexico* and *Conquest of Peru* are the archaeological, the ethnographic, and the anthropological. The volumes that were beautifully written and historically sound were weak in their introductory surveys of the Aztec and Inca civilizations. During the last quarter of the nineteenth century Lewis H. Morgan and A. F. A. Bandelier led the scientific assault on Prescott. The chiding and deriding accorded the romantic historian were essentially unfair in that the three sciences that contributed to our knowledge of the pre-Columbian cultures in later times had contributed very little prior to 1845. Judged by the lights of his day, rather than by the hindsight of subsequent generations, Prescott does not come off so badly.[46]

Some of his gilded and misguided views of the native cultures derived, quite probably, from the publication of Stephens' works. They so exalted the native cultures in Prescott's thinking that he tended, as he wrote, to give them the benefit of the doubt. Quite naturally some travel by Prescott could have reduced his tendency toward exaggeration. For failure to travel and study the settings and remnants of the native cultures, Prescott deserves considerable censure, the kind inherent in the statement, "His descriptions of customs, institutions, beliefs, and buildings are pure romanticism, with more imaginative and poetic than historic value."[47]

But his inability to anticipate the findings of generations of archaeologists, ethnologists, and anthropologists can admit of no sensible criticism. Today, despite the unsatisfactory nature of his introductions to the native cultures, Prescott's *Conquest of Mexico* and *Conquest of Peru* are essentially sound historical works.

---

Fernando Ramírez, "Notas y esclarecimientos a la Historia de la conquista de México del señor W. Prescott," in *Obras,* 3 vols. (Mexico, 1898), 1: 293–537; and C. H. Gardiner, "Prescott ante el mundo," *Revista Estudios Americanos,* no. 101 (1960), p. 130.

[46] Lewis H. Morgan, "Montezuma's Dinner," *North American Review,* 122 (April, 1876): 265–308; A. F. A. Bandelier, *The Romantic School of American Archaeology* (New York, 1885); Philip Ainsworth Means, "A Re-examination of Prescott's Account of Early Peru," *New England Quarterly,* 4 (October, 1931): 645–666; and William Charvat, "Prescott's Reputation," in Charvat and Kraus, *Prescott; Representative Selections,* pp. cxviii–cxxvi.

[47] Lohmann Villena, "Notes on Prescott's Conquest of Peru," p. 67.

Their continuing popularity is attested by the fact that the *Conquest of Mexico* has been published, in 10 languages, more than 200 times, and the *Conquest of Peru*, in 11 languages, more than 160 times.[48]

## 6

On his initial call at Fitful Head, Carter entered the plain square room—about sixteen feet square—which, with desks for both of them and hanging shelves for the books, constituted Prescott's study. That first day Carter read between one and two-thirty from Robertson's *Charles V*. Invited to dine with the historian, the reader-secretary sat down to an impeccably served meal. To his customary two glasses of sherry, Prescott, in a mood for celebration, added a glass of champagne. Chatting and joking while eating moderately and leisurely, he related that the damp atmosphere at Fitful Head permitted him without injury to drink twice the amount of wine that he consumed in Boston. Only at the conclusion of the meal and after the withdrawal of the female Prescotts, did the historian enjoy his daily mild Havana cigar. Before their cigars burnt out, the pair moved to the veranda. There the historian paced about as he conversed. Discarding his cigar, he was ready for his afternoon exercise.

On other days at Nahant, Carter read, in addition to Robertson, Robert Watson's *Philip II* and part of Leopold von Ranke's *Ottoman and Spanish Empires*. Prescott routinely interrupted, dictating notes. In this manner he derived from Watson a basic chronology of Philip's life and reign. Carter copied this synopsis in a large, legible hand so that the historian could study it. Apparently he memorized it.

On historical topics, Prescott invited expressions of opinion from Carter. Such discussion stimulated the historian and increased his enthusiasm for his subject. Politics, however, was a different matter. Although Carter scanned the paper for him daily, no discussion ensued. That might have been endless and pointless, between a die-hard conservative Whig and an equally adamant Free Soiler.

At Nahant, in addition to working with Carter and relishing the spate of reviews sent by the Harpers, Prescott gave time to society and correspondence. Sir Richard Pakenham, whose hospitality he had en-

[48] Gardiner, *Prescott—Bibliography,* pp. x, 59–128, 153–204.

joyed in Washington, was a dinner guest. Rhode Islander Henry Wheaton, recently recalled from Prussia where late in his decade of diplomatic service he had furthered the historian's acquisition of data on Philip II, was a day-long visitor. In mid-July Prescott passed several days at Newport.[49]

"My eye grows so dim that I think of putting myself under Elliott, the New York oculist's care before long," William told London-based George Bancroft. "It is my last hope, and that is faint, for my faith is weak, and faith you know is essential to the miracle-working efficacy. Yet I do not fear blindness, as my other eye will answer for all purposes but reading."

Uncertain vision encouraged intellectual dawdling at Nahant, even though Prescott was considering his project about Philip II. In correspondence with Count Circourt, he renewed his interest in the manuscripts relevant to Philip in the Granvelle papers. In addition to Circourt, Prescott applied for assistance from the American minister to France, Richard Rush, and from Narcisse Achille, the Comte de Salvandy, neither of whom he knew personally. Aside from letters which sought to pile even higher the materials in his library, the historian scarcely touched the big new project. To Gayangos he reported that, even though the summer was going off pleasantly in the *dolce far niente*, he was ill at ease and soon hoped to get to work.

Carter's services having proved satisfactory, a contract was drawn up. "It is understood," the agreement read, "that Mr. Carter will read and write for Mr. Prescott for five hours a day, for two years, the hours to be selected by Mr. Prescott. In return for which, Mr. Prescott agrees to pay him four hundred dollars a year, and all that his board shall cost him, out of Boston, over three dollars a week.

"The time of the commencement of this engagement, to be the first day of September, eighteen hundred and forty seven."[50]

William and Susan were at Pepperell when eighty-year-old Catherine Prescott reached a decision. Resigning her role as the lady in charge of the household at Fifty-five Beacon Street, she wrote, "It is proper

---

[49] [Frederick C. Hicks], "Henry Wheaton," *Dictionary of American Biography,* 20: 39–42; and Wolcott, ed., *Correspondence,* pp. 654–656, 663, 664.
[50] Gardiner, ed., *Papers,* p. 241.

my dear Son that your wife should be the Mistress of your family, your Children should consider her the head to guide and direct in every thing." In her way, mother Prescott had been as strong a personality as the Judge. His death had elevated his forty-eight-year-old son to the role of head of family, but it had not made Susan head of the household. Some of Susan's reticence was native to her nature. Some, however, surely resulted from her being relegated so completely to the background by her vigorous and dominant mother-in-law. The surrender of that role within the family must have been difficult for Catherine Prescott. Even so, she stubbornly retained her independence.

"Wherever I live, I chuse to pay my board," she informed her son and daughter-in-law, "and all extra expenses, such as the coal I burn in my chamber, half the wine, my taxes, hackhire or any other supernumerary I may incur and in case of sickness, which eventually must come, to pay doctors, nurses, and all other after charges and expenses."[51]

Meanwhile the historian received praise and encouragement. "But what the extraordinary (though perfectly natural) success of your last attempt should encourage you to," Count Circourt wrote, "is not to abandon the glorious and crowning enterprise you have set your face towards, the life and reign of Philip II, . . . which you alone, among the pillars of the House of History, are fully competent to accomplish." Another prod came from the Harpers who, three months after publishing the *Peru,* asked when the next work would be ready. Prescott, yet to put the first word on paper, replied that it would be a long time, in fact his health might eliminate the prospect completely.[52]

Two difficulties plagued his sight: a deposit of lymph partially obscured the retina, and incipient amaurosis, decay of the nerve, had set in. His physician and his oculist offered different assessments, the latter being the more optimistic. Torn between medical opinions, as well as the uses to which he might dedicate limited vision, he spent much time thinking, waiting, hoping.

"I am going to New York next month," he wrote John Kenyon in

[51] *Ibid.,* p. 248.
[52] Wolcott, ed., *Correspondence,* pp. 667–668, 669–671; and Gardiner, ed., *Papers,* p. 249.

September, "to put myself under the care of an eminent oculist, for a drowning man will catch at a straw. But the eye is nearly worn out I fear, and the hand that made it, can alone repair it."[53]

Otherwise, joys came with the autumn. In the dark-painted study on the second floor of the old house at The Highlands, Prescott and Carter continued their study of the English-language sources on late sixteenth-century Spain. The leafy limbs that darkened the study meant different things to the two men: to Carter, eyestrain; to Prescott, the changing colors that constituted one of the delights of the country. The joys of Nature pleased him, and walking and riding the historian daily made much of them. Another pleasure derived from the success of the *Conquest of Peru.* In five months the Harpers had sold 5,000 copies; and in England, where Bentley's 2,500-copy edition was triple the size of the average English edition of an historical work, the success was likewise spectacular.

7

The Nahant-Pepperell season of 1847 had been different. Ordinarily the salt air whipped up a commendable measure of intellectual activity which was matched, if not exceeded, in Pepperell's glorious shade. The return to Boston usually posed the question: can the momentum achieved at shore and in country be maintained despite the winter social season? In 1847, however, Fitful Head and The Highlands had generated nothing, the final proof of which was the complete void in the historian's memoranda.

In Beacon Street he instructed Carter to remove from the library to the study all the books and manuscripts relevant to the Spanish project. The acquisition of those materials represented a lively story. Now the issue was—could Prescott extract the lively history they contained? Item by item, Carter checked the lot and arranged them chronologically. Next he surveyed the title pages and tables of contents, pausing to read anything in which the historian expressed an interest. They retained many items, but they pushed aside numerous others—com-

[53] WHP to J. Kenyon, September 30, 1847, The New-York Historical Society.

pilations, latter-day syntheses, and so forth. A more vigorous and complete analysis of the desirable sources developed.

The better his acquaintance with the collection, the more Prescott wanted to work. However, the enormity of his theme, combined with the abundance of materials on hand and the state of his vision, understandably influenced his plan of attack.

"There is so much incident in this fruitful reign, so many complete and interesting episodes, as it were, to the main story," Prescott concluded, "that it now occurs to me, I may find it expedient to select *one* of them for my subject, instead of attempting to grapple with the whole." Themes ran through his mind: the colorful expedition of Don Sebastian in the conquest of Portugal, the chivalric siege of Malta, the glorious revolution in the Low Countries. "This last," Prescott mused, "is by far the greatest theme, and has some qualities— as those of unity, moral interest, completeness, and momentous and beneficent results, which may recommend it to the historian."[54]

But that which he himself found attractive, Prescott had vouchsafed another. In 1847 John Lothrop Motley was much taken with the idea of writing about the Dutch. Beyond their chance meeting in Boston society, the historian knew him as a writer of romances. With the amiable generosity so deeply rooted in his nature, he discussed with Motley their individual hopes and plans and insisted that Motley proceed with his project. Underscoring this endorsement of a quasi competitor, Prescott offered him books. In this decision of 1847, Prescott approximated Irving's of 1838–1839: a small kindness from a recognized writer became the generous act which was critically important in the career of a younger man.[55]

Meanwhile, Prescott was certain about two matters: he was weary of dawdling, and, at fifty-one, he could not think of turning his back completely on creative endeavor. Pondering his problem, moving in society, and maintaining his correspondence, he also occupied himself by writing a biographical notice of his friend the late John Pickering.

[54] Gardiner, ed., *Literary Memoranda*, 2: 179.
[55] For a fuller statement of Prescott's relations with Motley, see Gardiner, "Prescott: Authors' Agent," *Mid-America,* 41 (April, 1959): 80–83.

The Massachusetts Historical Society, having commissioned this labor of love, expected it for its next volume of *Proceedings*.

Other eulogies of Pickering had preceded Prescott's in print, but none exceeded its warmth. Both Pickering and Prescott had known Salem as birthplace and Harvard as Alma Mater. Nineteen years Prescott's senior, John Pickering had spent almost a half decade in diplomacy in the late 1790's—first in Portugal, later in England. Then it was that he established his love of languages and literature, his appreciation of foreign cultures, and his broad range of scholarly interests. The two men naturally had many friends in common. Their interests in literature and language and their frequent contributions to the *North American Review* guaranteed this. In addition, lawyer Pickering frequented the world of lawyer William Prescott. Pickering had been one of those special friends who not only read and criticized the manuscript of William H. Prescott's first book but also helped to launch *Ferdinand and Isabella* on waves of favorable criticism.[56]

Discharging a debt of friendship and complying with the charge laid upon him, Prescott also did something else as he produced his memoir of Pickering: for the first time in four years he wrote something unrelated to his historical studies.[57] Whereas previous articles generally represented unwelcome interruptions, this one was written while he was between projects. Accordingly it just might contribute to the work habits which he needed to reawaken if he were to give serious attention to Philip II.

In this period Prescott's relations with his New York publisher also evidence capacity for business detail. Many halts in Prescott's daily walk to Boston's downtown district seem to have occurred before booksellers' shopwindows or within the shops themselves. How else could the historian proclaim to the Harpers, "Your *Peru* is out in some

[56] [John Pickering], "Prescott's Reign of Ferdinand and Isabella," *The New-York Review*, 2 (April, 1838): 308–341.

[57] William H. Prescott, "Memoir of the Honorable John Pickering, LL.D.," Massachusetts Historical Society *Collections,* 3rd ser., 10 (1849): 204–224, also published separately in Cambridge, 1848; and Mary Orne Pickering, *Life of John Pickering* (Boston, 1887), pp. 321, 520–22.

of our shops"?[58] After all, the best promotion came to naught if the commodity itself was beyond reach of the potential customer.

In Boston, a Prescott day, as far as regular activities were concerned, fitted into a somewhat rigid schedule. Rising early, he walked thirty minutes before breakfast. Doing so alone, meditating, the historian often followed a fixed route. Breakfast concluded, Susan read to him for an hour, generally from some novel. This session ended at 10 A.M., and Prescott walked another thirty minutes, alone and on a different course from the prebreakfast stroll. At ten-thirty, six days a week, Carter appeared. The historian often opened their day with some such remark as "Let us see what is in the 'Respectable Daily' this morning." Taking his cue, Carter read as much of the *Boston Daily Advertiser* as the historian cared to hear. On certain days the semiweekly *National Intelligencer*, the only other newspaper to which Prescott subscribed, received similar attention. Dispatching the news, they next turned to other work—letters to be read, letters to be written, books to be read.

Opening the incoming letters himself, Prescott glimpsed the signature on each and then passed it to Carter. Often the historian interrupted the reading of long letters, dictating memoranda for his reply. The letters to be written, like those received, concerned correspondents in many countries. In this period, Prescott rarely wrote more in his own hand than brief complimentary closes and signatures.

At noon Carter and Prescott separated, the latter off on a walk which usually took him in the direction of State Street on business errands. At 1 P.M. he returned to his study and worked until the dinner hour, two-thirty. After a leisurely meal he relaxed amid clouds of cigar smoke and listened as Susan read more light literature. He next took his third thirty-minute walk, bringing the daily stint up to approximately five miles.

Carter reappeared at 6 P.M., to work with him in the study until 8 P.M. By then Carter had put in his allotted five hours, and Prescott was disposed to call a halt to the workday.

Late in January 1848 the historian and his aide constructed a list of

[58] WHP to Harpers, drafts, November 22, 26, December 27, 1847, Prescott papers.

those items which Prescott, on his death, bequeathed to Harvard College. The 287-item catalogue of books and bound manuscripts covered that segment of his research library which related exclusively to the reign of the Catholic Kings.

As in times past, Prescott often mulled over his historical projects with friends, sometimes in person, sometimes via correspondence. The 5 P.M. dinner party of Thursday, February 24, 1848, typified such activity in this period. Present were Jared Sparks, soon to resign his professorship for the presidency of Harvard; Charles Sumner, whose reputation as crusader was widening; and Henry Wheaton, weary, ill, and within a month of his grave.[59] Sumner continued a select correspondent to whom Prescott fired notes teeming with familiarity and problems.

"I have been poddering over my Philip the Second collection," he informed Charles. "It is a mammoth one—too big by half. I doubt if I shall attempt to cook the monster whole. I fear in my blind state, I should burn my fingers. So, I am looking round for the fattest slice to carve out of him. . . . all good pickings enough, though too well-seasoned with gun-power for your philanthropic nostrils."[60]

The Prescott-Gayangos exchanges, once charged with ideas and challenges, slackened, bogging down in polite trivia. In May 1848 Prescott lessened the reason for a continuing correspondence with Gayangos when he wrote, "I do not make an additional appropriation, as I consider the investigation now brought to a close." Still refusing to believe this, the Spaniard continued to tempt him by reporting manuscript finds.[61]

For weeks in the spring of 1848, Ticknor's work on Spanish literature, topic of conversation at Pepperell the previous autumn, oc-

---

[59] Later the tenth item in Prescott's will provided for this bequest; see Gardiner, ed., *Papers*, pp. 402–403. Except for five items which could not be located, these were transferred to Gore Hall on June 3, 1859; [Anon.], "Prescott's Library," *American Publishers' Circular*, 7 (February 18, 1860): 75; WHP to J. Sparks, February 19, [1848], Sparks papers; and [Hicks], "Henry Wheaton," *Dictionary of American Biography*, 20: 39–42.

[60] WHP to C. Sumner, [February, 1848], Sumner papers.

[61] Penney, ed., *Letters to Gayangos*, pp. 72, 73–74, 76; and P. de Gayangos to WHP, June 19, 1848, Prescott papers.

cupied Prescott's attention. Hearing it and studying it was the least that he could do for the friend whose inspiration and criticism had enriched all of his own creative efforts. Moreover, George's theme greatly interested him. His friendly survey of the Ticknor manuscript concluded, William gave George the benefit of his criticism in two forms, nineteen pages of notes and an eight-page letter. Pleased with Ticknor's manuscript, Prescott prophesied for it "an important and permanent place in European literature." The plan adopted by Ticknor appealed to him. And when his mind, often considering the prospect for his own books, included the idea of an abridgment of Ticknor's hefty work, he indicated the areas which he felt could be scissored. The work was least attractive to William on the score of style. He felt, among other things, that George left "too little to the reader's imagination, by filling up the minute shades, instead of trusting for effect to the more prominent traits. If you don't understand me, I can better explain myself in conversation."[62] They might have conversed about style, but the fact remains that Ticknor was essentially no stylist and any effort by Prescott to make him one was wasted.

By early June 1848—nine months after they had signed a two-year contract—the reader-secretary and the historian parted. Carter, the only one to explain the rupture, indicated that the impairment of his eyesight in the course of reading manuscripts during the evenings dictated his resignation. That, however, may be but a half-truth. One suspects that he also was weary of the routine. Eleven years later, upon Prescott's death, Carter wrote the most lively portrayal of Prescott produced by any of his reader-secretaries. In 1859 Carter, very much the journalist, wrote a splendid story of Prescott's personality, residence, work schedule—all. Sympathetic and graphic, his account was full of rich detail: instances of Prescott's charitable nature, his account books, his gay good humor, the color of the sofa in the study, why anthracite coal was used in the grates in the evening, and so on.

In his effort to give a full and fascinating account of the historian, Carter detailed the very manner in which Prescott presumably wrote the first chapter of the first volume of his *Philip II*. But the truth is

[62] Hillard, ed., *Life, Letters, and Journals*, 2: 251–253.

that Prescott never put the first word of that work on paper until almost a year after Carter's departure.[63] Not only is some of Carter's unique account fictitious, but all of his experience with Prescott, it must be remembered, was in a period of planning rather than real achievement. Oddly, the best contemporary statement of Prescott at work concerns an interval in which Prescott achieved next to nothing. The only thing he wrote during Carter's tenure was the eulogy of Pickering, an essay which flowed from the heart, not his historical processes. Indeed, the interval of Carter's service as reader-secretary constituted the least productive period in the quarter-century of Prescott's creative career.

On June 9, 1848, John Foster Kirk, recommended by Carter, signed a contract with Prescott.

It is understood that Mr. Kirk will read and write for Mr. Prescott, for five hours a day, for five years, the hours to be selected by Mr. Prescott. In return for which Mr. Prescott agrees to pay him four hundred dollars a year for the first year, four hundred and fifty dollars for the second year, and five hundred dollars a year, for the remaining three years, and also, all that his board shall cost him when the parties are out of Boston over three dollars a week.

It is further understood that, in case of Mr. Prescott's death previously to the expiration of this agreement, the contract shall be closed by the payment of a year's salary to Mr. Kirk.

The time of the commencement of this engagement to be the first day of September, eighteen hundred and forty-eight.

A few days earlier Prescott, appraising the nothingness of his life in recent months, had declared, "What next—idler?"[64]

---

[63] Gardiner, ed., *Literary Memoranda,* 2: 191. Also see [Anon.], "Mr. Prescott's Method of Literary Labor," *American Publishers' Circular,* 7 (February 12, 1859): 75; and [Anon.], "Prescott the Historian," *Boston Cultivator,* February 19, 1859. Both accounts were taken from the *Boston Transcript.*

[64] Gardiner, ed., *Papers,* p. 251. Also see [Frank Monaghan], "John Foster Kirk," *Dictionary of American Biography,* 10: 428–429.

*. . . the most brilliant visit ever made to England . . .*

ADHERING TO THE ANNUAL ROUTINE, Prescott evacuated hot, dusty Beacon Street the fourth week in June. More than twelve months had passed since he last had written any history. Yet, however lackadaisical his recent reading, the new contract with Kirk foreshadowed renewed determination. He planned to tackle the big Spanish project—otherwise why arrange for an aide for five years? The day following his arrival at Fitful Head, he resorted to a resolution, one of his oldest challenges to a lazy nature. Taunting and mocking himself, he underscored portions of this latest admonition.

But work he did. Viewing the total reign, via Evaristo San Miguel's *Historia de Felipe II Rey de España*, Prescott once more sought to determine whether he should encompass the complete subject or simply a part of it. At this time his eyes served him but one hour daily, in ten-minute intervals, inspiring the lament, "So I snail it along."

Late in July Charles King of New York relayed from General Winfield Scott to the historian an invitation to write a history of the late war, for which the general would make his papers available. The offer flattered but did not tempt Prescott. With finality he declared that he "had rather not meddle with heroes who have not been under ground—two centuries—at least." He might have added, as far as wars were concerned, that the one with Mexico, far from attracting him, distinctly repelled him. (To Lord Morpeth, during the course of the war, he had mentioned its eventual outcome in terms of "dirty superfluous acres" and "still more barren glory.")[1]

Early in August Prescott plunged into writing, dashing off a stack of letters of introduction for twenty-two-year-old Will, who, having won admission to the Suffolk County bar the last week in July, was about to tour Europe. In addition to more than a score of letters, his father gave him a sheaf of commissions and instructions. Plans called for Will's return before the end of the Pepperell season of 1849, a schedule which afforded him approximately fifteen months abroad. "Write me a letter the first day of every month," father told son, ". . . and I will write you as often." He also charged Will to write some other member of the household at least every two weeks. More than a little of the historian's own experience in Europe shone through in the words, "Your letters will serve as a journal, detailing your movements and observations." In addition, the historian reminded him, "You will keep a good account of your drafts and your expenditures."[2] Added to the emotional strain of farewells on a close-knit family were some special concerns of the day—albeit a little exaggerated in most American minds—the cholera and the revolutions of 1848.

Minus the shipboard member of the family, the Prescotts returned to Nahant, the historian to his reading. One title, Leopold von Ranke's *The Ottoman and Spanish Empires in the Sixteenth and Seventeenth Centuries*, meant most to Prescott. "His book contains inestimable materials for a more minute and expanded history," he observed. "It is a sort of skeleton—this bone-work of the monarchy. It must be studied." To do that, Prescott had selected portions, aggregating about two hundred pages, printed in exceptionally large type.[3]

[1] WHP to Lord Morpeth, April 30, 1847, Lord Carlisle papers, Castle Howard, Yorkshire; and Gardiner, ed., *Literary Memoranda*, 2: 180, 181. For the general background for the interval treated in this chapter, see *ibid.*, pp. 180–207.

[2] Davis, *Bench and Bar*, 1: 452; WHP to R. Bentley, August 5, 1848, Bentley papers; and Gardiner, ed., *Papers*, pp. 251–253.

[3] Gardiner, ed., *Literary Memoranda*, 2: 182; and Morison, ed., "Carter's

Will, meanwhile, had crossed the Atlantic in record time. The voyage satisfied a couple of his persistent appetites, for good food and numerous cigars, but it produced twinges of homesickness. "Give my best love to Lizzie," he wrote his mother, "and ask her to remember me to *all* my lady friends."[4] His affection for the fair sex marked him a direct descendant of his father. Fulfilling his promise, the historian wrote Will monthly, reporting those tidbits of family activity and community gossip which earlier writers had not pre-empted. Along with pen pictures of family life went advice. "I hope you thumb the guide-book well, so as to understand the full import of every spot that you tread," the historian wrote to the son who was then in the German states. "The more you are thrown among the people of the country where you are travelling, and the better you understand their ways—their nationality—the better you will like them."[5]

Unmentioned in such letters were the bookish activities to which the historian tried daily to assign hours. Yet that optimistic determination with which he normally went to The Highlands led him to exclaim, "Now cannot I *Phillipise* in these shades?" As at Nahant, the reading of background materials was the extent of that labor. As autumn advanced and Boston beckoned, Prescott's love of Pepperell swept him into reverie. "Monadnoc [*sic*] and his brotherhood of hills seemed to look gloomily on me as I bade them farewell," he wrote in late October. "What may betide me—of weal or woe—before I see them again!"[6]

On October 25, three days before the Prescotts returned to Beacon Street, a gala civic celebration took place in the Common, almost opposite their front windows. Rejoicing in the inauguration of the public water system, Mayor Quincy, flanked by Daniel Webster, Nathaniel Hawthorne, Ralph Waldo Emerson, James Russell Lowell, and other dignitaries, mounted a platform over Frog Pond. Lining the water's edge was the crowd of adults and children who earlier had paraded

---

Recollections," *The New England Quarterly,* 32 (September, 1959): 381–382.

[4] W. G. Prescott to S. A. Prescott, August 10, 1848, Prescott papers.

[5] Gardiner, ed., *Papers,* pp. 255–257.

[6] Gardiner, ed., *Literary Memoranda,* 2: 182–183.

through the streets of Boston. The climax of the day came amid loud huzzas when the jet of water leaped high. A school chorus sang Lowell's ode, written for the occasion, which announced, "My name is water." All this, plus cannons, rockets, and bells, the historian missed. Of one aftermath, however, he bore witness in an early letter to Will, "The magnificent jet in the Frog Pond . . . burst the pipes, so that we have not had a drop since."[7] Soon, however, the waters of the Cochituate resumed their flow.

A quieter kind of neighborhood matter, the death of Harrison Gray Otis, friend of three generations of Prescotts, deeply touched the historian. Otis was buried on the morning of October 30, the evening of which witnessed a noisy torchlight procession of Whig supporters of General Zachary Taylor. Because the parade route did not include their part of Beacon Street, the Prescotts watched the spectacle from the Amos Lawrence residence in Pemberton Square. Through muddy streets thousands of Whigs marched, carrying blazing torches. From the illuminated houses, Roman candles and rockets greeted the marchers.

"We were all brim-full of patriotism," William wrote Will, "and dying to serve our country."[8] This tongue-in-cheek statement represented the historian's maximum identification with the political campaign of 1848. Happy that the war with Mexico had ended and enraged at its territorial outcome, Prescott's routine endorsement of the Whig Party—lacking real enthusiasm for an ill-educated military man out of the West—was a lesser-of-evils proposition. Politics also dominated a letter to Pascual de Gayangos. "The triumph this time comes on the side of the Whigs—the conservative party,—as the Tories are the true levellers. What is there in a name? The Tories, or Locos, have their way, usually, three-fourths of the time, till the machine has got so much out of joint that it will hardly work; then comes a good Whig dynasty to tinker it up, and set it off again on a constitutional track for a few years, when the democracy are sure to run it off again."

---

[7] WHP to W. G. Prescott, October 29, 1848, Prescott papers; and Howe, *Boston Common*, p. 53.

[8] WHP to W. G. Prescott, October 31, 1848, Prescott papers.

Shifting his attention to Europe, he continued, "The consolidation of the German empire is a noble idea; is it practicable? The liberation of Italy from the barbarians is a beautiful old dream; can it be realized? The republicanism of France is a chimera, I fear."

Concerning his Spanish project, he told his distant aides, "The subject grows larger and larger as I contemplate it, and I feel somewhat disposed to pick out a fat slice, instead of 'going the whole hog,' as we say in Kentucky."[9] Previously he had always evolved firm, detailed conceptualizations of his projects. Without one as yet for Philip, he could do, and did, nothing.

Socially, however, he did everything—weddings, receptions, dinners, waltzing parties, whist clubs, visits. Sunday after Sunday, in the evening, the Prescotts had their quota of invited callers at Fifty-five Beacon Street. A *"very elegant dinner,"* said actor Macready as he recalled the Prescott affair which included Ticknor, Hillard, Felton, William Amory, and others. Among those invited by the Prescotts on Sunday evening, December 3, were Tyrone Power, the Irish player, Uncle William Amory and Aunt Anna from a few doors up the street, and the amiable George Hillard, lately returned from the European tour which soon appeared in book form.[10] If conversation turned from the theater and Europe long enough to pronounce the name "Harvard," it possibly embraced the resignation of the sensitive Edward Everett and the knowing rumor which mentioned Jared Sparks as the next president.

A few days before Christmas the historian wrote a special letter, his second eulogy of Reverend Dr. John S. J. Gardiner. Eighteen years before, shortly after his friend's death in 1830, William had eulogized him in the *Columbian Centinel*. Now, at the request of William Buell Sprague, he wrote his recollections of the man whom he termed "my preceptor in my early days, and afterwards my minister." A simple restatement of what he had published earlier, the letter of December 21, 1848, was important only as a demonstration of continuing affection. Of the small number of men about whom Prescott wrote eulogies, Dr. Gardiner uniquely was the subject of two. Yet another special air attaches to the letter because, though written more than ten years before Prescott's death, it appeared in print only after his death.

Weary of rounds of whist, *tableaux-vivants,* waltzing parties, and the like, Prescott was not alone in welcoming the opera. It proved, however, much inferior to the delightful company of 1847. Will's brother unblushingly aired his prejudice, saying, "I think with you that good vaudevilles are worth all the operas in the world."[11] Amory's candor much resembled that of grandmother Prescott. She, upon hearing that the late Mr. Brooks had left none of his estate, valued at $1,-800,000 to either the Female Orphans' Asylum, her pet charity, or to any other public institution, observed that he had no chance of going to Heaven.

During the entire winter of 1848–1849 the historian was in the doldrums. A week before Christmas he challenged his listlessness by summarizing his labor during the eighteen months since the publication of *Peru.* Chiding himself with truth, he tried, among other things, to prick his pride. What happened? He did so little during the ensuing eight weeks that he never added a word to his memoranda. In mid-February 1849 he confessed, "Dosed into another year." Then, from the depths of physical disability and social dissipation, up came the first sign of renewed vigor. He declared, "I have now made up my mind to take the subject—the whole subject—of Philip II."[12] But words alone could not effect the metamorphosis from lotus-eater to historian.

In a letter to Will he recited the kinds of activities which he needed to curtail, if not eliminate.

The town began to be wide awake about three weeks since. Three different lady-clubs have been set on foot, to supply the dearth of dances and merrymakings. I am going to one at your Aunt Ticknor's to-morrow evening. It is called the *sans cérémonie,* and each lady invites a couple of gentlemen and

[11] WHP to William Buell Sprague, December 21, 1848, in "John Sylvester John Gardiner," *Annals of the American Pulpit,* 5: 365; and W. A. Prescott to W. G. Prescott, January 20, 1849, Prescott papers.

[12] Gardiner, ed., *Literary Memoranda,* 2: 184.

a lady. I believe they card it first, and then dance. It is all one to me, who do neither. They chose me honorary member of one of these clubs, but I declined the honour, having more visiting on hand than I care for already. On Wednesday I dine with a lady party at our neighbour Appleton's, and last week dittoed at Mrs. Sears.

Will, wintering in Paris and enjoying Europe—despite a recurrence of the throat trouble which had often plagued him at home—requested an extension of his trip, from the autumn of 1849 to the following spring. To cover the tourist's expenses, his father added £250 to his account, raising it to a total of £850. And to previous remittances to cover commissions, the historian now added twelve dollars for the Parisian shirts which Amory hoped would come in red and blue striping.

Beyond the simple request that his trip be lengthened, Will's love of foreign scenes had led him to consider a career in diplomacy. The historian, besides abhorring an idea so alien to his Boston-based nature, viewed it dimly because it led nowhere in terms of a total career. To clinch his point, he added, "Lastly, I have no influence, if I had the wish, to get you into a diplomatic post. 'Kissing goes by favour'—at Washington—and I have no claims of electioneering services to show." Odd, by coincidence, was a letter which William H. Prescott received in this season. Writing from Madrid for her absent husband, Fanny Gayangos said, "We think a new ambassador-minister will come over next year. It seems so appropriate to have you named that I shall be disappointed if it is not so."[13] Fanny was disappointed, and so was Will. Closing the diplomatic door on Will, the historian began to lay plans.

Emphasizing the most important and interesting aspects of Philip's reign, he planned but sparing consideration of ecclesiastical, fiscal, and constitutional details. As the unifying and dominant interest, he planned to utilize Philip and his leading policies, especially the furtherance of Roman Catholicism and royal absolutism. The subject teemed with dramatic events, at home and abroad. Numerous figures also invited the pen of the historical portrait painter.

[13] Gardiner, ed., *Papers*, pp. 262–263, 265–267.

"It is one advantage to take the whole subject," he observed to himself, "—that I may carve out the dainty pieces, hardly noticing the poorer, and thus, make up a rich bill of fare throughout."

The project suggested four volumes. If he worked four hours daily for eight years, he should complete it. In order to break the routine—and sell more copies—the first pair of volumes might be published upon completion. That also would further pre-empt the theme for the slow historian. The weakened state of his eyes greatly influenced such thinking.

"I am not sure that it will not be better for me to call the work *Memoirs,* instead of history, &c. This will allow a more rambling style of writing, and make less demand on elaborate research; and so my eyes and my taste both be accommodated." Completing his preliminary call to action, the historian constructed a general synopsis.[14] As the architect, upon completion of the plans, gives way to the builder, Prescott the projector needed to yield to Prescott the writer. But months passed, winter turned into spring, and spring so advanced that talk turned to Nahant, and the writer never became ascendant in his nature.

Will's enquiry—so much like his father's questions to little brother some thirty years earlier under similar circumstances—led Amory to report his school activities. Under the instruction of Mr. Ingraham, in a group of about fifteen students—one of whom was cousin Arthur Dexter—Amory was winning little distinction. His disinclination for study was so considerable that the family did not include Harvard in his future. Compared with Will's casual reference to an encounter with an Italian countess, so phrased as to lift the reader's eyebrows, Amory's social life was less than scintillating—tea at Mrs. Bourne's, cards and roasted oysters at Mrs. Thayer's. Accompanying everything was gossip related to the recent inauguration of President Taylor. Abbott Lawrence, having declined the post of Secretary of the Navy, was mentioned as the next minister to London.

Beyond the Atlantic, Will planned his extended stay in Europe. Father and Uncle Ticknor showered ideas and itineraries upon him. Ticknor mentioned Switzerland, the Rhine, Scotland, even Ireland.

---

[14] Gardiner, ed., *Literary Memoranda,* 2: 186–189.

Many of those places the historian had not seen, and, coupling prejudice with limited experience, he expressed himself differently. "As to Germany, Spain, &c., &c.," he told Will, "I think you must be content to give them up . . . . Better to see a few of the best places thoroughly than to run like a courier over half of Europe . . . As to Ireland, I would not bother my brains about that."[15] The anti-Irish sentiment was a characteristic one, Prescott never having a kind word for the sons of Erin, despite the fact that many of his gifts went to alleviate the suffering of poor Irish families in Boston.

Mail kept the historian abreast of publishing developments in London. Bentley complained that, after four years, the *Miscellanies* had not yet paid expenses. Rumor of a reprinting of *Ferdinand and Isabella* by Henry G. Bohn suggested that he and Prescott agree to fight fire with fire. And, of course, Bentley wondered about the book on Philip.

Troubled about the threatened piracy of *Ferdinand and Isabella* in Britain, Prescott sought legal counsel. Passing the American legal opinion on to Bentley, for what it might be worth to him, he did not make the prospect of cheap competition more palatable when he remarked, "I trust you will not belittle the book by a duodecimo edition."[16] In dire straits, Prescott stood by his standards.

Mid-April took William, Lizzie, and Amory off for a week to New York and Philadelphia. Gowns for Lizzie and shirts for Amory served as excuses for their going. Dining and dancing kept them up until midnight or later every night. One evening, at the Astor's, the historian again saw Washington Irving. Returned to Boston, Amory went to bed with scarlet fever. In early May the marriage of one of Will's friends provoked a typical reaction from the Boston historian— "I doubt whether a New York *belle* will make the best wife for a Boston lawyer."[17]

[15] WHP to W. G. Prescott, March 19, 1849, Prescott papers.

[16] R. Bentley to WHP, March 23, 1849, Prescott papers; and WHP to R. Bentley, May 14, 1849, Bentley papers.

[17] WHP to W. G. Prescott, April 1–2, 1849, Prescott papers; and Gardiner, ed., *Papers*, pp. 269–272. This is but one of many indications of the nature which could place Prescott, along with many others, as archetype for John P. Marquand's *The Late George Apley* (New York, 1940).

In June politics and intellectual curiosity caused New Yorker J. Trumbull Van Alen to call upon the master of Fifty-five Beacon Street. One of the earliest workers on behalf of Taylor's political candidacy, Van Alen recently had been designated American minister to Ecuador. Believing that the historian of Peru surely had books which could supply the information which he desired about contemporary Ecuador, he traveled to Boston. The happy thought that the library crowded with sixteenth-century South American materials also teemed with nineteenth-century data was, however, a mistaken one. Prescott had nothing that helped the fledgling diplomat, nor could he direct Van Alen to such sources.

Despite his loyalty to the Whig Party, Prescott penned a letter on behalf of a Democrat. The recent removal of Nathaniel Hawthorne from his post at the port of Salem saddened, even sickened, the historian. To Daniel Webster he confided, "Many respectable Whigs here do not see any good grounds for the removal . . . Will you allow me, therefore, to request your interest in his behalf?" Immediately the Massachusetts senator turned to Secretary of Treasury William M. Meredith. As he transmitted Prescott's letter, Webster added, "This letter is from Mr. Prescott, the Historian; a man, not more distinguished for learning and ability as a writer, than for amiable manner, generous affections, true friendships—in fact, 'For every virtue under Heaven.' I hope you know him.

"I suppose it will be best to leave Mr. Hawthorne where he is, for the present."[18]

Apparently this appeal was Prescott's initial invasion of the political arena. Totally unsupported is the idea that "It may have been to the desire of the historian William H. Prescott for data on Nicaraguan antiquities that Squier primarily owed his assignment" in Central America.[19] In 1849, few things were farther from Prescott's mind than were Central American antiquities.

---

[18] WHP to [?], July 18, 1849, Duyckinck collection; Gardiner, ed., *Papers,* pp. 272–273; and D. Webster to William M. Meredith, June 23, 1849, Meredith papers.

[19] Holman Hamilton, *Zachary Taylor—Soldier in the White House* (Indianapolis, 1951), p. 193.

2

The fourth week in June a dyspeptic historian exchanged the dusty heat of Beacon Street for the rolling vistas at Fitful Head. On the eve of his departure from the city, William informed Gayangos, "There I hope to break ground with Philip II." To himself, however, he confided despairingly, "I have even ceased to make good resolutions— that last infirmity of feeble minds."

Eyes and general health contributed to the uncertainty. He continued to record his memoranda in his own hand—the better to say bluntly the critical things which might goad him to action—but that was about the limit of his use of his eyes for literary purposes. His dyspepsia was of short duration, but another ailment succeeded it, a vague organic disturbance which produced mounting pain if he spent as much as thirty minutes in position for writing.

"Yet I am determined," he told himself, "to make one serious trial before relinquishing the glorious field—on which I have won some laurels—and on which I had promised myself a long career."[20] For all his wealth and social position, Prescott, it will be recalled, belonged to a generation of Boston aristocracy that believed in the dignity and necessity of continuing work. Furthermore, in the course of countless self-appraisals, he clearly realized that his life had real meaning only when he was engaged in literary activity. However difficult it was to proceed, it was impossible to stop.

Chewing anew on his plans, he began to focus his attention on those materials needed for an introductory chapter. In mid-July he was working three hours daily, thirty minutes with his own eyes. Much of this labor called for focusing thought. After having been out of harness for more than two years, he found it indescribably difficult.

When yet another of Sumner's vigorous antiwar orations arrived in printed form, it reactivated the friendly relations which had drifted in recent months. Many proper Bostonians had recently joined the ranks of Sumner's enemies, and the crusader wondered about William H. Prescott, who had not called at his office for two years. Reminding

---

[20] Penney, ed., *Letters to Gayangos,* p. 89; and Gardiner, ed., *Literary Memoranda,* 2: 189.

Charles that in that interval he had not been in the office of Hillard, Gardiner, or any other friend except on business, he declared, "You ought to have known there could be no meaning in this. My intercourse with you, I rejoice to say, has never been ruffled by an unfriendly word or act; and where I may have differed from you as to some of your sentiments, or as to your manner of expressing them, I have always done justice to the elevation of your views and to the integrity of your motives."[21] As sensitive as he was loyal, the historian was pained by Sumner's vague imputation.

In the stuffy atmosphere of Boston society, which commonly correlated political outlook and social acceptability, Prescott was refreshingly liberal. He was one of few Boston aristocrats warmly friendly toward that traitorous political rebel George Bancroft. In like manner, despite Sumner's break with the Whigs and his association with the Free Soilers, Prescott remained his friend. The historian ignored the unwritten rule of Boston society that political apostasy spelled social ostracism. He liked and always would like Bancroft and Sumner for the breadth and depth of their intellectual interests, for their rich conversational gifts, for their social charms, for their *savoir-faire* and *savoir-vivre*. Politically Prescott had been and would continue conservative—much removed from both Bancroft and Sumner. To cite his friendship with them as proof of his political liberality is sheer nonsense.[22] Instead, it is better to view those friendships as demonstrations of the complex nature of the Whig-scholar-gentleman-socialite of Fifty-five Beacon Street.

"I trust, also, you will have the opportunity of seeing something of English country life," father wrote son. "An Englishman in town shows one phase of his existence. But you must see him in the country, surrounded by his tenants, and living with rural hospitality, to appreciate him rightly. It is there only you see him in his true national

[21] Gardiner, ed., *Papers*, pp. 273–275.

[22] Illustrative of this false deduction is Morison's statement "In politics he was a steadfast liberal." ("Prescott: The American Thucydides," *The Atlantic Monthly*, 200 [November, 1957]); 172. For a balanced and unified account of Prescott's political outlook, despite the fact it is derived solely from published materials, see Michael Kraus, "Political Ideas," in Charvat and Kraus, *Prescott; Representative Selections*, pp. ci–cxiii.

costume, the one by which he is recognized as an Englishman." This word to Will about the two dimensions of English life soon touched the historian himself.

Reacting to news of European revolutions, as well as suggesting that Will give more attention to Britain, the historian recommended changes in his Continental itinerary—the abandonment of Switzerland and the inclusion, next winter, of Spain. One of William H. Prescott's basic evaluations of travel he phrased tersely, "You see men and manners, which are, after all, more worth seeing than rocks and mountains." He also wrote letters for Will to use in Spain.[23]

"How much I would give to see the inside of an English country house," Will wrote his father, "but I am afraid that I must be contented with taverns. How different it would be if you were here and the more I am the more I regret that you will not come. How you would be received everywhere and how well you have earned it. I am sure that you would fascinate and be fascinated with the highest and most cultivated of the English aristocracy." Unknown is the exact weight to be assigned this sentiment in connection with the historian's decision of 1850, but Will could not have been more direct than when he said, "Pray come and early in the Spring give Philip the Second a vacation and enjoy what I know you will. Do not say that you are too old for you would be a young man here and you would see such charming young ladies."[24]

At Nahant, meanwhile, Prescott finally had broken ground on the new work. At 6 P.M. on Thursday, July 19, he wrote the opening passages of the initial chapter. Once adjusted, the literary harness complemented rather than competed with Prescott's other activities at Fitful Head.

At Pepperell, in addition to sustaining his historical labors, Prescott had to review a book, Ticknor's *magnum opus*. From an early moment, Prescott knew that he would review the *History of Spanish Literature* for the *North American Review*. "I shall review it in the North American—a thing I abominate," he wrote Will. "But I would

[23] WHP to W. G. Prescott, July 2, 1849, Prescott papers; and WHP to Alexander Burton, September 15, 1849, Wilkinson collection.

[24] W. G. Prescott to WHP, August 31, 1849, Prescott papers.

not have his argosy get afloat without a friendly breeze from one whose sails have been filled with many a kind, steady one from him."[25] Waxing expansive, Prescott considered the work at hand, its organization, its abundant proof of the literary wealth of Spain—all with liberal quotations from Ticknor. "Mr. Ticknor has now, for the first time," his friend declared, "fully surveyed the ground, systematically arranged its various productions, and explored their character and properties." Even Ticknor's style, which he privately had found undistinguished, drew praise. "It is clear, classical, and correct, with a sustained moral dignity that not unfrequently rises to eloquence."

"We predict with confidence," the historian continued, "that it will be speedily translated into Castilian and into German; and that it must become the standard work on Spanish literature, not only for those who speak our own tongue, but for the Spaniards themselves."[26] No daring attached to the first part of the Prescott prophecy because Gayangos was already translating it from another set of proof sheets.

This, his longest review, Prescott declared would also be his last. Although, from the beginning, he had intended to write it *con amore*, there is less evidence of it here than in his writings on Scott and Italian literature. Behind his words, however, was a remarkable demonstration of love. To avoid the pain which besieged him in a sitting position, he had written much of this article while on his knees. In 1850, he ordered stereotype plates for the addition of this review to his *Miscellanies*.

"Now Muse of History," he penned in his memoranda, "—never more will I forsake thy altar—yet I shall have but little incense to offer."[27]

---

[25] Gardiner, ed., *Literary Memoranda,* 2: 191–192; WHP to C. Sumner, August 16, 22, 1849, Sumner papers; Penney, ed., *Letters to Gayangos,* p. 91; WHP to W. G. Prescott, September 2, 1849, Prescott papers; and [WHP], "Ticknor's History of Spanish Literature," *North American Review,* 70 (January, 1850): 1–56.

[26] *Ibid.,* pp. 54, 55, 56.

[27] William H. Prescott, *Biographical and Critical Miscellanies* (Boston, 1855), pp. 639–729; and Gardiner, ed., *Literary Memoranda,* 2: 193.

3

A few weeks elapsed following the return of the Prescotts to Beacon Street and, in the midst of arrangements for a dance in their home, they were settling into their wintertime routine when all Boston experienced a shock of frenzied excitement.

Shortly after noon on Friday, November 23, tall, prosperous Dr. George Parkman left his Beacon Hill home on Walnut Street—a long stone's throw from the Prescott residence—for an appointment with Dr. John White Webster at Harvard's Massachusetts Medical College on North Grove Street, in Boston. Obsessed by a penchant for a style of living which he could not afford on his annual salary of twelve hundred dollars, chemistry professor Webster, wallowing in debt, had borrowed money from Dr. Parkman, Robert Gould Shaw, Catherine G. Prescott, and William H. Prescott, among others. For the historian the well-being of the Websters was a matter of more than normal concern because Mrs. Webster was his aunt, his mother's half-sister. To the Prescotts, Professor Webster owed $437.50.[28]

Although his brother-in-law Robert G. Shaw offered a substantial reward when Dr. Parkman failed to reappear, nothing relieved the mystery. Then, on Thanksgiving Day, college janitor Ephraim Littlefield, suspicious of the professor for reasons of his own, dug through a brick wall into a vault. There he discovered portions of a body which, identified as that of Dr. Parkman, led immediately to the arrest and jailing of the protesting Webster.

"I have seen him twice in person," the historian wrote, reporting the matter to Will, "the first time, much overcome; the second, tranquil—protesting his innocence. I was today at Cambridge with his distressed family—distressed, indeed, though firmly believing his innocence—their only comfort. Their friends are all most ready to show

[28] George Bemis, comp., *Report on the Case of John W. Webster* (Boston, 1850), p. 425; and additional references to the Prescotts are in *ibid.*, pp. 38, 151–152, 274. The Parkman murder has attracted many writers; three recent accounts, none of which relates the Prescotts to it, are contained in Stewart Holbrook, "Murder at Harvard," *The American Scholar* (1945); Morison, *Three Centuries of Harvard*; and Amory, *Proper Bostonians*.

their sympathy."[29] In addition to being talk of the town, something to pass on to Will, the case had yet another special tie to Will because he had traveled recently with Dr. Parkman's son.

Awaiting the coroner's report, Boston buzzed with speculation regarding the outcome of any trial which might develop. Lawyers and laymen alike discussed the evidence, the character of the professor, his motives, and so forth. Early in the Parkman-Webster furor the Prescotts canceled social activities, including their dance. In those same weeks the historian unavailingly tried to resume his historical labors. Out of spirits and unable to put stylus to noctograph, he admitted in his memoranda, "But my nerves have been much shaken by the late melancholy event."[30] For Webster the darkness deepened when the coroner's report led the grand jury to return a true bill charging him with murder. The suspect remained in custody.

Meanwhile Amory informed Will that Professor Webster "eats a very good dinner which he gets from Parker's, and which father has the pleasure of paying for."[31] Closer to the tragedy than most, all the Prescotts, and especially eighty-two-year-old Mrs. Prescott, felt it keenly. However, they did resume, on a limited scale, their social ways.

Edward Twisleton, charming and intelligent in the British manner which ever appealed to the historian, visited him early in December. Amory attended dinner parties and longed for dances. Lizzie, despite the fact that more and more of her friends were either married or engaged, flitted about in a manner which suggested that her heart was hers alone. "On New Year's Eve," the historian wrote Will, "we had a pleasant rollicking party at Sam Eliot's, with the old Pepperell games."[32] Apparently no Prescott ever outgrew blindman's buff. In intellectual circles the year closed with attention directed at George Ticknor's book.

Another melancholy circumstance, the plight of Nathaniel Hawthorne, also touched Prescott that winter. The efforts of many prominent persons notwithstanding, his dismissal of June 1849 remained in

[29] Gardiner, ed., *Papers,* pp. 279–281.
[30] Gardiner, ed., *Literary Memoranda,* 2: 194.
[31] W. A. Prescott to W. G. Prescott, December 16, 1849, Prescott papers.
[32] WHP to W. G. Prescott, January 8, 1850, Prescott papers.

effect. On the heels of that misfortune, the sensitive forty-five-year-old author also had lost his mother. By December, friends and admirers were contributing to his support. "I enclose you ten dollars, with pleasure, for poor Hawthorne," Prescott wrote Sumner, leader of yet another good cause. "I wrote to Webster in behalf of Hawthorne, I remember, last summer," the historian continued, "—with the success, it seems, I might have expected."[33]

Brightening the drab and melancholy season for those at Fifty-five Beacon Street were Will's lengthy letters. Beyond the happy experiences in rural England and Scotland which had lengthened to three months, Will had briefly glimpsed Ireland. "Tell Father," he wrote, "that I have seen in many of the principal [railway] stations copies of his works."[34] Crossing to Paris, he fell in with numerous traveling Bostonians, as well as the prominent Frenchmen to whom he bore letters. The winter dampness and cold again brought on the throat ailment to which he was highly susceptible. He tarried in Paris for medical reasons, among others.

While still in the French capital, Will began to look forward to Spain, having "made the acquaintance of a most beautiful Spanish lady with eyes as large as teacups and that dark complexion which lights up so well by candlelight."[35] In mid-February 1850, armed with Spanish grammar and the letters supplied by his father and others, Will headed south. As he neared Spain and saw sights never glimpsed by his father, the historian made numerous suggestions, none more important than one reading, "I want you to be among natives—not with a Yankee *clique,* who keep you still at home while you fancy yourself abroad." While awaiting Will's first reports from Spain and likewise the opening of the Webster trial, the congressional debates in Washington stirred the historian's political instincts as nothing had since the outbreak of the war with Mexico.

"There is a very bad feeling in Congress on the slave question between North and South," he wrote Will. "Mr. Clay has brought in a

[33] WHP to C. Sumner, December [blank], 1849, Sumner papers.
[34] W. G. Prescott to S. A. Prescott, October 25, November 8, 1849, Prescott papers.
[35] W. G. Prescott to WHP, January 23, 1850, Prescott papers.

compromise bill . . . . It is to be hoped that there are moderate men enough in both parties to carry this or some other compromise through." Later the historian took his place among the hundreds whose signed statement endorsed the sentiments in Webster's speech of March 7.[36]

Despite dozens of distractions, Prescott bent to his work and wrote the third and fourth chapters of the new history during the opening weeks of 1850. Amid all else, he maintained a massive and expanding correspondence. At first he fended off Bentley's request for a review of Ticknor's book—William's publishers on both sides of the Atlantic had published George's book—but the London publisher won out. "I wrote a little notice of the work," Prescott wrote Bentley, "for a newspaper here when it came out, which was printed in small type, among similar notices of new books, without my name. I have added about as much more; and if you like you can print it in your Miscellany."[37]

Every letter from Bentley in this period indicated that he was sending copies of recent books. Intended to foster the cordial relations which might help him obtain the contract for Prescott's next work, Bentley's kindness was self-defeating, in part, because the historian, in hearing them read, consumed hours which he could have dedicated to historical writing.

The opening of Professor Webster's trial in mid-March riveted Boston's attention on the second act of the dramatic and macabre case. Serving as counsel for the defense, at Prescott's expense, were Pliny Merrick and Edward D. Sohier, the former a Harvard classmate, the latter Susan's brother-in-law. Among those who crowded the courtroom of Judge Lemuel Shaw was William Appleton, Prescott's neigh-

[36] WHP to W. G. Prescott, October 29, 1849, January 8, 1850, Prescott papers; Gardiner, ed., *Papers*, pp. 282–285; and James Ford Rhodes, *History of the United States from the Compromise of 1850*, 7 vols. (New York, 1893–1906), 1: 156.

[37] R. Bentley to WHP, January 4, 1850, Prescott papers; Gardiner, ed., *Papers*, pp. 285–286; and WHP to R. Bentley, March 4, 1850, Bentley papers. The newspaper item was [WHP], in "New Publications," *Boston Daily Advertiser*, January 1, 1850; in expanded form it became [WHP], "History of Spanish Literature," *Bentley's Miscellany*, 27 (1850): 385–387.

bor. On the second day of the trial, Appleton wrote in his diary, "They will not convict him I think; so it looks now." Ten days later he wrote differently. "The trial of Dr. Webster brought to a close; after hearing the Charge of the Judge, I went to prepare Mrs. Prescott for the news of the sad event."[38] The Professor was sentenced to death.

The Webster trial attracted nationwide publicity and provoked much criticism. Susan Prescott, writing her absent son—"Willie" to her—referred to the widespread sentiment south of Boston "that the case has been conducted in a cruel, and unjust manner—by Counsel, Judge and Jury," and she added, "your father is troubled every day by letters and newspapers to that effect."[39] In general, opinion in Boston held that justice had been served. Mrs. Webster, accompanied by her three daughters—one of whom was named for Aunt Catherine G. Prescott—appealed unavailingly to the governor for a pardon for the condemned man.

On top of all else, the troubles besetting their retired domestic, Nathan Webster, shocked the Prescott household. Nathan's wife, considerably his junior, had deserted him to join a Mormon caravan. For the Websters, it was a bad season in Boston, and the historian, upset and yet unable to do anything in either case, possibly sought relief in the travel which he speedily undertook.

Leaving Boston on April 8 with a party which included nineteen-year-old Amory and Elizabeth, then nearing twenty-one, he leisurely journeyed to Washington. The first evening in that city, Friday, April 12, with Lizzie on his arm, he was guest of English Minister Sir Henry Bulwer. Another honored guest at the diplomat's table, Henry Clay, was celebrating his seventy-fourth birthday. The senior senator from Kentucky held a high place in Prescott's affections. Some of that affection derived possibly from Clay's friendly calls at Prescott's quarters and the Kentuckian's obvious delight in the company of the ladies. Following the Bulwer dinner, the visitors from Massachusetts attended the President's levee at the White House.

[38] Wolcott, *Jottings,* p. 83; Loring, ed., *Diaries of William Appleton,* p. 139; and Gertrude Euphemia Meredith, *The Descendants of Hugh Amory 1605–1805* (London, 1901), genealogical chart.

[39] S. A. Prescott to W. G. Prescott, April 14, 1850, Prescott papers.

Succeeding days brought other dinners—with Winthrop, King, the Calderóns, Webster, and others, visits to the capitol, Secretary of Treasury Meredith's reception, a ball given by the Tayloes at The Octagon. The stay in Washington closed with Prescott's attendance at a White House dinner presided over by the President's charming daughter, Mrs. Mary Elizabeth Bliss, who was but a few years older than Lizzie Prescott. Seated at the President's side, the historian fended off the old warrior's suggestion that he write a history of the war with Mexico. Zachary Taylor was the third occupant of the White House to receive Prescott. The historian's impression of him was more favorable than that of either John Quincy Adams or James Polk.[40] " 'Rough and Ready' is a very pleasing old soldier—of kindly and most cordial manners—very simple, yet with nothing vulgar in his air," he wrote Will. "The result of all the hospitality I experienced," Prescott wrote Sumner, "is that I have come home Rough and Ready to the backbone . . . If you were to spend half an hour with the old chief's daughter, who does the honors of the house, I think you would be a convert too."[41]

On the homeward trip, four days in New York City permitted a renewal of social contacts. On the edge of Greenwich, at Seventeen West Twenty-first Street, the George Bancrofts elegantly entertained Prescott. Recently returned to this country, the ex-diplomat was enjoying life. George and William talked of many things—mutual friends in England, the kindnesses which Bancroft had extended Will Prescott in London, and the historical labors which meant much to both of them. At another New York dinner, Prescott and Washington Irving once more exchanged pleasantries. By the time he reached Boston on April 24, Prescott teemed with delightful memories and with renewed awareness of the joys of travel.

[40] WHP to S. A. Prescott, [April 9, 14, 16, 21, 1850], Prescott papers; Gardiner, ed., *Papers,* pp. 286–287; and Massachusetts Historical Society *Proceedings,* 2nd ser., 4 (1887–1889): 236–237.

[41] WHP to W. G. Prescott, April 28, 1850, Prescott papers; WHP to C. Sumner, [n.d.], Sumner papers. Prescott's admiration of the firm, courageous, honest, sociable, thrifty, proud Taylor (see Brainerd Dyer, *Zachary Taylor* [Baton Rouge, 1946], scarcely included the democratic, informal, and uncultivated sides of that man's nature.

The historian and Lizzie unpacked their things, ready to settle down for a while, but not so Amory. For him the return was but prelude to departure. Lacking any desire to go to Harvard, the youngest Prescott talked of the Orient, specifically of the Calcutta trade. For generations, including generations of Prescotts, the India trade had been on the tongues and in the lives of Massachusetts men. Some of the fortune which promoted the ease of the Prescotts had come from profits in the India trade. To Susan and the historian, their boy's long absence became more palatable through their realization that his health, somewhat frail of late, might be improved by the long voyage. To him the historian entrusted a sum of money to be invested in goods. The little "adventure" might do much to determine his prospects as a business man.[42]

### 4

On April 29, the day that Amory began his long voyage, Will, already absent for twenty months, was in Seville. After a leisurely trip down the Guadalquivir River, he visited Cádiz and enjoyed kinsman Burton's hospitality, expecially his delicious sherry. Then followed Tangiers and Granada before doubling northward for England prior to shipping for America. Will's unhurried itinerary was devoid of schedule. In Boston, meanwhile, a schedule was in the making.

For years rumor of a trip to England had surrounded the historian almost as regularly as the grass greened. Urged repeatedly by American and English friends to make the trip, he had backed down on every occasion. Now he buttressed the usual spring rumor with firm resolve —May 22 was his sailing date. "The greatest pleasure in prospect is that of seeing you," he wrote his son. "Indeed I should not go unless you were to be there."[43]

Preparations for the epochal trip absorbed every energy. To Abbott Lawrence, the American minister in London, went a request that arrangements be made at the Clarendon or one of the other fine hotels for a parlor and two bedrooms. In order to have the comforts of home

[42] Gardiner, ed., *Papers*, 287–290.
[43] W. G. Prescott to S. A. Prescott, May 10, 1850, Prescott papers; and Gardiner, ed., *Papers*, pp. 291–292.

away from home, he also requested Abbott to obtain a good servant for him. For the trip he allotted approximately six weeks in London and a like period in the English countryside. By returning in September he would not sacrifice the joys of Pepperell.

Supplementing the aid extended by the current minister in London was the advice of former ministers George Bancroft and Edward Everett. Sailing from New York, Prescott hoped to see Bancroft immediately before departing, "to ask some scores of questions of your wife and you as to proprieties, *convenances* &c in the London world." To Edward Everett, in Cambridge, the historian proposed to go posthaste. "I should like to ask half an hours worth of questions of you, touching men and manners in London," he wrote Everett. "Shall I come out and see you tomorrow at twelve?" Everett answered the many questions and gave him letters of introduction to Macaulay, Lord Ashburton, Lord John Russell, and the Duke of Northumberland. Although Prescott's literary contacts in England virtually eliminated the need of letters of introduction, he nonetheless welcomed a few which opened political and fashionable circles to him. He also sought letters from Bancroft.[44]

On Tuesday, May 21, Prescott and reader-secretary John Foster Kirk, his traveling companion, entrained for New York. The Bancrofts entertained Prescott at dinner and answered his thousand-and-one questions as best they could. When he left their place late that evening, he carried a dozen or more letters. By noon, May 22, Prescott and Kirk had boarded the British mail packet *Niagara*. Beyond Halifax the wind increased, the sea roughened, and Prescott sickened. "This sea life is even worse than I thought it was," he wrote Susan. "I had forgotten half its miseries. I will never trust a man hereafter who talks complacently of it."[45] Travel strengthened his vision, but a touch of rheumatism reinforced the miseries of his uncertain stomach.

[44] *Ibid.*, pp. 292–294; WHP to G. Bancroft, draft, May 16, 1850, Prescott papers; and WHP to E. Everett, May 16, 20, 1850, E. Everett papers.
[45] WHP to S. A. Prescott, May 22, June 3, 1850, Prescott papers.

5

In England, the historian was very much at home. In 1816 he had gone there pro-British—a Federalist who considered the War of 1812 an American mistake, a lover of English literature, an admirer of British legal institutions, a young man who equated good manners and correct speech with English standards. Now, in 1850, his attachments multiplied, Prescott considered England the most truly civilized place on earth. The literary reputation which he had sought and won there had produced an ever-widening number of English correspondents. In America, in recent years, he had personally come to know Sir Charles and Lady Mary Lyell, Lord Carlisle (formerly Lord Morpeth), Charles Dickens, Edward Twisleton, William Macready, and others. The kind of welcome which the deceased Sydney Smith had described did await Prescott.[46]

On June 5 the train trip from Liverpool to London reacquainted Prescott with English countryside—the woods, flocks, emerald green lawns, winding streams, hawthorn hedges, rustic cottages, lordly mansions, and all else. In late afternoon he settled into an elegant ground floor apartment at Mivart's Hotel, in Brook Street. His drawing room was larger than the Beacon Street library, and the other rooms were of ample proportions. In addition to these sumptuous quarters, Minister Lawrence had arranged for a servant and a brougham, the latter with a couple of horses. The servant, Penn by name, quickly demonstrated his skills as he unpacked the trunks, strapped the razor, cleaned boots, attended to clothing, ran errands—indeed waited upon his new master hand and foot from the morning call that summoned Prescott from bed to the late evening attention that tucked him into it. Prescott's only disappointment was Will's failure

[46] Prescott's stay in London between June 5 and July 19, 1850, is detailed in the following: WHP to S. A. Prescott, June 7, 9, 11, 18–20, 29, 30–July 4, July 11, 16–18, 1850, and WHP to C. G. Prescott, June 20–28, 1850, Prescott papers; Gardiner, ed., *Papers,* pp. 294–296; WHP to E. Prescott, June 14, 1850, WHP to G. Ticknor, June 26, 1850, and WHP to A. Ticknor, July 18, 1850, in Ticknor, *Prescott,* pp. 306–308, 312–316, 318–319; and Gardiner, ed., *Literary Memoranda,* 2: 194–198. Hereinafter, in this section, the notes relate to direct quotations only.

to greet him, a disappointment to which he was doomed for several weeks. Meanwhile the social whirl of the West End quickly engulfed the historian.

The evening of his arrival in London, Abbott Lawrence whisked him off to an affair at which the visitor immediately met numerous diplomats and cabinet ministers, among the latter kindly Lord Palmerston, then Secretary for Foreign Affairs. Breakfasting with Lord Carlisle the next morning, he learned that that nobleman was as affable in England as he had been in Boston—and that the dowager Countess of Carlisle reminded him of his own mother. In less than forty-eight hours, Prescott's table was covered with cards and invitations.

Two segments of society, those gravitating about political leaders and literary figures, drew his attention. One day he dined with Sumner's friend Sir Robert Inglis, a Tory politician of little ability and considerable prejudice who was active in many religious and learned societies. He dined with Sir Robert Peel, enjoyed the view of the Thames at twilight, and even more so the stroll through Sir Robert's collection of paintings. Abbott Lawrence's dinner introduced him to a Turkish envoy in a red skullcap and a Nepalese envoy who wore a necklace of rough emeralds, a scarlet petticoat garnished with pearls, and a headpiece made of the beak of a bird. From Lawrence's affair he hurried off to Lady Palmerston's reception. Invitations to breakfasts, luncheons, teas, dinners, receptions, interspersed with tickets to the opera and various exhibitions, an invitation from the Duke of Northumberland to see a gigantic lily at his house, and so on, moved Prescott in circles studded with diplomats, cabinet officers, dukes, duchesses, and lesser nobility. He enjoyed every minute of it.

Two writers interested in Spanish culture, Richard Ford and William Stirling, entertained the historian in their own special ways. With Ford, "the lunch was all Spanish—Spanish wines—delicious, Spanish dishes, which good breeding forced me to taste, but no power could force me to eat, for they were hotter than the Inquisition." At bachelor Stirling's elegant quarters, where the American found the food less

Spanish and more palatable, he enjoyed the "Spanish drawings, and copies well executed of the Spanish art."[47]

Numerous literary figures were met and assessed. Thackeray he found "a stalwart person, with a face not indicating his peculiar talent. His manners are not striking either, but quite unaffected. He talks of coming to America." Macaulay was "*brusque,* cordial, a stout, sturdy, square-built person, rather ungainly, not pleasing in the tones of his voice, but very pleasing to me for his heartiness." Of the Dean of St. Paul's he concluded, "I have not seen any of them, however, that I like better than Milman, so kind and genial." John Gibson Lockhart, son-in-law and biographer of Sir Walter Scott, struck Prescott as one who "has the remains of a handsome face; looks rather melancholy, and is piquant in his conversation." The eighty-seven-year-old poet Samuel Rogers, with whom Prescott had exchanged publications and letters, was in bed nursing injuries received in a street accident, but the witty old man was "full of salt, not to say cayenne. I was praising somebody's good-nature very much. 'Yes,' he said, 'so much good-nature, that there is no room for good-sense'." Historian Archibald Alison, cordial but with nothing striking in his appearance, was remembered as "a stalworth, light-complexioned, red-whiskered Scot."[48]

The socialite rather than the historian had made the trip from Boston, but Prescott nonetheless crossed the paths of two publishers. On a belated and brief call upon Richard Bentley, the historian learned of the sales and prospects of his books. Of the man who had alternately baffled, irritated, and cultivated him, he now wrote, "You can't imagine how civil Bentley is." Declining his own publisher's social invitations, he accepted one from publisher John Murray, whom he had long admired. On July 4 Murray's whitebait dinner at Greenwich brought together Ford, Stirling, Hallam, Lockhart, a diplomat, a wild-game hunter, and the American historian and his son, the last-named

---

[47] WHP to S. A. Prescott, June 11, 30–July 4, 1850, Prescott papers.

[48] *Id.* to *id.,* June 9, 18, 30–July 4, 1850, Prescott papers; and Ticknor, *Prescott,* p. 314. For pre-1850 relations between Prescott and Rogers, see P. W. Clayden, *Rogers and His Contemporaries,* 2 vols. (London, 1889), 2: 188, 236, 339–341; and Wolcott, ed., *Correspondence,* pp. 122, 293, 401, 661.

having turned up that very day after his long Continental rambles. "Such a dinner—fish and wines and jolly company—and came into London at midnight on the top of a coach, with a cigar in my mouth—not singing, however. Next morning I felt a snapping headache was due. Waked up bright as a bell, as clear in conscience as if I had been virtuous and fasting," he wrote Susan.[49]

The physical well-being about which he occasionally fretted never once troubled the historian during this siege of rich foods, late hours, bright lights, and other nemeses. Soon after his arrival in England, he had reported that his eyes and stomach were improved. Week after week his eyes continued to improve. After three weeks of the social whirl he reported, "My health every way—eyes, tongue, stomach—is much improved." Like the frequent trips to New York, Washington, and elsewhere, this one did not tax Prescott's vision. Early in June, and periodically thereafter, he registered his characteristic away-from-home complaint, "a home-sickness, which lies at the bottom of my heart; and I wish September were come."[50]

One of the visitor's capital moments came on Thursday, June 20, when he was presented at Queen Victoria's drawing-room at St. James's Palace. For the occasion he wore "a chapeau with gold lace—blue coat and white trowsers, begilded with buttons and metal. The coat buttons up single breasted to the throat,—sword—and patent leather boots." Lady Mahon gave him every instruction, but he could not quench the fear that he would trip over his own sword. "I was presented by our Minister, according to the directions of the chamberlain, as the historian of 'Ferdinand and Isabella'."[51] The sword did not trip him—rather, he enjoyed the occasion immensely. Somewhat fittingly, as a follow-up to his presentation at St. James's Palace, Prescott repaired to the sumptuous Stafford House as the luncheon guest of the Duchess of Sutherland.

Days later, in much the same court dress, Prescott attended the

---

49 WHP to S. A. Prescott, June 30–July 4, 16, 1850, Prescott papers. Concerning Murray, see F. Saunders, *Memories of the Great Metropolis* (New York, 1852), p. 50.

50 WHP to S. A. Prescott, June 9, 29, 1850, Prescott papers.

51 *Id.* to *id.*, June 18–20, 1850, Prescott papers.

Queen's ball at Buckingham Palace. Never one to care for dancing, he gave most of his attention to jewels, lights, chandeliers, and the passing parade of notables.

Midway through the stay in London, the historian found himself posing for portraits, at the request of Lord Carlisle and William Stirling. For George Richmond, the popular portrait painter whose ideal of "the truth lovingly told" led to some conscious flattery of his subjects, Prescott sat four times. Henry Wyndham Phillips, working in oil, required a like number of sittings. In mid-July, both portraits were viewed and Richmond's crayon work, commissioned by Lord Carlisle, was pronounced perfect. Comparing it with earlier portraits, as well as with Phillips' oil canvas for Stirling which he did not particularly like, William wrote Susan, "It is the only portrait in which I recognize the gentleman I shave every morning. And it is such a gentlemanlike portrait—such a good tie to the cravat."[52] When the vain visitor who never looked his age had additional years subtracted by Richmond, the resulting portrait proved flatteringly acceptable.

True to the nature so often exhibited in Boston, New York, Washington, and elsewhere to the west of the Atlantic, Prescott gave the ladies of London more than passing attention. No sooner had he met Lord Carlisle's young sister Mary than he pronounced her "pretty and pleasing." Lady Lyell, his companion on many occasions and his hostess on others, remained the charming individual he had found her in Boston. Dean Milman's wife was also charming—"so modest, and unaffected, and intelligent!" At Ford's, the historian's dinner partner was "one of the most pleasing women I have seen here—very pretty, and animated in conversation—Lady Mahon." Returned from a small party at the Countess Grey's, William wrote, "There was also a charming lady there to whom I lost my heart, dear wife, some three weeks since. Don't be jealous—she is over 70—Lady Morley—a most natural, lively benevolent body."[53]

The greatest English tribute to Prescott, historian and man of letters, took place on Monday, June 24. In order to confer honorary degrees upon Prescott and Lord Northampton, Oxford held a special convo-

[52] *Id.* to *id.,* July 16–18, 1850, Prescott papers.
[53] *Id.* to *id.,* June 7, 11, 18–20, July 16–18, 1850, Prescott papers.

cation in the theater. In flaming red robes, the honored men processed through the public street with the faculty. Professor Joseph Phillimore expounded on Prescott's merits, and the degree of D.C.L. (Doctor of Civil Law) was awarded. Of all the honorary degrees received by Prescott, this was the only degree-conferring ceremony that he ever attended. Before returning to London with Minister Lawrence, he learned why it was that the award had not occurred earlier, in the regular academic season. Someone, with doubts about the historian's religious beliefs, had turned to Dean Milman for an opinion. That churchman's temporary absence from London so delayed his answer that the special convocation became necessary. In 1850 the granting of an honorary degree to a Unitarian was no trifling matter at Oxford.

Along with significantly memorable moments were miscellaneous ones which evidenced the American visitor's tastes and nature. Shortly after his arrival in London, he prodded Ford about the review of Ticknor's book which he was doing for the *Quarterly Review*. Remembering George's efforts on behalf of *Ferdinand and Isabella* in Britain in 1838, Prescott tried to do as much for the *History of Spanish Literature*. Of three other Bostonians, Prescott thought in different terms as he ordered Stilton cheeses sent to them.

The visitor neither liked nor pretended to like everything. On June 13 he was in the throng at Ascot which witnessed the widely heralded race for the Emperor of Russia's trophy. To the knowledgeable it was between Lord Eglinton's Flying Dutchman and Lord Stanley's Canezou. Five horses started the $2\frac{1}{2}$-mile race. Flying Dutchman won by such a wide margin that *The Times* termed it "a most hollow affair." Prescott put his estimate of the occasion in the words, "I would not go to another race, if I could do it by walking into the next street; that is, if I had to sit it out, as I did here, for three mortal hours. How hard the English fine people are driven for amusement!" A slightly more charitable view was taken of the upper house of Parliament. "On the whole the House of Lords is not as imposing a body in its appearance as the U.S. Senate. Many of the Members are clownish and countrified in dress and demeanor."[54]

[54] *The Times*, June 14, 1850; Ticknor, *Prescott*, p. 307; and WHP to S. A. Prescott, June 18–20, 1850, Prescott papers.

Always one to enjoy good food without disastrous effects upon his waistline, the historian declared himself on the subjects of confectionery and breakfasts. "You know I have a failing in the way of confectionery, and the English have varieties that would make the fortune of a Yankee. Would it not be a patriotic thing to send over some one to supersede our old-fashioned trumpery?" Apparently he enjoyed the confections from the first moment, but not so something else. "I have changed my mind somewhat in regard to London breakfasts. Nothing can be more easy and lively. A variety of dishes, meats, are often handed round—little touched. The guests generally lay out their strength on such simple fare as cold, dry, toasted bread, or the stale wheaton loaf, which each one cuts a junk off with a carving knife. Yet I would give a gold sovereign to exchange any dozen of them for the dipped toast and hot cakes—abominable as they are—in Beacon Street."[55] More than one London literary breakfast had introduced him to the heady kind of conversation which reminded him of Club meetings and afterdinner sessions in his own library.

Beyond the tidbits that occupied him daily, Prescott occasionally reflected and summarized his experiences. The day before he closed out six weeks of socializing, he wrote William H. Gardiner, "Well, what shall I tell you of London life? A singular society it is—wealth, rank, fashion, beauty, scholarship, with a good share of pretension, arrogance, narrow-mindedness, triviality, &c. &c., with plenty of leisure to have them all jumbled together in every possible way . . . . All talk politics—women and all. . . . The politics they talk are wholly English. They rarely send their views beyond the little island . . . The bigotry of the English surpasses everything since the days of Ferdinand and Isabella."[56]

To Anna Ticknor, who had sampled society in London on more than one occasion, he also summarized his thinking. "I have now seen life in London and its environs, wealth, wit, and beauty, and rank; sometimes without either; women talking politics, men talking nonsense; literary breakfasts, fashionable dinners, convivial dinners, political dinners; lords without pretension, citizens with a good deal,

[55] *Id.* to *id.,* June 30–July 4, 16–18, 1850, Prescott papers.
[56] Gardiner, ed., *Papers,* pp. 294–295.

literary lions, fashionable lions, the Nepalese, the hippopotamus, &c., &c. But I have not seen an old woman. As to age, nobody, man or woman, is old here. . . . It is a nation of *castes*, as defined as those in India. But what cordial hearts are sometimes found under the crust of shyness and reserve!"[57]

Months later, at Pepperell, the historian reflected, "With my reception there I had every reason to be gratified, not on the mere score of vanity, but on the reasonable conviction that my writings have been read and highly appreciated by the cultivated circles of my fatherland."[58]

6

Prescott's unfinished book encouraged his departure from London.[59] Accompanied by Kirk and Penn, he took train for Folkestone, crossed to Boulogne, and entrained for Paris. Will had preceded him to the French capital where he had suffered another of his throat ailments.

Dimmed by the passage of more than thirty years, the historian's memory of Paris was jolted by reality—"so brilliant and beautiful— a perpetual fete—more soldiers and music, and dancing, and frolicking of all sorts in the streets through the Sunday that I was there than I saw in the streets of London during my six weeks' residence." Still basically hostile to the French, and especially so in view of their penchant for recurring revolution, he viewed Paris with mixed reaction. "Talk of its misery and its dilapidation! I saw no sign of it. If the decay is anywhere it is not in the purse—at least not in the luxuries that the purse buys. But it is not the most moral place in the world certainly. Its revolutions have not turned up the moral side yet. There is one vice, however, they cannot be charged with—hypocrisy."

Failing to find at home either of two scholars about whom he inquired, Prescott gave the day to Will, the city at large, and the revival of his recollections of it, "so that they will now go down bright with me through the remainder of life."

<hr>

[57] Ticknor, *Prescott,* pp. 318–319.

[58] Gardiner, ed., *Literary Memoranda,* 2: 196.

[59] The interlude on the Continent is treated in the following: WHP to S. A. Prescott, July 23–30, 1850, Prescott papers; and WHP to E. Prescott, July 28, 1850, in Ticknor, *Prescott,* p. 323.

After fewer than forty-eight hours in Paris, Prescott and Kirk and the servant departed for Brussels, to undertake the quick tour which basically had inspired this Continental interlude. The unfinished history which lay in the study in Beacon Street concerned, among other places, the Low Countries. By glimpsing this region, Prescott did something which he had ignored in reference to Spain, Mexico, and Peru—he was studying, at firsthand, the terrain of his historical theme.

In Brussels he stepped into the Middle Ages, reveling in the grandeur of the Hôtel de Ville. Both there and in the cathedral, modern times melted away and the historian of the sixteenth century felt at home. Of the magnificent windows in the cathedral, he wrote, "The glass was of the time of Charles the Fifth, and I soon recognized his familiar face—the wapper-jaw of the Austrian line. I was with my own kith and kin, was I not?"

Between Brussels and Antwerp, Prescott enjoyed the rich countryside, of which he remarked, "It beats England all hollow." From Antwerp he sailed to Rotterdam. Beyond that city the trio quickly visited Delft, the Hague, Haarlem, and Amsterdam, aided on every occasion by his ubiquitous servant.

Refreshingly unlike his London experience, the hurried glimpse of Belgium and Holland stimulated the historian in Prescott. What he said of Brussels, he could easily have applied to all of the Low Countries, "If I don't make something out of my visit . . ., I don't know what there is in eyesight."

7

Returned to London following his hurried ten days on the Continent, Prescott ate a memorable dinner at the table of Lord Carlisle. Macaulay, Thackeray, the Earl and Countess of Clarendon, the Duchess of Sutherland, and Lady Mary Howard helped to make it a merry one.

The dinner went through the usual courses—the eternal turbot and shrimp-sauce—eight or ten *entremets*—much like those with us—then the regular saddle of mutton—then ducks and hare—then frozen pudding, and half a dozen nondescript confectionery things, with ices, strawberries and coffee —neither as good as ours—then a rich dessert of grapes, pines, strawberries, peaches—all such as are hardly to be found out of England—except, indeed, peaches. We had sherry after the soup, then champagne over and over again, superbly frozen—they drink, by the bye, always in flat glasses, then other wines, the madeira always bad. Sweet wines are handed round with the dessert, or it may be cordials. Ale and port with the cheese, which is as constant as mutton. I have run on with this bill of fare as a sample of what we had not only here, but, with little variation, everywhere in London.[60]

The next morning he set out for Hams Hall, the Warwickshire country place of Mr. Charles Bowyer Adderley. In so doing, Prescott began the second phase of his English visit. For six weeks in June and July he had enjoyed the brilliance of West End society. Now, with Parliament prorogued, he planned to spend an equal interval in rural Britain. So many invitations had been extended that, as in London, he had been forced to pick and choose, accept and decline. His first host in the country was a thirty-six-year-old Member of Parliament who was related to the historian's acquaintance Edward Twisleton.

One day Adderley and his guests sallied to Warwick Castle, to Stoneleigh Abbey, and Kenilworth. At Kenilworth the historian's thoughts centered upon Sir Walter Scott. Another drive, the next day, and he confessed, "The English live in the open air. They look on our ladies as Chinese, who never walk."

Two things which impressed Prescott at one country seat after another first drew his attention at Hams Hall: the numerous servants in colored livery and the morning prayers in which master, family, guests, and servants all participated. Days of gentlemanly ease, of unhurried excursions, of fascinating landscapes, succeeded one another. "The only bore I have met with was in the shape of my lady hostess's album—as much my horror as a dinner speech. I perpetrated a couple of verses, and this will be a memento of the Yankee stranger."

A long train ride to the north and the historian found himself in Alnwick, close to the coast of the North Sea in Northumberland, the guest of Everett's friend the Duke of Northumberland.[61] The ancient

---

[60] WHP to S. A. Prescott, August 3–8, 1850, Prescott papers. The account of the visit at Hams Hall is in *ibid*.

[61] For the visit at Alnwick Castle, see WHP to S. A. Prescott, August 3–8, 1850, Prescott papers; and Ticknor, *Prescott,* pp. 324–328.

castle of the Percys stood at the edge of town, its turrets adorned by stone figures of warriors, defenders of the castle. The tall, friendly host had musicians from London and a houseful of guests.

Between great houses and distinguished hosts, Prescott, en route to The Highlands, visited Abbotsford, Melrose Abbey, and Dryburgh Abbey. A note from Lockhart enabled him to see much more of Scott's home than was shown to the usual visitor. Of it he wrote, "Abbotsford is a disappointment to those who examine it architecturally. But I thought of it only historically, in the light of its association with its author. And it is a most characteristic work in all its detail—as well as in its books, furniture, old knick-knackery, rusty jackets, &c.—the very type of the national feeling of the poet and antiquarian, whose spirit seems still to linger around the scene he so fondly created."[62] Via Stirling and Loch Katrine, he entered The Highlands.

At Inveraray Castle, on Loch Fyne, Prescott visited the Duke and Duchess of Argyll. From atop a castle tower the banner of the head of the Campbells floated, and in the hall Prescott encountered "a stout, stalwart, fellow, dressed in the Campbell tartan with kilt and plumed bonnet and his little poniard in his belt." The young duke and duchess had no such crowd of guests as the historian had encountered at Hams Hall and Alnwick Castle, and he enjoyed the quiet ease with which he and Will settled into the routine of the household. Hours in the billiard room preceded leisurely drives, one of which took them to famed Loch Awe. So enjoyable was the stay at Inveraray that the Prescotts lingered a full week before departing southward.

Lord Carlisle met his American guests at Naworth Castle, one of the most picturesque properties of the Howard family.[63] Close to Hadrian's Wall and the rich old ruins of Lanercost Abbey, Naworth, befitting a border fortress, was set in wild country. "Our table was laid on the dais—the upper part of the long hall, with a great screen to keep off the cold; and a fire such as belted Will Howard himself

[62] *Ibid.*; and WHP to S. A. Prescott, August 18, 1850, Prescott papers. The account of the visit at Inveraray Castle is in *ibid.*

[63] For the visit at Naworth Castle and Castle Howard, see WHP to S. A. Prescott, August 24–28, 1850, and WHP to E. Dexter, August 25, 1850, Prescott papers; and Gardiner, ed., *Papers*, pp. 297–299.

never saw—for it was of coal, of which Lord Carlisle has some mines in the neighborhood—blazed in the chimney. The chimney—which has a grate to correspond—is full twelve feet in breadth—a fine old baronial chimney, at which they roasted whole oxen, I suppose." The next morning Lord Carlisle and his guests set out for Castle Howard.

Some seventeen miles from York, Castle Howard was a mighty monument to the architectural genius of John Vanbrugh. A princely establishment set in appropriately proportioned parkland, Castle Howard was being prepared for the royal progress which would bring Queen Victoria, Prince Albert, and their entourage there on August 27. Amid the hubbub of preparations, all of which he enjoyed immensely, Prescott registered one of his more unusual social feats.

Last night we played billiards [he wrote Susan] the game of pool—a number of gents and ladies. Each person has three lives. All had lost their lives but Lord Dufferin and myself. He had his three, and I had only one. The pool of sixpences could go to the victor. There was a great sensation, as he, being a capital player, had deprived many of their lives—that is, pocketed their ball. I struck him into a pocket, which cost him one life—a general shout—the whole house was there. He missed his stroke and pocketed himself; thus he lost two lives and we were equal. The stir was great—all shouting, as I played, 'Hit him there, you can't fail, kill him!' &c. &c. We fought round and round the table, and he took off his coat. So did not I, but buttoned up mine. As he missed a hazard and left his ball exposed, the silence was breathless. I struck him into the pocket amidst a shout that made the castle ring again. It was just twelve o'clock when I retired with my laurels and sixpences.

The narrative historian put aside none of his literary talents as he reported his trip via the many long letters which he, Kirk, and Will alternately penned.

The royal visit to Castle Howard began with the late afternoon rain-drenched arrival of the royal party. Dinner, at eight, in full dress, was a brilliant affair. Of Queen Victoria, the historian wrote:

I was as near the Queen as at our own family table. She has a good appetite, and laughs merrily. She is very plain, with fine eyes and teeth, but short and dumpy,—with a skin that reddens easily with the heat of the room. She was dressed in black, silk and lace, with the blue scarf of the Order of the Garter across her bosom. [After dinner] . . . she did me the honor to come and talk with me, asking me about my coming here, my stay in the castle, what I was doing now in the historic line, how Everett was and where he was, for 10 minutes or so; and Prince Albert afterwards a long while, talking about the houses and ruins in England and the churches in Belgium and the pictures in the room and I don't know what. I found myself now and then trenching on the rules by interrupting &c; but I contrived to make it up by a respectful 'Your Royal Highness' 'Your Majesty' &c.

Traveling southward from Yorkshire, the Prescotts glimpsed Chatsworth in the absence of the Duke of Devonshire and continued on to the Duke of Sutherland's place at Trentham in Staffordshire.[64] That Italianized seat delighted the historian. Complying with the Duchess of Sutherland's request, he planted a large cypress in her garden.

Time was running out for the visitor whose plans had long included a September 7 sailing for New York. Accordingly he hastened his gait, catching something more than passing glimpses of Lord Clarendon's place, Baron Parke's seat at Ampthill, and that of the Marquis of Lansdowne. Before reaching Liverpool, his six weeks at a succession of choice country seats had confirmed his belief that English life at its best was English life in the country.

8

Boarding the *Niagara*, he braced himself for the torments of an Atlantic crossing, but the weather favored the returning traveler and the passage was rendered fairer still by the historian's capacity for winning friends. On Friday, September 27, the *Niagara* docked in New York.[65]

On the whole [Prescott soon wrote] what I have seen raises my preconceived estimate of the English character. It is full of generous, true, and

---

[64] For Prescott's trip between Castle Howard and Liverpool, see WHP to S. A. Prescott, September 5, 1850, Prescott papers; and Gardiner, ed., *Papers*, pp. 297–299.

[65] WHP to Lady Lyell, September 30, 1850, copy of Lyell letterbook, Prescott papers; and Nevins, ed., *Diary of Philip Hone*, p. 905 .

manly qualities, and I doubt if there ever was so high a standard of morality in an aristocracy which has such means for self-indulgence at its command, and which occupies a position that secures it so much deference. In general they do not seem to abuse their great advantages. Their respect for religion, at least for the forms of it, is universal; and there are few, I imagine, of the great proprietors who are not more or less occupied with improving their estates and with providing for the comforts of their tenantry—while many take a leading part in the great political movements of the time. There never was an aristocracy which combined so much practical knowledge and industry with the advantage of exalted rank . . . .

The character of the people . . . has some disagreeable points, which jar unpleasantly on the foreigner not accustomed to them. The consciousness of national superiority, combined with natural feelings of independence, gives him an air of arrogance—though it must be owned that this is never betrayed in his own house—I may almost say in his own country. But abroad, where he seems to institute a comparison between himself and the people he is thrown with, it becomes so obvious that he is the most unpopular, not to say odious person in the world. Even the open hand with which he dispenses his bounty will not atone for the violence he offers to national vanity.

There are other defects . . . his bigotry . . . the exclusive, limited range of his knowledge and conceptions on all political and social topics and relations. The Englishman, the cultivated Englishman, has no standard of excellence borrowed from mankind . . . The English—the man of fortune—all travel. Yet how little sympathy they show for other people or institutions, and how slight is the interest they take in them. They are islanders, cut off from the great world. But their island is indeed a great world of its own. With all their faults, never has the sun shone—if one may use the expression in reference to England—on a more noble race, or one that has done more for the great interests of humanity.[66]

The historian's trip of 1850 had been a memorable one, and the friendships and correspondence which resulted from it continued to color his living all the remaining days of his life. Prescott himself recognized it as the trip of a lifetime.

From birth he had been nurtured amid pro-British sentiments; in the 1810's he had seen the external side of English life; in the 1820's he had become aware of English standards of criticism; in the 1830's

[66] Gardiner, ed., *Literary Memoranda*, 2: 204–206.

he had longed for literary acceptance in England; in the 1840's that reputation had been solidly won in England; and then, in 1850, he saw the inner nature of English society.

The summer of 1850 was the pinnacle of the English factor in Prescott's life, the season in which he enjoyed, as Ticknor termed it, "the most brilliant visit ever made to England by an American citizen not clothed with the *prestige* of official station."[67]

[67] Ticknor, *Prescott,* p. 339. At the March 14, 1929, meeting of the Massachusetts Historical Society, Mr. Roger Wolcott, great-grandson of the historian and owner of the Prescott papers in the collection of the Society, read extracts of the correspondence of William H. Prescott under the title "Prescott in England, in 1850." See Massachusetts Historical Society *Proceedings,* 62 (October, 1928–June, 1929): 86.

XIII

*The evening of life is coming over those of ...*

PRESCOTT QUICKLY CAME ABREAST of development on the home-front. Locally, at the end of August, the hanging of Professor Webster had closed the Parkman case; but nationally, President Taylor's death, in July, had plunged the nation into mourning. Millard Fillmore had thrown the weight of the presidency on the side of compromise, and by late September the national scene was less agitated than it had been for months, but not so Massachusetts. When Daniel Webster had left the Senate to become Fillmore's Secretary of State, the handsome Robert Winthrop eased into Daniel's seat. An autumn battle shaped up for the seat in the House vacated by Winthrop; and although victory belonged to the Whigs, defeated Free Soiler Charles Sumner was striding nearer to the Washington scene.

The historian's first days at home found the Prescotts in happy confusion. They emptied the trunks and portmanteaus of his European wardrobe and purchases and immediately packed them for Pepperell. Three weeks later than usual the Prescotts set out for The Highlands, accompanied by a party of young people who promised to heighten the enjoyment of the autumn days.

Aside from the confusion attending a houseful of guests, it was too soon to renew the assault on the reign of Philip II. Instead, recollections of happy times in England inspired a flurry of letters. Via instructions to Bentley, Prescott remembered many of his recent hosts and hostesses. To some, copies of the new edition of the *Miscellanies* would go, to others complete sets of his writings.[1]

October, his favorite month, summoned its customary charms for the historian, his family, and guests. In addition to Lizzie and Will, there were four Peabody girls—Josephine Augusta, Martha, Lizzie, and Clara, plus James Lawrence, Leverett Saltonstall, and R. D. Rogers. The nine gay spirits frolicked over the rolling acres, launched absent Amory's leaky boat on the Nissitisset, teased and loved his dog Sancho, played games, and became rowdy enough that several windowpanes had to be replaced. For Will, who repeatedly had proclaimed from abroad his intention of remaining a bachelor, there was Josephine Augusta Peabody, his bride within thirteen months. And for Lizzie, laughingly condemned by Will to spinsterhood, there was Abbott Lawrence's son James, who became Lizzie's husband in less than eighteen months.

All autumn the historian enjoyed the good health which he attributed, in large measure, to the European trip. From it he had returned weighing 154 pounds—that same record weight which he had attained once in the Azores in 1816. The only two entries in his memoranda in a period of three months recalled the pleasures of his English visit.

The new year, ushered in without resolution—much less a return to writing—redirected Prescott's thinking to copyright, this time in England. "The pirates seem to be attacking us on all sides," he wrote Bentley. In answer to Bentley's query, he listed the exact date of the publication by the Harpers of the *Conquest of Peru*, one of the threatened titles. Bentley, meanwhile, was one of several seeking a memorial from distinguished literary figures in favor of international copyright.[2]

While copyright uncertainties plagued his published writings, Pres-

---

[1] WHP to R. Bentley, October 29 [1850], Bentley papers.

[2] Gardiner, ed., *Literary Memoranda,* 2: 203; WHP to R. Bentley, January 13, 1851, Bentley papers; and R. Bentley to WHP, February 3, 1851, Prescott papers.

cott was doing little that pointed toward future publication. From friend Sumner he requested a copy of the letter which he had written from England. He needed it to round out the file of letters written from England. "I am having them copied into a big book, which may afford some gossiping entertainment for my grandchildren."[3]

Despite appearances which suggested he was too busy reminiscing to write, Prescott buckled down and wrote two chapters before spring officially arrived. More should have been achieved, and he freely blamed the lazy disposition and the temptations of the town which so readily converted him into dawdler. Writing in his memoranda for the first time in four months, he declared, "But I will not spoil the page by making new resolutions."[4]

Undaunted by the historian's refusal to accept their hospitality at the annual meeting in 1850, the Maryland Historical Society renewed their invitation the next spring. Declining this second invitation, he sent a toast: "American History: The best lesson which it teaches us is the value of the Union."[5]

That same season Prescott, demonstrating the unity of Bostonians, recommended a title to his London publisher. Twenty-eight-year-old Francis Parkman, son of a wealthy and socially prominent Boston family and a recent student of Jared Sparks at Harvard, had readied another manuscript for publication. After his memorable *Oregon Trail*, Parkman had written a second book-length manuscript. "My friend Mr. Parkman, of this city," Prescott wrote Bentley, "proposes to send out by this steamer the proofsheets of a new work of his relating to the occupation of this country by the French, and their intercourse with the Indians." Prescott recommended the Parkman product on the score of subject matter, style, and authenticity.

Reacting favorably, Bentley speedily published Parkman's *History of the Conspiracy of Pontiac*. One year later it was evident that the

---

[3] WHP to C. Sumner, March [blank], 1851, Sumner papers. All of the letters to which Prescott referred are extant but no unified copy of them is available.

[4] Gardiner, ed., *Literary Memoranda,* 2: 208.

[5] WHP to J. P. Kennedy, B. Mayer, and J. M. Harris, May 1, 1851, and WHP to J. P. Kennedy, April 3, 1850, Kennedy papers; and WHP to J. P. Kennedy, May 1, 1851, Brown autograph collection.

new work, like Parkman's former one, had failed to win an English audience, its sale totaling only 153 copies.[6]

The unproductive mood that included another leisurely trip to Niagara Falls continued, and Prescott did nothing related to history that season at Nahant. A changed mood set in at Pepperell. Beyond the fact that, more than any other place, it was associated with quiet reflection and intellectual achievement, Prescott had other reasons for arousing himself. He could ignore Bentley's repeated queries about the new work, but not so the progress of certain historians. Bancroft was well advanced on another volume of his history; and Macaulay, nearing publication day for two volumes, was plainly ahead of the schedule he had discussed with Prescott. Envy of brother historians prodded Prescott as little else could. "I take this envy for a good symptom," he confided to his memoranda, continuing, "Then the late [British] decision in favor of foreign copyright appeals to my avarice, if my ambition should go to sleep—for it will put some thousands into my pocket. So on the whole the signs are favorable for a regeneration."[7] Fitting action to words, he wrote the concluding chapter of part one of the new history.

Two kinds of planning occupied his closing weeks at Pepperell. He turned some thought to part two of his history, wherein he would discuss the Netherlands. "A fit subject," he entered into his memoranda, "for an independent history—as Motley will show the world before my limping volumes come out."[8] Quasi competitor Motley afforded another reason for buckling on his historical nature.

---

[6] Gardiner, ed., *Papers,* p. 305; R. Bentley to WHP, June 19, 1851, Prescott papers; Mason Wade, *Francis Parkman: Heroic Historian* (New York, 1942), pp. 299, 308; Van Wyck Brooks, *From a Writer's Notebook* (New York, 1958), pp. 103–104; Clarence Gohdes, *American Literature in Nineteenth-Century England* (New York, 1944), p. 131; and Gardiner, "Prescott: Authors' Agent," *Mid-America,* 41 (April, 1959): 74–75. Busy admiring Parkman, Mason Wade, unfortunately and untruthfully, belittles Parkman's contemporaries, as in the statement, "Today Prescott and Motley seem stiff and wooden, and are read only as romance and rhetoric." (Wade, *Francis Parkman,* p. v.)

[7] Gardiner, ed., *Papers,* p. 307; WHP to R. Bentley, August 19, 1851, Bentley papers; and Gardiner, ed., *Literary Memoranda,* 2: 208.

[8] *Ibid.,* p. 209.

The second set of plans concerned the Prescotts at large and Will in particular. The announcement by Mrs. Joseph Augustus Peabody of the engagement of her daughter Josephine Augusta to William Gardiner Prescott spelled joy, social activity, and wedding preparations in Salem and Boston. On Thursday, November 6, Will and Augusta—as the Prescotts knew her—became husband and wife. Nothing at this stage of Will's life could have pleased his parents more than his marriage to a Peabody of Salem. The newlyweds moved into a pretty house in Chestnut Street, so near, the historian wrote Lady Lyell, "that I look down on their drawing-room from my study."[9]

The social flurry of the Peabody-Prescott nuptials had scarcely subsided before plans got underway for Lizzie Prescott's marriage to James Lawrence. A graduate of Harvard in the class of 1840, James had amassed considerable experience within his father's business. The wedding was planned for late winter.

Meanwhile, during the closing weeks of 1851, Prescott had resumed his historical project. He not only closed out the year in a working mood, he sustained his determination, thus launching 1852 more auspiciously than any recent year. Early in February, having concluded four chapters of the second part of the history, he baited himself, "Can I not bag 400 pages this year? The last two chapters have been at that rate."[10]

Neither Philip II nor Lizzie's wedding arrangements consumed all of his energies. In an effort to help the town of Pepperell win an appropriation from the state for a monument to Colonel William Prescott, he turned to Jared Sparks, a respected scholar whose opinion might help to loosen legislative purse strings. For decades generations of Prescotts had worked on behalf of the Bunker Hill Monument. Now it was equally fitting that the historian do his bit for Pepperell and his grandfather. He did it out of loyalty to both the man and the place.[11]

[9] WHP to Lady Lyell, November 19, 1851, copy of Lyell letterbook, Prescott papers.

[10] Gardiner, ed., *Papers*, pp. 310–311; WHP to A. Lawrence, draft, December 29, 1851, Prescott papers; and Gardiner, ed., *Literary Memoranda*, 2: 210.

[11] Gardiner, ed., *Papers*, pp. 311–312.

On March 6 the marriage of Elizabeth to James Lawrence took place, and, with Amory's departure from town soon thereafter, none of the historian's children was with him at Fifty-five Beacon Street. With every best wish for each child's happiness, their gregarious father was lonely.

2

For some reason—perhaps loneliness as much as desire—Prescott renewed his assault on the reign of Philip II. In March he completed three chapters, composing, for fourteen days, at the rate of five pages daily. In addition to encouraging him, this led to the belief that the production desired for 1852 was attainable. By mid-April, he concluded the first volume of the new work. Reporting to Lady Lyell, he wrote, "I have never fairly put myself in harness since 'Peru' was launched till this winter." Reading, organizing, and writing, he pushed on. Then, just when the historian rejoiced in his victory over the distractions of Boston, his work stopped.[12]

Shortly after noon on May 17, Catherine Greene Prescott, almost eighty-five years of age, expired. Her first attack had come a few days before Elizabeth's marriage. Determined to attend the wedding of her only granddaughter, she did even more—she danced at the wedding party. But other attacks occurred, driving her for days to bed and drugs. On that Monday in May the end came. Along with Boston's elite, many poor old women and orphan children, recipients of the charitable labors of the deceased, called at the Beacon Street address. The Reverend Dr. Alexander Young conducted the funeral service at the New South Church. She was buried beside her husband in a crypt in St. Paul's Episcopal Church—where, seven years later, the historian rejoined his parents. Madame Prescott's newest in-law, James Lawrence, accurately appraised her life as he wrote, "She is a great loss, not only to us, but to hundreds, I may say thousands, who were fed and clothed by her."

As when, more than seven years before, his father had died, the historian was overwhelmed by grief. Now, as then, he wrote a summary

[12] WHP to Lady Lyell, April 18, 1852, copy of Lyell letterbook, Prescott papers.

—of her youthful spirit, sympathetic nature, physical stamina, love of books, and power for doing good. Few women of any station in Boston had identified themselves more completely with that city's humanitarian needs. For decades her particular charities had been the Lying-in Hospital and the Female Asylum. She had served on the board of the latter institution for thirty-nine years and as its directress the last seventeen years of her life. Full of fun, free from vanity, she had been a quiet but rich asset of the community. From wellsprings of enduring love, the son who had lived all fifty-six years of his life near her wrote, "She had errors, no doubt—though I have not been long enough with her to find them out."[13]

The bow-faced mansion was empty and quiet, despite the comings and goings of the Dexters, the William G. Prescotts, and the James Lawrences. For sorrowing loneliness, the historian sought solace in his work. Cold and dreary, Nahant also depressed him. The waters which he often remembered for their sails dancing in sunlight were a desolate waste. Pounding waves, which once, in pulsing rhythm, had urged him to industry, sounded like a dirge. Bedford Street had been crowded with memories of his father, and now recollections of his mother overran Fitful Head. Yet the resolve to work was also at Nahant.

Nothing kept Bentley from renewing his enquiries about Prescott's writing. And despite reiterated insistence that he never intended to become a slave to a publisher's timetable, the historian gave Bentley an entering wedge. "The last year," he wrote, "I have got into harness again, and I am now on my second volume. If I keep the steam up as I propose, I shall hope to complete it by the autumn of next year."[14]

Guests were few that season at Fitful Head. In time the bleak setting, the inner loneliness, the urgings of Bentley, and the resolution to move ahead combined to bestir Prescott. He ground out the notes for several chapters and wrote a new one. Unable to develop either en-

[13] Wolcott, *Jottings,* p. 84; Kitty Lawrence, quoting James Lawrence, to Mrs. Benjamin Smith Rotch, June 2, 1852, typescript, Prescott papers; and Gardiner, ed., *Literary Memoranda,* 2: 213.

[14] R. Bentley to WHP, June 16, 1852, Prescott papers; and WHP to R. Bentley, July 20, 1852, Bentley papers.

thusiasm or momentum, he confessed, "Dull sailing—I fear dull writing." Displeased with his performance at Nahant, he headed for Pepperell mindful of the Spanish battle cry, "St. Jago and at them!"[15]

Santiago's support, legendary among hard-pressed Spanish warriors of the sixteenth century, did not embrace Pepperell. Prescott put only one chapter on paper while there. Somehow, during the last twelve months, he had reversed his accustomed routine of achieving at Nahant and Pepperell and dawdling in Boston. On November 12 William Makepeace Thackeray reached Boston, and almost immediately Prescott invited him to dinner. The novelist tramped snowy streets two days later with a copy of his newest work under his arm. The *Henry Esmond* was a gift for his host. Before his return to England, the lecturing author was repeatedly the guest of the historian.[16]

In the meantime, Bentley's mounting interest in the unfinished work inspired more than one query which Prescott ignored. To quiet the eager publisher, he finally wrote, "Touching the contract of Philip the Second, it seems to me there is no occasion at present to bother our brains about the matter." It satisfied Bentley, however, to learn that Prescott intended to accord him preferential consideration. A beautiful phrase by Bentley possibly guaranteed that Prescott continue of that mind. "It is from the lustre of your name as an author that I as your publisher derive an honorable position among the publishers of the Nineteenth Century," the publisher told the historian.[17] The truth of the statement did not lessen its appeal to the vanity of the historian.

In time Prescott not only took wintry Boston in stride, he also pushed his agate stylus across his noctograph. For months he slowly plugged away, with a regularity that produced an impressive accumulation of pages. Having completed two chapters by early February, he wrote, "Nothing to brag of—but better than the doings of the past months." In March he added another chapter and by mid-May two

[15] Gardiner, ed., *Literary Memoranda*, 2: 214.

[16] Gordon N. Ray, ed., *The Letters and Private Papers of William Makepeace Thackeray*, 4 vols. (Cambridge, Mass., 1946), 3: 112–113; and James T. Fields, *Yesterdays with Authors* (Boston and New York, [1900]), p. 17.

[17] Gardiner, ed., *Papers*, pp. 317–318; and R. Bentley to WHP, December 14, 1852, Prescott papers.

more.[18] Two consecutive seasons in Boston had proved productive.

Naturally, all was not work, and Club still figured prominently in Prescott's life. On Washington's birthday, at 5:30 P.M., the faithful gathered under his roof. In this season, too, he and Susan routinely had "a little party of half a dozen friends once a week to dine." Upon request the historian sent a bust of himself to grace the Prescott House, which was scheduled for a June opening in New York City.[19]

Boston, meanwhile, was moving toward a sort of intellectual bedlam. The proposal to unite the venerable Athenaeum with the city library which was a-borning, much favored by George Ticknor, drew vigorous opposition. A goodly percentage of the six hundred member-subscribers of the Athenaeum met and voted unanimously to maintain that body's separate identity. Sardonic humor and patrician taste mingled in Prescott's words, "I could not but think if a subscription paper had made its appearance how soon the hall would have been cleared of those zealous friends of the institution. I was one of those, however, who could not make up their minds to throw open the doors to the many-headed."

More than mere holder of certificates 76 and 655 in the Boston Athenaeum, Prescott had been associated with the institution in ways which evoked memories and induced attitudes. As a trustee, he had worked for the growth of its library and art holdings and its removal from Pearl Street. When the cornerstone of the new building was laid in 1847, he was serving his fifteenth and last year as trustee.[20] Beyond those years of formal service, however, his affection for the Athenaeum continued. Alongside the tangible record of his use of its library was the equally significant, though intangible, influence which the art-conscious Athenaeum possibly essayed in a career related to richly illustrated books and artistic concepts of bookmaking. On more than one count, he owed the Athenaeum the vote he gave it in March 1853.

[18] Gardiner, ed., *Literary Memoranda*, 2: 215.

[19] WHP to C. Folsom, [February, 1853], Folsom papers; WHP to Lady Lyell, February 1, 1853, copy of Lyell letterbook, Prescott papers; and Gardiner, ed., *Papers,* pp. 319–320.

[20] *Ibid.,* pp. 322–323; and Quincy, *Boston Athenaeum,* pp. 181, 245.

3

The same spring he sent his portrait to the Harpers, who were fitting up their new counting room, William H. Prescott was furnishing a newly purchased house on the shore at Lynn. There was much more to the move than a simple transfer five miles northward from Nahant. The vigorous breezes at Fitful Head, which long had so toned his system as to reduce his dyspepsia, had plagued his advancing years with increased rheumatism. Gentler and less damp breezes of warmer air, and less water—hence less glare—were among the physical attractions of the mainland. In addition, just as the change in Boston from Bedford Street to Beacon had been in part a desire to cast off depression brought on by his father's death, so the shift from Nahant, so soon after his mother's death, seemed a conscious effort to put at rest the ghost of memory.

Bigger and more elegant than the cottage at Fitful Head, the residence at Lynn, only briefly lacking a more picturesque name, was referred to often simply as "the villa." The sea before it could be enjoyed from numerous windows as well as from the piazza, which encompassed two sides of the house. In another direction stretched inviting lanes which led pedestrian and horseman to wooded areas. The initial investment in the 1-year-old Lynn residence was small, $1,-346.67 for the house and 4-acre lawn and $522.51 for furniture. Because the property lacked shade—having but one old cherry tree, many young trees were immediately planted. While they struggled to attain size, the historian's twin loves of walking and shade described a path about the cherry tree. Among the prime attractions of the villa, which could comfortably house the married children and their families, were its special facilities for infants.

Late in June 1853 the Prescotts first moved into the new residence. Of course it was considered ideal for historical pursuits. However, the historian early tempered his prospects of realizing much progress there when he exclaimed, "But what shall I do with two nurseries—grandchildren—and a' that!"[21] One nursery sheltered James Lawrence, born

[21] Harpers to WHP, May 3, 4, 1853, Prescott papers; Gardiner, ed., *Papers,*

March 23 and affectionately called "Jemmie"; the other one housed Edith Prescott, born April 20, 1853. Twice a grandfather in less than a month, the historian was unusually excited.

Much of the summer he dedicated to society. First Sir Charles and Lady Mary Lyell, making another descent upon America, visited the Prescotts. Other guests at Red Rock, as the villa quickly came to be known, included Lord and Lady Ellesmere. Like Lady Lyell, Lady Ellesmere was attractive to William. As soon as she departed, however, he looked longingly toward another lady.

"Now for that exacting old dame—the Muse of History—who will not go halves with any lady," he told himself. Before leaving Red Rock, he composed three chapters and some footnotes. The shift to Pepperell imminent, he assessed the initial summer at Lynn. It had been hotter than he found comfortable, and his dyspepsia and rheumatism had continued to torment him. If the family returned to Fitful Head the next year—it had been abandoned, not sold—a bigger establishment would be required. Doubts beset the historian as he closed Red Rock, but he would return there. Creature of habit, he required more time for adjustment. When James and Elizabeth Lawrence built a residence scarcely a stone's throw from Red Rock, that adjustment was speeded, for Susan, too.

His historical steam up, he transferred to his favorite residence for his favorite season. Although he stayed commendably close to his work schedule, not all of the labor concerned Philip II. Ties of friendship laid another claim upon him. Hillard's *Six Months in Italy* needed friendly puffs for its offing. Often declaring and violating his intention of never reviewing another book, the historian reviewed Hillard's. The Italian theme was rather threadbare for a travel book, but Prescott, supported by his love and memories of Italy, warmed to the book and his task. Climaxing his opinion of Hillard's book, he declared, "It is destined, by its stores of solid instruction, its curious criticisms, and the beautiful forms in which they are conveyed, to take a permanent place among the classics of American literature."

---

p. 333; WHP to Lady Lyell, February 13, 1853, copy of Lyell letterbook, Prescott papers; and Gardiner, ed., *Literary Memoranda*, 2: 215–216.

Prescott did even more for Hillard. His letter to Murray encouraged that Englishman to publish Hillard's volume on a half-profits arrangement. Time proved the truth of Prescott's rich endorsement. Five American editions in less than three years and an eventual record of more than twenty editions did categorize it as a standard work among travelers' guidebooks.[22]

Focusing anew on his own writing, the student of Philip II calculated that he was more than three-fourths of the way through his second volume. Given the urgings of publishers, the long interval since his last work, and the likelihood of poachers, he renewed his desire to publish at the earliest opportunity two volumes of *Philip the Second*. Turning to the siege of Malta, a gloriously romantic and action-packed theme, the joys of Pepperell spurred him on.

After his return to Boston, Prescott placed his ailing eyes under the care of Dr. Turnbull. Weeks passed before the historian assessed the oculist's efforts and stopped the treatments. He and Susan celebrated Thanksgiving with the Lawrences in Park Street and kept Christmas in festive fashion at Fifty-five Beacon, with the Lawrences, the Paiges, Mr. and Mrs. David Sears, Jr., and all the Prescotts in high glee—"Scotch reeling it till midnight." The Puritanical strain of the Prescotts had yielded to the Amory influence as Christmas came to mean as much as Thanksgiving to the historian as a festive occasion for family and friends. Among his intimate friends now were the Abbott Lawrences, of whom he said, "How easily one's children bring one into new combinations."[23]

Meanwhile, between Thanksgiving and Christmas, Prescott suddenly worried about one of his publishers. When the mammoth Harper establishment went up in flames on December 10, the historian's concern smacked of sincere sympathy for his publisher as well as interest in his four sets of stereotype plates. Fortunately the plates survived the

[22] WHP to Lady Lyell, November 12, 1850, January 11, July 20, 22, August 29, 1853, copy of Lyell letterbook, Prescott papers; Gardiner, ed., *Literary Memoranda,* 2: 216; [WHP], "New and Interesting Work," *National Intelligencer,* October 6, 1853; and Gardiner, "Prescott: Authors' Agent," pp. 77–78. Prescott's review is yet another previously unidentified publication by him.

[23] WHP to Lady Lyell, October 10, November 8, 1853, copy of Lyell letterbook, Prescott papers; and Gardiner, ed., *Papers,* pp. 328–331.

holocaust, and the Harpers promised new printings of his titles in the very near future. Even as family joys and publisher calamity occupied him, he had done some writing. At end of year, however, another kind of account, the record of income and expense, also occupied him. His income for 1853 had been $27,739.00, his expenses, $22,819.24.[24]

4

As the holidays receded, Prescott marshaled time and determination behind his historical project, despite the urban vanities. He accomplished four chapters, texts and notes, before spring arrived. Behind him were such bloody dramas as the siege of Malta and the Morisco rebellion. To conclude the second volume, he only needed to put the mystery of Don Carlos on paper. That, however, required three chapters and a greater number of months. Finally, at Lynn, he wrote, with some satisfaction, "Finished last note of last chapter of Volume 2d of History of *Philip the Second*."[25] Short on entries in his memoranda, these months found the historian not only plodding toward that terminal point but also occupied with publishing plans.

Aware that his successive historical titles had been in the bestseller category, Prescott desired better terms in both the English and American contracts for his *Philip the Second*. As he opened the negotiation with Bentley, the historian desired to sell the work outright, at £1,000 per volume for the English rights. Countering the friendly relations which had developed between author and publisher were two complicating circumstances: Aspinwall was no longer available as his agent, and more copyright confusion loomed on the horizon. Before tedium developed in the transatlantic exchanges, Prescott opened his negotiation with the Harpers.

The New York publisher was in a disadvantageous position. The

[24] Gardiner, *Prescott and Publishers*, pp. 31, 254; Allan Nevins and Milton Halsey Thomas, eds., *The Diary of George Templeton Strong; the Turbulent Fifties 1850–1859*, 2 vols. (New York, 1952), 2: 139–140; *New York Daily Times*, December 12, 13, 1853; Gardiner, ed., *Papers*, pp. 331–333; Carolina F. Ware, *The Early New England Cotton Manufacture* (Boston, 1931), pp. 81, 89, 301, 302, 320, 321; and stock purchase receipt, May 1, 1846, Prescott papers.
[25] Gardiner, ed., *Literary Memoranda*, 2: 218.

Harpers, holding all four sets of his stereotype plates on basically similar terms, automatically thought of any work as a simple extension of previous terms. In addition, the New York house still suffered from the effects of its disastrous fire, and desired concession regarding payment schedules. Since both author and publisher wanted more, the gap between them was wider than usual. So considerable was it, that Francis H. Underwood, hearing rumors that the historian would welcome overtures concerning both the new and old titles, urged his employers to approach Prescott.

The affable and dignified Moses Dresser Phillips, of Phillips, Sampson and Company, called upon Prescott at Red Rock and speedily reached an agreement with him. The contract of August 4, 1854, was at once the longest, most complex, and potentially most remunerative publishing arrangement ever reached by Prescott.

The basic six-year period of the agreement—fated to outlast the historian—anticipated early printings of all the old titles, in both octavo and duodecimo, as well as the first two volumes of *Philip the Second* in the larger form only. A minimum of twelve thousand copies of the new work would be printed during the first three years. For them, and additional copies, the author was to receive fifty cents per volume. For duodecimo printings of the earlier histories, the publisher guaranteed him six thousand dollars per year for six years. Always in a separate category, the *Miscellanies* were to appear in duodecimo, and bring Prescott six hundred dollars. Beyond the six-year period, the contract promised twenty-five and fifty cents per volume of duodecimo and octavo, respectively, for the author. Prescott had good reasons for asserting that this contract provided him at least fifty thousand dollars.

Harpers, to whom, as his current publisher, he gave preference, could not match, much less surpass, these terms which returned Prescott to Boston with his publishing arrangements.[26] To a proud and

---

[26] Gardiner, ed., *Papers,* pp. 337–338; John Townsend Trowbridge, *My Own Story* (Boston and New York, 1903), p. 241; J. C. Derby, *Fifty Years Among Authors, Books and Publishers* (Hartford, 1886), pp. 521–522; and Gardiner, *Prescott and Publishers,* pp. 83–87. The text of the contract of August 5, 1854, is in *ibid.,* pp. 302–309.

loyal Bostonian, that return was itself satisfying. Far from satisfying, however, was the negotiation with Bentley.

Any willingness on Bentley's part to meet Prescott's insistence upon £1,000 per volume was tempered by two circumstances: the business sense which always had enabled that publisher to reduce the author's initial demands, and the uncertainty attending the decision of the House of Lords on the copyright appeal then before it. In midsummer the Lords held that foreigners could not hold copyright in Great Britain. Prescott's price tumbled from £1,000 per volume to half that price. Bentley, harassed by cheap editions of Prescott's earlier works which Routledge had just thrust upon the market, feared the same fate awaited the new work. Accordingly he sought additional concessions from the author.

Late in 1854, after successive statements of contract terms had proved fruitless, author and publisher were in agreement, but far from happy. The competition of the cheap reprints, the Crimean War—which caused reader interest to shift to newspapers—higher taxes, the approaching end of the literary season—all suggested postponement of publication until the autumn of 1855. Bentley advanced that idea and Prescott accepted it, with the understanding that the English edition would appear before November 15, 1855.

In the meantime, Prescott was readying his two-volume manuscript for the printer. He made many final corrections at Pepperell. Returned to Boston, he contracted with Metcalf and Company of Cambridge, who began their work on the stereotype plates. As with *Peru*, the arrangement called for a steady flow of fourteen pages of proofs daily. Soon the daily stint dropped to ten pages. Charles Folsom played his accustomed role, as did the historian's reader-secretary, this time John Foster Kirk. Prescott's eyes held up, and by mid-February 1855 the first volume was finished. Maintaining a steady pace, they concluded the second volume on April 27. Four weeks later every loose end, including preface, illustrations, and final check of the plateproofs, was in order.

Once these volumes were complete, Prescott turned not to the third volume of his study of Philip II but to a new project. Inspired by recent publications and manuscript material which Gayangos had brought to his attention, the historian had determined to issue an edition of Robertson's *Charles V* to which he would append a study of the postabdication years of that monarch.

Prescott's plan called for about seventy pages of original writing, all to be executed at Red Rock. Friends, conversations, dinners, and grandchildren wrecked that timetable. He continued the project, first at Pepperell, then in Boston. When Beacon Street brought distractions in the form of dinners and theatrical performances, the historian reminded himself, "This is not the way they lived at Yuste."[27]

While Prescott thus consumed six months on his new project, and merely awaited the moment chosen by Bentley for the publication of *Philip the Second*, confusion re-emerged in author-publisher relations. It began when rumors reached Prescott that Bentley was teetering on the brink of bankruptcy. Willing to cancel their arrangement, the historian desired to retrieve those sheets of *Philip the Second* which Bentley had in his possession. Distrust rapidly dissipated the air of friendly trust, and Prescott, decidedly in need of an agent in London, turned to Russell Sturgis of the house of Baring Brothers. Prescott was adamant in his refusal to go to England to strengthen Bentley's position in reference to the new work. In August Bentley availed himself of Prescott's offer to rescind the contract. The effort of fifteen months had come to naught.

Sturgis quickly sampled the London market. Routledge, the house that once had led Prescott to expect £1,000 per volume, now offered £100 per volume for the work. In a free-for-all negotiation between agent and publishers, Bentley emerged victor, obtaining the two-volume work for £250. The author accepted the inevitable, but distrust and dislike of Bentley deepened, foreshadowing a later move.

Reviewing, long after the fact, this most disappointing of all his publishing arrangements, Prescott recited the high hopes that had tumbled from £1,000 to £125 per volume, adding, "The game was very adroitly managed by one of the parties certainly . . . Thus has evaporated *in fumo* one of the noblest contracts ever made by a history-monger for sales in a foreign market, I suspect."[28]

[27] Gardiner, ed., *Literary Memoranda,* 2: 223.
[28] Gardiner, *Prescott and Publishers,* pp. 88–95; [Anon.], "Complimentary

Prescott was essentially unfair in his derogatory estimate of Bentley. Much of the historian's hardship was of his own making. Because he abhorred politics and because he luckily had not been victimized early and widely by pirated editions, Prescott either failed to understand the chaotic state of international copyright or refused to believe that its distress might affect him. Prescott, it is true, had repeatedly placed his name on the side of justice in the copyright controversy, but he always had done so only upon the urgings of others and then in a mild, almost marginal sense of identification. The man who prided himself on his detachment from the ugly world of politics faced belatedly some ugly realities of the related financial world. Much of the joy which usually attended the launching of a new title was absent when Bentley finally issued the first pair of volumes of *Philip the Second*.

Six weeks later Phillips, Sampson and Company published the same title in Boston—on December 10, 1855, to the tune of a thumping advance sale. As the year closed, Prescott basked once more in the warmth of complimentary reviews. Behind the façade of polite approval, doubts might have cropped up about *Philip the Second*. Some uncritical reviewers, climbing on the bandwagon of Prescott's fame, automatically put the stamp of popular approval on this work. As with many other writers in different times and places, the aura of fame sustained Prescott beyond the peak of his powers. Furthermore, the incompleteness of the work—it was the only history he served up piecemeal—encouraged either a wait-and-see or a benefit-of-the-doubt approach by many who otherwise might have been more critical.[29]

This is not to say that *Philip the Second* lacked the elements of Prescott's prior successes. They were present, but in less sustained fashion

---

Dinner to Mr. George Routledge," *Publishers Weekly,* 33, no. 5 (February 4, 1888): 212; and Gardiner, ed., *Literary Memoranda,* 2: 223–224.

[29] Gardiner, *Prescott—Bibliography,* pp. 207, 208. For representative reviews, see [Anon.], "Prescott's Philip II," *Blackwood's Edinburgh Magazine,* 79 (April, 1856): 421–438; Prosper Mérimée, "Philippe II et Don Carlos," *Revue des deux mondes,* 2nd ser., 20 (April, 1859): 576–600; and [M. Guizot], "History of the Reign of Philip the Second, King of Spain . . . The Rise of the Dutch Republic: a History," *Edinburgh Review,* 105 (January, 1857): 1–24. One blistering indictment is in [Anon.], "Is Mr. Prescott an Historian," *Metropolitan,* 4 (1856): 81–86.

than in the earlier writings. Basic to the inferiority of this work were a number of factors which, in the aggregate, became exceedingly complex: so great had been his success that his incentive for achievement was so considerably reduced as to be virtually nonexistent; deteriorating health had played havoc with the regular work habits of which his best writing had come; the greater mass of materials available for this work had so overwhelmed Prescott that he, previously the master craftsman in matters of organization, never produced a satisfactory concept of this project; and finally, the historian never developed any real affection for his hero. Lacking affection for his subject, the uninspired historian often wrote in a mood of depression. "With all my good-nature," he wrote Lady Lyell, "I can't wash him even into the darkest French gray. He is black and all black."[30]

However aware he might have been that the new work was far from his best, Prescott was pained, nevertheless, by the treatment accorded him by the *North American Review*. The journal which once had rushed to review his titles almost simultaneously with their publication now waited more than six months. The journal which once had given a Prescott book more than eighty pages now accorded this one less than one-tenth that space.[31]

5

The flurry related to contracts, stereotyping, and publication notwithstanding, the years 1854–1855 meant more than just his own books to Prescott. Despite the fears entertained at the close of the first

[30] WHP to Lady Lyell, April 25, 1856, copy of Lyell letterbook, Prescott papers.

[31] Gardiner, ed., *Papers*, pp. 358–359; and [Anon.], "History of the Reign of Philip the Second, King of Spain," *North American Review*, 83 (July, 1856): 96–103. Prescott never saw it, because it entered a private diary three days after his death, but G. T. Strong's estimate of *Philip the Second*—"I am tired of history in dress coat and patent-leather pumps, Clio in hoops and powder"—also would have pained him. See Nevins and Thomas, eds., *Diary of George Templeton Strong*, 2: 435. For another private estimate of *Philip the Second*, see G. Otto Trevelyan, *The Life and Letters of Lord Macaulay*, 2 vols. (New York, 1875), 2: 323. For a broader estimate of Prescott by Macaulay, see Richard Croom Beatty, *Lord Macaulay—Victorian Liberal* (Norman, Okla., 1938), p. 375.

season, the Prescotts returned to Red Rock in 1854. More determined than ever to have a beautiful lawn, the owner ordered the removal of fifteen hundred loads of gravel from his four acres, substituting therefor an equal quantity of loam. In this season, too, Lizzie and James Lawrence erected a somewhat larger house close by. Not every Prescott lingered at Lynn, however. Amory departed for Europe in mid-July. The historian's youngest child, more than twenty-four years old, was rapidly developing a love of foreign lands.

At home and abroad political matters of which the historian did not approve drew his attention in mid-1854. Opposed, as ever, to territorial expansion, Prescott loathed the American designs on Cuba. That same sentiment he extended to the Fugitive Slave Law as he witnessed its operation in Boston.

Varying the winter routine, two more grandchildren arrived in February 1855. Lizzie bore a daughter on the nineteenth; and three days later Augusta bore the son whom they christened William Hickling Prescott.[32]

Honors continued to pour in. To his election to honorary membership in various societies he replied with thanks and copies of his works.[33] Another kind of honor which came often was the request for his autograph. In time, to fulfill such requests, Prescott had form letters printed. To them he simply added his signature. Of all those requests, none possibly intended greater honor than did that of young

[32] Gardiner, ed., *Papers,* pp. 334–336, 344–346; and WHP to Lady Lyell, April 7, June 11, July 15, December, 1854, copy of Lyell letterbook, Prescott papers. In the years 1854–1855, Prescott wrote Lady Lyell nineteen letters, a veritable encyclopaedia of social activities.

[33] Representative of the institutions electing Prescott to honorary membership in this period are the following: Sociedad Mexicana de Geografía y Estadística, the Royal Irish Academy, and the State Historical Society of Wisconsin; see their communications of September 15, 1851, December 28, 1852, and March 6, 1854, respectively, Prescott papers; and WHP to Wisconsin Historical Society, April 7, 1854, Draper-Wisconsin correspondence. The Prescott Literary Association of Philadelphia informed him of a similar honor on February 15, 1849. The Prescott Literary Society of Maysville, Kentucky, informing him on January 22, 1851, of his election as an honorary member, added, "We have called our Society after you because we know no name in our Country more honored or so justly distinguished, at home and abroad, as an Historian." All these communications to Prescott are in the Prescott papers.

Augustus Wight. "Will you," he wrote, "favor one of your younger readers with your autograph?

"And will you allow him to return you his most hearty thanks and acknowledgments for having cured him of novel reading? I was a most desperate and determined peruser of the 'yellow-covered' until my good sister Agnes gave me all your histories . . . Dear Sir, you are a magician; again and again I go back and put myself under your delightful spell." Equally under Prescott's spell was young Lucilla Stanley Lincolne of Norwich, England, who mailed more than one lengthy letter of "undiluted panegyric" to the historian.[34]

When Samuel Austin Allibone requested a memoir of George Ticknor for his projected dictionary of literature, Prescott volunteered to write it. This was yet another way of repaying George's many kindnesses, one of which had been the account of Prescott in the volume *Men of the Time in 1852*. At first the historian acceded to Allibone's idea of attaching his name to the sketch of Ticknor, but he soon changed his mind. Learning that Ticknor's name was scheduled to be affixed to the biographical sketch of Prescott in E. A. and G. L. Duyckinck's proposed work, he wrote Allibone, "I think it will have an awkward effect for us to be chronicling each other. So that I should be better pleased not to appear as the author of the notice of him in your work." Exceeding the demands of his high regard for George was Prescott's testimonial on behalf of Allibone's *Dictionary*. One of seven —the others who wrote published testimonials being Irving, William Cullen Bryant, Sparks, Bancroft, Edward Everett, and Lieber—the Prescott name presumably possessed magical qualities in dictionary promotion as well as on the title pages of histories.[35]

---

[34] Gardiner, ed., *Papers*, pp. 323, 357–358; WHP to Lady Lyell, April 18, 1856, copy of Lyell letterbook and L. S. Lincolne to WHP, May 15, 1856, Prescott papers.

[35] [Anon.], *The Men of the Time in 1852* (London, 1852), pp. 333–334; Gardiner, ed., *Papers*, pp. 347, 348–349; WHP to S. A. Allibone, December 4, 7, 1854, February 21, 1855, Allibone papers; [WHP], "George Ticknor, LL.D.," in S. Austin Allibone, *A Critical Dictionary of English Literature and British and American Authors*, 3 vols. (Philadelphia, 1858–1871), 3: 2416–2418; and [Anon.], in *American Publishers' Circular*, 1, no. 16 (December 15, 1855): 244. Ticknor's sketch of Prescott is in Evert A. and George L.

Declining an invitation to a distant literary festival, scheduled for September 20, Prescott remarked, "If toasts should be in fashion, will you allow me to send you one?

"The Complimentary Festival to Authors and Publishers:—By their *fruits* ye shall know them."[36] Conceivably the day might come when he would tire of history, but of punning there would be no end.

Not long returned from the journey which had included Madeira, Portugal, Spain, and France, Amory sailed on November 9 to Europe for the third time. "I give him an allowance—such as I can afford," the historian wrote Lady Lyell, "and leave him to spend it on whichever side of the Ocean he prefers." Amory's preference for Europe clearly established, he was off to Paris.

A week before Amory sailed, however, his father faced the reality that his younger son possessed both a wanderlust and a capacity for spending money which required restraint. Point by point, in a document of which each retained a copy, they agreed: (a) that Amory should receive $3,500 during his first year abroad, beginning November 7, 1855; (b) that his annual allowance, thereafter—as long as he was away from home—would be $1,500, minus $100 a year "an interest on the money which I have borrowed"; (c) that William H. Prescott would refuse to pay any debt whatever contracted by Amory and would not authorize the quarterly installments of his allowance in advance of the dates on which they were due.[37]

Amory's departure and the publication of *Philip the Second,* many copies of which went to friends in England, shifted attention to Europe. Letters of thanks from remembered friends reactivated correspondence on many fronts. And as America went to England, in the form of Prescott's latest book, so, too, England, in the person of the lecturing Thackeray, came to America, to Boston, and to Prescott's table.[38] In due time Thackeray, returned to England, wrote *The Vir-*

Duyckinck, *Cyclopaedia of American Literature,* 2 vols. (New York, 1855), 2: 235–242.

[36] [Anon.], in *American Publishers' Circular,* 1, no. 5 (September 29, 1855): 75.

[37] WHP to Lady Lyell, November 8, 1855, copy of Lyell letterbook, Prescott papers; and Gardiner, ed., *Papers,* pp. 352–354.

[38] WHP to Lady Lyell, December 17, 1855, copy of Lyell letterbook, Pres-

*ginians,* the flattering opening passage of which attested his affection for the Boston historian.

6

Complimentary words about *Philip the Second* inspired Prescott to complete the supplement to Robertson's *Charles the Fifth.* The stylus glided across the noctograph, and by mid-January 1856, the writing done, he arranged for publication. With Phillips, Sampson and Company, he concluded a half-profits contract. Prescott and the publisher divided the cost of putting Robertson into stereotype, but Prescott paid for and owned outright the plates for his continuation. Should author and publisher part, the former had the right to buy out the latter's interest in the plates. To avoid competition with *Philip the Second,* as well as to ride the high tide of a new publishing year, they scheduled publication for December 1856. *Charles the Fifth* appeared on the eighth of that month, almost one year to the day after *Philip the Second.* Facing the truth inherent in this latest use of his time, Prescott confided to himself, "This is a speculation in which the *auri fames,* I fear, has had more to do than that fame—the last infirmity of noble minds."[39]

No one, on the other hand, could chide Prescott for the memorials which he raised to friendship, one of which, that honoring the recently deceased Abbott Lawrence, next occupied him. Prepared for the *National Portrait Gallery,* this nineteen-page sketch also was printed for private distribution by permission of the publisher.

All of Prescott's short pieces of the last decade and a half had resulted in one of two ways: to help a friend launch a book—as Bancroft, Fanny Calderón de la Barca, Ticknor, and Hillard; or to sketch the career of a friend—as Dr. Gardiner, John Pickering, George Ticknor, and now Abbott Lawrence.

The memoir completed, Prescott turned to the third volume of *Philip the Second.* Before the mid-June shift to Red Rock, he had com-

---

cott papers; and Hexter Thackeray Ritchie, ed., *Thackeray and His Daughter* (New York and London, 1924), p. 87.

[39] Gardiner, ed., *Papers,* pp. 355–356; Gardiner, ed., *Literary Memoranda,* 2: 224; and Gardiner, *Prescott—Bibliography,* p. 243.

posed almost 125 pages of text and notes—4 chapters. Even as he wrote, he viewed it dimly, labeling his writing "the narrative sort, such as might be run off 'by a penny-a-liner—at the rate of a ream' a day, with little cost of brain work."[40] Deriving so little pleasure from the product of his noctograph, it was surprising that Prescott kept at his labor. All the more was his diligence commendable when one considers larger matters that competed for his sympathetic attention: the caning of Sumner on the floor of the Senate in Washington, the account of the Battle of Bunker Hill penned by Bancroft, and the receipt of a presentation copy of Motley's *History of the Dutch Republic.* Motley received a letter of warm commendation.

With Susan and William at Lynn was Will's family, for whom Europe beckoned before the end of the summer. Regularly, after the evening drive, the historian plodded pensively along the sandy shore. The lawn at Red Rock was the best ever, despite unusually high temperatures. The nomination of Buchanan by the Democrats and the futility of the Whigs inclined him toward the infant Republican Party. "I am not quite settled," he wrote Lady Lyell in midsummer, "but I expect to be an enthusiastic Fremonter."[41] The one thing upon which he had settled that summer was his work.

Beginning July 20, he dedicated six weeks to correcting proofs from the stereotype plates for his continuation of Robertson's history. Before completing that labor, he informed three London publishers of the new work and invited their offers. Immediately Bentley offered £100. From Routledge, however, came an offer of £110 and he obtained the contract. For £10, Prescott turned his back on Bentley and did business with a house which previously had pirated his works. Emotion, more than money, prompted the decision. Prescott still held Bentley responsible for the collapse of the financial hopes which he had pinned on *Philip the Second.* Enraged, yet interested in still more of the unfinished *Philip,* Bentley was bitterly disappointed.

[40] William H. Prescott, *Memoir of the Honorable Abbott Lawrence* (n.p., 1856); [Arthur N. Holcombe], "Abbott Lawrence," *Dictionary of American Biography,* 11: 44–46; and Gardiner, ed., *Literary Memoranda,* 2: 225.

[41] George William Curtis, ed., *The Correspondence of John Lothrop Motley,* 2 vols. (New York, 1880), 1: 191–193; and WHP to Lady Lyell, August 1, 1856, copy of Lyell letterbook, Prescott papers.

Since Lynn had not advanced the third volume of *Philip the Second,* such was scheduled for Pepperell. To its perennial autumn charms— solitude, memories, brilliant leaves, dark blue mountains in the distance—this season added the presence of Elizabeth and James Lawrence and their children. They were enjoyed the more because of the recent sailing of Will and Augusta. Propitious as ever, Pepperell was not productive in the historical sense.

As a young man of conservative political outlook, Prescott regretfully had witnessed the demise of the Federalist Party; now the Whig Party, to which he had been loyal for decades, was in the throes of death. As issues crystallized increasingly on a regional basis and as the Republicans arose from the ruins of the Whigs, he was one of many more interested than usual in national politics. Having made up his own mind, the historian wondered about certain friends. To Sparks he wrote, "By the by, whom do you vote for in the next presidential struggle?"[42] Casting his vote for loser Frémont, the historian, aware of Buchanan's promises, declared, "if carried out, one may look for a train of evils foreign and domestic, that might give an ague fit to every lover of his country. Luckily I have a snug little place in the 16th century to which I can retreat when the storm is brewing." Promising retreat, he actually did otherwise. When the authors, editors, publishers, and booksellers of Boston called a meeting "to consult upon the best means for securing the blessings and privileges of Freedom to Kanzas [*sic*]," Prescott's name headed the list of sponsors.[43]

Back in Boston, he welcomed, at year's end, the American and English editions of *Charles the Fifth.* He likewise rejoiced in the excellent sale of his works. From Phillips, Sampson and Company came word and payment in support of the claim that they had marketed more than forty thousand volumes of his various titles, all in octavo. In London, Routledge protected his *Charles the Fifth* by releasing it simultaneously in four editions and price ranges.

[42] Gardiner, *Prescott and Publishers,* pp. 96–97; R. Bentley to WHP, October 2, 1856, Prescott papers; and WHP to J. Sparks, August 15, 1856, Sparks papers.

[43] WHP to Lady Lyell, October 10, November 11, 1856, copy of Lyell letterbook, Prescott papers.

The historian hoped to parallel the favorable record of his books by advancing his unfinished manuscript, but ill health and society deterred him. Beginning in December, rheumatic headaches plagued him for more than three months. Dr. Jackson, considering them just another manifestation of an almost inbred rheumatic nature, did little more than prescribe rest. In daily pursuit thereof Prescott stretched out, for varying intervals, on the sofa. This inactivity further reduced the will to complete *Philip the Second*. The headaches, however regular, did not alienate him from society. Indeed, now that the English-style dinner party, which permitted both sexes in the company, had become fashionable in Boston, Prescott found added delight in dining out. To Will he wrote, "I keep my footing in all the merry-makings from the nursery upward."[44]

Months passed without a single entry in the memoranda, hinting that literary labor was at a low ebb. However, the fact that Amory and Will and Augusta and their two children were all in Europe induced a lively correspondence. Susan and William, enjoying every report, eagerly phrased questions about the grandchildren. William, happy that Amory was so much in the company of Will and his family, reflected his pleasure by increasing his unmarried son's allowance. Referring to himself as "somewhat teased with headaches," the historian's recital of dinners attended, invitations refused, guests entertained, and the like suggested to absent ones that the situation at Fifty-five Beacon Street was normal.

Meanwhile love of the foreign scene had prompted Will to reactivate an idea which he had entertained almost a decade earlier, that of a career in diplomacy. The historian now looked more favorably upon it, but when asked to use his influence in Washington to obtain a secretaryship of legation for his son, he reminded Will that his support of Frémont, a matter of common knowledge, precluded his approaching the Buchanan administration. He would not submit to the humiliation of having a petition refused.

While patiently trying to wear off the siege of headaches, he lis-

[44] WHP to Lady Lyell, December 16, 1856, copy of Lyell letterbook, and WHP to W. G. Prescott, December 29, 1856, Prescott papers; and Gardiner ed., *Papers*, pp. 372–374.

tened as many books were read. He also occupied himself pleasantly
in other ways, attending Shakespearean readings by Fanny Kemble,
romping with Lizzie's children, and reclining on the sofa. One thing,
the diet which eliminated meat and wine and emphasized vegetables,
required some adjustment on his part. As one of the severest winters
on record came to a close, he won a bout with influenza, rejoiced in
the diminution of his headaches, and looked forward to full recovery
at Lynn. At Lynn he also planned to accelerate the recent slow progress
on *Philip.*[45]

Although destined to come to public attention somewhat later, the
spring of 1857 witnessed the second fundamental challenge thrown
at Prescott's historical labor. When Theodore Parker had challenged
him on the score of philosophy—a variable, however fundamental—
Prescott remained undisturbed. The challenge by R. A. Wilson, on the
other hand, he could not ignore. Wilson challenged Prescott on the one
ingredient without which the historian has nothing, namely, truth. It
all began in friendly fashion.

When lawyer Wilson, a British subject residing in Rochester, New
York, indicated that during a long illness he was turning to historical
writing, he invited and won Prescott's sympathy and assistance. When,
however, he asserted that he planned to write "the Conquest of Mexico, without the fable," Prescott had more than common caution as
reason for limiting the offer of his materials to the arrogant stranger.
With an offhand impudence to be sensed only from his exact words,
Wilson had written, "I took it for granted that you had fought your
Mexican battle, and that the market for your book had been supplied—
and that your Mexican library had become cast-off lumber." Prescott's
kindly nature still prevailed. He offered specific titles to Wilson. Indicating that "your views are certainly entitled to respect," he even
offered to help bring them before the public. Months passed and
Wilson concluded his manuscript and found a publisher. Briefly put,
Wilson's *A New History of the Conquest of Mexico* is a violently
biased anti-Catholic, anti-Spanish diatribe which suffers from short-

[45] *Ibid.,* pp. 353, 369–372, 375–377; and W. G. Prescott to WHP, January
21–22, 1857, and W. G. Prescott to S. A. Prescott, March 18, 1857, and WHP
to W. G. Prescott, April 6, 1857, Prescott papers.

ages of scholarship and truth. In 1859, Prescott could not reply to the attack which not only had impugned his work and honor but also had tried to capitalize upon his name by exploiting a Prescott letter as a testimonial for Wilson's book. Prescott's labor on Mexico, like truth itself, needed no defense; but John Foster Kirk and George Ticknor nonetheless vigorously attacked Wilson. Prescott was in his grave; but the same posterity that praises Prescott's *Mexico* has consigned Wilson's work to historical oblivion. But none of Wilson's base nature was evident as Prescott's friendly nature evidenced itself in the spring of 1857.[46]

The historian's cooperative spirit also shone through when he replied to the request put by Samuel D. Morgan, president of the Board of Commissioners for the erection of the new state capitol in Nashville, Tennessee. Morgan's request for his likeness, that it might be reproduced in the ornamental fresco of the State Library, was promptly filled. Prescott was one of few non-Tennesseeans so honored.

The summer at Red Rock was cool and wet, a boon to the struggling lawn and young trees, as well as to the historian's work. There, as the Atlantic surged outside his window, he wrote of the Battle of Lepanto. "I hope it will smell of the ocean," he confided to his memoranda, adding, "I have had the steam up most of the time. And as I fight—as metaphorically speaking Cervantes at Lepanto—with one hand crippled—my summer's work has been fair." He despatched more than one chapter while at Lynn.[47] With the coming and going of visitors, not to mention the Lawrences nearby, it was a joyous summer—until mid-August cast a pall of sorrow.

Franklin Dexter, husband of the historian's only sister and father

[46] R. A. Wilson to WHP, April 4, 1857, and WHP to R. A. Wilson, draft, April 16, 1857, Prescott papers; [John Foster Kirk], "Review of Wilson's *A New History of the Conquest of Mexico*," *The Atlantic Monthly*, 3 (April, 1859): 518–525, and (May, 1859), pp. 633–645; and George Ticknor, "Papers Discussing the Comparative Merits of Prescott's and Wilson's Research," in Massachusetts Historical Society *Proceedings*, 4 (1858–1860): 277–283. Ticknor's item also was published separately, Boston, 1861.

[47] S. D. Morgan to WHP, May 20, July 30, 1857, Prescott papers; and Gardiner, ed., *Literary Memoranda*, 2: 227. For one visitor's picture of Prescott at Lynn in 1857, see James Wynn, "William H. Prescott," *Harper's New Monthly Magazine*, 28 (December, 1863): 51–57.

of four grown sons, died after a lingering illness. More than brother-in-law, Frank Dexter had been genteel, sophisticated, urbane—a man of distinction professionally, intellectually, socially.

By summer the national economy had sickened, the expanding depression having severely hit the book trade. In 1856 the Boston publisher had sold between nine and ten thousand copies of *Philip the Second. Charles the Fifth* had soared to a sale of more than two thousand copies in its first two months. In early 1857 book sales continued strong, and Prescott had received seven thousand dollars from Phillips, Sampson and Company before the depression so reminiscent of 1837 set in.[48]

Despite the storm warnings, Phillips, Sampson and Company laid the plans in mid-1857 which culminated in the inauguration of *The Atlantic Monthly* later that year. Prescott figured in those plans as, indeed, he had once before when a publisher of his had launched a magazine. Then, on May 7, 1850, the Harpers had informed the historian that they planned to feature him, in words and picture, in the first number of a new magazine. The Harpers had planned their magazine as a tender of their business, and Prescott, a star in their galaxy of authors, had helped them launch it. Now, Phillips, Sampson and Company, for similar reasons, launched their magazine and turned to Prescott, their leading author. Reminded in midsummer of 1857 of his promise to give them a few pages of material, the historian was loathe to interrupt his work. To satisfy his publisher as well as himself, he offered M. D. Phillips "part of a chapter, equal perhaps to a dozen or fifteen or twenty pages, of my history—which I flatter myself would have more interest for the public than any hoozymoozy nonsense which I could manufacture."

Published in the second number of *The Atlantic Monthly*, "The Battle of Lepanto," like every other short piece by Prescott, was unsigned.[49] Many who sampled it knew that it was Prescott. Typical of

48 WHP to W. G. Prescott, April 13, June 2, July 2, 1857, and WHP to Augusta Prescott, August 17, 1857, Prescott papers; Crawford, *Famous Families*, 2: 150; Loring, ed., *Diaries of William Appleton*, p. 198; and Gardiner, ed., *Papers*, pp. 385–387.

49 *Ibid.*, pp. 291, 382–383; [Anon.], *Harper's New Monthly Magazine*, 1, no. 1 (June, 1850): 134–139; [Anon.], "Fifty Years of Harper's Magazine,"

him, that opening line—"It was two hours before dawn on Sunday, the memorable seventh of October, 1571, when the fleet weighed anchor"—carried the reader along, to high adventure in the long ago. Somewhat later this material appeared in the third volume of *Philip the Second*. Meanwhile, typical of his generous nature, Prescott had helped another publisher launch another magazine. This, however, was the only instance in his entire career that he published a segment of one of his histories in the form of an article.

Learning that Will, Augusta, and their children, having spent almost all of their time in Paris, planned to pass a second winter in the French capital, the historian expressed his displeasure. For Amory, entering his third consecutive year abroad in quest of health, in part, foreign residence was also becoming a questionable thing. In truth, Paris captivated him also.

The historian and Susan never quite faced up to one truth—namely, that neither of their sons possessed a fraction of the manliness of their father. To the wealth and doting nature of the parents, garnished many years by generous grandparents under the same roof, could be added the questionable health, spendthrift dispositions, and lazy natures of two who now were almost thirty years of age. Often the historian had chided himself for the dreamy, wasteful, *far niente* air in his own life, but he apparently never laid equivalent truths convincingly before his sons. To admit that the assurance of the good life without labor rather naturally engendered the unmanly natures of Will and Amory is to say, indirectly, that William H. Prescott had been a most remarkable person. He likewise had been assured the good life but nonetheless he had labored and achieved. His triumphs had been many, and high among them—way above his triumph over physical disability—had been his victories over a lazy nature and the temptations offered by wealth and position. Unfortunately the will to work and achieve is not an inherited trait, as Will and Amory so conspicuously demonstrated.

---

*Harper's New Monthly Magazine,* 100, no. 600 (May, 1900): 948; and [WHP], "The Battle of Lepanto," *The Atlantic Monthly,* 1, no. 2 (December, 1857): 138–148. This material also appears in William H. Prescott, *History of the Reign of Philip the Second, King of Spain* (Boston, 1858), 3: 332 ff.

That best spot on earth, Pepperell, was conducive to work. Although his theme had shifted from the gore of Lepanto to political intrigue, which required more time and care, the historian plugged away at *Philip*. When the time came for farewells to snowy Monadnock and trees whipped bare of their leaves, he anticipated additional achievement in Boston. "Under the gloomy pressure of a financial crisis unexampled in the United States," he wrote in his memoranda, "I shall have fewer temptations than usual to dissipation."[50]

As the year closed, the sun pierced the gloom: Susan's health, always a subject of complaint, was better than it had been for years; during the next year the children would return; taking a cue from rising stock prices, business, far from brisk, was on the upswing; and the third volume would be ready when the right moment arrived for launching it. Toward that end the historian salted away a few more chapters, between evenings given over to "bread and butter" and whist parties. At both, he was more conversationalist than either eater or player. His only physical discomfiture was an occasional "little headache."

On Thursday, February 4, 1858, the kind of day that usually brought both, there was neither work nor social activity. That day a stroke of apoplexy felled Prescott.[51]

7

Most unexpectedly the foul fiend, as the victim himself put it, laid him low. He had lacked all the common symptoms, being the reverse of plethoric, red-faced, portly. The attack affected both his sight and locomotion. The latter returned to normal almost at once, and the doctor soon decided that he had suffered no brain damage. The scare experienced by friends and relatives did not pass so quickly.

Veteran Dr. Jackson prescribed rigorous adherence to an all-vegetable diet. For weeks, as the historian told Lady Lyell, he was on a

50 WHP to Augusta Prescott, August 17, 1857, and W. G. Prescott to S. A. Prescott, September 17, November 26, 1857, Prescott papers; and Gardiner, ed., *Literary Memoranda*, 2: 228.

51 *Ibid.*, p. 229; W. G. Prescott to parents, December 1, 1857, and WHP to W. G. Prescott, December 8, 1857, Prescott papers; and Gardiner, ed., *Papers*, pp. 385–387.

"fare of pulse and water." Rest was a basic prescription, and rest he did. Added to the ministrations of Susan and the servants were those of Lizzie, for the Lawrences, awaiting the completion of their new residence nearby, spent the winter at Fifty-five Beacon Street.

In body and spirit the historian was much improved as winter expired. Indeed it was a spring tonic when Dr. Jackson added sherry to his diet. Amory's return, after a lengthy absence, so warmed the heart as to speed recovery. Meanwhile the Will Prescott family, assured of the historian's recovery, planned to remain in Europe until summer, when all would be reunited at Red Rock. Cheery word came in Bancroft's version of the Battle of Bunker Hill, the first to give Colonel Prescott the credit which his grandson had longed to see in print. By mid-April Prescott was again gingerly adjusting his historical harness. To the 470 pages already composed for the third volume he hoped to add about fifty more, to conclude his treatment of the government of Alva. He would work slowly, encouraged to do so because the book trade was still sufficiently out of joint that he was in no hurry to publish. Tentatively he selected December for the publication of the single third volume of *Philip the Second.*

In April he made arrangements with his Cambridge printers. The schedule for converting the manuscript to stereotype plates called for the handling of five pages per day. His altered way of life forced many changes—in mid-April he had to forego even the pleasure of attending Club. However, he did not plan to see his volume through the press without the aid of Charles Folsom. Once more he summoned the skills of the bald purist.

As one member of Club helped to convert manuscript into book, another, Theophilus Parsons, offered recipes for Prescott's more complete conversion to vegetarian. As he thanked Theop for his kitchen literature, he also extended his sympathy to him. "I am very sorry to hear that you had wounded yourself with a pruning-knife," he told Parsons, "and I trust long before this you have got over the effects of it. This is an accident that cannot befall me. The more's the pity. I wish with all my heart that I could get up a little horticultural gusto."[52]

---

[52] WHP to Lady Lyell, January 29–31, April 5, 1858, copy of Lyell letter-

Like Prescott the historian who never frequented libraries and archives, Prescott the lover of nature always had derived his fondness for trees and flowers and other growing things from a detached romantic contemplation rather than by digging and planting and cultivating.

Meanwhile the printer-editor-author routine got underway. As usual, the historian incorporated some and discarded many of Folsom's recommendations. "I bow before your authority," he wrote Charles, "or rather your reasons, in regard to the two first—or, to show you how much I profit by your teaching—first two points, and have made the alterations accordingly, to be introduced in the plates, which I suppose are now cast."[53]

Fending off Bentley's desire to discuss publication arrangements, Prescott stated that, as a concession to bad times, publication could not occur before December. By then, he hoped—despite contrary prospects—some change might take place on the copyright front. Offering the London publisher no encouragement about his own work, Prescott did take the opportunity to recommend John Gorham Palfrey's history to Bentley. The tall, balding Palfrey, member of Club and the owner of the *North American Review* in a period during which seven Prescott items had appeared therein, was yet another friend to whom Prescott extended a helping hand. Weeks later, when Francis Bowen visited London and Bentley—the latter in behalf of Palfrey's history— he carried a letter of introduction from Prescott. When naught came of this effort, Prescott contacted Routledge in Palfrey's behalf. Death, alone, would stifle Prescott's efforts to help his literary friends as they attempted to hurdle the barrier of publisher indifference.

Particularly welcome, after the cold, damp spring in the city, was the summer heat which greeted the Prescotts at Red Rock. The shuttling of proofsheets continued so punctually as to invite praise. "Those who have said you were not the most punctual of men know nothing about it," he told the Cambridge Aldus, "and I will take up the gauntlet for you on this quarrel whenever you desire it." Experiencing no frustrating delays—Folsom had been known to stop the presses

---

book, Prescott papers; Ticknor, *Prescott,* pp. 432–433, 435, 452; and WHP to C. Folsom, [April 13, 15, 1858], Folsom papers.

[53] *Id.* to *id.,* May 12, [June 8], 1858, Folsom papers; and Gardiner, ed., *Papers,* 389–390.

while debating the choice between comma and semicolon—the historian was most fortunate. The soaring July heat might have roasted the band at Red Rock if refreshing northeasters had not drenched Lynn occasionally with heavy rains.[54]

On July 19, Will, Augusta, Edith, and little Willie returned to the bosom of the Prescott family. The reunion, for the first time in years, of all the family further diminished the historian's will to work. No longer babbling infants, the grandchildren captivated their loving grandfather. Will and Augusta brought news from scores of the historian's English friends. To one of them, the lovable Lady Lyell, he wrote, "I have been very well of late, though I cannot occupy my mind for a long time without flushing the face and bringing on slight headaches—when I take the kind hint and indulge in a promenade." Now, with Lizzie, Will, Amory, James, and Augusta—as well as the quartet of preschoolers, he had a wide choice of companions on the beach. Those were days and weeks when he whipped no new chapter into shape on solitary strolls. Indeed, he never did compose the desired additional pages for the third volume.

In midsummer, Prescott did write one thing, a one-sheet fourth codicil to the will he had executed on January 5, 1854. Reflecting the length, complexity, and precision of his father's will, that of William H. Prescott called upon three faithful friends for its administration. He named George Ticknor and William Amory trustees, in charge of the trust funds which were to be created for Susan Prescott, William Gardiner Prescott, Elizabeth Lawrence, and William Amory Prescott. The historian named William Howard Gardiner as his sole executor. In less than three months, Prescott had prepared the first codicil, wherein he made adjustment in the trusts for his two sons. Toward the end of 1855 the second codicil, in addition to increasing certain legacies and naming James Lawrence as a third trustee, made further adjustments in the trust for Will and Amory Prescott. In the spring of 1857, additional adjustments in the trusts for his two sons went into the third codicil.

Now, on August 21, 1858, in light of his recent stroke and the re-

---

[54] WHP to R. Bentley, May 3, 1858, Bentley papers; Gardiner, "Prescott: Authors' Agent," pp. 83–84; and Gardiner, ed., *Papers*, p. 392.

turn of the boys from abroad and his latest assessment of their maturity and financial responsibility, the historian effected the fourth and last codicil to his will. By it he terminated the trust for Will and allowed all of his older son's share of his estate to go directly to him. For Amory, however, strict control of the majority of his inheritance was continued through a trust arrangement.[55]

At Pepperell the joy of having all the children and grandchildren under his roof continued. The daily routine called for little labor. To bring the smaller third volume up to the size of the previous pair, author and publisher decided to use heavier paper. Beyond that, in his only work at The Highlands, Prescott looked backward rather than forward. "I am now amusing myself," he confided to his memoranda, "with making some emendations and additional notes for a new edition some day or other of the 'Conquest of Mexico'."

He now concluded the negotiations, which he had initiated at Lynn, for English publication of the new volume. This time shifting thought led him to insist upon at least a two-day priority for American publication. Beyond that, for publication in December, the volume awaited the London publisher that tendered the highest bid. In case of equal offers, Bentley, publisher of the first two volumes, would get it. Bentley, however, tied his offer of £400 to his insistence upon two months priority. This contradicted Prescott's terms and the author discarded it in favor of Routledge's offer of two hundred sixty guineas. At home, meanwhile, the historian quickly reached an agreement with Phillips, Sampson and Company.[56]

Despite the presence of his loved ones and the plans for his book, Prescott yielded to melancholy at Pepperell. Monadnock rose as proud

---

55 *Ibid.*, pp. 402–428. The codicils are dated March 15, 1854, December 18, 1855, March 25, 1857, and August 21, 1858. In appointing Gardiner his executor, Prescott reciprocated an honor which Gardiner had accorded the historian in a will dated June 19, 1832; see William Howard Gardiner, Last Will and Testament, June 19, 1832, Gardiner papers.

56 WHP to Lady Lyell, July 23, September 27, 1858, copy of Lyell letter-book, Prescott papers; Gardiner, ed., *Literary Memoranda*, 2: 230–231; Gardiner, *Prescott and Publishers*, pp. 98–99. Enraged by his loss of Prescott's works, Bentley published some of his correspondence with the historian; see *Correspondence of William H. Prescott, Esq. with Richard Bentley, from August, 1856, to November, 1858* (n.p. [1859]).

and high as ever and breezes played through trees touched with riotous color. Every joy of his favorite month was present, but he so succumbed to memories and news of death that he did not enjoy it as in former years. Thoughts ran to his father and mother, brother Ned, brother-in-law Franklin Dexter, friend Abbott Lawrence, and others when he wrote, of Pepperell, how full the place was of "so many recollections of joys departed, and of friends, alas! that have gone with them." From England recent word informed him that Richard Ford, exactly his age, had died.

Not long before this season in which home was less homelike than ever before and work was but vaguely on the indefinite horizon of tomorrow, the historian summed up certain things for Pascual de Gayangos. "Spain . . . I have lived in . . . in spirit at least—the last 30 years—more of my time than in my own land." Elsewhere in that letter he told Don Pascual, "I . . . made it a rule, one indeed that I have generally followed, never to sacrifice pleasure to business. But in truth long habit makes me find business—that is literary labor—the greatest pleasure."[57]

Thanksgiving, once the only winter holiday that counted, passed quietly amid plans for a rollicking Christmas celebration. In the chatty, romantic vein that characterized his every letter to the Lyells, he wrote, "We propose to celebrate Christmas by calling children and grandchildren together under the patriarchal roof. Don't I write like an ancient?"

Tempering the hand of death which had taken Augustus Thorndike, a friend since boyhood, and threatened to take ailing Washington Irving, some rejoicing attended the publication of both the American and English editions of the third volume of *Philip the Second*.

Interested, as ever, in many things, the historian sent Mrs. Greenough his contribution to the Mt. Vernon Fund. Another sum, likewise for a good cause, went to friend Loring. "I am glad to get your summons for 'Club,' " he wrote Jared Sparks, "but it seems to me that P. should come before S." The better to make sure that he was not de-

---

[57] WHP to Lady Lyell, September 27, 1858, copy of Lyell letterbook, Prescott papers; and Penney, ed., *Letters to Gayangos,* pp. 140–141.

nied his chance to play host to Club, he turned at once to preparations for the gathering in January.[58]

The new year came in quietly, the flush of journalistic approval of his new volume encouraging no literary resolutions. Amory, seemingly unable to anchor himself in Boston, departed for New York. Deep winter took over in Beacon Street, the thermometer flirting with zero, drifts of snow on all sides, and life indoors as gay as ever. Wintertime Boston was normal, but not so William H. Prescott.

Declining the latest invitation from the Lyells, this one urging the historian and Susan to come to London in the spring, he was momentarily his gay old self, remarking, "As to my wife, a voyage to the moon would not be more chimerical in her eyes than a trip . . . across the Atlantic. She will die without ever having got so far as New York." But the mood shifted markedly, in the same letter, when he added, "Life is so stale when one has been looking at it for more than sixty winters!"

Even Routledge's communication, paying for the third and asking about the next volume of *Philip the Second,* did not jolt the ennui. "I have not broken ground on it yet; but shall soon do so," he replied, adding, "It must depend on my health, which is good now." A few days later he could no longer say that. In mid-January he suffered from chills and fever and spent many daylight hours reclining on a sofa. Sometimes Kirk read to him; often he conversed with friends, none of whom was more welcome or more frequent in his visits than George Ticknor.

Proudly he informed Sir Charles Lyell of Boston's effort to erect a museum. Frank Gray's will promised fifty thousand dollars toward the end so close to Professor Louis Agassiz's heart, and now the community was trying to subscribe an equal sum. Son-in-law James Lawrence was a leader in the cause.[59]

One day Longfellow "met him in Washington Street, just at the

---

[58] WHP to Lady Lyell, November 27, 1858, copy of Lyell letterbook, Prescott papers; WHP to J. Sparks, December 3, 1858, Sparks papers; and WHP to C. G. Loring, December 12, 1858, Loring papers.

[59] WHP to Lady Lyell, January 10, 1859, copy of Lyell letterbook, Prescott papers; and Gardiner, ed., *Papers,* pp. 397–398.

foot of Winter Street. He was merry, and laughing as usual. At the close of the conversation he said, 'I am going to shave off my whiskers; they are growing gray.' 'Gray hair is becoming,' I said. 'Becoming,' said he; 'what do we care about becoming, who must so soon *be going?*' 'Then why take the trouble to shave them off?' 'That's true,' he replied with a pleasant laugh, and crossed over to Summer Street.''[60]

Beyond the limitations imposed by his health, social activity at Fifty-five Beacon was restricted, first by the long illness, then death, of the historian's sister-in-law, Mary Dexter. Skipping the session of Club for which Loring was host and canceling a dinner intended to bring visiting English noblemen as well as stalwarts like Ticknor, Hillard, and William Amory to his table, Prescott donned his mourning clothes. Reporting the Dexter funeral to absent Amory, he expressed the sadness in his heart, "The evening of life is coming over those of our generation, and we must be prepared to say farewell to one another."

Three days later, the resolve to pitch into more of the life of Philip II was increasing, even though he was still listening to a travel book on Russia which Kirk was reading. Leaving Kirk momentarily, he exchanged words with Susan and his sister, who had dropped in for a visit. On his way back to his study, he was in an adjacent room when Kirk, hearing a groan, rushed to him. Laid unconscious by a second apoplectic stroke at 11:30 A.M., Prescott, carried to his room and speedily attended by several doctors, never spoke, never regained consciousness. At 2:30 P.M., January 28, 1859, he died.[61]

In fulfillment of his expressed wish, William H. Prescott, prepared for burial, was carried momentarily into his library. Beyond life, he wanted to be with his books. Beyond death, Prescott, in his books, is with us.

[60] Longfellow, ed., *Life of Longfellow,* 2: 377.
[61] Gardiner, ed., *Papers,* pp. 398–399, 401; WHP to C. G. Loring, January 25 [1859], Loring papers; and Ticknor, *Prescott,* pp. 440, 442–445.

# MANUSCRIPT COLLECTIONS CITED

This list locates and more fully identifies the manuscript collections cited in this study. Those manuscripts which are not within collections have been identified fully, as have all printed materials, in the notes. They are excluded from this list. Many materials, manuscript and printed, which were studied but not quoted, are unmentioned.

Adams papers
  Adams Family Papers, Massachusetts Historical Society, Boston, Mass.

Allibone papers
  S. Austin Allibone Papers, The Huntington Library, San Marino, Calif.

Bancroft papers
  George Bancroft Papers, Massachusetts Historical Society, Boston, Mass.

Bentley papers
  Richard Bentley Papers, Harvard College Library, Cambridge, Mass.

Brown autograph collection
  Charles A. Brown Autograph Collection, The University of Rochester Library, Rochester, N. Y.

Lord Carlisle papers
  Lord Carlisle Papers, Castle Howard, Yorkshire, England

Chamberlain autograph collection
  Mellen Chamberlain Autograph Collection, Rare Book Department, Boston Public Library, Boston, Mass.

Dexter papers
  F. Gordon Dexter Papers, Massachusetts Historical Society, Boston, Mass.

Draper-Wisconsin correspondence
  Draper-Wisconsin Historical Society Correspondence, The State Historical Society of Wisconsin, Madison, Wis.

Duyckinck collection
  Duyckinck Collection, The New York Public Library, New York, N. Y.

Ellis papers
  George E. Ellis Papers, Massachusetts Historical Society, Boston, Mass.

E. Everett papers
  Edward Everett Papers, *ibid.*

Folsom papers
Charles Folsom Papers, Rare Book Department, Boston Public Library, Boston, Mass.
Charles Folsom Papers, Massachusetts Historical Society, Boston, Mass.

Ford collection
Ford Collection, The New York Public Library, New York, N. Y.

Gardiner papers
William H. Gardiner Papers, Massachusetts Historical Society, Boston, Mass.

Goodhue papers
Goodhue Papers, The New York Society Library, New York, N. Y.

Kennedy papers
The John Pendleton Kennedy Papers, Peabody Institute Library, Baltimore, Md.

Lieber papers
Francis Lieber Papers, The Huntington Library, San Marino, Calif.

Loring papers
Charles G. Loring Papers, Harvard College Library, Cambridge, Mass.

Meredith papers
Meredith Papers, The Historical Society of Pennsylvania, Philadelphia, Pa.

Prescott papers
William H. Prescott Papers, Massachusetts Historical Society, Boston, Mass.

Sparks papers
Jared Sparks Papers, Harvard College Library, Cambridge, Mass.

Sumner papers
Charles Sumner Papers, *ibid.*

Ticknor collection
Ticknor Collection, Archives, Dartmouth College Library, Hanover, N. H.

Wilkinson collection
O. D. Wilkinson Collection, The Historical Society of Pennsylvania, Philadelphia, Pa.

# INDEX

abridgment of *Ferdinand and Isabella*: projected, 173–175; executed, 175

Achille, Narcisse: as aide, 270

Acosta, José de: book by, 150

Adams, John Quincy: 32, 91

Adams, Sir William: 32, 45

Adderley, Charles Bowyer: 310

Aikin, Lucy: *Memoirs of the Court of Queen Elizabeth* of, 99

Alamán, Lucas: as aide, 172; as annotator, 229

Albany, New York: trip to, 253

Alfieri, Vittorio: 72

Alison, Archibald: 303

Allibone, Samuel Austin: 335

American Antiquarian Society: membership in, 180

American Philosophical Society: membership in, 149, 179

American Stationers' Company: contract with, 134; publishes *Ferdinand and Isabella*, 138; bankruptcy of, 145; mentioned, 140

Ames, Joseph: portrait by, 213

Amory, N.: as travel companion, 36

Amory, Susan. SEE Prescott, Susan

Amory, Thomas C.: 16, 58

Amory, William: described, 15–16, 58; as travel companion, 112, 203; quoted, 112; as guest, 133, 283; as neighbor, 239; as trustee, 348; mentioned, 164, 238, 352

"Anika." SEE Ticknor, Anna Eliot

Appleton, Fanny. SEE Longfellow, Fanny Appleton

Appleton, William: 239, 296–297; quoted, 297

Argyll, Duke and Duchess of: 311

Ariosto, Ludovico: *Orlando Furioso* of, 72, 74; mentioned, 158

Ashburton, Lord: 300

Aspinwall, Col. Thomas: met, 32–33; described, 132; as guest, 132; negotiates contracts, 133–134, 175, 197–198, 199–200, 226, 258; letters from, 159, 200; letters to, 194, 222; quoted, 198, 222; mentioned, 194, 203, 328

Athenaeum (Boston): library of, 16, 81; supported, 69–70, 324; trustee of, 116; gift to, 152

*The Atlantic Monthly*: helps launch, 343–344

Awe, Loch: visited, 311

Azores: trip to, 26–30

Babbage, Charles: 261

Bancroft, George: at Harvard, 22; letters to, 79, 109, 120, 261, 270; school operated by, 87; as aide, 120, 133, 137, 148, 154, 300; *History of United States* of, 169, 346; example of, 174; honorary degree for, 202; guest of, 249, 298, 300; in England, 261; quoted, 261; testimonial by, 335; mentioned, 138, 163, 203, 238, 290, 337

Bandelier, A. F. A.: 268

Barante, Amable: *Histoire des Ducs de Burgoyne de la maison de Valois* of, 99; mentioned, 97

Baron, Alexander: novel by, 210

Barrow, Isaac: 61

Belfast, Maine: trip to, 254

Bentley, Richard: contracts with, 133–134, 175, 226; letters to, 151, 181, 194, 215, 232; suspicions regarding, 159; gifts from, 195, 296; tactics of, 199; quoted, 259; letters from, 287, 296, 322, 323; met, 303; negotiations with, 330, 331, 349; publishes correspondence, 349 n; mentioned, 156, 317

Benton, Thomas Hart: 248, 250

Berni, Francesco: *Orlando Innamorato* of, 72, 74; mentioned, 71

Bigland, John: 67

*Biographical and Critical Miscellanies*: published, 234. SEE ALSO *Miscellanies*

Bliss, Mary Elizabeth: 298

Boccaccio: *Decameron* of, 71; mentioned, 85

Bohn, Henry G.: 287

Boiardo, Matteo: *Orlando Innamorato* of, 72; mentioned, 71, 158

Boston, Mass.: described, 3–5, 194; as